AF477672

Studies in Economic Transition

General Editors: **Jens Hölscher**, Reader in Economics, University of Brighton; and **Horst Tomann**, Professor of Economics, Free University Berlin

This series has been established in response to a growing demand for a greater understanding of the transformation of economic systems. It brings together theoretical and empirical studies on economic transition and economic development. The post-communist transition from planned to market economies is one of the main areas of applied theory because in this field the most dramatic examples of change and economic dynamics can be found. The series aims to contribute to the understanding of specific major economic changes as well as to advance the theory of economic development. The implications of economic policy will be a major point of focus.

Titles include:

Lucian Cernat
EUROPEANIZATION, VARIETIES OF CAPITALISM AND ECONOMIC
PERFORMANCE IN CENTRAL AND EASTERN EUROPE

Irwin Collier, Herwig Roggemann, Oliver Scholz and Horst Tomann (*editors*)
WELFARE STATES IN TRANSITION
East and West

Bruno Dallago (*editor*)
TRANSFORMATION AND EUROPEAN INTEGRATION
The Local Dimension

Hella Engerer
PRIVATIZATION AND ITS LIMITS IN CENTRAL AND EASTERN EUROPE
Property Rights in Transition

Hubert Gabrisch and Rüdiger Pohl (*editors*)
EU ENLARGEMENT AND ITS MACROECONOMIC EFFECTS IN EASTERN EUROPE
Currencies, Prices, Investment and Competitiveness

Oleh Havrylyshyn
DIVERGENT PATHS IN POST-COMMUNIST TRANSFORMATION
Capitalism for All or Capitalism for the Few?

Jens Hölscher (*editor*)
FINANCIAL TURBULENCE AND CAPITAL MARKETS IN TRANSITION COUNTRIES

Jens Hölscher and Anja Hochberg (*editors*)
EAST GERMANY'S ECONOMIC DEVELOPMENT SINCE UNIFICATION
Domestic and Global Aspects

Mihaela Kelemen and Monika Kostera (*editors*)
CRITICAL MANAGEMENT RESEARCH IN EASTERN EUROPE
Managing the Transition

Emil J. Kirchner (*editor*)
DECENTRALIZATION AND TRANSITION IN THE VISEGRAD
Poland, Hungary, the Czech Republic and Slovakia

David Lane and Martin Myant (*editors*)
VARIETIES OF CAPITALISM IN POST-COMMUNIST COUNTRIES

Tomasz Mickiewicz (*editor*)
CORPORATE GOVERNANCE AND FINANCE IN POLAND AND RUSSIA

Tomasz Mickiewicz
ECONOMIC TRANSITION IN CENTRAL EUROPE AND
THE COMMONWEALTH OF INDEPENDENT STATES

Milan Nikolić
MONETARY POLICY IN TRANSITION
Inflation Nexus Money Supply in Postcommunist Russia

Julie Pellegrin
THE POLITICAL ECONOMY OF COMPETITIVENESS IN AN ENLARGED EUROPE

Stanislav Poloucek (*editor*)
REFORMING THE FINANCIAL SECTOR IN CENTRAL EUROPEAN COUNTRIES

Gregg S. Robins
BANKING IN TRANSITION
East Germany after Unification

Johannes Stephan
ECONOMIC TRANSITION IN HUNGARY AND EAST GERMANY
Gradualism and Shock Therapy in Catch-up Development

Johannes Stephan (*editor*)
TECHNOLOGY TRANSFER VIA FOREIGN DIRECT INVESTMENT
IN CENTRAL AND EASTERN EUROPE

Hans van Zon
THE POLITICAL ECONOMY OF INDEPENDENT UKRAINE

Adalbert Winkler (*editor*)
BANKING AND MONETARY POLICY IN EASTERN EUROPE
The First Ten Years

Studies in Economic Transition
Series Standing Order ISBN 0-333-73353-3
(*outside North America only*)

You can receive future titles in this series as they are published by placing a standing order. Please contact your bookseller or, in case of difficulty, write to us at the address below with your name and address, the title of the series and the ISBN quoted above.

Customer Services Department, Macmillan Distribution Ltd, Houndmills, Basingstoke, Hampshire RG21 6XS, England

Corporate Governance and Finance in Poland and Russia

Edited by

Tomasz Mickiewicz

First published 2006 by
PALGRAVE MACMILLAN
Houndmills, Basingstoke, Hampshire RG21 6XS and
175 Fifth Avenue, New York, N.Y. 10010
Companies and representatives throughout the world

PALGRAVE MACMILLAN is the global academic imprint of the Palgrave
Macmillan division of St. Martin's Press, LLC and of Palgrave Macmillan Ltd.
Macmillan® is a registered trademark in the United States, United Kingdom
and other countries. Palgrave is a registered trademark in the European
Union and other countries.

ISBN-13: 978–0–230–00795–6
ISBN-10: 0–230–00795–3

This book is printed on paper suitable for recycling and made from fully
managed and sustained forest sources.

A catalogue record for this book is available from the British Library.

Library of Congress Cataloging-in-Publication Data
Corporate governance and finance in Poland and Russia / edited by
    Tomasz Mickiewicz.
      p. cm. — (Studies in economic transition)
    Includes bibliographical references and index.
    ISBN 0–230–00795–3
    1. Corporate governance—Poland. 2. Corporate governance—Russia
(Federation) 3. Corporations—Poland—Finance. 4. Corporations—Russia
(Federation)—Finance. I. Mickiewicz, Tomasz.
HD2741.C774885 2006
338.7′409438—dc22   2006047269

10   9   8   7   6   5   4   3   2   1
15 14 13 12 11 10 09 08 07 06

Printed and bound in Great Britain by
Antony Rowe Ltd, Chippenham and Eastbourne

Contents

List of Figures and Tables

Figures

Tables

Acknowledgements

The origins of this book can be traced back to the conference on 'Finance and Corporate Governance: Economic, Managerial and Policy Perspectives' held at the Social Science Department, School of Slavonic and East European Studies, University College London. I would like to express my gratitude to the M.C. Grabowski Fund, which was the main sponsor of the conference and enabled this fruitful and interesting meeting to take place. In addition, my gratitude is to Dr Adam Śliwiński, for his organizational efforts that made the conference a success.

The book was discussed from the very beginning; it soon became obvious, however, that from one point of view we have had too much material for one volume, and from another too little as more coherence was needed. The organizers therefore decided to go simultaneously into two different directions, one of which led to this volume. At the end, only four chapters in the book can be traced back to the conference. Most of the others, however, draw from the research focused around the 'Managing Economic Transition' network and its continuing series of workshops.

My gratitude is also to my home department and University College London as a whole, for granting me research leave, which made completion of this work possible. I would also like to thank Professor George Kolankiewicz, the director of the School of Slavonic and East European Studies (SSEES) between 2001 and 2006, whose encouragement made me think about this project. I am also grateful to Dr Jens Hölscher, one of the editors of this series, and to the anonymous referees whose comments helped to restructure this volume.

TOMASZ MICKIEWICZ

Notes on the Contributors

Yuko Adachi is a Lecturer in the Department of Russian Studies, Sophia University, Tokyo, Japan. She holds a PhD from the School of Slavonic and East European Studies (SSEES), University College London (UCL). Her PhD dissertation is on informal corporate governance practices in Russia. Prior to her doctoral studies, she worked at the International Monetary Fund after obtaining an MA from the School of Advanced International Studies (SAIS), Johns Hopkins University, USA. She was an Obuchi Fellow at the Moscow School of Economic and Social Sciences in 2002–03. Her research interests include Russia's corporate governance, the development and growth of Russian firms, as well as business–government relations in Russia.

Maria Aluchna is an Assistant Professor in the Department of Management Theory, Warsaw School of Economics. She specializes in corporate governance of transition economies, including ownership structure, institutional investors and the role of supervisory boards. She spent fall semester 2001/02 at Universität Passau (Deutscher Akademischer Austauchdienst scholarship) and the academic year 2002/03 at Columbia University, New York (Fulbright scholarship). Currently, she teaches comparative analysis of corporate governance and strategic management (both in English).

Wladimir Andreff is Professor of Economics at the University Paris 1 Panthéon Sorbonne, a Researcher at the Centre d'Economie de la Sorbonne (CNRS), and Vice-President of the French Economic Association. In addition, he served as President of the European Association for Comparative Economic Studies during 1997–98. He serves on the editorial board of 13 economic journals. He has authored 11 economic books and 316 economic articles, and has edited 11 economic volumes. His research areas are: economics of transition, international economics and globalization, and the economics of sports. His most recent books are: *Privatisation and Structural Change in Transition Economies* (ed. with Y. Kalyuzhnova), Palgrave 2003; *La mutation des économies post-socialistes: une analyse économique alternative*, L'Harmattan 2003; *Analyses économiques de la transition* (ed.), La Découverte 2002; and *The Handbook on the Economics of Sport* (ed. with S. Szymanski), Edward Elgar 2006, forthcoming.

Maciej Bałtowski is a Professor in the Economics Faculty of the Maria Curie University, Lublin (Poland), and the Head of the Institute of Economics there. His research interests include privatization and restructuring of enterprises and economic transition in Poland. His multiple publications include: *Privatization of State Enterprises in Poland. Course and Evaluation* (PWN, Warsaw 1997, awarded

The Prize of Educational Enterprise Foundation for the Best Economic Publication in Poland in 1998); 'Privatisation in Poland: Ten Years After', in *Post-Communist Economies*, 2000, 12 (4), (co-author: T. Mickiewicz); *Privatized Enterprises in the Polish Economy* (editor and co-author; PWN, Warsaw 2002); 'All Roads Lead to Outside Ownership: Polish Piecemeal Privatisation', in D. Parker and D. Saal (eds), *Handbook of Privatization*, Edward Elgar, 2003 (co-author: T. Mickiewicz); and *Economic Transition in Poland*, PWN, Warsaw 2006 (co-author: M. Miszewski).

Jan Chadam is a CEO and Finance Director of Pro Futuro SA (Warsaw, Poland). The company Pro Futuro SA (an alternative telecommunications operator) was awarded the first place in the FAST 50 and the third place in the FAST 500 EMEA of the Deloitte Touche Tohmatsu 2005 Ranking. Dr Chadam has over 20 years' experience in management, restructuring enterprises, finance strategies, ERP systems implementation, and e-business. He has extensive experience in financial management, preparation and management of corporate restructuring processes and implementation of complex IT projects. He has participated in the implementation of two international projects financed by the Danish government and by the EU and at present is involved in a research project concerning capital groups in Poland. Among his Polish and international publications are about 30 papers and monographic studies on finance, restructuring, IT problems, competitiveness of enterprises, and capital groups. His two most recent publications include 'Elements of Knowledge Management in Multi-Entity Organisations', *International Journal of Management and Decision Making*, 7, 2006; and 'Marketing Aspects of Knowledge-Based Management in Groups of Companies: Case of Poland', *Industrial Management and Data Systems*, 7, 2005 (both with Zbigniew Pastuszak).

Igor Filatotchev is a Professor of Strategic Management at King's College, University of London. Before joining King's College, he held various academic positions at Nottingham University Business School, Birkbeck College (University of London) and the University of Bradford. He earned his PhD in Economics from the Institute of World Economy and International Relations (Moscow, the Russian Federation) in 1985. His research interests are focused on a fast-growing area in the management and economics literature relating to corporate governance effects on entrepreneurship development, strategic decisions and organizational change. Key research programmes currently in progress include analysis of resource and strategy roles of corporate governance; the corporate governance life-cycle; and a knowledge-based view on governance development in entrepreneurial firms. He has published extensively in the fields of corporate governance and strategy, in journals such as *Academy of Management Journal*, *Strategic Management Journal*, *California Management Review*, *Journal of International Business Studies*, and *Journal of Management Studies*.

Piotr Marek Jaworski is a Lecturer in Economics at the Napier University Business School in Edinburgh. Previously he worked in Britain at Birkbeck College and the School of Slavonic and East European Studies of University College London, and in Poland at the Warsaw School of Economics and Ministry of Finance. He graduated from the Warsaw School of Economics (MA), the London School of Economics and Political Science (MSc) and the University of Minnesota (MBA). His PhD thesis on economics of pension systems, written at the Warsaw School of Economics, was awarded first prize for the best Polish thesis by the BISE bank. He specializes in economics of transition, macroeconomics and insurance, commercial as well as social. His recent publications include 'An Insurance Policy – Case Study of Legal and Economic Interactions in Transforming Economy', *Post-Communist Economies*, 2004; and an edited volume *Polish EU Accession in Comparative Perspective: Macroeconomics, Finance and the Government* (co-editor: Tomasz Mickiewicz), published by University College London, 2006, in which he also has his article on Polish commercial insurance.

Rostislav Kapelyushnikov is Chief Researcher at the Institute of World Economy and International Relations of the Russian Academy of Sciences. He is Deputy Chief Editor of the quarterly bulletin *The Russian Economic Barometer* and is Deputy Director of the Centre for Labour Market Studies at the State University – Higher School of Economics, Moscow. His research interests are focused on labour economics, economics of transition, institutional economics and corporate governance. He is an author of several books including *Russian Unemployment: Dynamics, Composition, and Specificity* (2003) and numerous papers in Russian and Western academic journals.

Jens Köke is affiliated to the Allianz Group, Stuttgart, Germany, where he works as an investment strategist. Before joining Allianz Group, he was a researcher in the research department 'International Finance and Financial Management' of the Centre for European Economic Research (ZEW) in Mannheim, Germany.

Andrei Kuznetsov is Reader in International Business Management, Manchester Metropolitan University Business School. His research focuses on corporate governance, cross-cultural management, knowledge transfer and corporate social responsibility. He is on the editorial board of the *Journal of East–West Trade*. He has written and edited several books on post-communist transition, including *Russian Corporation: The Strategies of Survival and Development* (2001), and has published in journals such as *Europe–Asia Studies* and the *Journal for East European Management Studies*.

Olga Kuznetsova is a Senior Lecturer in the Manchester Metropolitan University Business School. Her research agenda includes corporate governance development, corporate social responsibility, institutional dimensions of the business environment and economic reforms, and the economic role of the state. Her research findings are reported in numerous publications.

Robert W. McGee is a Professor at the Andreas School of Business, Barry University in Miami, USA. He has published more than 40 books and more than 350 scholarly papers in the fields of accounting, taxation, public finance, economics, law and philosophy. Recent books include *Accounting and Financial System Reform in a Transition Economy: A Case Study of Russia* (Springer, 2005), *Accounting and Financial System Reform in Eastern Europe and Asia* (Springer, 2006) and *The Philosophy of Taxation and Public Finance* (Kluwer, 2004). Books currently in process include *Taxation and Public Finance in Transition and Developing Economies* (Springer) and *Accounting Reform in Transition and Developing Economies* (Springer). His research interests include transition economics, economic philosophy, business ethics, financial reporting, international trade and political philosophy.

Tomasz Mickiewicz is a Senior Lecturer in Economic Restructuring in the Department of Social Sciences, School of Slavonic and East European Studies, University College London, where he also coordinates the Centre for the Study of Economic and Social Change in Europe. He is also an affiliate of the CASE Institute at Warsaw and publishes on comparative economic systems. His most recent book is *Economic Transition in Central Europe and the Commonwealth of Independent States* (Palgrave Macmillan, 2005). He publishes in *Europe–Asia Studies*, *Post-Communist Economies*, *Economic Systems*, *Acta Oeconomica*, *Transnational Corporations* and others in English, Polish and Spanish. Recent articles in progress are available in the William Davidson Institute (University of Michigan) Working Papers series.

Ilya Okhmatovskiy is a doctoral candidate in the Marshall School of Business at the University of Southern California. He specializes in strategic management, organization theory and international business. His current research is on comparative corporate governance, networks and institutions. In his dissertation he compares intercorporate networks created by ownership and directorship ties among corporations in countries with different institutional environments. Another area of research is the emergence and evolution of industries in transition economies. He is studying the evolution of the Russian banking industry after the market reforms of the early 1990s, and his research has been published in *International Sociology* and *Academy of Management Best Paper Proceedings*. In summer 2006, Ilya Okhmatovskiy takes up post as an Assistant Professor in the Desautels Faculty of Management at McGill University.

Zbigniew Pastuszak is an Assistant Professor and manager of the Management Information Systems Laboratory at the Faculty of Economics, Maria Curie

University, Lublin, Poland. He lectures at the College of Enterprise and Administration in Lublin. Dr Pastuszak has over 12 years' experience in restructuring enterprises, logistics strategies, production management, e-business and MIS. He has participated in the implementation of six nationwide projects financed by the Scientific Research Committee in Poland and two projects funded by the EU. At present he is involved in research projects concerning the net readiness of the largest Polish companies and knowledge management and synergy in multi-entity companies. Among his Polish publications are three books and about 80 articles and monographic studies on restructuring, supply-chain management, competitiveness of enterprises, and e-business. Among his international publications are one chapter and five articles. Currently he serves as an Editorial Advisory Board member of *Industrial Management and Data Systems* (IMDS); as an Editorial Board member of the *International Journal of Intercultural Information Management* (IJIIM), the *Journal of International Technology and Information Management* (JITIM), the *International Journal of Service and Standards;* and as an Editorial Review Board member of the *Interdisciplinary Journal of Knowledge and Learning Objects.*

Slavo Radosevic is Professor at the School of Slavonic and East European Studies, University College London. His research interests are in the areas of science, technology, industrial change and foreign direct investments in countries of Central and Eastern Europe, and he continues to be involved in international projects in this area. He also acts as an expert for various international organizations. He has published extensively in international journals on issues of innovation and innovation policy in countries of Central and Eastern Europe. Dr Radosevic is the author of *International Technology Transfer and Catch Up in Economic Development*, Edward Elgar, 1999. He is co-editor of three recent volumes: F. McGowan, S. Radosevic and N. von Tunzelmann, *The Emerging Industrial Structure of the Wider Europe*, Routledge, 2004; S. Radosevic and B. Sadowski, *International Industrial Networks and Industrial Restructuring in Central Europe, Russia and Ukraine*, Kluwer, 2004; and K. Piech and S. Radosevic, *Knowledge-Based Economy in Central and Eastern Europe: Countries and Industries in a Process of Change*, Palgrave Macmillan, 2006.

Michael Schröder is the head of the research department 'International Finance and Financial Management', at the Centre for European Economic Research (ZEW) in Mannheim, Germany. His main research interests are: international capital markets, relationships between capital markets and economic fundamentals, capital markets in Central and Eastern Europe, quantitative methods for portfolio management, asset pricing, and socially responsible investments. Current projects deal with the European market in asset management, banking regulation in Europe, overconfidence amongst German stockmarket forecasters, and portfolio management of German charitable foundations. More details can be found at *www.zew.de*.

Anna Zalewska is a Professor of Finance at the School of Management, University of Bath. Having both a mathematical and economics background (she received a PhD in Mathematics at the Polish Academy of Sciences, Warsaw, and a PhD in Economics at the London Business School) her research interests cover a broad range, mostly in financial economics. In particular, Professor Zalewska works and publishes in the following four areas: (1) privatization, stockmarket valuation of regulated companies, and the sensitivity of market risk to regulation; (2) profitability, governance and managerial incentives; (3) emerging markets – development, efficiency and integration, and (4) the impact of pension reforms on the development of financial markets. Her publications include papers in the *Journal of Financial Economics, European Economic Review, Journal of Empirical Finance, Economics Letters* and *Economics of Planning*. She has also contributed to several books, most recently in the American Bar Association publication on *Issues in Competition Law and Policy*.

Part I

Russia and Poland in Comparative Perspective

1
Corporate Governance in Russia and Poland in Comparative Perspective: An Introduction

*Tomasz Mickiewicz**

Russia is a country that many love, some hate, but hardly anybody can remain indifferent about it. The largest country on earth, rich in natural resources, a nuclear superpower, a nation that participated in some of the most dramatic events throughout the twentieth century. Even cool-blooded economists become passionate as soon as they start discussing Russia, as well-exemplified by the recent heated discussion between Shleifer and Tresman (2004) and Rosefielde (2005). One is tempted to recall Conrad (1999 [1911]), who a century ago declared when introducing his novel about Russia: 'my greatest anxiety was in being able to strike and sustain the note of scrupulous impartiality' (p. lxxxiii).

Maintaining some acceptable level of impartiality is simpler for us, as this book is limited in its objectives. It deals with corporate governance. We aim to understand more about corporate control structures, the links between corporate governance and finance, its political economy and implications for performance, including some lessons that go beyond any individual country. That leads to the important characteristic of this volume. It is comparative. Which country should Russia be compared with? Shleifer and Tresman (2004), rather provocatively, point to Brazil. That we doubt. We have to look for a country that would share with Russia some sufficient similarity in terms of inherited institutional experience. There is no entirely satisfactory answer to this query, but we propose Russia's old and smaller neighbour, Poland. Between 1831 and 1915, most of Poland was sharing the Tzarist institutions with Russia. And again, the same applies to the period between *circa* 1948 and 1989, when both nations shared the experience of the Soviet command economy. It is equally easy to point out the differences. The command economy had a longer history in Russia, and Poland was more liberal since 1956. Yet, at the starting point of the systemic transition

---

*I am grateful to Yuko Adachi, Wladimir Andreff, Andrei Kuznetsov, Olga Kuznetsova, Robert McGee, Ilya Okhmatovskiy and last but not least to Anna Zalewska for comments and criticism. Obviously, all remaining errors are mine.

at the end of the 1980s, after the reforms initiated by Gorbachev, the economic systems in the two countries were very similar. What makes the comparison interesting is the fact that while the starting point was comparable, the corporate structures in both countries evolved in different directions. This book aims to enhance our understanding why.

We believe that those interested in Russia may learn from studying Poland, and equally importantly, those concerned with Poland may benefit from studying Russia. While marked differences may be found, one is also surprised by similarities.

The themes covered in this book should also be relevant to anybody interested in more general studies of corporate governance. Institutions are easier to understand by capturing the differences between the common and the idiosyncratic, and that is impossible to grasp without a comparative perspective.

Besides, we live in a world that is globalizing fast. While the characteristics may differ, both Russia and Poland are representative of the surge of trade and investment from abroad that followed the end of communism. Both economies have come a long way from the economic autarchy of the COMECON to become active players in the global economy.

The aim of this chapter is twofold. We present a snapshot of the corporate ownership structures in Russia and Poland, comparing them with the two other major Central European economies: the Czech Republic and Hungary. Next, based on this we introduce the main themes of this volume, and offer some conclusions.

Corporate ownership structures in Russia and Poland

Our discussion of corporate ownership characteristics draws on the sample of companies produced by the Business Environment and Enterprise Performance Survey (2002), available from the European Bank for Reconstruction and Development. The main advantage of this survey is that, unlike some other sources, the sample is not restricted to a small minority of companies that are quoted on the stock exchange. It also offers detailed information on owners' characteristics not available elsewhere.

For Russia and Poland, the sectoral composition of the survey is very similar, with about 30 per cent of companies in trade, 25 per cent in manufacturing, 15 per cent in construction, 10 per cent or slightly below in both transport and communication and in business services, and a few per cent in hotels and restaurants, other services and mining (the latter, in Russia only). The survey produced 487 usable questionnaires for Russia and 488 for Poland. However, we focus only on one-third of enterprises which are in the medium and large-size category (50 or more employees). This is where the ownership structures become more diversified, and the classic agency problems of corporate governance may emerge. In addition, we compare both Russia and Poland with two other major Central European Economies: the Czech Republic and Hungary (the BEEPS survey sample is smaller for both: 266 and 207 observations correspondingly).

Concentration of ownership

We are interested in three related dimensions of corporate control: concentration of ownership, identity of the owners and the institutional origins of the companies.

The first dimension is illustrated by Figure 1.1, which presents histograms of the share of the largest owner in equity for the four countries. Interestingly, the pattern is very similar for all four economies. Corporate ownership remains heavily concentrated; between 50 per cent and 60 per cent (the latter in Poland) of the dominant owners hold all or almost all equity alone.

One may also note an interesting local maximum in densities around 50 per cent of equity, being most visible in Russia, but noticeable in Poland and the Czech Republic as well. This may be seen as an indication that the choice of equity portfolio is partly driven by the private benefits associated with legal control – for the dominant shareholders, the 50 per cent threshold seems to be very relevant. In general, looking at the concentration of ownership we may infer that we are far away from the market-based, 'Anglo-Saxon' system of corporate control, where minority shareholder interests are well-protected and medium-size firms participate on the formal capital markets as the owners-founders-entrepreneurs diversify their holdings as soon as the opportunity arises (Shleifer and Vishny, 1997).

Thus, our first conclusion is that Russian and Polish companies share one important common attribute: concentrated ownership.

Interestingly enough, the two economies are not very different either when we look at the identity of the dominant shareholder (see Table 1.1). For the four major 'transition' economies, it is only Hungary that stands apart from the other three (as confirmed by χ^2 values from pairwise tests). The difference relates to the role played by foreign ownership in Hungary; 44 per cent of medium and large firms in Hungary are controlled by foreign companies, as compared with 22 per cent in Poland, 20 per cent in the Czech Republic and 16 per cent in Russia. This results from the privatization strategy chosen in Hungary and is consistent with macro data on foreign direct investment. Clearly, Hungary may be seen as representative of one of the stylized corporate governance models in Central Eastern Europe, as discussed by Andreff in the second chapter of this book.

Yet, while Russia and Poland are not very different with respect to the identity of owners, some characteristic features are noticeable. While the share of domestic companies in ownership is very similar, ownership by foreign companies is marginally more frequent in Poland. One may also notice that the share of employee ownership in Poland is twice as high as in Russia (6.8% versus 3.3%), and may be attributed to the choice of privatization methods (see again, the chapter by Andreff). Another interesting difference

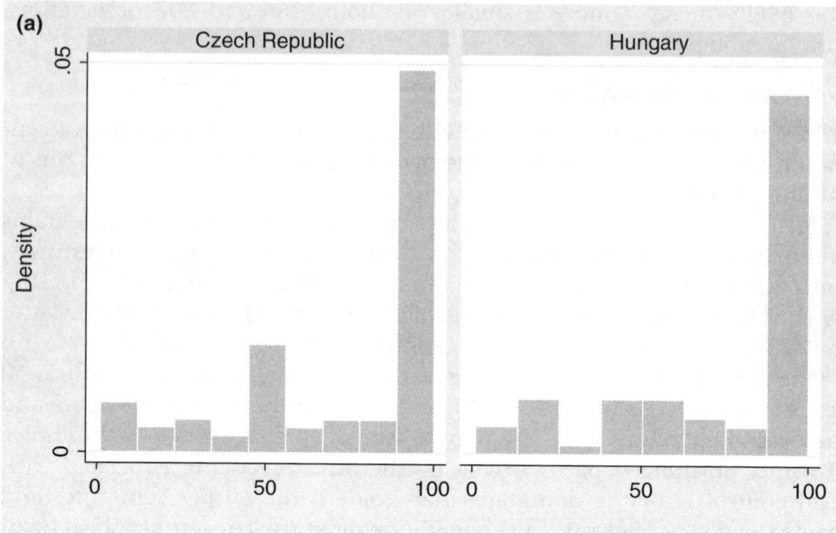

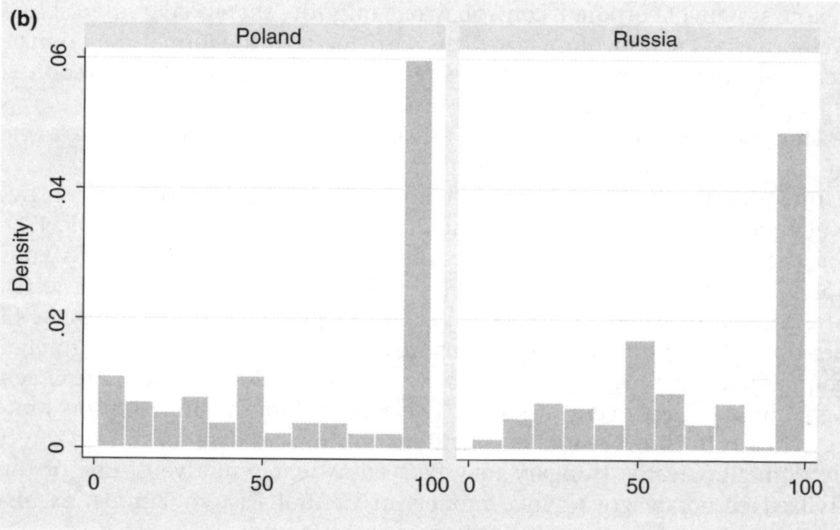

Figure 1.1   Percentage of equity held by the largest shareholder (medium-size and large companies, histogram)

relates to the fact that in Russia a larger proportion of medium-size and large companies is held by individual private owners (39% versus 25% in Poland). However, one has to be cautious when interpreting this result. The difference between private individual ownership, family ownership and employee

Table 1.1   Identity of the largest shareholder, based on EBRD BEEPS survey, 2002

Largest shareholder	*Czech Republic*	*Hungary*	*Poland*	*Russia*	*Total*
Individual	29	16	41	58	144
	33.33	23.53	25.47	38.67	30.90
Family	4	1	6	3	14
	4.60	1.47	3.73	2.00	3.00
Domestic company	16	13	20	17	66
	18.39	19.12	12.42	11.33	14.16
Foreign company	17	30	35	24	106
	19.54	44.12	21.74	16.00	22.75
Bank	1	0	0	1	2
	1.15	0.00	0.00	0.67	0.43
Investment fund	1	0	2	0	3
	1.15	0.00	1.24	0.00	0.64
Managers	2	1	2	3	8
	2.30	1.47	1.24	2.00	1.72
Employees	0	0	11	5	16
	0.00	0.00	6.83	3.33	3.43
Government	15	6	39	37	97
	17.24	8.82	24.22	24.67	20.82
Other	2	1	5	2	10
	2.30	1.47	3.11	1.33	2.15
Total	87	68	161	150	466
	100.00	100.00	100.00	100.00	100.00

Notes: Small companies (employment below 50) are excluded from comparisons. The first figure = cell count, the second (lower) figure = column percentage. For companies with two major shareholders (i.e. coded as three digit entries in the BEEPS survey answers), the identity of the first category is reported, i.e. 1 (individual) for 102 coding, 2 (family) for 207 coding etc). Pearson $\chi^2(27)$ = 53.0705 (probability = 0.002).
For pair-wise comparisons:
Czech Rep. v. Hungary: Pearson $\chi^2(8)$ = 13.8648 (probability = 0.085),
Czech Rep. v. Poland: Pearson $\chi^2(9)$ = 12.4455 (probability = 0.189),
Czech Rep. v. Russia: Pearson $\chi^2(9)$ = 10.5406 (probability = 0.309),
Hungary v. Poland: Pearson $\chi^2(8)$ = 22.5576 (probability = 0.004),
Hungary v. Russia: Pearson $\chi^2(8)$ = 28.9756 (probability = 0.000),
Poland v. Russia: Pearson $\chi^2(9)$ = 11.3838 (probability = 0.250).

ownership may not be clear-cut. The individual owners are not dispersed investors (like in the 'Anglo-Saxon' model), but would typically be related to the company they hold ownership stakes in. After privatization to employees, employees may leave companies and hold shares, and, even more importantly, may sell shares to other individuals with whom they are closely connected. Given that, a more appropriate statistic could be the joint share in ownership held by employees, other private individuals and families. When aggregated this way, it is still different, but less so (44% for Russia versus 36% for Poland). Correspondingly, a more cautious (and robust) conclusion is that institutional ownership plays a larger role in Poland.

And last but not least, there is one characteristic that makes both Russia and Poland similar to each other and different from the Czech Republic and Hungary: for the first two countries almost a quarter of companies still have the government as the dominant owner. This may be compared with 17 per cent in the Czech Republic and only 9 per cent in Hungary. The role of government in corporate governance will be analysed in chapters by Adachi and Bałtowski and Mickiewicz. Here, one is tempted to comment that the common tradition of big government that we referred to in the opening sequence of this chapter is still detectable in both Russia and Poland.

The new versus the old

Thus, are we to conclude that Poland and Russia share all in common with respect to corporate ownership characteristics? The answer is no. Table 1.2 sorts the medium and large-size companies by their origin (method of establishment). This time it is Poland which is different from the other three economies (again as confirmed by χ^2 values for the pairwise comparisons): 67 per cent of medium-size and large companies in Poland are *de novo* (new) firms, that were created from scratch by the owners/entrepreneurs, as compared with 56 per cent in the Czech Republic, 51 per cent in Russia and only

Table 1.2   Company origins, based on EBRD BEEPS survey, 2002

Company origins	*Czech Republic*	*Hungary*	*Poland*	*Russia*	*Total*
Privatized	19	28	32	39	118
	26.39	45.90	28.32	34.51	32.87
New private	40	20	76	58	194
	55.56	32.79	67.26	51.33	54.04
Subsidiary of	5	4	1	7	17
privatized company	6.94	6.56	0.88	6.19	4.74
Joint venture with	7	8	3	8	26
foreign company	9.72	13.11	2.65	7.08	7.24
Other	1	1	1	1	4
	1.39	1.64	0.88	0.88	1.11
Total	72	61	113	113	359
	100.00	100.00	100.00	100.00	100.00

Notes: Small companies (employment below 50) are excluded from comparisons. The first figure = cell count, the second (lower) figure = column percentage. Pearson $\chi^2(12) = 26.1384$ (probability = 0.010).
For pair-wise comparisons:
Czech Rep. v. Hungary: Pearson $\chi^2(4) = 7.7108$ (probability = 0.103),
Czech Rep. v. Poland: Pearson $\chi^2(4) = 10.1656$ (probability = 0.038),
Czech Rep. v. Russia: Pearson $\chi^2(4) = 1.5945$ (probability = 0.810),
Hungary v. Poland: Pearson $\chi^2(4) = 23.5710$ (probability = 0.000),
Hungary v. Russia: Pearson $\chi^2(4) = 6.1456$ (probability = 0.189)
Poland v. Russia: Pearson $\chi^2(4) = 9.8808$ (probability = 0.042)

33 per cent in Hungary. (A detailed discussion of the Czech Republic would take us too far afield; however the relatively high share of new private firms – second after Poland – is noticeable. The mass privatization programme became the trademark of Czech privatization, and the main theme of analysis and discussion. However, one should not overlook a very efficient early small privatization programme that produced similar results and dynamism as in Poland; for details see Frydman *et al.*, 1993 and Earle *et al.*, 1994.) It is not just that Poland differs from Russia; the former seems unique in this respect when compared with other transition economies (see the typology presented in the subsequent chapter by Andreff).

Why is that? The explanation has to take into account the interaction of institutions, policies and social attitudes. As mentioned already, Poland experienced a relatively larger margin of economic freedom than most of the other countries subjected to the command economy system. That created experience and partly explains social attitudes. In a survey across 'old' and 'new' Europe, reported by Blanchflower *et al.* (2001), Poles came out on top in terms of willingness to create their own enterprises. That effect was enhanced by two other factors: full freedom of entry was established there quickly, starting in 1989 (the first regulations were adopted in 1988), and state enterprises could sell assets to outside owners from 1990 onwards, which helped many new firms to build capital (Balcerowicz, 1995). The role of the new private sector as a source of dynamism in the Polish economy throughout the 1990s is well-described in Jackson *et al.* (2005; see also Mickiewicz *et al.*, 2005, on employment creation by firms). However, as strongly argued by Winiecki (2002) it is far from obvious how much of the initial liberalization of entry survived the wave of increased regulatory and tax pressure in the late 1990s. Whether Poland will be able to revitalize its initial dynamism remains an open question at the time of writing.

More details

We may get additional insights by cross-tabulating the origins of companies against the dominant owner, and this is presented in Tables 1.3–1.6, for the four countries we discuss. The results should be treated with some caution, as they are based on only a small number of observations. For Hungary (Table 1.4), we may again confirm the dominant role of foreign ownership, and we can now also see that it resulted more from the choice of privatization method than from the new entry of foreign firms, as already asserted. When we compare Hungary with Poland, we see immediately that 50 per cent of *privatized* firms are controlled by foreign companies in the former economy, against 22 per cent in the latter, even if the outcome already incorporates the post-privatization, secondary ownership transfers. On the other hand, the share of foreign companies in the *new entrants group* is more similar: 35 per cent for Hungary against 30 per cent for Poland. One may also note some impact of investment-fund-driven mass privatization programmes in

Table 1.3 Czech Republic: company origins (rows) and identity of the largest shareholder (columns)

	Individual	*Family*	*Dom.comp.*	*For.comp*	*Bank*	*Inv.fund*	*Managers*	*Other*	*Total*
Privatized	8	0	6	4	0	1	0	0	19
	42.11	0.00	31.58	21.05	0.00	5.26	0.00	0.00	100.00
New private	20	4	5	6	0	0	2	2	39
	51.28	10.26	12.82	15.38	0.00	0.00	5.13	5.13	100.00
Subsidiary of privatized company	1	0	3	1	0	0	0	0	5
	20.00	0.00	60.00	20.00	0.00	0.00	0.00	0.00	100.00
Joint venture	0	0	0	6	1	0	0	0	7
	0.00	0.00	0.00	85.71	14.29	0.00	0.00	0.00	100.00
Other	0	0	1	0	0	0	0	0	1
	0.00	0.00	100.00	0.00	0.00	0.00	0.00	0.00	100.00
Total	29	4	15	17	1	1	2	2	71
	40.85	5.63	21.13	23.94	1.41	1.41	2.82	2.82	100.00

Table 1.4 Hungary: origins (rows) and identity of the largest shareholder (columns)

	Individual	*Family*	*Dom.comp.*	*For.comp*	*Managers*	*Other*	*Total*
Privatized	7	0	7	14	0	0	28
	25.00	0.00	25.00	50.00	0.00	0.00	100.00
New private	9	1	1	7	1	1	20
	45.00	5.00	5.00	35.00	5.00	5.00	100.00
Subsidiary of privatized company	0	0	4	0	0	0	4
	0.00	0.00	100.00	0.00	0.00	0.00	100.00
Joint venture	0	0	0	8	0	0	8
	0.00	0.00	0.00	100.00	0.00	0.00	100.00
Other	0	0	0	1	0	0	1
	0.00	0.00	0.00	100.00	0.00	0.00	100.00
Total	16	1	12	30	1	1	61
	26.23	1.64	19.67	49.18	1.64	1.64	100.00

Table 1.5   Poland: origin of the company (rows) and identity of the largest shareholder (columns)

	Individual	Family	Dom.comp.	For.comp	Inv.fund	Managers	Employees	Other	Total
Privatized	4	1	9	7	2	1	7	1	32
	12.50	3.13	28.13	21.88	6.25	3.13	21.88	3.13	100.00
New private	33	5	10	23	0	1	2	2	76
	43.42	6.58	13.16	30.26	0.00	1.32	2.63	2.63	100.00
Subsidiary of privatized company	0	0	0	1	0	0	0	0	1
	0.00	0.00	0.00	100.00	0.00	0.00	0.00	0.00	100.00
Joint venture	0	0	0	3	0	0	0	0	3
	0.00	0.00	0.00	100.00	0.00	0.00	0.00	0.00	100.00
Other	0	0	0	0	0	0	1	0	1
	0.00	0.00	0.00	0.00	0.00	0.00	100.00	0.00	100.00
Total	37	6	19	34	2	2	10	3	113
	32.74	5.31	16.81	30.09	1.77	1.77	8.85	2.65	100.00

Table 1.6   Russia: origin of the company (rows) and identity of the largest shareholder (columns)

	Individual	Family	Dom.comp.	For.comp	Bank	Managers	Employees	Government	Total
Privatized	19	2	9	2	0	1	5	1	39
	48.72	5.13	23.08	5.13	0.00	2.56	12.82	2.56	100.00
New private	36	1	4	13	1	2	0	1	58
	62.07	1.72	6.90	22.41	1.72	3.45	0.00	1.72	100.00
Subsidiary of privatized company	3	0	2	1	0	0	0	0	6
	50.00	0.00	33.33	16.67	0.00	0.00	0.00	0.00	100.00
Joint venture	0	0	2	6	0	0	0	0	8
	0.00	0.00	25.00	75.00	0.00	0.00	0.00	0.00	100.00
Other	0	0	0	1	0	0	0	0	1
	0.00	0.00	0.00	100.00	0.00	0.00	0.00	0.00	100.00
Total	58	3	17	23	1	3	5	2	112
	51.79	2.68	15.18	20.54	0.89	2.68	4.46	1.79	100.00

Notes: Small companies (employment below 50) are excluded from comparisons. The first figure = cell count, second (lower) figure = row percentage. For companies with two major shareholders (i.e. coded as three digit entries in the BEEPS survey answers), the identity of the first category is reported, i.e. 1 (individual) for 102 coding, 2 (family) for 207 coding, etc.).

both the Czech Republic and Poland: these are the only two economies where we can trace firms that have investment funds as owners, albeit the numbers are very small.

In general, the majority of *new* medium and large firms are controlled by either individual owners or families in all these economies. The percentage is clearly the highest for Russia (64%), but not very different from the Czech Republic (62%). It is 50 per cent for both Poland and Hungary.

However, a more significant difference relates to the structure of control of *privatized* companies. 54 per cent of Russian privatized companies have either individuals or families as the largest shareholders. That contrasts with Poland, where the corresponding figure is only 16 per cent. Hungary and the Czech Republic are in between, with 25 per cent and 42 per cent, correspondingly. The difference in composition could be partly explained by the role of foreign owners (22% of *privatized* firms in Poland and 5% in Russia are controlled by foreign companies), and partly by employee ownership (22% of privatized firms in Poland and 13% of privatized firms in Russia). Still, one may risk an observation that both the post-privatization and post-establishment (in case of new firms) transfers of ownership went to some extent in opposite directions in Poland and Russia. For the first economy, it was not uncommon for the entrepreneur to sell stakes in his/her company to some institutional owners, foreign in particular (however, unfortunately, the BEEPS survey does not distinguish between the original foreign entry and this type of secondary transfer). On the other hand, corporate control by individuals emerges as a typical outcome of post-privatization evolution in Russia.

Emerging patterns of capitalism?

Can we infer anything about the wider systemic characteristics from the ownership data just discussed? In particular, can the dominant role of individual concentrated ownership of companies in Russia be linked to the skewed general distribution of asset ownership? Is concentrated ownership of assets hidden behind the institutional ownership in Central Europe as well? While some institutional ownership may also lead back to concentrated ownership by individuals via pyramid schemes, it is unlikely it would change our conclusion that much. The institutional owners in Central Europe may be represented by privatized companies, with relatively dispersed, stock-exchange based ownership, or by foreign companies (see the chapters in this volume by Aluchna and by Jaworski *et al.*). Thus, most likely, in Central Europe we do not (yet?) face concentrated private individual owners or families controlling large sections of corporate property. Thus, the Central European economies remain different both from some Asian economies and some continental 'old' EU economies (especially France and Sweden), where ultimate corporate asset ownership is heavily concentrated (Morck and Steier, 2005).

Thus, in terms of ownership (but not in terms of access to education, and generally in human capital endowment!), one could say that Russia may be evolving towards a Brazilian model. Still, Central Europe, Poland included, could be following the same path of inequality in asset ownership at a slower pace. With entry being more difficult in Poland now, there is less chance that fresh entrepreneurship could counterbalance the tendency for those already wealthy getting richer. It is possible that in some foreseeable future Poland would therefore evolve towards the corporatist model of continental 'old' EU, where inequality in control over industrial assets is balanced not by entrepreneurial opportunities and private job creation, but by the welfare state.

The main themes of the book

The themes just discussed are expanded in Chapter 2 of this book, where Andreff shows how the alternative paths of privatization and transition produced different models of corporate control and ownership. Our quantitative presentation of ownership structure above was intended as an introduction to this analysis and is broadly consistent with it. We see the distinctive pattern of foreign corporate control in Hungary, a mixed model of new entry and employee control in Poland, some role of financial institutional investors in the Czech Republic (albeit it seems to be transient) and concentrated individual ownership in Russia. Andreff places his analysis in the context of both the general (economic) corporate governance literature and the economics of transition. Along the first dimension, he accentuates the inadequacy of the bipolar (owners-managers) agency perspective, a model that is too narrow to enhance our understanding of the complex corporate control relationship in the 'transitional economies'. The second line of his criticism relates to a rather mechanistic perspective on privatization, which dominated the theoretical discussion early in transition, and implied that a transfer of property to new owners is a simple task, identity of the new owners is not an important issue, and speed is critical. That led to an early stress on fast privatization methods, voucher privatization in particular. Various variants of these schemes were implemented in the Czech Republic, Russia and (on a more limited scale) in Poland. However, this led either to petrifaction of employee/insiders control, or to dispersed individual ownership. Coupled with inefficient legal mechanisms protecting minority shareholders, both outcomes produced no significant efficiency gains, which in turn, led ultimately to some reexamination of the applied theoretical perspectives.

Privatization is a proper domain of political economy and Chapters 3 and 4 adopt this perspective. Chapter 3 by Adachi presents the case of Yukos Oil Company. After the assets were privatized in an almost haphazard way at the beginning of the 1990s, the company's dominant owners imposed their control on multiple subsidiaries at the cost of abuse of minority shareholder rights, producing a tightly controlled, well-functioning business group. The 1990s story of Yukos illustrates very well the ambiguities and trade-offs both in the privatization process and in corporate control design. The trade-offs are between speed and quality and between internal functionality/efficiency and negative externalities. The privatization of Yukos was effective in the sense that it was fast, but ineffective in two ways. Firstly, and similar to other large Russian companies, it was non-equivalent: an enormous amount of corporate wealth was transferred to new owners, creating a sense of social injustice, which made the whole privatization programme unpopular. Second, it was ineffective, in the sense that it created a dispersed control structure, with multiple bargaining problems, difficult to solve, given unknown values of assets and high transaction costs in the nascent, inadequate legal capitalist environment. Adachi shows clearly that given this environment, the abuse of minority shareholders was almost unavoidable in the process of turning Yukos into a functional, integrated business group. Nevertheless, the process, while improving internal efficiency and increasing the value of the company significantly, contributed (along with other cases) to the general climate of uncertainty and short-termism on the part of investors.

The second phase of the Yukos company history started in the early 2000s, when after the consolidation of control, the dominant owners promoted a new policy of corporate responsibility, transparency and protection of shareholder rights. From one point of view, this was to be expected. Regardless of the way the ownership is originally established, ultimately it is in the best interest of the owners to promote a business climate where the property rights are protected and transferable. And the latter requires not only the protection of dominant holdings, but also of the minority interests. This may also explain some ambition of the Yukos owners to influence politics. However, by the time the new Yukos strategy was implemented, the balance in the close relations between businessman and politicians in Russia shifted towards the latter. On the positive side, the government became consolidated and more effective. On the negative side, it adopted some degree of authoritarian and antidemocratic stance, and Yukos became a good opportunity for signalling the shifting balance of power. Recalling the irregularities from the early period, Yukos was effectively renationalized.

The key issue is the following. Performance is conditional on the long-term horizon of investors, and the latter in turn may be endangered by the abuse from private agents. However, it may also be endangered by the threat coming from those in control of state institutions of coercion. At the time of writing it is still difficult to assess in which direction Russia will evolve, and if both of these dangers are going to diminish or grow in the future.

While Russia has its problems with the political environment, so does Poland. In fact, as discussed in the opening section to this chapter, there is a common denominator between the two countries: both preserved a relatively high share of state ownership. Chapter 4 by Bałtowski and Mickiewicz looks more closely into the issue of corporate governance of the state-owned sector in Poland. At the beginning of the transformation, that is in the early 1990s, economic policy-makers assumed that fast privatization could easily solve the problem of state corporate governance leaving very little in the state domain. Correspondingly, while the practice of governance of state assets was initially based on sound principles, these were never embedded in strong legal foundations, as the necessity to exercise control over state assets was perceived as temporary.

Nevertheless, fast privatization turned out to be impossible to accomplish. The slow path of privatization in Poland during the 1990s may be attributed both to technical reasons and to the difficulty in politically negotiating the implied distribution of benefits resulting from wealth transfers. Moreover, for some state-sector firms (coal mining, metallurgy, transport), to remain in the state domain was a guarantee of continued soft budgeting. In addition, the state administration and other politically-connected stakeholders soon rediscovered that control over state assets is possibly the easiest way of realizing private benefits associated with political control. Interests became entrenched and a strong anti-privatization lobby emerged. When the early 'technocratic' reformist governments of 1989–93 (Mazowiecki, Bielecki, Suchocka) were voted out of power, subsequent governments, regardless of the declared ideological affiliation, were increasingly involved in reaping benefits from the state-owned companies. This approach was reflected in the across-the-board appointment of 'our own people' to the supervisory boards and management boards of state-owned companies after each change of government. The state dominion was used to strengthen the party influence. However, growing public pressure and criticism ultimately led to some positive developments and reforms that have taken place in 2003–04 in the area of corporate governance exercised by the state. Thus, a source of optimism is in the free media and the democratic process. These, while slow and inefficient, are still the only mechanisms in place that may ensure that the reforms continue.

While the two chapters just discussed focus on the issue of public failure, chapter 5 (by Jaworski and Radosevic) illustrates vividly the potential for private failure. The chapter discusses the case of Elektrim, once the largest nonfinancial company quoted on the Warsaw Stock Exchange, which became practically insolvent, and which, with a threat of bankruptcy hanging over it for a few years, had to sell the majority of its assets to survive. The case may be seen from different angles and this is what the chapter provides. It illustrates the importance of strategic management, and the importance of a 'strategic owner', that is an institutional owner with branch-specific knowledge and resources capable of imposing a sound business strategy on a privatized company. This was missing in Elektrim, which was floated on the stock exchange with corporate control first left to insiders, and then to a coalition of insiders and financial investors. The company strategy was first based on using privatization opportunities and cheap prices of assets to create a wide multi-sector conglomerate, and in the next phase to focus on the core business of telecommunications. Lacking financial resources themselves, the company managers did not want to transfer control to foreign corporate investors either. The company overextended itself and at the time of the downturn of the telecommunications market it collapsed.

As argued by the authors, the Elektrim case illustrates how undercapitalized privatized enterprises with limited management capabilities have difficulty in growing through generic expansion. If we take a look into other cases, we can conclude that there were possibilities to grow effectively, either at a slower pace using only domestic capital or choosing one strategic investor. Controlling insiders were clearly oriented on growth, without a proper weight given to profits. Not only was there a conflict of interest between managers and shareholders, but also the strategy of the company was evolving in a haphazard way following changes in management. Clearly, neither the nascent capital market mechanism nor dispersed owners were capable of pressing a coherent long-term strategy on the insiders.

A corollary to the presence of strategic corporate investors as dominant owners is the formation of business groups and networks, and this is the topic of Chapters 6 and 7, the first of which focuses on Poland and the second on Russia. In their contribution on Poland, Chadam and Pastuszak provide evidence for an interesting phenomenon, which we already discussed in the first section of this chapter: the Polish corporate system is characterized by the strong presence of newly created private companies. As the authors demonstrate, after 15 years of growth, a significant number of these companies is already forming capital groups. Thus, while privatized companies are typically reducing the scope of their operations, becoming more focused on their core competence business, the successful new private companies are expanding into *related* areas of activity, building capital groups in the process. The authors document two things. Firstly, that the capital groups centred around new private companies exhibit stronger financial performance than their counterparts built by the privatized firms. And, secondly, they look into management strategies, and find that the new private companies seem to utilize superior knowledge-management techniques, which may be one of the important factors of their competitive edge.

In Chapter 7, Okhmatovskiy presents characteristics of the corporate networks in Russia, which encompass links with the banking sector (and are therefore labelled 'financial-industrial' groups). By mapping the links between the boards of the companies, Okhmatovskiy demonstrates that Russian banks receive many directional ties created by the executives of industrial corporations on boards of banks. He argues that this finding should be analysed in the institutional context, which is very different from the mature market capitalism of economies like the United States. Arguably, the network position of Russian banks reflects a subordinate role of banks in today's Russian economy. Okhmatovskiy explains this subordinate role by the fact that Russian banks are dependent on large industrial corporations (first of all, exporters of raw materials) as the major source of financial capital. An empirical test of hypotheses provides support for this context-specific application of the resource-dependence argument. Once again, we see that a mechanical application of the corporate governance paradigm designed for the institutional context of mature market economies may lead to unrealistic conclusions. Okhmatovskiy argues that it is more productive to compare emerging industrial-financial networks in Russia with their counterparts from the similar early stage of capitalist organization some one hundred years ago in the United States than with a very different institutional setting of the latter economy as observed today.

Chapter 8 by Filatotchev and Mickiewicz may be seen as complementary to Chapter 7. The focus is still on close ties between the banking institutions and corporations, while we discuss performance implications. Building on the 'law and economics' literature, the chapter analyses debt financing in an environment where a dominant owner is able to extract *ex ante* 'private benefits of control'. A model is suggested that describes a possible collusion between entrenched dominant shareholder(s) and fixed-claim holders in extracting a 'control premium'. In this framework, ownership concentration results in lower efficiency, measured as a ratio of investment to a firm's debt, while this effect may be modified as it also depends on the identity of the largest shareholder. The analysis sheds new light on agency problems associated with the financial-industrial groups in emerging and transition economies. On the macro-economic level, one possible outcome of the collusion between banks and dominant shareholders is a 'crowding-out' of entrepreneurial firms from the debt market. Thus, in line with the previous analysis, a supporting argument is found to illustrate the contrast between an economic system based on close links between providers of fixed claim finance and corporate owners, and the system where finance is more market-driven and the scope for the entry of entrepreneurial firms is higher.

Chapters 9 and 10 (first on Russia and next on Poland) follow a similar theme and offer an interesting empirical illustration demonstrating that the role of concentrated ownership may be ambiguous. In their contribution, Kuznetsov, Kuznetsova and Kapelyushnikov focus on the business environment characteristics in Russia, and argue that the strategies of the dominant owners are predominantly conditioned by it. They find a negative association between the size of the dominant owners shareholding and such performance parameters as profitability, investment and capacity utilization. The authors argue that these findings reflect the insecurity of dominant shareholders and top managers. They may be well-aware that the size of the holding gives no immunity against raiders: the legal system offers inadequate protection of legitimate owners, even if they hold majority stakes. Therefore it might be the case that the incumbent owners are reluctant to see their firms as long-term commitments in spite of large ownership stakes. On the other hand, concentrated ownership facilitates wealth transfers from the company. As a result, the owners may use their position to drain resources out of the firm.

Interestingly, the effects of ownership concentration are also ambiguous in Poland, and Aluchna in Chapter 10 utilizes a unique dataset on ownership and performance of Polish quoted companies. While the ownership concentration of quoted companies may be lower than for the joint sample of both quoted and privately held companies, it is still relatively high. The dominant shareholder holds on average a stake of 41 per cent of votes, whereas the three biggest shareholders control almost 60 per cent of votes. The civil law tradition of Poland supports ownership concentration and makes it consistent with the continental 'old' EU. Moreover, the results indicate that the ownership concentration has been growing over the analysed period of six years. The concentration calculated by the stake of the dominant shareholder as well as by the stakes of the three and five biggest shareholders increased. The stake of the dominant shareholder rose from 34 per cent in 1997 to almost 41 per cent in 2002, whereas the position of the three biggest shareholders increased from 52 per cent in 1997 to 59 per cent in 2002. At the same time, the free float calculated as the stake hold by shareholders who own less than 5 per cent fell from 43 per cent in 1997 to merely 33 per cent in 2002.

In addition, Aluchna applies simple but robust econometric techniques to demonstrate that it is not the ownership stake of the largest shareholder, but that of the second largest that may have a positive impact on the firm's performance. Owing a significant stake, the second biggest shareholder can monitor the dominant shareholder, may outweigh his/her impact on the company, and exert influence that leads to better performance. In contrast, unchecked dominant shareholders (holding large stakes, having full control over the company and not being monitored by strong minority shareholders) may engage in value-destroying practices. This finding is consistent with some cases in recent Polish corporate history where the dominant shareholder was successfully challenged by strong minority shareholders, typically investment funds, to block some value destruction, tunnelling, and other practices (transfer pricing, share dilution).

The latter conclusion leads us naturally to the Chapter 11 by Zalewska, which deals with the implication of pension reform for stockmarket development. It was the pension reform in Poland that led to the emergence of pension funds as important players on the stockmarket. However, their potential for exerting a disciplining impact on the dominant owner is conditional on the existence of a credible exit option. Unfortunately, as argued by Zalewska, the latter has been limited by the restrictions on the freedom of pension funds' investment decisions. In particular, the government enforces a home bias in investment behaviour (as is also the case in Russia).

The chapter not only provides a non-technical introduction to home bias and its role in stockmarket development, but also uses the Polish experience as a case study. It discusses the main arguments for portfolio diversification, the primary side effects that emerge from locking funds into underdeveloped equity markets, and highlights the problems the Polish pension funds face as a result of the 'enforced' home bias policy of the Polish authorities. The findings support the view that an enforced home bias has a negative impact on local stockmarket development, on the performance of pension reform and on corporate governance.

With Chapter 12 by Köke and Schröder we move to a more general perspective, discussing the capital markets in Central and Eastern Europe. These are fast-growing emerging markets, although they still exhibit a relatively low market capitalization and turnover compared to Western European exchanges. The high speed of expansion corresponds to strong economic growth in Central and Eastern Europe. Another important reason might be the membership in the European Union and expectations on a future EMU membership as well as an increasing integration into the world economy. The best-developed stock exchanges are those of the Czech Republic, Hungary and Poland, and among these, the Polish Stock Exchange clearly merits a top ranking. The Warsaw Stock Exchange has the highest capitalization, the largest official market segment, which is particularly interesting for foreign and institutional investors, and a liquid index future on the blue chip index WIG20, which allows investors to efficiently hedge stockmarket risk.

Building on this discussion, the authors offer a more detailed analysis of the sources of corporate finance. This shows that the CEE firms finance the largest fraction of investment internally. Compared to Western countries, only Hungarian companies finance a similarly large fraction of gross fixed capital formation externally (about 50%), that is without relying on internally generated funds such as retained earnings. This fraction is much lower for Poland (25%), the Czech Republic (11%) and the Slovak Republic (4%). Closer analysis of the sources of external finance reveals that the largest part is obtained by taking new credits, and a much smaller part by issuing equity or debt securities. In Hungary and Poland, new credits significantly contribute to financing investment, while in the Czech Republic the issue of domestic debt securities is particularly relevant for corporate finance.

The dominance of credit finance is confirmed in a case study of all nonfinancial corporations listed by the Warsaw Stock Exchange. It has also been growing in significance in recent years and, compared to earlier years of transition, internal funding has declined significantly. While finance by equity issues has declined over the period 1994–2000, it still contributes strongly to corporate finance and its significance may be growing again alongside stronger economic growth and revitalization of the Warsaw Stock Exchange in the early 2000s.

Köke and Schröder's findings are well-complemented by the contribution by McGee (Chapter 13), who discusses corporate governance regulations. Based on the careful analysis of the Reports on the Observance of Standards and Codes (from the World Bank) and other sources, the author concludes that corporate governance practices in Hungary and Poland seem to be somewhat better than corporate governance in the Czech Republic. Another clear conclusion is that all three countries are in need of improvement in some areas of corporate governance. This chapter points out which areas of corporate governance are strong and which are weak for each of the three countries, and provides a discussion of why this is the case.

It is likely that corporate governance practices in all three countries will continue to improve, perhaps markedly, in the next few years. One impetus for improvement is membership in the European Union; pressure from EU bureaucrats will force changes in corporate structure and governance practices. The adoption and implementation of IFRS and International Auditing Standards will help improve corporate financial reporting practices. Assistance in the improvement process will also come from within, as top management seeks foreign investment. The Big-4 accounting firms, which audit most of the larger firms in these countries, will help enterprises in these countries climb the learning curve, thus facilitating the process of corporate governance reform and improvement. It would not be too much of a stretch to predict that in a decade, if not less, the corporate governance practices of the Czech Republic, Hungary and Poland will be more or less on a par with practices in the older members of the EU, at least as far as the large companies are concerned.

Chapter 14, also by McGee, focuses on corporate governance rules adopted in Russian companies, and on transparency in particular. As noted by the author, the passage of time, moving up the learning curve through trial and error, plus advice from the large international accounting firms and international organizations have all helped Russian companies increase both the quantity and quality of disclosure. Contrary to some stereotypes, in terms of governance practices, Russia's score is now on a similar (or even higher) level than in several Central European countries, Poland in particular, and clearly higher than China. The quality of Russian financial statements is getting better, and an increasing number of Russian accountants are seeing the value of good reporting practices. Nevertheless, there is a long way to go to achieve the standards prevailing in high-income OECD economies.

In addition, the chapter focuses more closely on two aspects of transparency: completeness and timeliness. The financial statements of selected Russian companies are examined to determine the extent and timeliness of disclosure, two key aspects of transparency.

Conclusions

Obviously, it is difficult to summarize a number of interesting themes included in this volume in a short statement. Nevertheless, we intend to highlight a few points, with some arbitrariness and a serious risk of specification error and selectivity bias. Our intention here is to highlight some areas, which may still be controversial and deserve further research.

Corporate governance may improve either bottom-up, by voluntary adoption of good practices by large companies, or top-down by improving the standard of government regulation and enforcement. Interestingly, as of today, the largest Russian companies while still a long way from the best world practice, have improved a lot by their own actions and their corporate governance practice looks *better* than that found in Central Europe, Poland included, contrary to some stereotypes. After all, as noted by McGee, Russian companies that want to attract foreign investment, or even a loan from the local bank, need to disclose financial information. Paradoxically, however, it may well be that it is the instability that one finds in the business environment that provides the largest Russian companies with a strong incentive to counterbalance it with the stability of their own accounting and corporate governance practices.

Investors are concerned by the risk originating both from within and outside companies. The latter source of risk implies that our understanding of corporate governance is enhanced as soon as we extend it towards the political economy perspective. Ultimately, the providers of finance may be expropriated both by majority shareholders and by government officials. Self-regulated capital markets may be the ideal solution, but for such an institution to work well, one needs a rather long time. And even where good corporate governance practice is adopted, it still may not lead to wider economically efficient outcomes if more basic protection and stability of property rights is endangered. Thus, a well-functioning market left alone in the absence of the state is an illusion: a limited state is impossible where state institutions fail. A weak state is not a limited state, rather, it is an unpredictable state.

In this respect Russia and Poland have few things in common, and a few things that make them different. Both share a common tradition, which is one of extensive state control and interference coupled with limited predictability. Unlike several other major transition countries, both have extensive state corporate ownership, which, unlike some Western economies, is not yet subject to the same corporate governance rules as the private sector. In both countries, corruption and realization of political private benefits has been rampant albeit the scale is smaller in Poland.

With all the similarities there are also differences, however. The rich natural resource base in Russia is both an advantage and a disadvantage. An advantage, if properly used, is that it may result in a lower tax burden and a better business environment in the non-resource sector. It is a disadvantage if rent-seeking and rent extraction results in concentrated control of assets, with oligarchic structures not interested in competition, freedom of entry and promoting new entrepreneurship.

The second difference relates to the characteristics of the political system. Russia is a much larger country and a strong presidential system may be an advantage if it facilitates reforms and change. And some corporate governance reforms have indeed been introduced in Russia. However, with concentrated political power, there is also a risk that Russia may be going back from democracy to some form of authoritarian political capitalism. And democracy, with all its inefficiency, is still a more efficient mechanism for institutional improvement.

One general lesson from this book is that from the point of view of economic efficiency, both new entry and balance of power are good. This we see on the micro level. Newly created capital groups perform better than the old ones, centred around privatized enterprises. Along a different cross-section, companies where the dominant owners' influence is balanced by a strong minority stockholder base seem to perform best.

On a purely formal plane, corporations are not that different from polities. Thus, these two general findings may apply in the latter case as well.

2

Corporate Governance Structures in Postsocialist Economies: Towards a Central Eastern European Model of Corporate Control?

*Wladimir Andreff**

Fifteen years after the dawn of postsocialist economic transformation, corporate governance structures differ significantly across Central Eastern European countries (CEECs) and the Commonwealth of Independent States (CIS) members. The observed differentiation is to a large extent due to the variety of methods that have been used to privatize former state-owned enterprises (SOEs). In addition, the growth of the *de novo* private sector and the extent of residual state property also had an important impact on governance structures. In the new private start-ups, a strong corporate governance structure – the monitoring of a single or a few owner(s) – tends to prevail while in privatized firms (that is former SOEs) a managerial corporate control is widespread. In our country sample, corporate governance structures change very slowly since the emerging capital markets are not yet functioning properly and the set of appropriate institutions is not comprehensive and not fully enforced. Fifteen years after privatization has begun, the corporate governance structures in CEECs can be described using the following stylized models: a foreign capital controlling stake, managerial control (sometimes with the cooperation of banks), an outsider–insider coalition governing the enterprise, and/or an employee governance and strong owner-managers position in newly created firms. In recent years, some converging tendencies towards an 'average' Central Eastern European model of corporate governance have shown up; its two major pillars are a strong foreign investor control over big corporations, combined with strong governance by a single owner over genuine small and medium sized *private* enterprises (SMEs).

---

* An earlier version of this paper was presented at Amsterdam Research Centre for Corporate Governance Regulation (ARCCGOR) Inaugural Workshop, *Vrije* Universiteit Amsterdam, 17–18 December 2004.

The impact of privatization on corporate governance structures

The corporate governance structure of a Soviet enterprise was rather simple: the state, as the single owner, assigned all management decisions to a single firm's executive director who was assisted in his work by some engineers and executive managers. While in charge of fulfilling the enterprise plan, the executive director was subject to different checks and controls from his tutelage industrial ministry, from the state bank (*Gosbank* in the USSR) and from the communist party. Due to information asymmetry, all enterprise directors were at any time capable of cheating (biasing all information transferred to controlling bodies) during both processes of building-up and implementing the plan. Such a cybernetic weakness was one basic source of inefficiency in the former centrally planned economies (Andreff, 1993).

The economic reforms launched by Gorbachev in the Soviet Union attempted to alleviate the causes of economic inefficiency through increasing the decision-making autonomy given to enterprise directors and managers; that is – in terms of a property rights analysis – through fully transferring the cash flow right (or *usus fructus*) over the enterprise's assets to them. In some other socialist countries, such as Hungary and Poland, an elected employee committee was entitled to supervise the current decisions (or *usus*) made by the director and managers, whereas Yugoslavia adopted its special form of self-management in granting supervision and cash-flow rights to the enterprise personnel (however, the control right or *abusus* never got out of state hands). Thus, during the last years of the communist regime, in nearly all CEECs, corporate governance was taken over by insiders, either managers (the director included of course) or employees (or both). The only exception to insider governance was regarding the control right over the enterprise's assets, namely the right to sell them, which was kept by the state administration, although it was partially alleviated by newly introduced schemes of leasing and renting assets.

In the early years of postsocialist transition, privatizing SOEs was envisaged as the major tool for changing not only ownership, but also management and governance in order to improve economic efficiency through asset restructuring and labour shedding. However, even before privatization laws had been passed, a significant development of so-called spontaneous or *nomenklatura* privatization sprang up in all post socialist economies in transition (PET). This meant that the director and managers immediately used their supervision and cash-flow rights in such a way as to take over all the enterprise residual revenue, tunnel it into private companies they had just set up on purpose, to strip the most interesting assets from the SOE to their own newly settled private firms. Spontaneous privatization strengthened the consensus that the privatization drive should proceed at the fastest speed, whatever the price to be paid, so that communist managers and politicians could not transform their former political power into economic ownership. The long-run consequences for corporate governance of such an accelerated, if not forced[1], privatization process remained unheeded, at least in the mainstream economic literature, for several years. Nevertheless, some time was required to elaborate on and adopt privatization laws and, usually, they were not passed early enough to avoid or prevent spontaneous privatization from occurring.

On the other hand, some economists have advocated since the very beginning a slower development of the private sector, stressing the role of new enterprises created from scratch (Kornaï, 1990) and privatizations exclusively implemented by means of asset sales, the only way not to generate serious corporate governance problems (Andreff, 1991, 1992). Their recommendations were ignored or criticized by the mainstream and rejected by international economic organizations until the late 1990s[2]. In their survey of the literature, Shleifer and Vishny (1997) conclude that an effective corporate governance structure (that triggers restructuring and turns a loss-making SOE around) requires a 'hard core' of controlling blockholder(s), as the only feasible alternative to a well-functioning capital-market based indirect corporate governance mechanism (neither present nor possible to introduce quickly in PET). The emergence of this core of blockholder(s) can only be the outcome of firm privatization through direct asset sales to strategic investor(s) or initial public offerings followed by a market acquisition of the newly issued shares by those investors who wish to take over a majority or minority blockholding position. At odds with the previous conclusion, during the 1990s, Washington international organizations and their experts prioritized simple quantitative criteria such as the speed of privatization and the number of firms privatized and assumed them to be guaranteeing the political objective of an irreversible change in ownership.

This approach is well-exemplified by Jeffrey Sachs (1991), who argued that the initial economic conditions in PETs made it impossible to efficiently privatize SOEs through asset sales and recommended resorting to non-standard methods of privatization, supposedly enabling a rapid transfer of SOE ownership to new private proprietors. The so-called non-standard methods are mass privatization, management and employee buy-out (MEBO) at preferential prices, and restitution (to former (pre-communism) owners, or their heirs).

However, the problem is that MEBO transfers those property rights (*usus* and *usus fructus*) previously acquired by SOE managers ... to the same incumbent managers while adding the *abusus* to their former rights. As to mass privatization, it generates a widespread capital scattering since vouchers (then redeemed into shares) are allocated free to the whole population. When the vouchers are redeemed into shares, managers are used to take benefit from their insider information in such a way as to acquire significant blocks of shares. If they succeed in such endeavours, mass privatization then comes out with the same result as MEBO, that is a transfer of property rights from incumbent managers ... to incumbent managers.

Given the economic importance rapidly reached by the private sector in GDP (Table 2.1), and the fact that this sector's growth is partly due to privatization, the variety of current corporate governance structures in PETs is strongly determined by those privatization methods that have been adopted in each country.

At the peak of the initial privatization impulse, by mid-1990s, the distribution of privatized assets according to privatization methods in PETS was as follows (Andreff, 1999a): only 13 per cent had been privatized through asset sales, 43 per cent through MEBOs, 24 per cent through mass privatization and 20 per cent by means of other methods such as restitution, heirs' (financial) compensation and municipalization of assets. Since then, the distribution has evolved towards a higher share of asset sales due, in particular, to an increased participation of foreign investors. However, mass privatization is still the primary method, which has been used so far in eight PET and MEBO

Table 2.1   Major privatization methods in transition economies

Country	Share of the private sector in GDP in 2004*	Direct asset sales	Mass privatization	MEBO
Albania	75%	Tertiary	Secondary	Primary
Armenia	75%	Tertiary	Primary	Secondary
Azerbaijan	60%	Secondary	Primary	No
Belarus	25%	No	Secondary	Primary
Bulgaria	75%	Primary	Secondary	Tertiary
Croatia	60%	Tertiary	Secondary	Primary
Czech Republic	80%	Secondary	Primary	No
Estonia	80%	Primary	Secondary	No
Georgia	65%	Secondary	Tertiary	Primary
Hungary	80%	Primary	No	Secondary
Kazakhstan	65%	Secondary	Primary	No
Kyrgyzstan	75%	Tertiary	Primary	Secondary
Latvia	70%	Secondary	Primary	No
Lithuania	75%	Secondary	Primary	No
Macedonia	65%	Secondary	No	Primary
Moldova	55%	Secondary	Primary	No
Poland	75%	Primary	Tertiary	Secondary
Romania	65%	Secondary	Tertiary	Primary
Russia**	70%	Secondary	Tertiary	Primary
Slovakia	80%	Tertiary	Secondary	Primary
Slovenia	65%	Tertiary	Secondary	Primary
Tajikistan	50%	No	No	Primary
Turkmenistan	25%	Secondary	No	Primary
Ukraine	65%	Tertiary	Secondary	Primary
Uzbekistan	45%	Secondary	Tertiary	Primary

* Estimation: EBRD (2005).
** Three-quarters of mass privatization turned out to be MEBOs.
Source: Vagliasindi (2003); private sector shares: EBRD (2005).

in 13 of them. Asset sales, including to foreign investors, has really been privileged only in Hungary and Estonia, even though it has become a significant privatization method in Bulgaria and Poland in recent years; it is also going to outstrip all other methods in the Czech Republic with bank privatizations very much open to foreign capital since 1999 (Bednarova, 2001). Corporate governance structures have been diversified further in PETs by the skyrocketing growth, though uneven from one country to the other, of start-ups in the *de novo* private sector (Duchêne and Rusin, 2003; Dallago and McIntyre, 2003). On the other hand, some SOEs appear to be so much 'unprivatizable' that the state has kept, willy-nilly, a significant share in their capital stock (residual state property), whereas some other SOEs will remain in a state of ongoing privatization for a rather long time, and a last group of SOEs many still avoid privatization because the government declares them 'of strategic importance', in particular being unwilling to sell the shares to foreign investors.

The overall result is – insofar as various privatization methods have been experimented with – a variety in the forms of ownership and in the distribution of property rights (Aukutsionek *et al.*, 1998), and a diversity in corporate governance structures, both in each PET and across all PETs.

Diversified corporate governance structures

Thus, corporate governance structures are now complex and diversified in all PETs. An overview of these structures is exhibited in Table 2.2 in which they are classified from the strongest as assessed by the principal-agent model (those structures where shareholders are assumed to have the strongest monitoring power) to the weakest (where the shareholders' supervising power is the most alleviated, diluted and ineffective).

The economic analysis of corporate governance in PET is difficult so far because there is no device that compares either to the 20-F form in the USA (which encompasses one section about control/governance to be filled by the informant) or to the European Directive 88/627/EEC on big holdings (Becht and Mayer, 2002). In the future, quantitative analysis will be facilitated for the eight PET which have been admitted to join the European Union (EU) in May 2004, since they will have to implement the aforementioned European Directive.[3] Better information about shareholders' votes and their possible concentration will then be available even though information regarding the concentration of stock ownership may remain partly undisclosed (which is especially impenetrable in PET so far). Meanwhile, studying the outcome of privatization can provide an insight into the whole spectrum of governance structures that exist in postsocialist firms.

The first configuration is one in which a private owner, often the only owner or a few associated owners, hold the entire enterprise stock (capital) and exert all the prerogatives of an (owning) boss, that is as chief executive officer (*usus*), as residual claimant (*usus fructus*) and as possible seller of his/her enterprise

Table 2.2   Corporate governance structures in East European enterprises

Enterprises	Ownership acquired through	Enterprise governed by	Representative countries
Private	Creation from scratch	Owner (single)	Poland
	Small privatization: auction sale asset by asset	Owner (single)	All countries
Privatized	Restitution	Former owner, heir	Czech Republic
	Initial public offering	Institutional investors*	Rare in any country
	Direct asset sales	Foreign investors	Hungary, Estonia
		Outsiders or local FIGs**	Russia
	MEBOs	Employees	Poland, Croatia
		Managers	All countries
	Mass privatization	Investment funds	Czech Republic
		Managers	Russia, Kazakhstan
		State holdings	Poland
	Loans for shares scheme	Banks, FIGs*	Russia
Mixed	Ongoing privatization (the state is the single or majority shareholder)	State representatives	All countries
	Residual state property	Unspecified	All countries
Public	Nationalized after self-management	State representatives	Slovenia, Croatia
	State-owned (not yet corporatized)	State-appointed managers as before	Belarus Turkmenistan

* pension funds, investment funds, insurance companies, etc.
** FIGs: Financial-industrial groups.

(*abusus*). It is so in *private enterprises* created from scratch (start-ups) whether they are privately held enterprises or small corporations (SMEs). It is a strong governance structure, which is similar to that of SMEs in Western market economies. Where do the assets come from in such small enterprises? Their origin can be legal or not, the assets provided to the start-up can result from a primary accumulation of capital by the new entrepreneur or from asset-stripping and tunnelling from a SOE in which he/she was previously (or still is) employed. The major problem with these new private SMEs is that their access to banking and other finance is hindered by their tiny or non-existing collateral for loans. Nevertheless, the creation of start-ups has been of tremendous magnitude, mainly in Poland (Rusin, 2002) and then the Czech Republic (Vincensini, 2003), as well as Hungary, Slovenia, Bulgaria, Romania and Slovakia.

A variant of small private enterprises are those owned by a single or a few associated owners emerging from the process of *small privatization*. The latter refers to the state releasing retail shops, hotels, restaurants, cars, lorries, buses and small craft production either through public auction sales or property transfers to employees.[4] Small privatization also encompasses the state selling the physical assets of beforehand-dismantled SOEs such as various machine tools, equipment goods, buildings or workshops that can be of interest for some private purchaser.

Small privatization has brought about millions of mushrooming SMEs. If one can speak of a major success story in postsocialist privatization, small privatization shows up in the foreground. The only dark side of the story is that private SMEs are facing high mortality rates, due to their lack of finance and/or expertise that is not compensated by their high birth rates (Rusin, 2002).

Strong corporate governance, with a strict shareholder monitoring of managers, is rarer in *privatized firms*. When it comes to restitution to a former owner or his/her heirs, the outcome is ambiguous. In a number of cases, the former owner or heir has flown away from the communist regime long ago and stays abroad; he/she may only be interested in closing down the factory and making all workers redundant. He/she may intend to restructure or change the nature of the business, or may simply resale the assets obtained in the restitution process. Whatever the decision, the owner enjoys non-alleviated property rights despite a possible resistance on the side of managers and employees. In addition, restitution is in direct conflict with any other privatization method that would result in some non-equivalent transfer of shares to insiders. Few PET, except the Czech Republic, engaged in ambitious restitution programmes. Elsewhere, as in Hungary for instance, those entitled to restitution did not receive physical assets but were compensated with privatization vouchers enabling them to participate in the privatization of SOEs that were for sale (with voucher redemption into shares). They then entered the stockholding of privatized corporations, most often as minority shareholders excluded from corporate governance.

Privatization based on *initial public offerings* was eventually rather rare in PETs since, when the privatization drive was launched, the stock exchange either did not yet exist, or if launched early (Hungary and Poland) it was still too underdeveloped to become a major channel for privatizations. The newly emerging stockmarket was tiny in terms of (not even daily) transactions. All the more so since, at the very beginning, institutional investors were few, apart from state banks, state insurance companies and state financial institutions. Gathering a hard core of monitoring blockholders remained, in most cases, an unresolved issue because this hard core could not rally non-state shareholders and foreign investors (whose acquisitions were restricted or sometimes even forbidden in most privatization programmes, except in Hungary and Estonia). Moreover, domestic or local capitalist tycoons, capable of buying a substantial block of shares, were very few or non-existent at the onset of transition. The most efficient corporate governance structure coming out from privatization has been acquisition or take-over[5] by foreign investors. Take-overs have nearly always resulted from a direct asset sale negotiated by the state with a foreign firm and practically never from the latter's raid by swiftly buying shares of the targeted domestic firm at the stock exchange. In such cases the monitoring blockholder is a foreign transnational corporation, capable of supervision and used to efficiently supervise its foreign subsidiaries' managers.

A number of assets have been directly sold by the state to domestic or local investors, that is to domestic outsiders. However, at the dawn of the privatization process, sales to domestic outsiders were rather few and undesirable because they boiled down to transferring assets to incumbent *nomenklatura* leaders and managers or, even worse, to those who had previously illegally enriched themselves to accumulate enough wealth in the second (underground) economy or in the *Mafia* to be able to invest it in a substantial share of a privatized corporation. In some PET, the law or the programme of privatization forbid the sale of SOEs' assets to incumbent communist leaders and rulers. After some time, however, since the mid-1990s, circumstances changed and privatized corporations have been acquired or taken over by domestic outsiders. The number of '*nouveau riche*' has substantially increased thanks to legal, illegal or borderline transactions in formal or informal emerging markets; such individuals' capacity for investing in the property of privatized corporations has improved. After the initial MEBO and mass privatization programmes, share resale transactions expanded, sometimes in the stockmarket, more often off the market[6]. This opened up an opportunity for domestic outsiders such as the *nouveau riche*, but also for insiders using their own private 'screen companies' and oligarchs heading the new financial-industrial groups (FIGs) to acquire substantial – often controlling – blocks of shares in privatized enterprises. All these share purchasers were looking for a sizeable block-holding, which – with some alliances – could enable them to take over all strategic decisions in the targeted privatized enterprise; that is to exert a strong corporate governance in spite of the wishes, hopes and intents of both incumbent managers and minority shareholders. Although all share re-sales did not end up with a corporate governance dominated by a hard core of monitoring blockholders, they increased the proportion of corporations under outsider and FIG control, as in Russia for example (Table 2.3).

The trickiest issue of corporate governance in privatized firms surged after MEBO and mass privatization. In PET with a self-management tradition (former Yugoslavia, Poland), MEBO was the tool for transferring most firms to their personnel. Then, those who govern the enterprise are easily identified – that

Table 2.3   Corporate control of big privatized corporations in Russia

Proportion of total assets under the control of:	*1994*	*1996*	*1998*	*2000*
Insiders	60%–65%	55%–60%	50%–55%	30%–35%
Outsiders	12%–25%	30%–35%	35%–40%	50%–55%
The state	15%–20%	9%–10%	5%–10%	10%–12%

Source: Radygin (2000).

is employees and managers; but with MEBO we may say that enterprise assets are 'socialized' rather than genuinely privatized. Of course, employees become private owners of their enterprise but their main objectives are different from those of a capitalist owner. In acquiring ownership, and corresponding property rights, employees look to maintain jobs, secure current wage rates, and safeguard working conditions. Such a corporate governance structure is weak or inefficient, not likely to pave the way for high firm profitability. Most studies based on enterprise samples in PET show that employee-owned firms on average underperform other enterprises, even SOEs, as regards productivity and profitability, except for a few noticeable exceptions in Poland (see a survey of these sample studies in Djankov and Murrell, 2002; Megginson and Netter, 2001). On the other hand, employee ownership has triggered an interesting effect: it has markedly reduced, in particular in Poland, asset-stripping by incumbent managers before, during and after privatization (Nellis, 2002a).[7] As regards quality of owners, employees have submitted managers to strict supervision in such a way as to prevent their attempts to loot the firm's assets. However, such managerial discipline obtained by employees did not primarily aim at profit or shareholder value maximization – as uses to be the case with capitalist shareholders.

Anyway, a more frequent way out of MEBO is managerial governance over privatized enterprises. In the most common schemes, former communist enterprise managers have transformed their political power into economic capital.[8] Either altogether the managers hold a significant share in the privatized firm's stock, or they acquire it by purchasing shares from employees. Often, managers have simply utilized their authority over employees to take over all governing decisions or acquire employees' shares at low prices (managers are used to threatening with redundancy those employees who intend to sell their shares to outsiders, promising to keep jobs for those who will sell them their shares, etc.). In some countries, such as the Czech Republic, employees were excluded from MBOs (management buy-outs); managers were the only ones allowed to purchase assets. Sample studies have shown that manager-controlled (owned) firms on average outperform employee-owned enterprises and SOEs as far as productivity and profitability are concerned, although they underperform outsider-owned firms and do markedly worse than enterprises taken over by foreign investors (Andreff, 2003). The *managerial firm* is the predominant corporate governance structure emerging from privatization so far. This is confirmed when looking at mass privatization.

In all those PET which have privileged *mass privatization*, the results today are disappointing, standing very far from what has been expected 10 or 15 years ago. The objective was to offer free, or nearly free, to the whole population, privatization vouchers redeemable into shares that would give the right for anyone[9] to participate in the acquisition of state-owned assets. An initial and egalitarian distribution of property rights was supposed to evolve, in accordance with the Coase theorem[10], through share re-sales in the stockmarket, in such a way as to favour the emergence of blockholders. The latter were assumed to be willing to invest in privatized enterprises and purchase the shares of those citizens not interested or unfitted for business. Contrary to these expectations, in all PET, mass privatization paved the way, directly or not, for corporate governance dominated by managers in privatized firms.

For instance, in Russia, three options were available in the framework of mass privatization. According to option 1, 40 per cent of corporate stock was offered to the personnel at a preferential price. In option 2, employees could immediately get 51 per cent of the stock at a higher (than the book value) price, and option 3 preserved 30 per cent of the stock to a managerial group committing itself to turn the enterprise around and avoid bankruptcy. In each case, the remaining part of the stock was to be sold against privatization vouchers until June 1994, and for money 'cash' privatization afterwards. Option 2 was chosen by over 73 per cent of the roughly 15,000 enterprises involved in the mass privatization programme, while option 1 was adopted by 25 per cent of privatized firms, leaving only less than 2 per cent in option 3 (Blasi *et al.*, 1997). In nearly all circumstances, managers have kept a firm hand over corporate governance since the remaining stock was so widely scattered. Moreover, they have proceeded to a capital concentration in their hands by acquiring the shares held by the personnel (under threat, see above). Thus, strong managerial entrenchment has been the key result of mass privatization (Filatochev *et al.*, 1999; Labaronne, 1998). It was strengthened by the opportunistic and strategic behaviour of managers. In Russian privatized firms, managers exerted strict supervision over who bought their enterprise shares; most enterprises did not use independent shareholder registers; and most managers declared they had opposed financial disclosure and majority ownership by an outside investor with enough capital to turn the firm around. Inadequate legal and regulatory frameworks and poor protection of minority shareholders' rights increase managerial benefits to be gained from holding controlling stakes. When legal rules fail to constrain the actions of controlling managers, the latter are used to engage in self-serving activity such as the transfer of assets at arbitrary prices to manager-owned private firms. This, in turn, dilutes minority claims further. Incumbent managers have also circumvented the law: we have listed (Andreff *et al.*, 1996; see also the list provided in Blasi *et al.*, 1997) more than 20 varieties of violations of the corporate law in Russian privatized enterprises, from not convening shareholder meetings to votes by show of hands.[11] Due to its weakness and unpredictability, the Russian court system has not been able to put a brake on these violations.[12]

In other PET, corporate governance was taken over by managers as an indirect result of mass privatization. In the Czech Republic, about three-quarters of all privatization vouchers have been purchased for the citizens by Privatization Investment Funds (PIFs), which thereafter have redeemed them into shares. At first sight, becoming major shareholders, these newly created institutional investors (that is the PIFs) seemed to have taken over most privatized firms.

Therefore, the PIF's managers were in a position to monitor the decisions made by the managers running the firms belonging to the PIF's portfolio but, as Stiglitz (2000) stressed, the problem then became 'who monitors the monitors?' (that is, who monitors the PIFs' managers?). In the context of the Czech Republic, the response was quite clear since many PIFs had a major (often only one) shareholder, which was a state bank or a state insurance company. Thus, a Czech Minister for the Economy (Mertlik, 1996) once said that mass privatization is the fastest track to transfer state property ... to the state. As regards corporate governance, it was transferred from former (now privatized) SOEs' managers to PIFs' managers and eventually to state banks' managers, in other words from incumbent *nomenklatura* to *nomenklatura*.

In the Polish (limited-scale) variant of mass privatization, the state set up 15 National Investment Funds across which the assets of would-be privatized firms have been allocated. Polish citizens could not acquire shares in the privatized firms' stock but they were entitled to become shareholders of the Funds. Attempting to circumvent the issue of monitoring the monitors, each Fund is managed by a management consortium comprised of foreign and Polish banks and audit agencies. The resulting governance structure *a priori* seemed stronger than the one with the Czech PIFs, since each management consortium was given the explicit objective of increasing the value of the asset portfolio held by its Fund. However, all the Funds behaved in such a way as to disinvest from the least profitable firms in their portfolio and to invest in the most profitable ones instead of, as expected, restructuring and modernizing the most obsolete firms. In fact, they adopted the behaviour of an institutional investor (such as, say, an American pension fund) and did not involve themselves in the corporate governance of those firms they were supposed to monitor; as a result, restructuring is lagging behind in Polish mass privatized firms.

Finally, Russia experimented with the most criticized privatization method, the so-called 'loans for shares' scheme, even though it ended up with a strong corporate governance structure. The scheme was suggested in 1995 to President Yeltsin by Vladimir Potanin, the Uneximbank CEO, and involved the Russian State depositing in Russian banks significant blocks of shares from the stocks of the most valuable Russian SOEs (oil companies and other energy and raw materials producers). Banks would consider the stock they held as collateral for the loans that they offered in order to bail out a serious fiscal deficit. For each company involved in this device, an auction was opened and the winning bank got a block of shares, remitted the price as a loan to the state, while holding the shares until September 1996. If, on this date, the state had not reimbursed the loan, the bank would be allowed to sell or definitively keep the shares (and ownership in an oil trust, etc.). Since the state obviously was not capable of repaying its debt, banks gained through this scheme the ownership of the 'crown jewels' of the Russian industry, for a nominal sum[13], insofar as auctions were rigged and not exempt from collusion. All the winning banks were owned by a small group of financial oligarchs well-acquainted with the President of the Russian Federation (Nellis, 2002b). Some of these transactions were so fraudulent that the Moscow arbitrage court invalidated them. Nevertheless, a small group of oligarchs, including Roman Abramovitch, Evgueny Ananiev, Boris Berezovski, Mikhaïl Fridman, Vladimir Goussinski, Mikhaïl Khodorkovski, Igor Malatchenko, Vladimir Potanin, Alexander Smolenski, Oleg Deripaska, and others, appropriated the finest jewels of Russian industry. The 'loans for shares' scheme definitely discredited the Russian privatization drive which was both disapproved of by the World Bank and overtly criticized by the great bulk of the Russian population, and became infamous outside Russia.[14] While absolutely questionable from a moral or business ethics point of view, the scheme brought about the integration of valuable firms into oligarchic FIGs with a strong corporate governance structure (privatized enterprises are then monitored by the core bank of the FIG or by an oligarch – major shareholder – himself). It has contributed to increasing the outsiders' share in the overall control over Russian enterprises (Table 2.3) and to the emergence of a new economic and financial 'elite' (Andreff, 2004b; see also the more detailed discussion in Yuko Adachi's contribution in the present volume).

Until now, a number of enterprises remain in *mixed ownership* in PET, with both private owners and the state sharing their stock. First, there are those firms whose privatizations have been launched and are still ongoing, but some part of the stock is still in state hands. Second, there is the category of state residual property. In several privatized enterprises the state has kept a share in the stock ownership for one or another reason: the state may wish to avoid a take-over of the enterprise by foreign investors, and keeps a golden share or a minority blockholding; the state may not have been able so far to find enough purchasers to sell them the whole stockholding; or some of those entitled to benefit from MEBOs or from redeeming their vouchers into shares might not have acquired the shares they have a right to, and their shares remain in state hands. We therefore find some state representatives sitting on the boards of directors of such firms, in proportion with the stockholding share still in state ownership. A serious issue of corporate governance derives from this situation. Either incumbent managers govern the firm or state representatives in the board of directors adopt a strategic behaviour which dissuades private owners to invest further in the firm (or even incites them to sell their shares). Since the state representatives on the boards are usually civil servants, academics from state universities or state experts appointed by a ministry, they may not have the required financial, juridical, accounting and managerial skills to act as efficient enterprise executives. Moreover, as soon as appointed they make up a group of stakeholders with its own interests within the board of directors, interests that often conflict with those of private owners. As an in-group they may lean towards halting the privatization process of the firm (of course a comprehensive privatization of the stock would entail the phasing out of their participation in the board of directors, and a loss of influence and directors' fees). Besides this, the sustained relationships between these state representatives sitting on the boards and the state administration from which they come may harm independent corporate governance in partially privatized firms. It also happens that state residual property paves the way for an ambiguous corporate governance structure due to a lack of consensus or missing alliances between conflicting interests of managers, private shareholders and state representatives in the board (see also Bałtowski and Mickiewicz's contribution in this volume).

The last subset of firms in PET encompasses *public enterprises*; they still represent about 20 per cent of GDP in Hungary and over 80 per cent in Belarus and Turkmenistan. Their survival may be traced back in various ways. First, in the successor states of former Yugoslavia, Poland and some others, the self-managed enterprises were in 'social ownership' so that the first step before privatization was frequently to nationalize ('corporatize') them in order for the state to have full ownership at its disposal and then only privatize the newly state-owned enterprises. However, since privatization has taken some time, meanwhile, the boards of directors comprised only of state representatives remained in charge of running the corporations. On the other hand, in all PET, primarily in Belarus, Turkmenistan and Uzbekistan, a number of SOEs have not even been corporatized, in which case state-appointed managers, as before, dominate corporate governance. From the standpoint of the property rights theory and the principal–agent model, such a governance structure is assumed to be weak and inefficient, since managers are not monitored, and cannot be monitored, by many shareholders (here the assumption is that the whole population owns each SOE). An alternative view is to regard SOEs as having a single unique shareowner – the state – which is then in a strong position to lay down governance guidelines onto the managers, that is a strong governance structure. For instance, in China (Djankov and Murrell, 2002), the state is used to provide SOEs' managers with very strong incentives to behave in such a way as to maintain the enterprise in the black, while threatening them with heavy disciplinary and financial penalties if it is in the red; sanctions can go as far as the death penalty in cases of abuse of power! On the contrary, sanctions are less stringent and often deferred, sometimes non-existent, *vis-à-vis* SOEs' managers in Central and Eastern Europe and CIS countries.

In the same vein, we have recommended privatizing the management of public enterprises (Andreff, 1992, 1995) when the privatization of assets is not immediately feasible or is not desirable. What does this mean? Privatization of management consists in managing a public enterprise in such a way as to put a full stop to any current deficit, and then make profits in order to invest in restructuring the assets, eventually into foreign subsidiaries abroad; in other words, it means managing public enterprises according to exactly the same criteria as a private firm. Privatization of management is only feasible if the state, as the single shareholder, adopts an efficient corporate governance structure by providing appropriate incentives to SOEs' managers; that is, incentives which drive them to 'manage as in the private sector', and firing them overnight otherwise. A recent World Bank report (World Bank, 2002a) acknowledged that, often, it would have been preferable to leave assets in state hands – instead of swiftly launching mass privatization and MEBOs – long enough to identify reliable strategic investors and, only then, to sell SOEs to them. Unfortunately, the World Bank was not open to accepting such advice when it was suggested ten years ago (see among others Andreff, 1991, 1992).

Post-privatization corporate governance and performance

The overall picture of corporate governance in PET that we have screened above is put in somewhat static terms and only describes governance structures during the first decade of transition (that is, the 1990s). Of course, corporate governance structures are dynamic and usually evolve over a period of time. In emerging market economies, such as PET, the initial absence of appropriate rules and institutions that regulate changes in corporate governance and, later, their inadequate enforcement, have put limitations on the dynamics of corporate governance structures.

The key institutional deficiency relates to a lack of developed and tightly regulated capital markets in most PETs, more than one decade after the early days of transition (see contribution by Köke and Schröder in this volume). A tiny stockmarket not only delivers a distorted – disequilibrium – price for each quoted share (contrary to what is assumed when a great variety of shares are traded among very numerous traders), but it is often plagued by connected trading and speculative bubbles, and circumvented by vast off-market transactions. Regulating bodies of the stock exchange, when they are existent, have little experience and are often incapable of ensuring that transactions are fair or simply legal. Lacking a facilitating role of the stockmarket up to the end of the 1990s, take-overs, mergers and acquisitions between firms based in the same PET or in different PETs (transborder mergers) remained as exceptions, while an important wave of (including transborder) mergers and acquisitions flooded the global economy and world capital markets from 1994 to 2000. Since the end of the 1990s, concentration through take-overs and acquisitions started to develop in PET and, as a consequence, corporate governance has evolved in acquired or merged firms, switching from managers to outsiders and FIGs. For instance, in the Czech Republic the number of take-overs and acquisitions increased from 67 in 1997 to 196 in 1999, 221 in 2000 and 158 in 2001. In Russia as early as 1996–97, the state supported some take-overs and the setting-up of big holdings in key industries such as electricity, hydrocarbons and telecommunications (Nestor, 2002).

On the other hand, underground alliances between different groups of interests still exhibit the inertia of former networks between communist leaders, managers and bureaucrats. These alliances gather either insiders (primarily managers) or outsiders (primarily bankers and oligarchs), or only outsiders. So far there is practically no study that systematically identifies who exactly are those involved in such alliances. However, in a work by Bałtowski and

Mickiewicz (2000), three types of alliances appear to be widespread across Polish privatized firms: (1) alliances between a group of outsiders and representatives of the State Treasury (which holds the shares corresponding to residual state property), often opposed to the firms' personnel; (2) alliances between managers and employees against the representatives of the State Treasury; and (3) alliances of employees and the representatives of the State Treasury against either an outsider or the managerial team. Further studies monitoring blockholders and interlocking directorates need to be conducted when fuller information about them (for a first and partial attempt, see Mesnard, 1999).

More generally, the evolution of ownership structures is slow, and the pattern of corporate governance that is emerging in PET is path-dependent, reflecting the means used to privatize SOEs, the laws that have been enacted or revived, and the institutions that have emerged – or not – to facilitate corporate governance (Brada and Singh, 1999).

In particular, it is mostly due to national specificities in institutional environment that various empirical surveys produce a very scattered picture of the link between a privatization and restructuring in PET. The picture is more clear-cut for CEECs, as a number of surveys based on firm samples have reached the same sort of findings: microeconomic profitability has improved after privatization, and privatized firms have outperformed existing SOEs. However, in most surveys the result is subject to a selection bias. Was it privatization that fostered better enterprise performance, or was it better performance that led enterprise to be selected for privatization? Privatized firms were not randomly selected. The choice of a standard privatization method often reflects the fact that the firm is viable and potentially or really profitable under market conditions. Several enterprises sampled as privatized may well be still under state control (via residual state property), so that differences in performance between genuinely privatized and state-run firms may be partly levelled off. This occurs for example when some major adjustment efforts in state firms have been achieved, including redundancies and wage control in loss-making firms, under the pressure of the elimination of open-ended subsidies.

Profitability and productivity are supposed to reflect the scope and depth of restructuring, and thus the quality of corporate governance. The hypothesis then follows, often tested in enterprise surveys, that privatized firms perform better than SOEs, and those outsider-controlled outperform insider-controlled firms in terms of profitability and productivity. The most robust finding in various surveys so far is that foreign owners outperform former SOEs and all privatized firms in strategic restructuring (Bornstein, 2001) by bringing in expertise, technology and capital. On average, privatized firms are more profitable than SOEs, in line with the principal-agent model. Across privatized firms, more surveys exhibit insider-controlled firms engaged in survival-oriented adjustment than the other way round. Outsider-owned firms enjoy an advantage over SOEs. Firms with investment funds as the largest owners perform rather well, but firms owned by domestic non-financial companies often exhibit a weaker performance. Insider-controlled firms shed labour at significantly lower rates than either SOEs or other privatized companies, and do even worse on costs and revenues. Employee-owned firms even underperform SOEs in terms of labour shedding. This backs a strong mainstream case against the efficiency of employee buy-out privatization. However, worker councils in Polish enterprises have ultimately proved to be a positive force, namely in keeping an eye on managers and hindering them, if not totally preventing them, from asset-stripping and spontaneous privatization (Nellis, 2002a) that has pervaded privatizations in most PET. Worker control in this country eventually seems qualitatively more efficient than managerial control, at odds with the mainstream view. Contradicting the mainstream hypotheses as well, some surveys have found strategic restructuring in all ownership types, including SOEs and insider-controlled firms. Managers, under the pressure of new market conditions, unexpectedly initiated restructuring, at least defensive restructuring, in not-yet privatized SOEs (Pinto and van Wijnbergen, 1995).

Despite the number of studies on the relationship between ownership and corporate governance, and performance in transition, the results have been weak and rather mixed so far. This indicates that the theoretical relationship between corporate governance and restructuring postulated by the bipolar principal–agent model is probably too restrictive. In the real world, this relationship is not stable due to frequent changes in the shareholding of each single corporation (share sales, take-overs, acquisitions). The same agent may modify his/her economic behaviour depending on macro- and micro-circumstances, including the threat of a take-over, the redistribution of shareholding, the appointment of new enterprise boards, the result of a proxy fight, the emergence of a FIG, loopholes in corporation law, opportunities for corruption, and the claims of non-residual claimants. More or less regular bonuses, premiums, perks and bribes can link insiders to outsiders (Blasi *et al.*, 1997) in a not-yet fully-fledged market-oriented enterprise, in a way difficult to capture by a simple bipolar version of the principal–agent model, so that profitability is often a meaningless variable, not to speak of profit distortions in a still imperfect competition. Lower profit may reflect the existence of a coalition between outsiders and insiders involved into a profit-hiding tax-evasion strategy.

Most restructuring in Russia was confined to shedding labour and rehabilitating firms' existing production capacity (Aukutsionek *et al.*, 1998), since strategic restructuring calls for important investment that exceeds the finance available to firms. The capacity of many enterprises to upgrade or expand their capital stock was severely constrained by a lack of finance from internal or external sources. In particular, banks were reluctant to lend money to unrestructured insider-controlled firms, fearing that credit would be allocated to wage increases or managerial appropriation. On the other hand, such credit should have been the first step towards strategic restructuring. Therefore, most enterprises have to rely on self-financing – hence on short-term profitability – to invest in the modernization of their production capacity. A strong limitation is that insider-controlled firms are less or non-profitable. Those firms involved in FIGs, and benefiting from a privileged access to credit of a 'pocket bank' belonging to the group, did not engage in strategic restructuring either (Perotti and Gelfer, 1999). Thus, except when foreign investors stepped in, privatization had not triggered much strategic restructuring. As a result, firms changed little, by a lack of both in-house restructuring and intensive take-over deals.

In the background of slow restructuring, we find top managers that have really taken over enterprises and own many of them, including firms where employees apparently hold more shares than managers. In many circumstances, managers and employees have actually colluded to save insider control over privatized enterprises. Managers have purchased employee shares; some top managers have bought up stock without the employees' knowledge and have used 'pocket companies' to buy shares quietly. The shares had not been traded anonymously (Aghion and Blanchard, 1998) and, at the end of the day, managers were among the main buyers. Therefore, managerial entrenchment is a widespread result of privatization in all PET. Entrenchment seems to be a common attitude of most managers, although some managerial turnover has been observed in privatized firms. Pre-tax profits, rates of return on capital, export sales and other economic indicators do not produce statistically significant effects on managers' intentions to buy shares from employees, while entrenchment proxies proved to be very significant determinants of a managerial strategy aimed at preserving their control over companies (Filatochev *et al.*, 1999, on Russia). Increased managerial ownership can cause increased entrenchment detrimental to strategic restructuring.

When facing managerial entrenchment in a joint-stock company in a Western market economy, shareholders may follow several strategies to get rid of incumbent incompetent managers since there is a competitive market for managerial talent, an efficient capital market and a possible threat for the enterprise to be taken over if unsatisfied shareholders sell their shares. In privatized firms in PET, incumbent managers utilize legal, illegal or borderline means for guaranteeing their own entrenchment (Labaronne, 1998). Loopholes in the new legislation on joint-stock companies have been used by incumbent managers to avoid disclosure (Klipper, 1998) and, thus, alleviate small shareholders' property rights. They have not been disciplined by the threat of bankruptcy since the law is often not enforced.

Beyond the bipolar principal–agent model

To understand the corporate outcomes in PET, one has to reach beyond the bipolar version of the principal–agent model developed for advanced economies, taking a very different institutional environment as granted. However, alternative theoretical explanations of corporate governance exist. First, we may look for the theory of corporate control developed for the less-developed stage of Western market capitalism (as an example, the contribution of Okhatovskiy in this volume offers very interesting comparisons between the banking system in the early stage of development in the USA, and Russia). Second (and complementary to the first approach), one can also reach beyond the bipolar version of the principal–agent model and consider the literature on coalitions within economic organizations. In the quite peculiar ownership structures of PET firms, what matters is not only the concentration of ownership, but also the identity of the owners. Who personally are the new owners and in how many different corporate boards are they involved? How many shares do they personally own? What are their alliances or interest groups?

The theory of corporate control applicable to the earlier stages of capitalism development distinguished insider (usually managerial) and outsider control, the latter being in the hands of a hard core of strategic shareholders, the tycoon's family, banks, or institutional investors. The whole issue not only depended on the concentration or dispersion of shares, but was also based on distinguishing majority and minority control of shares (and on pointing at the blocking percentage of shares). The basic hypothesis was that corporate governance structures are not static or fixed forever, they move due to mergers, acquisitions, take-over bids and, in the most sophisticated versions, to proxy fights for appointing the firm's boards (Andreff, 1996). Though moving, the financial capital structure interlocks a number of industrial firms and banks, through cross-ownership, into FIGs. This should be a valuable analysis for PET today, as well as the analysis of interlocking directorates (again, see Okhatovskiy in this volume).

The focus on coalitions (Mintzberg, 1983) enables us to analyse how, among the participants in a firm, some subsets or groups can coalesce around a mutual target of satisfying results under the hypothesis of a bounded rationality of economic agents. At any moment, some coalition dominates the enterprise but can be removed by another in the making. The type of coalition in power and contingencies of the economic environment determine the kind of target, which must reach a satisfying level in the firm: for example efficiency, survival, autonomy, growth, asset value, and so on. The emergence of a new dominating coalition within the enterprise can obviously change the prevailing target. Although survival usually characterizes insider coalitions and profit-making outsider coalitions, the real picture in a corporation is often blurred when managers are shareholders, when employees own shares, when there is discord within the management team or the corporate board, or when alliances tie some managers to core shareholders. Once all these factors are taken into account, the objective functions of insiders and outsiders might well overlap. A deeper analysis of the ruling coalitions in various privatized firms would help in detecting a revealed (probably multi-variable) objective function for each type of coalition. A first step in this direction is the above-mentioned survey of Polish privatization by Bałtowski and Mickiewicz (2000). Here we are far beyond the simplistic bipolar distinction between the profit-seeking behaviour of residual claimants and managerial rent-seeking. Though old-fashioned, the analysis of intra-firm coalitions is of interest in nascent market capitalism.

Within a firm, shareholders and other stakeholders may collude. In fact the latter may be compared, to some extent, to shareholders if one considers that a firm needs both finance capital and human capital to function, and thus both are residual claimants and must be rewarded as such out of the firm's revenue. This is the core argument of an attempt to renew the analysis of corporate governance (Blair, 1995). According to Blair, even most Western modern corporations do not fit the mainstream model of corporate governance and the underlying analysis of the bipolar principal–agent model, because in practice shareholders are rarely the only residual claimants. If assets such as finance capital and human capital are dependent on each other, co-specialized, by definition neither has much value without the other. The firm (that is, capital shareholders) must share with employees some of the economic rents or quasi-rents from their common enterprise. Therefore, the mainstream model wrongly overemphasizes the potential conflict between shareholders and managers. This is the stakeholder management nexus that is important, whoever the stakeholders (managers, employees and shareholders) are.

Towards a Central Eastern European model of corporate governance?

Systemic change in PET cannot reduce itself to the issue of ownership transformation, although the latter is crucial. The privatization outcome has frequently left a sort of overall 'neither social, nor private' ownership regime. If so, PET are mixed economies, in the sense of having a mixed – private and public – ownership, often with some employee ownership. The widespread managerial control over privatized firms gives to these countries a flavour of managerial capitalism but, in many PET, managers are not gaining control through acquiring a sizeable stake of property, but are acquiring a sizeable property in order to keep and strengthen the control they exercise. Now the question is to know whether a typical Central Eastern European model is emerging after systemic change.

However, opposing an outsider system of external monitoring to an insider system of inner control is too sharp when it comes to analysing the heterogeneous corporate governance structures that we have observed in PET as well as those witnessed in EU countries (Pollin, 2003). Sometimes, governing coalitions in a firm gather both outsiders and insiders in PET privatized firms so that the delineation between outsider and insider control is blurred, just like it appears to be now in Western capitalism (Becht and Mayer, 2002). The borderline between an outsider-dominated and an insider-controlled corporate governance structure is disrupted by the power positions acquired together by blockholders and managers (Boutillier *et al.*, 2002) or, in PET, by alliances between oligarchs and incumbent managers. From this point of view, some similarities emerge between the prevailing corporate governance structure in Western and Eastern Europe. Crowding-out minority shareholders from decision-making is a common feature. However, this is not enough to conclude that all corporate governance structures are converging towards a single European model, since such a conclusion is not even valid across Western European countries (Boutillier *et al.*, 2003; Plihon *et al.*, 2001) where there are several hybridizations of the Anglo-American and German models. The driving force of a new hybrid model is the rising power of institutional investors (Geoffron, 1999; Jeffers and Plihon, 2001), imposing a return norm on the shareholder value. PET firms do not converge towards this new hybrid model given the low level of development of local institutional investors and the very modest investment of foreign institutional investors in local companies so far (see, however, the contribution by Zalewska in this volume). Regarding institutional investors as 'potential agents of a (retired) employee shareholding' that determines 'a socialised property of corporate companies' (Aglietta, 1997), they appear as a sort of Western counterpart of MEBOs which have *directly* transferred the company's shares to employees in PET.

Could we at least assume that there is some sort of convergence towards a Central Eastern European model of corporate governance? During the last decade, corporate governance structures have markedly differentiated in PET. If we except those countries where privatization is lagging behind (Belarus, Turkmenistan, Uzbekistan), as well as the issue of residual state property (see Bałtowski and Mickiewicz, in this volume), it seems that the privatization drive has generated, in a context of tiny financial markets, four stylized corporate governance models:

A A model of *foreign corporate control* (FCC), or the 'Hungarian' model. About 150 out of the biggest 200 corporations in Hungary exhibit an influential foreign participation in their stockholding (and a majority blockholding in 50 out of the biggest 100 corporations). Today, foreigners own 46.7 per cent of the overall stock of all corporations based in Hungary. Besides, foreign owners wholly own 61 per cent of those firms showing a foreign participation to their stock (100% of the stock). Still in Hungary, foreigners (62% in Estonia) hold 72 per cent of the overall stock exchange capitalization value as against 34 per cent in Poland and even less in all other PET.

Hungary and Estonia are the two PET where shareholders exert the strongest supervision of managers (Vagliasindi, 2003) and where monitoring shareholders are mainly foreign. The precondition for building up the FCC model is the important magnitude of inward foreign direct investment (FDI) compared with GDP or per capita; its emergence is facilitated when there is no regulation that prevents foreign firms from buying assets in local firms in the process of privatization (as in Hungary and Estonia from the very beginning, and contrary to all other PET). Therefore, the great bulk of Hungarian and Estonian firms are governed by mighty foreign outsiders, which are transnational corporations and banks, and not by institutional investors. Such a corporate governance structure is typically strong and capitalist and stands as the closest scheme to the above-mentioned hybrid model of corporate governance, fully immersed in current economic globalization.

B A model of *banking and managerial control* (BMC), or the 'Czech' model. Privatized firms are monitored by their managers who are supervised by the privatization funds' (now holdings) managers, these holdings being a proxy or a substitute to non-existing genuine institutional investors. The managers of those banks, which have set up the former privatization funds, supervise holdings' managers, in turn. Since most of these state banks have been privatized since the late 1990s through take-overs and acquisitions by foreign banks, the BMC model converges towards the previous FCC model in the long run (see, for instance, the increased significance of inward FDI in the Czech Republic, in Table 2.4). On the other hand, managers in privatized firms resist supervision by the funds (holdings) in utilizing their

Table 2.4   Inward foreign direct investment in transition economies, 1993–2002

Country	Inward FDI stock/GDP (%)			Inward FDI stock per capita ($)		
	1993	*1997*	*2002*	*1993*	*1997*	*2002*
CEECs						
Bulgaria	1.4	9.4	24	18.7	117.4	511.7
Czech Republic	7.7	22.8	54.8	260.2	896.5	3,733.0
Estonia	6.3	24.5	65.9	164.7	765.3	3,018.6
Hungary	13.6	34.7	38.2	514.0	1,557.1	2,417.4
Latvia	0.6	23	32.4	13.1	508.8	1,134.6
Lithuania	0.4	10.9	31.4	5.9	281.4	1,105.8
Poland	3.5	11.6	23.9	78.0	428.8	1,169.7
Romania	0.8	10.4	20.5	9.3	160.0	394.0
Slovakia	3.2	8.2	43.2	76.2	295.7	1,893.5
Slovenia	1.8	12.1	23.1	117.4	1,154.7	2,670.5
CIS countries						
Armenia	n.a.	8.4	28.7	n.a.	40.00	206.06
Azerbaijan	n.a.	48.8	86.4	n.a.	238.31	686.41
Belarus	0.1	2.4	11.2	1.63	30.96	155.53
Georgia	n.a.	4.2	19.9	n.a.	32.50	135.80
Kazakhstan	1.0	27.3	62.9	14.71	324.64	919.40
Kyrgyzstan	n.a.	15.7	25.9	n.a.	59.78	86.46
Moldova	0.7	9.6	45	6.89	40.91	162.95
Russia	0.4	3.2	6.5	9.43	97.46	155.61
Tajikistan	n.a.	2.2	14.8	n.a.	7.38	24.18
Turkmenistan	n.a.	9.5	19.1	n.a.	96.74	247.45
Ukraine	0.6	4.2	12.9	7.69	40.95	110.64
Uzbekistan	0.4	2.6	13.8	3.86	25.21	52.03

Source: Calculated from UNCTAD (2002).

privileged insider information and knowledge. Holdings re-concentrate a property that has been scattered by mass privatization and organize it into FIGs. Cross-ownership, off-market trading of shares, managerial entrenchment and a corporate governance that takes care of stakeholders' interests (for years, the Czech Republic was distinguished by showing the lowest unemployment rate in PET) make the BMC model not that far from the German model of corporate governance.

C A model of *control by an outsider–insider coalition* (COIC), or the 'oligarchic-managerial' model detrimental to (small) minority shareholders is typical in Russia and several CIS countries. Here a great number of firms are under the inner control of insiders (primarily managers) while others are integrated in one or two hundred FIGs and holdings governed by new tycoons, financial oligarchs and bankers. Numerous insiders are at the same time outsiders in other companies in which they have invested their new wealth (or companies that they have started up on purpose), whereas interlocking directorates and outsider–insider alliances (between oligarchs, bankers, CEOs and managers) strengthen a network structure of governance (see Okhatovskiy in this volume). The issuance of shares off the market to the exclusive benefit of blockholders and managers (Kogut and Spicer, 2002) is a tool for such networking. The resulting networks are the more long lasting the more they are connected to political power (see Adachi in this volume). Then, they put a brake on FDI inflows into the stockholdings of big Russian industrial and financial trusts and hinder the emergence of new private start-ups. Generally speaking, FIGs, managerial networks and oligarchic power are not supposed to facilitate a blossoming competitive market economy. A major potential driving force which may push forward this model into significant changes might well be the globalization of Russian firms and FIGs by means of their outward FDI (Andreff, 2003).

D A mixed model based on *'employee and start up' control* (ESUC), or the 'Polish' model. Changes of political power between parties (Andreff, 1999b) and a postponement of mass privatization until 1996 created a vacuum which was soon filled by small privatizations and MEBOs; that is by creating new start-ups and an inner supervision of the firm by its employees (and not only managers as in Russia). The outcome has been a widespread dispersion of ownership among employees who are both shareholders and stakeholders. They attempt, often successfully, to lock-in the existing stockholding and corporate governance and they participate in current management; their success is evidenced by few social conflicts registered at the level of enterprises in Poland. On the other hand, a rather efficient institutional framework (the 1934 commercial and bankruptcy laws have come into force again, and an anti-trust law was passed in 1990) facilitates starting up *de novo* private enterprises. New SMEs have mushroomed, mainly from 1990 to 1993 (Rusin, 2002); in

1993, all these start-ups were concentrating 18.4 per cent of overall employment in Poland. Afterwards, the momentum of the new private sector relied on both the emergence of new start-ups and the increasing size of those which survived the harshness of competition. In 1996, the SME sector reached 31.7 per cent of overall employment (three times more employment than in privatized firms). In 1997, the number of Polish SMEs was 1.398 million. The ESUC model paradoxically combines the supposedly weakest governance structure (employee self-supervision) and the supposedly strongest, that is the SME monitored by its own boss(es). However, similarly to the BMC ('Czech') model, the ESUC model may be a temporary phenomenon. In the early 2000s, the Polish entrepreneurial sector was no longer creating employment. On the other hand, employees kept selling their shares (Bałtowski and Mickiewicz, 2000) while foreign capital involvement was steadily growing, resulting again in some convergence towards the FCC model.

A sort of inertia affects corporate governance structures in PETs, which is due to absent or weak institutions that would facilitate or trigger their change and improvement so that a convergence towards a single model is slowed down. However, in recent years some omens of a possible convergence of FCC, BMC and ESUC[15] models towards a prevailing corporate governance structure have emerged in Central Eastern Europe. The latter would combine a strong foreign stake in the biggest corporations with a large number of SMEs monitored by their bosses (and fewer and fewer former privatized SOEs). In other words, it would be a hybrid of the 'Hungarian' and 'Polish' models (referring to the latter's start-ups component).

Indeed, we observe (Table 2.4) that Poland and the Czech Republic have hosted more FDI than Hungary in recent years. Both countries, with some delay compared to Hungary, have launched wide programmes of bank privatization (after 'cleaning' bank assets from bad debts) through selling their assets to transnational banks[16] (Bednarova, 2001; Dudzinski and Szymkiewicz, 2003). Since 1998, the Czech Republic has also favoured the sale of strategic enterprises to foreign investors so that the FDI share in privatization has grown from 1 per cent in 1997 to 23 per cent in 1999 and 28 per cent in 2001. At the same time, the share of privatization funds (then holdings) has dramatically reduced in the ownership structure of Czech enterprises in which they now behave as sleeping partners – and thus increasingly resembles West European institutional investors (Vincensini, 2003). In 1997, Polish authorities decided to give more momentum to privatization and sell strategic enterprises, henceforth without any restriction against foreign investors. As a consequence, foreign-owned firms grew from 1.8 per cent of overall employment in Poland in 1996 to 3.6 per cent in 1999. Besides increasing inward FDI, the convergence towards a common Central Eastern European model of corporate governance is influenced by spreading globalization of governance standards and, in recent years, by outward

FDI of new transnational corporations from PETs (Andreff, 2002). Adopting global strategies, PET enterprises do converge, in some sense, towards the above-mentioned hybrid model prevailing in Western economies (Plihon *et al.*, 2001).

A second strong tendency is embedded in the development of new start-ups, both individual enterprises and SMEs. Such small firms characterize the 'Polish' model (ESUC) of governance, but they are also widespread and growing in Hungary, the Czech Republic, Bulgaria, Romania and Slovakia (Table 2.5). In 1995, 1 million Czech individual enterprises employed 11.2 per cent of overall working population; in 2000, 1.471 million individual enterprises were employing 13.2 per cent of the overall working population. The same year, in Hungary, 9 per cent of the overall working population was employed in 381,000 individual enterprises (51% in all SMEs and individual enterprises) as against 5.6 per cent in 1992 (43% in all SMEs and individual enterprises in 1994).

Therefore, FCC, BMC and ESUC models exhibit, in recent years, a convergence towards a Central Eastern European model of corporate governance characterized by both an important foreign stake in the ownership of – and foreign control over – big businesses and by single bosses monitoring their own SMEs. If such a converging tendency prevails in the future, then FCC, BMC and ESUC models have to be regarded as *transitory* governance structures emerging from privatization; strict managerial control, employee supervision, banks' monitoring and other *ad hoc* forms (privatization investment funds, state-run holdings, mixed enterprises) will disappear after some time. In the wake of convergence, the increasing significance of foreign ownership is likely to adjust the governance structure to international standards of governance; that is the characteristics associated with the aforementioned hybrid

Table 2.5   Small and medium-sized enterprises in Central and Eastern Europe, 1995

Country	% of SMEs in total number of firms	Population density of firms*
Bulgaria	96.0	39
Czech Rep.	85.6	68
Estonia	78.2	21
Hungary	83.2	56
Latvia	80.3	11
Lithuania	75.1	18
Poland	87.8	37
Romania	95.3	17
Slovakia	92.1	42
Slovenia	75.4	37

* Number of active enterprises per 1,000 inhabitants.
Source: Rusin (2002).

model. For instance, after privatization, investment funds have eventually transformed into genuine institutional investors setting up a building block of the hybrid model. It remains to be seen whether it will be enough to solve all the unresolved issues of corporate governance that have accumulated during the first 15 years of transition.

Notes

1 Often, managers and employees first reacted with some resistance to privatization, since they expected it to reduce overmanning in their SOE, which meant a threat to their jobs.
2 A strategy of 'organic development' (Kornaï) of the private sector and an economically efficient privatization (through asset sales) was only supported by a small group of economists in the early 1990s, including Wlodzimierz Brus, David Ellerman, Kazimierz Laski, Ronald Mc Kinnon, Lubomir Mlcoch, Peter Murrell, Gérard Roland, David Stark, and later Joseph Stiglitz (2000) ... and of course myself. Their economic analyses and recommendations remained unheeded until a World Bank (2002) report recognized that mass privatization and employee-management buy-outs (nearly for free) turned out to be inefficient privatization methods. Since this report, the Bank gives its support to those market institutions which facilitate entry by new start-ups and privatization through direct case-by-case transactions.
3 And the same applies to Bulgaria and Romania, which are assumed to join the EU soon (at time of writing).
4 Even in the latter case an efficient outcome is to be expected, as most of the small firms operate in highly competitive markets and face hard budget constraints. In this respect, small employee-bought firms may not be very different from larger employee-bought companies. In addition, the governance and coordination problems associated with employee ownership may be far less significant in small companies.
5 Under certain conditions, monitoring over managers and a prevailing decision power over other shareholders can be reached with a minority share (see Andreff, 1996). A 'blocking minority', usually defined in each corporate law (for instance, it is fixed at 25% of total stock – votes – in Hungary), can sometimes be enough for a foreign investor to prevail in managerial and financial decisions, but it can also create a conflict of interest with domestic shareholders or with the state when it keeps some share (as has been witnessed in Hungary, Poland and other PETs).
6 About 90% of share resale in the Czech Republic and Russia occurred off–market after mass privatization.
7 Note, however, an endogeneity issue here. *Both* better checks on potential managerial theft *and* choice of EMBOs as a privatization method may follow from a strong initial position of workers' representation, trade unions in particular (in Poland: 'Solidarity'). See discussion in Bałtowski and Mickiewicz (2000).
8 According to a large EBRD survey, hardly one-third of former managers have been replaced in privatized firms, in all PETs. Among the new executive managers, 40% come from outside the firm while 60% have been promoted within the same enterprise (EBRD, 1999b). Poland may be an exception, again thanks to the strong position of the 'Solidarity' union (see: Mickiewicz, 1996).
9 We can also see in this privatization scheme as a sort of 'egalitarianism', either a strong whiff of socialism and communism or the effect of the theory of property

rights regarding the whole population as the true owner of SOEs. In some circumstances, free distribution of vouchers was thought of as a tool for overcoming popular resistance against the privatization programme (Boycko *et al.*, 1995) or as a means, for political parties in power, to 'purchase' their success in the next democratic elections (for example in the Czech Republic).

10   We elaborate elsewhere (Andreff, 2004a) on a critical analysis of the Coase theorem on the grounds of both some inconsistencies between the so-called theorem and the Coasian theory of the firm (Coase, 1937) and the inapplicability of the assumptions underlying the Coase theorem to the economic situation in post-Soviet economies (extremely high transaction costs, an absent stockmarket, etc.).

11   Note that remedies for illegal self-dealing by managers or board members include criminal sanctions in some OECD countries.

12   Williamson (2002, p. 178) states: 'courts will refuse to hear disputes that arise within firms – with respect, for example, to transfer pricing, overhead, accounting, the costs to be ascribed to intra-firm delays, failures of quality and the like. In effect, the contract law of internal organization is that of forbearance, according to which a firm becomes its own court of ultimate appeal'. As long as market institutions are not fixed and laws are not enforced, the boundary of the firm remains blurred between the nexus of internal contracts (mentioned by Williamson) and outside contracts (including share ownership). Then, its inability to be perceived as an identifiable entity by other economic agents creates important transaction costs for the economy as a whole.

13   Since the auctions were rigged the shares were sold at extremely cheap prices. For instance, Mikhail Khodorkovski is suspected to have paid $300 million for obtaining the ownership of assets now valued at about $10 billion.

14   Keeping Khodorkovski in jail and circulating rumours about Abramovich and other oligarchs might give the feeling that President Putin's administration is now willing to put the most fraudulent acquisitions of Russian enterprises into question. An alternative assumption, however, is that we are witnessing a harsh struggle for redistributing assets between a part of this administration (the 'security' services) and oligarchs. For more on this see Yuko Adachi's contribution in this volume.

15   In Russia and CIS countries, the relative significance of inward FDI is markedly smaller and those institutions that favour the legal start up of new private enterprises are less stabilized (and more circumvented) than in Central Europe.

16   For example, in the Czech Republic, Nomura has purchased 36% of Investicni a Postovni Banka's stock (1998), the Belgian bank KBC has acquired a 65.7% stake in Ceskoslovenska Obchodni Banka (1999), Erste Bank a 52% stake in Ceska Sporitelna (2000) and Société Générale 60% of Komercni Banka (2001). In Poland, 48 out of 71 active banks in 2001 were under the monitoring of foreign owners.

Part II
The Political Economy of Corporate Governance

3

Corporate Control, Governance Practices and the State: The Case of Russia's Yukos Oil Company

Yuko Adachi *

Introduction

Although the issue has been on the agenda for more than half a century, globalization of the market and the increasingly international character of investment seem to have highlighted the importance of standards of corporate governance. There is growing awareness both in the advanced market economies, also, and perhaps especially, in emerging and developing economies. It has been emphasized that good corporate governance allows greater access to global financial markets, which play an important role in economic growth (Millstein *et al.*, 1998; Cornelius and Kogut, 2004).

Against this background of increased concern over standards of corporate governance, Russia came under the spotlight in the 1990s. It was considered that there were serious obstacles to Russia's efforts to achieve deeper integration into the world economy. Corporate practices in Russia such as share dilution, limiting shareholders' access to votes, asset-stripping, transfer pricing and other corporate governance abuses of shareholders have became widely known and heavily criticized (OECD, 1999b, 1999c). Russia achieved notoriety for its non-transparency in corporate governance, which were seen as deterrents to investment (Nestor and Jesover, 1999). The Yukos Oil Company, which grew to become Russia's largest oil company before its dismemberment in 2004, was particularly associated with corporate governance abuses during the 1990s.

The objective of this chapter is to demonstrate the development, the rise and the fall of Yukos Oil Company from a corporate governance perspective, which is placed in the broader political economy context. First, the chapter shows that the corporate governance practices in Russia, which were well-publicized as abuses of minority shareholders, aided the establishment of Yukos as a coherent vertically integrated company under the conditions of

*The author is grateful to Tomasz Mickiewicz for valuable comments on an earlier draft and Alena Ledeneva and Slavo Radosevic for helpful discussions.

institutional weaknesses following the disintegration of the Soviet economic system.[1] Secondly, this chapter goes on to examine the paradoxical aspects of the Yukos Oil's eventual fate. When the dominant owners consolidated their control, Yukos was transformed from a company notorious for its poor corporate governance to becoming one of the most respected Russian companies with a strong commitment to good corporate governance and transparency. However, in a campaign against the company and its core owners that began in 2003, Yukos became a target of expropriation by the Russian authorities. This chapter examines the rise and fall of Yukos in the context of state–business relations in Russia.

The chapter is organized as follows. The next section discusses the corporate governance problems that have beset Russia, and I then move on to demonstrate how Yukos suffered from the prevailing lack of organizational integrity, and also how its consolidation as an effective vertically integrated company was achieved through corporate governance practices such as share dilution, transfer pricing and limiting shareholders' access to votes. Yukos Oil's transformation to a model of good corporate governance and transparency is then discussed, followed by an examination of the possible link between improved transparency and expropriation, and its implications for government's relationship with big business in Russia. In the final section the main argument is summarized and some concluding remarks presented.

Corporate governance problems in Russia

What is good corporate governance and what is meant by corporate governance abuses? Studies of corporate governance have predominantly been approached from the point of view of the principal–agent problem, which emerges from the separation of ownership and control. In this view, shareholders and managers of a large corporation are in a principal–agent relationship: corporations are owned by the shareholders (principals), who are often dispersed, and who delegate day-to-day control of the firm to managers (agents). This separation of ownership and control is a source of agency problems. According to this approach, shareholders, who make a financial investment in a company, need protection against the risk of expropriation by opportunistic managers (Shleifer and Vishny, 1997; Boycko, Shleifer and Vishny, 1995; Grossman and Hart, 1986). In this context, the critical focus of corporate governance becomes the question of how to assure shareholders that they receive a return on their financial investment (Shleifer and Vishny, 1997: 773). More specifically, the major issue for corporate governance is how to protect shareholders' rights and to design mechanisms to control management behaviour (Hart, 1995a).

There are some compelling criticisms of the usefulness of a principal–agent approach to the analysis of corporate governance (Allen and Gale, 2000; Aoki, 2000, 2001; Berglof and von Thadden, 2000). Nevertheless, the analysis of corporate governance based on the principal–agent view has had a strong influence on how the corporate governance problem is perceived in policy debates. Examples include the corporate governance framework defined by the World Bank, and the Organisation for Economic Co-operation and Development's (OECD) *Principles of Corporate Governance*. The World Bank (2000) emphasizes the need for a governance mechanism to address the principal–agent problem that arises from the separation of ownership and control. The *OECD Principles of Corporate Governance* (1999) provide a set of good corporate governance practices and aim at developing a common international understanding. The *Principles* focus on relationships amongst shareholders, managers, the board of directors and other stakeholders, and are designed to be applicable to listed companies, though they could be applied to improve corporate governance in non-traded companies. Although non-binding, they delineate a set of good practices in corporate governance, based on the principles of: (1) the rights of shareholders; (2) the equitable treatment of shareholders; (3) the role of stakeholders; (4) disclosure and transparency; and (5) the responsibilities of the board.[2]

As global concern over the standard of corporate governance increased, Russia's corporate governance practices in newly privatized firms became a subject of critique during the 1990s. Facts abounded about informal practices, such as share dilution, asset-stripping, transfer pricing, non-transparent ownership structures, cash-flow diversion, limiting shareholders' attendance at meetings, and using bankruptcy as a take-over instrument, all of which have come to constitute corporate governance abuses (Radygin, 1999; Fox and Heller, 1999; Black *et al.*, 2000; Ikonnikov, 2001; Sprenger, 2000; Vasiliev, 2001; Krastnitskaya, 2000). As the OECD reported:

> Abuse of corporate governance remains a common problem in Russia. Investors have often seen their shares diluted by insiders and major shareholders. Companies have seen their assets stripped by various means of transfer pricing. The interests of creditors have not been adequately protected and the mobilisation of capital has been hampered. (OECD, 1999b: 5)

Corporate governance in Russia is considered especially problematic because of the wide discrepancy between the standards of good corporate governance and the actual practices. As McCarthy and Puffer (2003: 407) put it, in Russia 'most tenets of good corporate governance were badly abused'. Seen from the point of view of good corporate governance as exemplified by the *OECD Principles*, the relevance of the corporate governance problem in Russia is acute, with the basic rights of shareholders not well-protected, and lack of equitable treatment of shareholders (Nestor and Jesover, 1999).

Russia's corporate governance problems have been particularly detrimental to Russia's investment climate (*Moscow Times*, 2 November 1999). The following quote from Mark Mobius, a well-known international investor, captures the sentiments of investors:

> the number and scope of corporate governance violations in Russia is appalling. Russia has certainly not been the safest market to invest based on economic and political criteria, but it has become infamous for the huge number of minority shareholder rights abuses perpetrated by the voracious and corrupted company managements and controlling shareholders. (Mobius and Filatov, 2001: 65)

Consequently, such practices as share dilution, asset-stripping and transfer pricing have become the key criteria used by rating agencies and investment houses to assess Russia's corporate governance risks (Brunswick UBS, 2000; Institute of Corporate Law and Corporate Governance www.iclg.ru; Troika Dialog, 2001; Standard & Poor's, 2002). The extent of the problems was reflected in the increased awareness by policy-makers of the need to improve corporate governance. Since the late 1990s, various private and public institutions – both domestic and international – have made substantial efforts to improve corporate governance in Russia, and in 2002 Russia's Federal Commission for the Securities Market (FCSM), with the assistance of several international organizations, published a national *Corporate Governance Code* based on the *OECD Principles*.[3]

Corporate governance practices in the 1990s: the case of Yukos Oil Company

Background to the development of Yukos

During the 1990s, Yukos Oil came to be seen as a 'corporate governance nightmare' (Troika Dialog, cited in Yousef-Martinek *et al.*, 2003) due to the way the company treated its minority shareholders. The corporate governance problems that became prominent in the Russian oil sector, and particularly in Yukos Oil, had their roots in the two-tiered privatization that had occurred; that is, privatization at the level of the subsidiaries of the oil holding companies, and at the level of the holding companies. This two-tiered privatization led to multilevel ownership and control structures within Yukos, and shareholders with conflicting interests.

Two-tiered privatization in the oil sector

Following the break up of the Soviet Union, a reorganization of the disintegrating Russian oil industry took place. President Boris Yeltsin issued decree 1403 in November 1992, which contained specifications for the corporatization and privatization of oil enterprises. The first pillar of the reorganization policy was the establishment of holding companies to create vertically integrated oil companies (VIOCs). Vertically integrated companies were designed to encompass an entire production linkage 'from the well to the gas station' (Moe and Kryukov, 1994: 93). Such a structure was in part modelled on the vertically integrated Western oil majors (Dienes, 1996: 10; Moser and Oppenheimer, 2001: 305). The decree established VIOCs consisting of holding companies, under whose umbrella the existing enterprises dealing with oil production, refining and the distribution of oil products were organised as subsidiaries. The first three VIOCs to be established were the Yukos Oil Company, Lukoil and Surgut Holding. Yukos Oil comprised a dozen subsidiaries, including oil production enterprises such as Yuganskneftegaz, Samaraneftegaz and refineries such as Kuibyshevnefteorgsintez. The name of the company was derived from Yuganskneftegaz and Kuibyshevnefteorgsintez.

The creation of VIOCs was promoted by the general directors of former Soviet oil enterprises who wanted to maintain their newly gained autonomy and control over their enterprises. They opposed a plan to create a unified state oil monopoly on the lines of Gazprom, Russia's gas monopoly (Moser and Oppenheimer, 2001). At the same time, the establishment of VIOCs was in part a policy priority in the face of a chaotic economic situation and weakened central control over the oil industry (Dienes, 1996). Because the oil industry was seen as a strategic sector in the national economy, the government felt strongly that some degree of state control was essential (Presidential decree 1403, November 1992). Federal government sought to exert a large measure of influence over these VIOCs through substantial share ownership in the newly created holding companies (Dienes, 1996). The state shares in separately privatized subsidiaries became the charter capital of the holding companies, enabling the state to have a controlling interest in them (Lane and Seifulmulukov, 1999: 17–8). Furthermore, given the disintegration and uncertainty in the sector, the creation of VIOCs was seen by the government as a way of restructuring the Russian oil industry into several vertically integrated holdings, which would eliminate the discord among the existing entities dealing with oil exploration, development, and refining stages – something that had plagued the Soviet oil industry when different ministries were responsible for each of these activities (Dienes, 1996: 10).

The second pillar of the reorganization policy was corporatization and privatization of the enterprises engaging in oil production, refining and marketing. These former state-owned enterprises became open-type joint stock companies and were organized as subsidiaries. The controlling interest in each enterprise remained with the state for the first three years of reorganization (Lane and Seifulmulukov, 1999). In the case of Yukos, its oil production subsidiaries, such as Yuganskneftegaz and Samaraneftegaz, were corporatized into joint-stock companies and went through the privatization process (*Russian Petroleum Investor* (RPI), June 1994: 50). This meant that shares were issued both at subsidiary and holding company level. For example, Yuganskneftegaz became an independent state enterprise in 1991, and an open joint-stock company in June 1993 (Yugankneftegaz, 1994: 3). Its shares were divided 25 per cent preferred non-voting stock and 75 per cent common voting stocks. Thirty-eight per cent of this common stock of shares contributed to the Yukos charter fund (RPI, June 1993: 48–51), and since this constituted more than half of the 75 per cent of voting shares, the holding company had the controlling stake (51 per cent) of Yugankneftegaz. Thus, Yukos, as the holding company, obtained controlling stakes in its separately incorporated subsidiaries.

A further round of privatization of the oil holding companies began in 1995 via the investment tenders and loans-for-shares auctions, which represented the second phase of Russia's privatization policy, the first having consisted of voucher privatization. The loans-for-shares programme implemented in 1995, reflected the shift from rapid, mass privatization to a more selective selling off of the largest and most profitable enterprises to maximize state budget revenue (Gustafson, 1999: 43).[4] In exchange for bank loans, the government offered its shares of valuable oil and metal-sector enterprises through a series of auctions. The loans-for-shares programme was largely criticized as being nothing less than a rigged auction, which allowed shares to be transferred at a fraction of their potential market value to a select small circle of politically well-connected buyers (Allan, 2002; Freeland, 2000; Goldman, 2003). As a result of the loans-for-shares programme in the oil sector, companies such as Yukos, Surgut Holding, Lukoil, Sidanco and Sibneft were privatized.

The Menatep group became the new owner of Yukos and, thereby, the controlling shareholder of Yukos Oil's subsidiaries. The Yukos loans-for-shares auction was run by Menatep, and by excluding through a technicality outside bidders from participating, involved only two bidders, both proxy companies founded by Menatep (Allan, 2002: 152–3; Freeland, 2000: 175–7). The Menatep Bank, headed by Mikhail Khodorkovskii, had become one of the leading Russian banks in the period when the banking business had been very profitable, and was regarded as being the only Russian bank that from the outset had had an industrial orientation (Pappe, 2000: 129). Menatep began to acquire shares in Yukos Oil in 1995, and by the beginning of 1997 more than 85 per cent of Yukos shares were owned by the group (Lane and Seifulmulukov, 1999). As its shareholdings in Yukos increased, the top management of Yukos came to be dominated by representatives of Menatep. In April 1996, Khodorkovskii was made the first Vice-President and chairman of the board of directors of Yukos. Other Menatep representatives occupied leading positions in the oil company (Kryukov and Moe, 1998). However, the new owners still had to establish corporate control over Yukos Oil as a whole. In other words, Menatep needed effective administrative control over all of the constituent subsidiaries of Yukos. Although Menatep had obtained majority stakeholdings in these constituent subsidiaries, it controlled them only in a legal sense (*Moscow Times*, 23 September 1997).

Yukos without an effective administrative hierarchy

Yukos Oil suffered from a lack of internal cohesion and organizational integrity from its establishment (Kryukov and Moe, 1998). The lack of internal cohesion between the holding company and Yukos's constituent enterprises was in part due to the privatization method, which created a multilevel governance structure at both holding and subsidiary levels, and created different groups of management and shareholders, including minority shareholders. This two-tiered scheme resulted in a situation where even though the holding company had a director and board members, its subsidiaries, being independent legal entities, could choose not to recognize them (Moser, 1996: 28). As a result, the subsidiaries effectively maintained operational independence, which the management of Yukos could not penetrate. Yuganskneftegaz, the main subsidiary of Yukos, had its own company charter, management and board of directors, and continued independent operations (Yuganskneftegaz, 1994). Yukos was unable to control Yuganskneftegaz's resource and financial flows as it did not exert administrative control over the subsidiary: Yukos Oil's management even sought state intervention to deal with this lack of internal cohesion (Kryukov and Moe, 1998: 13).

When Yukos was established as a VIOC, several of the entities responsible for business functions, such as production, refinery, exploration and distribution, were assembled under the Yukos umbrella. Yuganskneftegaz, for example, was a former production association, itself composed of several oil and gas production units such as Yuganskneft and Pravdinskneft (Yuganskneftegaz, 1994: 3). In addition to these oil-producing units, the Novokubyshev refinery, and several distributors of oil products were pooled under the umbrella of Yukos Oil. The holding company also included the research and development (R&D) function (Gokhberg, 1999: 48). However, to achieve synergy, these business functions needed to be integrated and organized within one administrative framework. Yukos had no such effective administrative framework. Subsidiaries maintained their operational independence, and this led to a disintegrated corporate management within Yukos as a whole. Due to this lack of a proper administrative hierarchy and administrative control over the subsidiaries, various of the business functions were not effectively integrated within Yukos.

The company's lack of administrative control over subsidiaries hindered its ability to organize the chain of production linking crude oil production to refining, and refining to distribution. Despite the fact that Yukos had been established as a vertically integrated company, it was vertically integrated in name only in the sense that the production chain from the well to the gas station was not closely linked within the structure of Yukos. The constituent subsidiaries of Yukos were independent legal entities, which also operated outside Yukos. For example, refineries that belonged to Yukos were buying oil from other companies, refusing to restrict their purchasing to their holding company (Moser, 1996: 28). There were production chains operating outside of Yukos: according to Latynina (1999), at Nefteyugansk, the town that became established around Yuganskneftegaz, crude oil was being stolen from the wells, and the distribution of oil involved about 20 intermediary firms (established to tunnel profits outside the holding), half of which belonged to a recognized criminal. To make production linkages work, and to become a truly vertically integrated oil company, successive stages of the industrial process had to be brought together within the administrative framework. Therefore, the production chain had to be reconstructed and brought within the boundaries of Yukos. In order to achieve this, the company required an effective administrative hierarchy controlled by a single management (Adachi, 2006).

Restructuring Yukos as a functioning VIOC

Use of transfer pricing for cash-flow control

The government recognized that there was a lack of organizational integrity and a lack of internal cohesion amongst holding companies and their subsidiaries as a result of the two-tiered privatization (Moser, 1996). Presidential decree 327, issued in 1995, was intended to complete the first stage of privatization and reorganization of the Russian industry. The decree allowed the oil holding companies to issue additional shares in order to enable them to transform their constituent subsidiaries from independent joint-stock companies into wholly-owned subsidiaries of the holding companies. Thus, all holding companies were permitted to consolidate the shares of their subsidiaries into a single stock issue representing the entire company (Moser, 1996: 28). By this means it was hoped that the problems resulting from an ineffective administrative framework and disintegrated administrative coordination between holding companies and subsidiaries would be overcome. This was particularly important in facilitating the establishment of the production chain within the company, and consequently in allowing vertical integration both in name and in substance.

However, although Yukos management announced its intentions to make subsidiaries wholly-owned, the actual process of consolidation was arduous. In order to convert the shares of a subsidiary into a single share, it was first necessary for Menatep to take firm control of what often were clearly independent subsidiaries. Because these subsidiaries were operating independently, Menatep had to establish control over their revenue streams in order to centralize cash flows within the holding company, so that all product and revenue streams were under direct control of Yukos management, rather than the managements of the individual subsidiaries.

As a first step, Yukos management sought to limit independent transactions by the subsidiaries that were selling and buying oil outside of the Yukos framework. In order to centralize material and financial flows, the new owner-management team at Yukos first ensured that subsidiaries would not be allowed to deliver oil to anywhere but the holding company: the holding company then became responsible for distribution to both domestic and international markets. Only the holding company was allowed to sell oil to its own traders, which it was hoped would stop side contracts being entered into at the level of subsidiaries.[5] Then the question of the price at which Yukos would buy oil from the subsidiary became important. Forcing subsidiaries to sell at a very low price meant that the subsidiaries were even more dependent on the holding. With the aim of transferring oil cheaply from the subsidiary to the holding, Yukos classified what it was buying from the subsidiaries as 'liquid from the wells' (*skvazhinnaia zhidkost'*) (Latynina, 1999). In other words, a product that the subsidiaries on paper sold to the holding was not 'crude oil', but a much less expensive product. By this means Yukos set an 'intra-corporate price' for the purchase of 'liquid from the wells' from its own subsidiaries.[6] It should be noted also, that a direct effect of this manipulation of transfer pricing was a reduction in tax burden of the holding company.[7] The result of the output of these subsidiaries being sold to the holding company at below-market prices, was that the operating costs and debts remained with the subsidiaries while the profits accrued to the parent company (Moser and Oppenheimer, 2001: 316). With the use of intra-corporate transfer pricing between the holding company and its constituent subsidiaries, Yukos was centralizing financial flows, but in effect making a profit at the expense of subsidiaries (*Moscow Times*, 17 February 1998).[8]

Use of transfer pricing for single share conversion

After establishing cash-flow control over the subsidiaries, Yukos Oil's management attempted to cancel the separate listings of subsidiaries' shares in order to make subsidiaries wholly-owned by Yukos. Consolidation envisaged a single share conversion – a swap of subsidiaries' shares for a holding company. This would eliminate the situation where shareholders of subsidiaries and shareholders of the holding company coexisted within the framework of a single VIOC.

However, not surprisingly, the attempts to accomplish this single share conversion were hampered by the fact that Yukos was receiving little cooperation from the minority shareholders in its subsidiaries. The two-tiered privatization scheme gave rise to a conflict of interests between the management of Yukos and subsidiaries' minority shareholders who owned separately listed subsidiary stocks. The conflict of interests between Yukos and one minority shareholder group, led by an investor called Kenneth Dart, became particularly acute (*Moscow Times*, 1 June 1999).

Following voucher privatizations, Dart's group had obtained shares in the subsidiaries (*ibid.*), and through his various investment entities his group reportedly held some 12 to 14 per cent of the shares or Yukos's three production subsidiaries of Yukos: Yuganskneftegaz, Samaraneftegaz and Tomskneft (Moors, 1999).[9] Dart had reportedly approached Khodorkovskii in 1997 at the time of Russian stockmarket boom and offered a buy-back of these shares

(Nechaev, 1999). However, it was reported that the parties could not agree about terms for the buy-back, and this served to fuel the conflict (Nechaev, 1999). In early 1998, Dart's group demanded an audit of Yuganskneftegaz (*Moscow Times*, 6 March 1998). The group accused Yukos of asset-stripping via manipulation of transfer pricing with subsidiaries (*Moscow Times*, 1 June 1999). Dart's group was losing on its investment and was taking a stand about shareholder's rights (*Moscow Times*, 1 June 1999).

While transfer pricing practices were detrimental to share values from the point of view of minority shareholders in subsidiaries, the management of Yukos was keen to proceed with consolidation of a vertically integrated company by making subsidiaries wholly-owned, and maximizing the value of subsidiaries which was in the interests of minority shareholders did not fit. The owner-managers of Yukos saw the subsidiaries' minority shareholders as hindering the process of consolidation. In fact, at an extraordinary shareholder meeting of Tomskneft in January 1999, a Dart-controlled group that owned 13.9 per cent of Tomskneft proposed a change in a composition of the board of directors controlled by Yukos management, and elected a new board (*RPI*, March 1999: 57).[10] It attempted to change the Tomskneft charter, which granted Yukos the right to manage Tomskneft, and in addition it sought to freeze the 51 per cent of Tomskneft shares held by Yukos (*ibid.*). This blocked the attempts of Yukos's management to establish an effective administrative hierarchy (*Vedomosti*, 25 June 2002).

Under the circumstances, it seemed impossible to both establish internal cohesion and build a truly vertically integrated firm, and protect the interests of minority shareholders. However, with abusive treatment of minority shareholders, the management of Yukos risked losing some of the sources of Yukos's equity financing. Good corporate governance, which gives strong protection of shareholder rights, reduces agency costs, and reduction in agency costs is important for obtaining financing from shareholders. However, during the 1990s, and particularly before the financial crisis of 1998, Russian businesses were not reliant on equity finance. As Nash (2001: 119) pointed out, 'Equity investment in the sense of oversight and company valuation simply had no impact on firm behaviour'. In addition, Russia's market-supporting institutions were underdeveloped (World Bank, 2002). Rather than trying to attract financing from shareholders, managers strove to establish cash-flow control, which enabled them to obtain cash that was generated from assets. Obtaining cash-flow control was more important than adding value to the assets at the time, given the political and economic uncertainty. Thus, for the Yukos management, establishing administrative control by installing an effective management structure and controlling the production chain appeared to be of greater priority at that time than increasing market capitalization. The cost that would be incurred from violating shareholders' rights seemed to be less significant than the benefits to be derived from removing the influence of minority shareholders. By eliminating the influence of minority shareholders and concentrating ownership, the management hoped to establish strong administrative control. It should be borne in mind however that if expropriation of minority shareholders' rights becomes frequent, the investor confidence is damaged and the investment climate suffers. Thus, there were negative externalities attached to this strategy.

Given the plan to cancel the separate listing of subsidiaries' shares, the transfer-pricing scheme became a precondition for single share conversion. As noted above, by making subsidiaries cost centres, the share value of subsidiaries went down. Shares in production subsidiaries were relatively liquid and readily available to brokers, generally at fairly high prices (*Moscow Times*, 23 September 1997). Of course, the higher the market price of subsidiaries, the more costly it was for the holding company to do the share exchange. Therefore, it was advantageous to the holding company owners to minimize the value of the subsidiaries. If the market price of subsidiaries could be reduced, the holding could accomplish the share exchange on more favourable terms (Moser and Oppenheimer, 2001: 315).

Use of share dilution, asset-stripping and limiting shareholder access to votes

To facilitate the consolidation of Yukos, share-dilution practices were used to eliminate the influence of minority shareholders, including the Dart group. A series of extraordinary general shareholder meetings was held at Tomskneft, Samaraneftegaz and Yuganskneftegaz in March 1999. 'Undesirable' minority shareholders were not invited to attend these meetings, where decisions were taken to increase the number of shares in order to dilute the proportion of shares held by minority shareholders (Hoffman, 2002).[11] Another decision made at these meetings was to transfer unspecified company assets to more than a hundred obscure new companies during 1997 to 2001 (Fedorov, 2000). These actions – share dilution combined with asset-stripping – became well-publicized examples of Yukos's corporate governance abuses. The decisions about new share issues were taken at a time when the conflict between Yukos's owners and Dart was intensifying. Yukos reportedly was explicit that its aim was to dilute the stake held by Dart's companies to smooth the process of single-share conversion: for example, the new issue would reduce the proportion of Dart's shareholding in Yuganskneftegaz to less than 5 per cent (Fedorov, 2000).

It should be emphasized that the weak judicial system in Russia contributed to the use of share dilution and limiting voting rights. Some minority shareholders tried to challenge the court ruling that barred them from participating and voting at shareholder meetings, as they believed that the judge had been guilty of several violations of the legislation. Minority shareholders lodged an appeal against the ruling with the General Prosecutor's Office and filed a complaint against the judge's actions with the Grievances Commission and a higher-level regional court (Fedorov, 2000). However, their protests either went unheeded or were sent to the same judge against whom the complaints were made. As a result, a representative of NAUFOR (National Association of Professional Participants of Securities Market) concluded that 'None of the legal Russian instruments for appealing against a judge's unlawful actions proved to be of any effect' (Fedorov, 2000: 75), indicating the flawed judicial system that made share dilution workable.

The minority shareholders attempted to prevent the FCSM, which was responsible for registering newly issued shares, from registering Yukos Oil's new share issue. The offshore entities chosen to receive the new shares, although not connected formally with Yukos, were suspected of being affiliated to its core owner-managers (Fenkner, 1999). Therefore, if it could be established that these offshore entities were connected with owner-managers of Yukos who had participated in the vote to transfer the newly issued shares to those entities, then the transactions would be interested party transactions and this would allow FCSM to refuse to register these new share issues (FCSM, 1999). However, circumvention of the interested-party rule was generally possible by setting up a non-transparent network of offshore entities in which other shareholders did not participate. Dmitrii Vasiliev, the head of the FCSM at that time, was convinced that the objective of Yukos in issuing the shares was to transfer them to affiliated offshore companies (*ibid.*). However, it proved impossible to show that the sales of the additional shares to these offshore companies constituted interested-party transactions. Noting that the Yukos share-dilution case involved multiple offshore jurisdictions, Vasiliev stressed the need for a mechanism that would help FCSM to establish the identities of the real individuals behind the offshore companies in order to prevent transactions involving interested parties (*ibid.*). In Russia, real owners often disguise their ownership by buying shares through one or more offshore shell-companies that cannot be traced back to them (Nestor and Jesover, 1999: 5). Chains of offshore companies or affiliates are often arranged in such a way that the real owners do not appear on the ownership registration (Radygin and Sidrov, 2000: 52).

Furthermore, the state did not live up to the expectations of minority share-holders in terms of its role in protecting their rights. Despite attempts by the FCSM to investigate the legitimacy of the share issue at Yukos Oil's sub-sidiaries, the Commission did not have sufficient investigative power. Other Russian government agencies refused to provide FCSM with information that might assist the investigation: For example, the Fuel and Energy Ministry and the State Tax Service ignored requests from FCSM for assistance (Hoffman, 2002: 455). In fact, it appears that the state authorities ultimately took no action to prevent the investments of minority shareholders from being diluted. To prevent the issue of new shares, a group of minority shareholders sought help from the state authorities, filed claims with the General Prosecutor's Office, and sent a joint letter to the government. However, government did not respond; the Prosecutor's Office was silent, and apart from the FCSM no government agencies were willing to help minority shareholders (Fedorov, 2000). Thus, there was at least a tacit condoning of Yukos Oil' actions by the state.

Yukos with effective administrative hierarchy

With the use of practices such as transfer pricing, share dilution and limiting shareholders' access to votes, the Yukos management strengthened its administrative control over subsidiaries, eliminating minority shareholders' influence and concentrating ownership, eventually establishing a workable administrative framework. By June 2000, Yukos had control of over 90 per cent of the stock in its Yuganskneftegaz, Samaraneftegaz and Tomskneft subsidiaries (*Moscow Times*, 6 June 2000). During 2001, Yukos Oil announced that it had 'substantially completed its plan to acquire 100 per cent of the voting stock in its key production, refining and marketing subsidiaries' (Yukos, 2002: 76). Yukos, in turn, was owned by a group of core owner-managers who had built up an equity stake following the loans-for-shares auction (Boone and Rodionov, 2001: 14). They owned Group Menatep, which, through one of their entities called Yukos Universal, owned Yukos. The core shareholders, as of early 2001, held nearly 70 per cent of Yukos Oil's shares (Salter, 2002: 12).

The achievement of complete control over its subsidiaries enabled Yukos to effectively coordinate and manage Yukos's oil production activities from 'the well to the gas station' within a single Yukos framework (*Profil'*, 2 September 2002). Yukos E&P (Exploration & Production), an upstream division of Yukos, initially established in 1998, took control of the oil extracting subsidiaries (Yuganskneftegaz, Samaraneftegaz and Tomskneft), and was able to manage the upstream chain of production (*Moscow Times*, 3 September 1998; www.yukos.com). Yukos R&M (Refining & Marketing), another operating segment, was able to manage the downstream chain of production, with control over the Kuibyshev, Novokuibyshev, Syzran and Achinsk oil refineries and Yukos's sales network (www.yukos.com). Yukos E&P and Yukos R&M were under the management of Yukos-Moskva, a management company wholly-owned by Yukos, which was responsible for developing strategy and for decision-making on major strategic issues (*Moscow Times*, 29 March 2000). Thus, the company had managed to establish an effective administrative hierarchy, with the activities of subsidiaries being brought together under a single management within the framework of Yukos as a whole (Adachi, 2006).

The rise and fall of Yukos in the context of state–business relations

From corporate governance disaster to corporate governance success?

After gaining supermajority control, Yukos Oil's focus shifted towards increasing market capitalization. The emphasis on increasing market capitalization and enhancing corporate value is a tendency that emerged around 2000, among those who had concentrated ownership stakes during the late 1990s. Following the financial crisis of 1998, the combination of devaluation, which increased the purchasing power of Russian companies, and the low valuation of Russian shares, facilitated this concentration of ownership. A substantial portion of Russian industry was consolidated into a small number of core owner-managers (Boone and Rodionov, 2001; Dynkin and Sokolov, 2001; World Bank, 2004).[12] Although this did not mean the end of the asset contest and the process of redistribution of ownership (Barnes, 2003), these owner-managers who had successfully gained control over substantial assets, became more aware of the value of assets. Now, from the owners' perspective, ownership concentration motivated them to achieve higher share value (Boone and Rodionov, 2001; Nash, 2001).

Yukos Oil's new drive to increase transparency and to boost capitalization included the introduction of a corporate governance charter of the company in 2000, and the appointment of independent directors, and foreigners as board members. The company adopted a clear dividend policy and stock-option programme for top management. In order to increase transparency and improve its corporate reputation, which had been badly tainted by corporate governance problems, Yukos in two years reportedly spent approximately US$300 million on efforts to improve its corporate image (*Ekspert*, 18 February 2002). Since 2001 the company started to issue regular quarterly US Generally Accepted Accounting Principles (GAAP), and the company launched a Level-1 ADR (American Depositary Receipt) programme in March 2001 (Yukos, 2002).

Yukos began to create a more transparent ownership structure. The highlight of these efforts occurred in June 2002 when the company disclosed the names of both the core shareholders of the company, and the beneficiary owners. It was announced that Mikhail Khodorkovskii, Platon Lebedev, Leonid Nevzlin and three other individuals were among the owners of Group Menatep, which owned Yukos Oil Company through entities called Yukos Universal. This event was seen as a bid to be listed on the New York Stock Exchange, which requires strict corporate disclosure (*Vedomosti*, 20 June 2002). The move also reflected the owners' desire to legalize their ownership stakes, that is to make their stakes legally secure and reduce the risk of their being confiscated by the state or rival businesses; in other words to help them to hang on to what they had come to own (Radygin, 2004). Boone and Rodionov (2001) argue that this drove some of the new, propertied elite to become a key lobbying point for stronger property rights.

As a result, Yukos was hailed as one of the best-governed and most efficient companies in Russia. Meanwhile, the consolidation of the holding resulted in efficiency gains. Since production had bottomed out in 1998, the company had delivered the largest absolute production increase in the Russian oil sector. It kept operating costs low and generated higher profit margins by adopting Western know-how in oil production (O'Sullivan *et al.*, 2003).[13] The value of Yukos Oil increased about 1,000 per cent between 1998 and 2003 (Goriaev and Sonin, 2005: 6); Yukos had emerged as the clear leader among the Russian corporations. Its success was dubbed 'yukosization' – the process through which a poorly managed, non-transparent Russian company 'cleans up its act' (Freeland, 2003). Russia's Investor Protection Association in 2001 named Yukos the best company with the best dividend policy, and the best company with most improved corporate governance. Khodorkovskii won an award for the best manager. (www.yukos.com/exclusive/exclusive.asp?id=6095). Thus, Yukos was hailed as having achieved the transformation from 'corporate governance nightmare', to 'a leader in Russian corporate governance' with a strong commitment to continued good corporate governance (Yousef-Martinek *et al.*, 2003; Salter, 2002).

Fall of Yukos and the nature of relations between the state and big business

However, with the onset of what came to be known as the 'Yukos Affair', Yukos Oil Company, once Russia's largest and the most profitable oil producer, suffered dismemberment. In 2003, the Russian authorities initiated a criminal investigation of the top executives of Yukos. Platon Lebedev, the head of Menatep and a business associate of Khodorkovskii, was arrested in July on charges of embezzlement of state assets in the 1994 privatization deal of the mineral fertiliser producer Apatit. In October 2003, Khodorkovskii himself was arrested on charges that included fraud, embezzlement and tax evasion. In 2004, Yukos was presented with claim for back taxes. By the end of 2004, the company's tax claims amounted to US$25 billion (*Financial Times*, 29 November 2004). In December 2004 Yuganskneftegaz, Yukos Oil's main and most attractive production subsidiary, which accounted for about 60 per cent of Yukos Oil's production, was sold at auction (77 per cent of Yuganskneftegaz was auctioned off). The buyer was a previously unknown company called Baikal Finance Group. Eventually, Rosneft, a state-owned oil company, announced its purchase of Baikal Finance Group, and the head of Rosneft subsidiary Purneftegaz was appointed the new head of Yuganskneftegaz. The 'Yukos affair' was interpreted as a politically motivated attack on Khodorkovskii and Yukos by the Kremlin. Regarded as the most successful of the oligarchs, it was emphasized that Khodorkovskii was targeted because of his political ambitions, which included the support for non-pro-presidential parties, and Yukos Oil's commercial interests (see below) which did not attract the Kremlin's support (Aron, 2003; Rutland, 2005).

The paradoxical aspect of Yukos Oil's 'fall from grace' (*Financial Times*, 29 November 2004) was that it became a target of what is widely viewed as politically motivated attack and expropriation by the Russian authorities at a time when it had achieved a transformation from a company associated with corporate governance abuses to one of Russia's most respected companies with a strong commitment to good corporate governance and transparency. Questions arise, therefore, about a possible link between improved corporate transparency and expropriation by the state, and what this implies about the nature of state–business relations in Russia.

Although, in principle, non-transparency was a strategy commonly adopted by Russian companies to shield themselves from possible interference from the state authorities and rival businesses, improved transparency and corporate governance seem to have contributed to an exit strategy for those dominant owners who achieved corporate reorganization and consolidation. This exit strategy consists of the Russian owners-mangers selling large stakes to foreign investors in order to diversify their own wealth and improve liquidity. The improved transparency was seen as enhancing capitalization, which in turn would create favourable conditions if core owners decide to sell their stakes to foreign investors. In addition – the argument went – if reputable foreign investors participated in the share capital the company would be protected from a sudden and selective expropriation from the state, because higher involvement of foreigners would make it politically more difficult for the state to launch such an attack (Negodonov, 2001). However, from the owners' perspective, the timing was difficult: as Guriev and Rachinsky (2004: 140–1) argue, 'Selling too early would bring too little as the assets are initially undervalued. Delaying the sale in order to restructure the company and improve transparency would raise the price, but would also increase the risk of expropriation by the Russian government'.

Considering the Yukos case *ex post*, increased corporate transparency turned out to be self-defeating. Although a link between transparency and expropriation is multifaceted and not straightforward as will be shown, many specialists have in part attributed the legal and political attack on Yukos to its improved transparency. Makarenko, Shevtsova and Urnov (2003) argue that the primary reason why Yukos was attacked was because the company 'started to come out of the shadows and was able to become a model for others' when Russia's bureaucracy was not yet ready for transparency (Makarenko *et al.*, 2003). In Aron's (2003: 7) words, 'International accounting standards and audits by top Western accounting firms leave little, if any, "slush" funds for bribery'. Radygin (2003) points out that Yukos achieved the highest level of corporate transparency and independence among the Russian companies, and questions how such a company could fit into the idea of a 'strong state' in the current Russian context, where there is a tendency toward what the author calls 'state capitalism' (Radygin, 2004).

Thus, greater transparency could be seen as a firm's increased independence from the state. This is in line with the observation that 'the expanded disclosures and additional scrutiny that come with issuing foreign securities might be at odds with close political ties at home because these ties can best be exploited when little is disclosed about the firm' (Leuz and Oberholzer-Gee, 2003). As Stulz (2005: 1614) puts it, 'The ability of the state to favour some firms and expropriate others can make a lack of transparency more advantageous for the firms that are favoured by the state than those that are not'. In other words, from the point of view of the state, transparent businesses are much harder to control than those that maintain close ties with the state.

A notable feature of the state–business relations developed in post-Soviet Russia has been the 'conflation of state and business' (Erickson, 2001), with the boundary between the private and the public blurred (McFaul, 1997). During the Yelstin era, it was emphasized that the state had fallen prey to 'state capture', where special interest groups, such as powerful businesses, were able to shape the regulations to their own advantage (Hellman *et al.*, 2000). As a result, business engaged in efforts to forge a close integration with state structures, and to have representatives on government or legislative bodies that support particular business interests (Yakovlev, 2003). State institutions have become too closely involved with business, and vice versa.

While the Russian state has been non-autonomous and 'captured', it has exerted a potent 'grabbing hand', 'empowered to impose on business a variety of predatory regulations' (Frye and Shleifer, 1997: 355). Through excessive red tape or prohibitive tax rates, for example, state officials were able to reap benefits from firms that were seeking preferential treatment from the state in the form of tax exemptions, and so an. As Tompson (2002: 937) points out, Russia has a weak state but strong officials, where 'The patronage dispensed by individual officials ... has been enormous, while the weakness of the administrative machinery has made it easy for them to use its power for private gain at state expense'.

Emphasizing the interpenetrative, two-way process of interaction between state and business, Rutland (2001) argues that the pattern of interaction is more top-down, because it is the state that creates and maintains big business. In fact, the initial development of Russia's big businesses, which came under the control of business tycoons known colloquially as oligarchs, owes much to the fact that these individuals were 'authorized' by the state to be rich (Kryshtanovskaya, 1996; Kryshtanovskaya and White, 1996). By the mid-1990s, the oligarchs were able to accumulate wealth as heads of 'authorized banks', which were given exclusive privileges to handle the finances of various government agencies. Moreover, the loans-for-shares privatization programme, through which the state handed over the most profitable enterprises (including Yukos) to a select few who were politically well-connected, can be seen as another such 'authorization' process. In the words of Peter Aven, former Minister of Foreign and Economic Relations and head of Alfa bank, in Russia 'you are appointed a millionaire' (quoted in Black *et al.*, 2000: 1743–4).

What emerged in Russia was a particular type of interaction between the state and large business. Volkov (2003) notes that the relationship between the state and big business was based on an intricate system characterized by unwritten agreements and exchanges: the Yeltsin administration aided the rise and protected the expansion of big business, such as the Yukos Oil Company, and the presidential administration could be seen as the Kremlin's 'roof' (*krysha*, or protection) protecting the oligarch's business interests. In return, oligarchs provided the resources that helped the administration to maintain power in the government (Volkov, 2003). In this connection, an alleged tacit pact struck between Putin and Russia's big businesses in the summer of 2000 – reassurance that their property rights would be respected in exchange for their staying out of politics – appeared to imply the top-down character inherent in Russia's business–state relations.

In short, big businesses – especially those operating in the natural-resource sectors – have largely been 'authorized' by the state for development, and the Yukos affair seems to confirm the continuity of this systemic dependency of big business on the state in the Putin period. The difference between the Yeltsin and Putin periods, however is the increased degree of state dominance, as Hanson and Teague (2005) point out. They argue that business–state relations in Russia under Putin have become more one-sided enabled by Putin establishing central control over the machinery of state, and Russia's economic recovery since 1998, which strengthened public finances. The unpopularity of rich businesspeople with the Russian public, which regards their wealth as having been accumulated mostly by dishonest means, provides the state with further leverage over them (Hanson and Teague, 2005). Moreover, because most large businesses depend on revenue from natural resource-based exports, they may be particularly vulnerable to state interventions (Hanson, 2005). Natural resources are not the private property of big companies, and as Breach (2005) points out, the infrastructure to extract those resources was built by the state and not by the assets' recent private owners.

Since becoming Russia's President, Putin has endeavoured to rebuild the state, to strengthen its economy and to re-establish Russia's status as a great global power (see Tompson, 2003, 2005b; Tsygankov, 2005). Big business has been expected to contribute to this project by fulfilling the role expected of them by the state. In this context, there are various analyses indicating that Yukos Oil's owners pursued commercial interests 'at the expense of state assets and/or interests' (Kraus, 2003: 3). It has been alleged that Yukos Oil's expansion plans to become a global energy conglomerate put pressure on state-controlled companies such as the pipeline monopoly Transneft, the state oil company Rosneft, and the gas monopoly Gazprom (Kraus, 2003; Lelyveld, 2003; Woodruff, 2003). In 2003, when the Anti-Monopoly Ministry approved the merger of Yukos and Sibneft to create the world's fourth-largest producer after BP, ExxonMobil and Royal Dutch Shell, it was widely believed that Yukos Oil's owners were negotiating the sale of a large stake of Yukos to a Western oil major (*Ekspert*, 13 October 2003). When a question was raised about this possible transaction in an interview in October 2003, Putin said 'As regards purchasing part of the Yukos company ... we are talking about a possible major deal here, and I think it would be the right thing to do to have preliminary consultations with the Russian government on this matter' (quoted in Tompson, 2005b: 201; see also www.kremlin.ru/eng/speeches/2003/10/04/1345_53478.shtml). This does not mean that the President considered that foreigners should be completely excluded from the Russian oil industry, as the creation of TNK-BP and ConocoPhilips' purchase of Lukoil stakes indicates; on the contrary, foreign partners bring technology and expertise much needed to develop Russia's oil and gas industry (Henderson and Radosevic, 2004). Rather, the Kremlin appears to see the oil as the country's strategic sector, in which the oil companies' major plans are expected to be coordinated with the state. As Olcott (2004: 3) argues, 'While Vladimir Putin recognizes the importance of market forces and the need to protect private property, he believes that both must be managed to insure that neither takes precedence over the interests of the state'.

For the state administration, establishing firm control over the natural resource sector means securing a source of income and power. The state administration can take an increased share of natural resource rents by imposing higher taxes or/and enforcing and auctioning state licences. Or it can use those rents to fund tax cuts for the rest of the economy. Moreover, Russia's natural resources, oil and gas in particular, are attractive as a foreign policy lever to assert influence internationally, thus enhancing Russia's geopolitical power (Balzer, 2003; Weafer, 2005).

In terms of a systemic implication of the Yukos affair on the relationship between the state and big business, it seems that unwritten agreements and exchanges continue to be crucial in obtaining *ad hoc* security for the pursuit of business interests. However, such a situation can be at odds with providing certainty in the longer term, and the state's role could be destabilizing for business. For example, a condition of what Ledeneva (2001) terms 'suspended punishment' contributes to the potentially destabilizing role of the state. Because of the pervasiveness of informal practices that are in some violation of the formal rules, business actors are continually under threat of reprisals; actual punishment is suspended but might be enforced at any time. The authorities can apply and enforce the formal rules selectively (Ledeneva, 1998, 2001). Such a condition of 'suspended punishment' and the possibility of selective enforcement increase the insecurity of property rights for businesses. As Hanson (2004: 425) puts it: the state can 'maintain the power to intervene *ad hoc* in at least some sectors of the economy ... by preserving a large gap between formal and informal rules, so that the state is not constrained by an independent legal system'. As far as the state is concerned, it can sustain informal order by keeping business insecure and vulnerable.

Conclusion

In this chapter, the rise and the fall of Yukos Oil Company has been analysed from a corporate governance perspective, focused within the wider political economy context. During the course of the 1990s, Yukos was mostly associated with corporate governance abuses. However, the use of corporate governance practices that constituted abuses to minority shareholders helped restructure the company, which, when it was established as a VIOC by presidential decree in 1992, lacked organizational integrity and was vertically integrated in name only. This chapter has shown that these practices aided the consolidation of Yukos as an effectively operating vertically integrated company under the conditions at the time.

By the end of 2001, Yukos emerged as a company that had undergone an impressive makeover from 'corporate governance nightmare' to 'investor darling'. It was perceived as the most transparent company in Russia. It turned around its operations and became the largest and most profitable oil producer in Russia. However, the company became a target of expropriation by the Russian authorities and faced dismemberment. This chapter illustrated that Yukos Oil's increased transparency signalled its independence from the state, and that its increased independence risked the loss of 'authorization' from the state in a system where the relationship between the state and big business is considered to be maintained by informal understanding and mutual support, with the state exhibiting the upper hand.

The case of Yukos is significant from a corporate governance perspective since Yukos Oil's earlier corporate governance abuses arguably had some positive effects on its internal technical and economic efficiency, while by receiving an award for excellent corporate governance, the company was singled out for expropriation by the authorities. One of the implications of the story of Yukos seems to be that a 'well-governed company' can be context-specific, especially in a weak institutional environment. From the principal–agent point of view, protection of shareholders' rights, as well as transparency and disclosure, reduce corporate governance risks for investors. However, in a situation where the rule of law is weak and the property rights are fuzzy, and businesses are in a condition of 'suspended punishment' such as in Russia, it appears that reduction of political risks becomes fundamental for the good governance of a private company to be sustainable.

Notes

1   For an analysis of the ambiguous effects of corporate governance abuses in the Russian economy of the 1990s, taking Yukos, Siberian (Russian) Aluminium, and Norilsk Nickel as case studies, see Adachi (2006).

2   A revised version of the *Principles* was published in 2004 adding 'Ensuring the basis for an effective corporate governance framework' as a fifth principle to ensure that the corporate governance framework should promote transparent and efficient markets, be consistent with the rule of law and clearly articulate the division of responsibilities among different supervisory, regulatory and enforcement authorities.

3   The *Code* is developed as recommendations, and most of its provisions, according to the *Code* (2002: 5), have already been reflected in the Russian legislation. The European Bank for Reconstruction and Development (EBRD), in its effort to promote improved corporate governance in Russia, helped the FCSM to develop the country's Corporate Governance Code, and the code-drafting process was EBRD's single largest legal reform project (EBRD Press release, October 2001).

4   Allan (2002) emphasizes the government's need to raise revenue for the budget, while Freeland (2000) emphasizes the exchange of property for political support

ahead of the presidential election in 1996 as the main explanation of this loans-for-shares scheme. The revenue from the loans-for-shares auction turned out not to be substantial, and Pappe (2000) argues that what was actually achieved through the scheme, was (a) the formation of strong ties between the banking sector and industry; (b) the emergence of domestic 'strategic' owners with longer-term interests in companies; and (c) the securing of a political alliance between the government and business.

5   Author interview with a Russian oil analyst at an oil consultancy firm in Moscow, January 2003. Hoffman (2002: 445–6) cites an account of a former Menatep official, who said that when Khodorkovskii acquired Yukos, he dispatched 300 of the best security personnel to Siberia to physically take over the company's wells and refineries: Khodorkovskii personally visited every single financial controller and chief accountant in all the subsidiary daughter companies and made sure that it was known and accepted that he was the new owner.

6   According to Latynina (1999), this intra-corporate price was set at 250 rubles (US$10.2) per ton, while the domestic market price was 800 rubles (US$32.6) per ton, and the international market price was US$73.0 per ton.

7   For example, by reducing the profits made by subsidiaries through the transfer pricing scheme, and by decreasing the amount of profit for regional authorities to tax subsidiaries located in an oil extraction region, the holding company could choose to pay taxes in Moscow, the location of Yukos head office, where greater political and economic benefits were available for the holding company (Shleifer and Treisman, 2000: 132–3).

8   According to Yukos's financial statement audited by Pricewaterhouse, in 1996 the holding company recorded an after-tax profit of US$91.5 million, while the subsidiary minority interests recorded a combined loss of US$345 million, in which Yuganskneftegaz in 1996 lost an estimated US$195 million through transfer pricing (Moser and Oppenheimer, 2001: 316).

9   Tomskneft was originally a subsidiary of holding company Eastern Oil Company (VNK), which held a 51 per cent stake in Tomskneft. In 1997, Yukos acquired the controlling stakes of VNK, which made Tomskneft a subsidiary of Yukos (*Moscow Times*, 30 May 2002).

10   In January 1999, the two parties – Yukos and the minority shareholders – held parallel meetings, both of which claimed to be legitimate (*Moscow Times*, 16 January 1999).

11   According to Hoffman (2002: 448–9), Yukos planned to issue: (1) 77.8 million new shares in Yuganskneftegaz, additional to the existing 40 million, (2) 67.4 million new shares in Samaraneftegaz, additional to the existing 37.6 million, (3) 135 million new shares in Tomskneft, additional to the existing 45 million. Black, Kraakman and Tarassova (2000: 1170) note that a proposal was passed at each of the three meetings for 'a massive new share issuance to obscure offshore companies, at dirt-cheap prices that valued the companies at 1% or less of their true value, and perhaps 10% of their depressed trading prices'.

12   For example, the World Bank (2004) study shows that the 23 largest private owners controlled 36 per cent of sales and 38 per cent of employment in the sample of industrial firms which account for three-quarters of total sales in the sub-sectors covered in the survey.

13   At the same time, it should be noted that Yukos Oil's 'short-termism', that is its strategy of maximizing current output at the expense of prospecting and exploration focusing on the long-term, was being criticized. See Dienes (2004).

4
Politicians or Administrators? State Corporate Governance in Poland

*Maciej Bałtowski and Tomasz Mickiewicz**

Introduction

Over the last 15 to 20 years, corporate governance (CG) has become one of the most prolific areas of economics, business, management and law research (in particular, see World Bank, 1995). CG principles and procedures are strictly related to those features of the economic system that are defined by ownership rights and by the ways these rights are exercised. Understood as the modes of supervision over publicly held companies, the CG models and standards were developed independently in such countries as the United Kingdom, Germany or France and still differ greatly from one to another (Charkham, 1994; Chew, 1997).

Since the late 1990s, international institutions (mainly the OECD and ICGN – the *International Corporate Governance Network*) have demonstrated an active commitment to the unification of CG principles and procedures, plucking from the different national models their best, proven attributes. OECD experts drew up the *OECD Principles of Corporate Governance*, a document that in May 1999 was adopted by ministers representing 29 OECD member states. The *Principles* describe uniform fundamental standards of CG, which – in the opinion of the OECD – should be applied to the operation of public companies throughout the world.

In more recent years, concurrently with the implementation of the uniform CG standards for listed companies, there have been attempts to transfer some of the proven CG principles and procedures to other companies, notably those operating in the public sector – that is, in the area where public services (that is, those with public goods or merit goods attributes) are created and delivered to consumers. The concept of *Corporate Governance in the Public Sector* became well-established in economic writings (see Hodges *et al.*, 1996; IFAC, 2000), and the corresponding research addresses such issues as stakeholder

---

* We are grateful to Rick Woodward for helpful comments and criticism. Needless to say, any remaining errors are ours.

relations, operational transparency and the appointment of governing boards of public-sector entities. Where the state is the sole owner, for obvious reasons, some of the issues that are significant in the 'traditional' corporate governance sense, for example the issue of the rights of minority shareholders, do not apply. In general, the overall objective of the public-sector governance rules is to improve the effectiveness of the public sector and put in place mechanisms preventing corruption.

In 2000, the OECD's Advisory Group on Privatization was transformed into the Working Group on Privatization and Corporate Governance of State-Owned Assets and embarked on a project of developing a set of non-binding guidelines and best practices for corporate governance of state-owned assets, which is to complement the *OECD Principles of Corporate Governance* referred to above.

A similar rationale (that is, improving effectiveness and preventing corruption) is behind the transfer of the CG principles and procedures to state-owned enterprises (SOEs), operating not in the public sector (as defined above), but on the competitive markets.

In the developed Western economies, the latter is a relatively marginal issue, for the reasons listed below:

- state-ownership of companies is marginal (4–8% of the employed in the business sector of the economy); in addition, these, as a rule do not operate on the 'normal' competitive markets, instead they enjoy either a monopoly position or command such a major share of their respective goods and services markets that they remain the focus of attention of the general public and media which, in a sense, perform some monitoring role, becoming, to a degree, a substitute for the government's corporate governance (railways, urban transport, postal services, power generation);
- many of these companies operate in established and static markets, i.e., in industries in which, as a rule, repetitive activities and easily monitored routine operations are performed, thus reducing the significance of the agency problem and rendering corporate governance much easier (of which postal services are the best example);
- in some cases, where enterprises operate in a competitive environment, the latter includes on a well-established corporate culture and the appropriate institutional environment; in particular, the well-functioning market of managerial talent ensures that the controlling stakeholders in the state-owned companies may face incentives that are not very different from these experienced by the managers of privately owned corporations: these two groups overlap, thanks to the managerial job market;
- the exercise of property rights by the state in respect of these enterprises has for years been subject to strong, most often formalized supervision, being a feature of the well-established government administration with relatively well-defined relations to politics that limits the amount of short-term rent-extraction by politicians;[1]

- and last but not least, the number of SOEs in Western economies is also generally smaller than in the CEE economies; in the former case, typically, the state owns only a dozen or so large enterprises; in contrast, in the early 2000s, despite progress in privatization, the share of the state-controlled enterprises in output of the CEE countries still accounts for double the percentage of Western Europe.

In Poland, the share of the state enterprises is even higher than in the neighbouring countries; they represent over 20 per cent of the economy, measured by the proportion of the employed or the contribution to value-added (see also Chapter 1 by Mickiewicz in this volume). The state is the owner of dozens or even hundreds of smaller enterprises. Due to the size and complexity of the state sector, the potential for supervision of the general public and media is in these countries incomparably weaker than in the developed economies of Western Europe.

Second, in the economies undergoing transformation, state enterprises operate in a rapidly changing, unstable environment. Many large enterprises have been privatized and they are shaking off the burden of the command economy; however, this proceeds gradually and as a result their corporate culture still leaves much to be desired. Oftentimes in a specific industry (in Poland for example in hard coal mining, power, heavy chemical industry), the state continues to own a major proportion of enterprises. Therefore, the disciplining effect of product-market competition is weak, because either there are not that many private companies to compete with, or those that exist are not yet sufficiently efficient. Thus, on many occasions the only feasible competition comes from imports, but the potential for the latter is sector-specific.

Third, as a rule the institutional environment (for example anti-monopoly agencies or auditing organizations) is less-developed than in Western Europe and hence its impact on the evolving corporate governance is far weaker.

Fourth, in the majority of the former COMECON countries, formalized proven principles of state-owned assets management in the economy were either not developed or were not adequately applied at the outset of transformation. The case of Poland demonstrates (to be elaborated further in this chapter) that there was no political will to create clear transparent rules governing the exercise of property rights by the state. It appears that this was due to two factors, ironically, each motivated by a very different combination of interests and ideas:

- initially, there were concerns that devoting too much attention to the operational problems of state enterprises may contribute to ingraining the old patterns of the economy, creating an obstacle to the progress of privatization which (at least in the early stages of economic transformation) was seen as a priority of the economic policy;

- the absence of clear corporate governance policies made it possible for the SOEs to be used as a sort of political bounty by the successive governments. The discretionary appointment of several thousands of supervisory board members in companies with State Treasury participation and the reaping of other benefits deriving from the existence of the state dominion in the economy became a tacit privilege and attribute of power.

And, fifthly, in the transition economies the scale of soft financing of SOEs has historically been and – while diminished – continues to be more extensive and its principles less transparent than in Western European economies. Soft financing is provided by means of subsidies, tax breaks, tax payment arrears, access to easy credit and bad debt being tolerated for long periods without restructuring, and – in cases of the dominant position in the market – by the ability to pass costs onto consumers via price increases. As a rule, a situation of soft budget constraint is more likely to apply to SOEs than to private-sector enterprises, both because the process is less visible for the general public and because – given the channels of influence of politicians on state-owned firms – it is more likely that politicians and state-sector managers will trade soft budgeting for some private political rents or for benefits delivered to some crucial political constituencies. The latter phenomenon would typically imply increasing labour costs beyond the level determined by profit-maximization, either in the form of higher wages, higher employment or both (Shleifer and Vishny, 1994).

Over the last several years, the problem of corporate governance of state-owned assets in transition economies triggered a special interest of the OECD in this issue. More specifically, it seems that this resulted for several concurrent reasons:

- the expansion of corrupt practices, in particular at the point of contact between the state and the private sector in the Central and Eastern European countries, which either have joined the EU, or have applied for EU membership;
- the development in these countries of public and private partnerships, often based on EU funds; and
- the rapid opening up to the world of the Chinese economy where the absence of the rules of corporate governance exercised by the state represents a significant obstacle to the safety of foreign investors (Clarke, 2003; Lin, 2001).

In this chapter, we build on some of the insights referred to in this introduction and analyse the state corporate governance in Poland. In the next section we discuss both the origins of the state corporate governance system in the market environment established in Poland in the early 1990s, and subsequent developments seen in the political economy perspective. We shall than present an early 2000s attempt to reform the state CG system, before building on our discussion of the institutional evolution to present a more systematic assessment of the government corporate governance in the early 2000s. A final section concludes.

Political economy of the state corporate governance in Poland

It was already at the very start of the economic transformation in Poland that the reforms of state corporate governance came up against two barriers, resulting from the historical heritage of the command economy.

First, over 8,000 SOEs that existed at the time Communism was crumbling were in fact 'state' by name only, as – pursuant with the provisions of the law effective at that time – they were actually in the hands of their workforces (thus, being effectively the workers' self-management enterprises). Furthermore, these enterprises, particularly the large ones, were seen by their workforce (and even more importantly, by their representation: the Solidarity Trade Union, the major force behind the political and economic transformation) as their own. It was not a coincidence, therefore, that already in 1989 at the onset of regime change, that the employee buy-out privatization concept emerged and attracted many supporters. These ideas, if implemented in full, could hamper the development of the capital market but also erode the power of the state administration over state enterprises (Bałtowski, 1998; Mickiewicz and Bałtowski, 2003).

Second, the society professed an across-the-board disrespect for the state, and in particular for state property, a legacy of the Poland's partitions further strengthened by the communist regime. State property was nobody's property, and a transgression against state property was perceived by the general public as far less reprehensible than a transgression against any other type of property. Therefore, it was difficult to raise interest and build consensus around the protection and good governance of state assets, even as a measure to ensure that their value is preserved until the privatization process is completed.

However, the problem of corporate governance exercised by the state returned to the forefront of policy discussion in the autumn of 1990, when it was decided that employee-buyouts (EBOs) would not become a dominant form of privatization for large enterprises. Instead, while EBOs remained a popular method of privatization for medium-size companies, the largest SOEs were expected to be transformed into limited liability companies 100%-owned by the state (that is, corporatized or commercialized), under the provisions of the Privatization Act adopted in July 1990. The commercialization clarified or rather reinstated formal ownership of these companies, even if enterprises remained the property of the state.

It is telling, however, that neither in 1990–91, that is during the years of rapid commercialization, nor at any time afterwards until 2004, there was any legal act that would regulate in a comprehensive manner the exercise of ownership control by the state, although the need for such an act would seem quite obvious, firstly given the size and significance of the state dominion in Poland, and secondly because knowledge, skills and experience in exercising the ownership role by the state were in short supply. As has already been mentioned, such legal acts have been adopted in the majority of Western European countries, although the number of state enterprises is far smaller there.

One has to admit that it was already at the very start of the transformation period that certain practical measures of corporate governance of state assets were taken, perhaps being more administrative than legal in nature. The Ministry of Ownership Transformation under the supervision of Drygalski compiled a list (together with a system of selection and recruitment) of candidates for supervisory board (SB) members (based on an open invitation to apply) and the Committee for Supervisory Board Appointments in State Treasury Companies was set up. A system of examinations for SB member candidates was introduced. The Ministry of Ownership Transformations (jointly with the Privatization Centre Foundation) launched a specialized newsletter *State Treasury Companies* intended for members of supervisory boards and management boards of State Treasury companies, containing guidelines (oftentimes acting as *prawo powielaczowe* – ministerial circulars posturing as law) on corporate governance.

In 1991–92, the system was relatively effective, meeting the expectations of policy-makers. Examinations for supervisory board member candidates were treated seriously and were difficult to pass. As a result, those political cronies who did not have adequate business and legal training were prevented from joining the candidate list. On appointment of SB members, the Ministry complied with the candidate list requirement, while the selection itself was usually made in such a way that three SB members appointed for a given company included a lawyer, an economist and a specialist from a given industry. At that time, supervisory boards had quite extensive powers (as provided for under the Commercial Code and the Act on Privatization of SOEs), while the (potentially politically motivated) interference of the Ministry, particularly as far as smaller companies were concerned, was limited.

This system, which was initially quite effective, was nevertheless not embedded firmly in supporting legislation, and therefore easy to dismantle. For the latter reason, the system begun to erode quickly following frequent changes of the privatization ministers, and in the autumn of 1993, after power was seized by the coalition of Democratic Left Alliance and the Polish Peasants Party (replacing previous weak, multiple parties coalitions), the process of deterioration rapidly accelerated. Criteria based on merits and skills soon gave way to political considerations. The publication of the *State Treasury Companies* newsletter was discontinued. Soon, the SB member candidate exams became a mere formality and in fact simply a farce. When the requirement to hold the exams was included in the new Act on Commercialization and

Privatization of State Enterprises in 1996, it did not have much positive impact on the already established practice of distributing the supervisory board seats according to political criteria.

The absence of a strong CG state system, coupled with a slowed-down pace of privatization (which left the large state sector difficult to monitor), led to confusion and opportunities for discretionary opportunist behaviour, which became a common practice of politicians across all the political spectrum. In this way, the dilution of the written and unwritten CG principles progressed fast, and the concept of political capitalism was endowed with quite a tangible meaning.

The Act on Commercialization and Privatization of State Enterprises enacted in 1996 introduced a possibility of commercialization for other purposes than privatization. This simply legitimized the existing practice, according to which the control of many large enterprises had been moved from workers' councils to the ministry administration without privatization in sight. The new Act contained very brief new provisions on corporate governance exercised in relation to the companies set up as a result of commercialization. At the same time, as part of the reorganization of the administrative centre, the Ministry of Ownership Transformation was replaced with the Ministry of State Treasury. The new ministry was granted statutory powers to manage the assets of the State Treasury, and to exercise supervision over state property held by corporate organizations.[2]

The emergence of the 'Solidarity' government in 1997 did not improve things in the area under review. On the contrary, the computer database of the personal details of SB candidates was liquidated, decreasing the transparency of the process even further. The appointment of members of the supervisory boards of State Treasury companies became from then on the key prerogative of heads of political teams of the successive ministers.

As a result, the scale of private benefits extraction became rampant. However, this in turn drew the attention of the media and, as a consequence, a wave of criticism of the State Treasury supervisory activities followed. With new elections already in sight, in the spring of 2000 the Act capping the remuneration of, *inter alia*, members of management boards of companies wholly-owned by the State Treasury was adapted.[3] The Act covered wholly-owned companies of the State Treasury and companies wholly-owned by local government units, companies in which the State Treasury or local government units held more than 50 per cent of shares, and companies with an indirect controlling interest of the State Treasury or local government units. In addition, Article 15 of the Act was very important for the transparency of corporate governance and public life; it stipulated that the information on the remuneration of members of management and supervisory boards of companies in which the state had a majority interest was made publicly available and was thus exempted from the provisions of the personal data and trade-secret protection law. However, the regulation had a *vacation legis* clause built in; it was to be implemented after two years' delay (that is after the 2001 parliamentary elections).

At the same time, however, the Minister of the State Treasury, Wąsacz, amended Articles of Association of the majority of the State Treasury companies to subordinate them to the general meetings of shareholders (that is, to himself, representing state shareholdings) so that the decisions on appointment of management board members, which earlier fell within the powers of supervisory boards, were now under centralized control. In this way, the minister (read: his political sponsors) became endowed with far-reaching powers over appointments of corporate officers and gained control over the associated distribution of benefits. As a result, state corporate governance found itself even more at the mercy of politicians; this time, not only at the level of supervisory boards, but also at the level of management executive boards, affecting daily operation of state firms. The successive ministers of the State Treasury eagerly maintained these provisions in force.

Reform attempts

In the autumn of 2001, 'Solidarity' suffered a severe electoral defeat and was replaced again by the coalition of the Democratic Left Alliance and the Polish Peasants Party. While the practice of state governance deteriorated further after the parliamentary elections, at the same time, new legislative initiatives were launched, aiming at reform.

It was already in the first months of its term of office that the new government of Miller started to work on a report about the situation in some of the major companies in which the State Treasury had strong shareholdings ('Opening Report': State Treasury, 2002) which – it seems – was intended above all as a tool of political criticism of the previous government and its state-owned assets management policy.[4] The cases of mismanagement widely described in the Report were investigated by the Supreme Audit Commission (NIK), which – generally speaking – did not confirm the allegations. On the other hand, NIK did find that the way the Ministry of State Treasury conducted its daily business was unsatisfactory from the point of view of both meeting legal standards and managerial efficiency (NIK, 2003). The document, that was widely publicized by the media, provided evidence not so much on the violation of the law and political capitalism of the previous government (which was its original objective), but exposed inherent mismanagement of the state administration in respect of the companies controlled by it (directly or indirectly), regardless of which party was in control. The Report also revealed the absence of coherent, comprehensive solutions in the area of corporate governance exercised by the state, and triggered off a public debate on the issue (see for example Drygalski, 2002; Walendziak and Bałtowski, 2003).

The 'Opening Report' of the government pledged the establishment of an 'effective and efficient system of state-owned assets management, based on free market principles, capable of fast and effective response to the changing conditions as well as to potential threats and irregularities'. The Report also listed the constituents of a new desirable system of corporate governance. The government announced that the Ministry of the State Treasury would implement 'new, uniform standards and mechanisms of corporate governance encompassing all the state assets, regardless of which state body exercises corporate governance and under which statutory provisions' (State Treasury, 2002, pp. 47–48).

In the spring of 2002, the Law and Justice opposition party submitted to the Polish parliament a Bill containing an amendment of the Act on Commercialization and Privatization of State Enterprises, focusing above all on improving the corporate governance in the State Treasury companies.[5] The bill envisaged expanding the powers of supervisory boards at the expense of the Minister of the State Treasury. In smaller companies, supervisory boards were to be slimmed down to three members, which was allowed by the Commercial Companies Code, that had recently come into force. It was proposed that a recommendation list of supervisory board member candidates should again be compiled, including individuals with outstanding expertise in economics, management, finance, banking and law. According to the Bill, in each company at least one member of the supervisory board would have to be chosen by the minister from among the candidates on the recommendation list, to ensure that the boards include some external directors. The Bill aimed at unifying corporate governance, addressing the issue of scattered control over state assets exercised by multiple state organizations, in addition to the Ministry of the State Treasury. Each appointment of a member of the supervisory board was to be preceded by a qualification-verifying procedure. The proposed Bill also included ample anti-corruption provisions and regulations aimed at improving the operational transparency of companies wholly-owned by the State Treasury.

Shortly after, the Ministry of the State Treasury produced its own reform proposal, a working document entitled *Target Model of Corporate Governance of State-Owned Assets* (August 2002). While it did not propose any groundbreaking changes in corporate governance exercised by the state, the document included a number of interesting proposals, oftentimes concurrent with the Law and Justice propositions:

- improved transparency of the State Treasury companies to a level comparable with the disclosure standards of listed companies;
- wider public disclosure of information on the public enterprise sector on the website of the Ministry of the State Treasury;
- adopting the rule of appointment of management board members of State Treasury companies, guided by competition; and
- improving the monitoring procedures of companies supervised by the state administration.

In December 2002, the Polish parliament adopted an amendment of the Act on Privatization and Commercialization of SOEs (Dz.U. no. 240, item 2045) that included, *inter alia*, a compilation of the proposals put forward by both the government and Law and Justice on the improvement of corporate governance exercised by the state. Among others, it included an important provision (Article 19a) requiring mandatory verification of qualifications in the case of appointment of management board members in companies where the state holds over half of the shares. In February 2003, the Council of Ministers issued an implementing regulation,[6] which provided the details of the qualification procedure, as well as the conditions that management board member candidates were required to meet. Finally, after ten years, the government relinquished discretionary appointment of management boards of the majority of the largest state enterprises[7] and returned to the initial idea of selection via competition.

Another important step towards normality was taken later the same year. On 1 July 2003, following a two-year *vacatio legis*, the provisions of the Act on Access to Public Information came into force.[8] The provisions impose on all the companies in which the State Treasury or local government units have a dominant position the obligation to disclose information on:

- the identity of members of their corporate boards and their powers;
- ownership structure of these companies; and
- assets they have and hold.

In the spring of 2004, the government work on regulating corporate governance was perceptibly stepped up further. *Principles of Corporate Governance in Companies with State Treasury Interest and Other State Owned Corporate Organizations*[9] was published in April 2004. This represented – as rightly indicated by its authors in the Introduction – 'the first attempt to compile and structure the principles which should be followed while exercising corporate governance'. It should be added, however, that the document, being a model of best practice for corporate governance of state-owned assets, applied only to companies supervised by the Minister of the State Treasury. Thus, the promised unification of corporate governance of the whole state-owned domain did not materialize.

In the autumn of 2004, when Socha, the former chairman of the Securities and Exchange Commission for many years, and proponent of the introduction of the principles of corporate governance, became the Minister of the State Treasury, the website of the Ministry published for the first time in the history of the Polish corporate governance exercised by the state detailed consolidated information on the individuals representing the State Treasury on supervisory boards of companies.

To summarize the above: in 2001 the departing 'Solidarity' government extended the discretion over state-sector corporate appointments, and that was willingly accepted by the subsequent government. As a result, political corruption was further facilitated and expanded, but it also drew attention of the media and therefore became one of the key factors that contributed to the plummeting popularity of the government. The best-known example of a political corruption scandal related to Orlen plc., the largest Polish petroleum company, where secret services were apparently used to facilitate the transfer of control to new political cronies, an event that triggered proceedings of a special parliamentary commission (2004). Perceiving the problem, attempts at reforms were launched, as discussed above. However, too little and too late was done to restore the credibility of the government and the Democratic Left Alliance suffered a massive electoral defeat in autumn 2005. Apart from unsatisfactory economic results (high unemployment), the corruption issue was one of the key factors leading to this outcome. As a result, and consistent with a striking regularity in Polish politics, it was the turn of this group of political entrepreneurs to depart in disarray after four years in power, following the democratic choice of the voters.

Main weaknesses of state corporate governance

The brief historical review presented above suggests a number of drawbacks of the state corporate governance. While the system became subject to partial legal reform in 2003–04, it is too early to assess if that will induce an improvement in practice. Over a dozen or so years of economic transformation in Poland, the state corporate governance did not operate effectively. It seems that there were three main factors that were significant here:

1   the absence of uniform principles of the CG system;
2   the arbitrariness of the CG system; and
3   insufficient disclosure of information.

Absence of uniform principles

A number of strategically important companies, which are formally owned by the State Treasury, remain under the control of various ministers, other than the Minister of the State Treasury. These mainly include ministers of infrastructure (for example the Polish rail company PKP S.A.) and of the national economy (for example the entire hard coal mining industry) as well as the Minister of Finance and the Minister of National Defence. At the time of writing, there are no common principles of CG for all the organizations representing the State Treasury. The reform introduced in 2004 applied only to the companies supervised by the Minister of the State Treasury.

It also needs stressing that some provisions of the law treat differently companies set up through commercialization and those set up in some other way. The best example is the Regulation of the Council of Ministers referred to above concerning the qualification procedure (competition) for members of management boards, which applies to those companies which were set up by commercialization, while the same provisions are not applicable to companies whose establishment followed a different path. Also, the composition of supervisory boards of the two types of companies differs, as the companies set up by commercialization are required to have employee directors.

In addition, over the 15 years of the transformation process, no system for the management of minority shares owned by the State Treasury in companies was developed. Such shareholdings continue to be very numerous – the State Treasury at the end of 2003 was a minority shareholder in over 1,000 companies, including some 400 in which it was a significant shareholder with over 25 per cent of the shares. The Industrial Development Agency manages some of the minority interests, however uniform principles of reasonable utilization of these state-owned assets have never been introduced despite repeated announcements of the government that it intends to do so. On the contrary, random or arbitrary ownership decisions are taken, and in many cases the only reason for which the minority interests are retained at all is the right to appoint 'our man' to the supervisory board of such a company, fuelling political corruption.

Very frequently, state-owned corporate organizations, above all wholly-owned companies of the State Treasury, companies in which the State Treasury holds a controlling interest, as well as state-owned enterprises, set up subsidiaries. There are some 350 of such daughter companies, including such major ones as the life-insurance company PZU Życie S.A. There are no principles governing the supervision and monitoring of such companies, and experience demonstrates that the cases when such companies act contrary to shareholders' interests are not at all infrequent.

A separate problem is the exercise of corporate governance in municipal companies by local government units. This area of the corporate governance policy of the state was, and continues to be, deprived of any overall principles governing the exercise of CG by the state.

Excessive concentration

Despite dispersion in control of some assets, which leads to an opaque and murky CG system as discussed in the previous section, at the same time the system of corporate governance exercised by the state in the Polish economy retains enormous unchecked control in the hands of the central government, mainly the Minister of the State Treasury. At the end of 2003, the State Treasury directly held the shares of some 1,600 companies, including the majority shares of some 500 companies. The Minister of the State Treasury exercises supervision not only over the strategic companies generating an annual turnover of a billion or more PLN, but also over companies which are one hundred times smaller, of a mere local significance. The exercise of ownership rights in relation to all these companies – appointment of some 2,500 members of supervisory boards, appointment of management boards, decisions over distribution of profits and formulation of the strategic objectives of their development – is concentrated in the Ministry of the State Treasury in Warsaw, and so effectively these decisions are taken by the political and administrative circle of advisors of the Minister.

Experience demonstrates that the management of the largest and most important companies owned by the State Treasury is in fact the art of compromise, reconciliation of contrary interests – above all over position filling – the informal negotiations being conducted in the Ministry of the State Treasury and government offices. A variety of political groupings take part in the game – the political team of the current Minister of the State Treasury, the PM's circle, and government coalition members. In some important cases, the Minister of Finance or even the President's circle join in.[10]

Local branches of the Ministry of the State Treasury, existing since 1991 (until 1996 as branches of the Ministry of Ownership Transformations), deal mainly with direct privatization issues and have virtually nothing to say when it comes to corporate governance, even in the case of small companies of local significance or minority interests of the State Treasury in such companies.

Insufficient disclosure of information

Corporate governance is one of the spheres of economic and social life where transparency should go as far as possible (see also Chapter 14 by McGee in this volume). State-owned enterprises represent common property, and efficiency of their operation is enhanced by public control which is conditional on disclosure of information on their operation.

Decisions on donations granted by large state-owned companies (for example to various politically-connected foundations) or on the appointment of suppliers (for example advertising agencies with politically-connected owners) from the private sector for a number of years gave rise to much criticism and undermined the already weak confidence of the general public in the state and government leading to the widespread and justified perceptions of 'political capitalism' and corruption. Corporate decisions on the appointment of management board and supervisory board members of companies wholly-owned by the State Treasury, which were taken in an unclear and non-transparent manner, provoked a similar response among the public. The justification for the appointment of a prominent activist of a coalition party, with no experience in business, to the position of the chairman of the management board of one of the largest Polish companies of the State Treasury, provided at the end of 2001 by the Minister of the State Treasury – 'let Stan have his go in business' – became a symbol of arrogance and political corruption, epitomizing corporate governance decisions of the state (*Rzeczpospolita*, 2002).

Summary and evaluation

The experience of the entire period of transformation clearly indicates that the operation of SOEs and corporate governance exercised by the state is more than just an economic problem – it is a problem of the quality of the government, as it determines the way the general public perceives state authorities, and consequently the extent of confidence the citizen has in the state authorities. Corporate governance exercised by the state becomes a reflection of the fundamental issue of relations between the state and the economy.

State corporate governance was one of those constituents of state functions that had to be developed from scratch in the period of transformation. This area of the state's involvement in the economy remains inadequate, partly due to the legacy of the earlier command economy period when the government administration was both weak and arbitrary in its decisions. It was weak when facing large enterprises due to informational asymmetries and state capture by industrial interests. However, wherever its position was stronger, it acted in an arbitrary manner as the legal system gave state officials unchecked power over many decisions, appointments in particular (see Mickiewicz, 2005, ch. 1).

At the beginning of transformation, that is in the early 1990s, economic policy-makers assumed that fast privatization could easily solve the problem of state corporate governance leaving very little in the state domain. Correspondingly, while the practice of governance of state assets was initially based on sound principles, these were never embedded in strong legal foundations as the necessity to exercise control over state assets was perceived as temporary.

However, fast privatization turned out to be impossible to accomplish, partly due to technical reasons: the experience of other countries (the Czech Republic, Russia) demonstrated that the available methods of fast privatization did not produce satisfactory results. This suggested a difficult trade-off between the speed and efficiency of privatization.

With the benefit of hindsight, we may argue that not implementing strong legal provisions on state corporate governance focused on limiting the arbitrariness of government officials and enhancing disclosure was a policy mistake made early in the reform process.

However, the slowdown of privatization in Poland over the 1990s has to be attributed to more than just purely technical reasons. For some state sector firms (coal mining, metallurgy, transport), to remain in the state domain was a guarantee of continued soft budgeting. In addition, the state administration and other politically-connected stakeholders soon rediscovered that control over state assets is an easy way of realizing private benefits associated with political control. Interests became entrenched and a strong anti-privatization lobby emerged. When the early 'technocratic' reformist governments of 1989–93 (Mazowiecki, Bielecki, Suchocka) were voted out of power, subsequent governments, regardless of the declared ideological affiliation, repeatedly preached the policy of 'active state ownership' which in reality either turned out to be nothing more than hot air, or produced grossly mismanaged groups of state companies. After 1993, all the governments in Poland, were increasingly involved in reaping direct benefits from the existence of the state-owned company sector, treating it as a political bounty won with victory in the elections. This type of approach was directly and universally reflected in the across-the-board appointment of 'our own people' to the supervisory boards and management boards of state-owned companies after each change of government. State dominion was used to strengthen party influence.

J. Drygalski, one of the architects of the Polish economic transformation, was right when he wrote (with some degree of self-criticism) that

> corporate governance exercised by the state … is the epitome of reforms started and never completed, the clashing of contradictory interests of ministerial and business pressure groups … It is a hybrid combining features of the system prevailing in the 1980 and of the free-market economy. It is an example of social and systemic barriers that reformers come up against. (Drygalski, 2002)

Some positive developments and reforms that have taken place in 2003–04 in the area of corporate governance exercised by the state were driven by growing public pressure. Accordingly, the only important source of optimism is that free media, division of power (see the role of the Supreme Audit Commission discussed above), elections and democratic processes in general, while slow and inefficient, may still ensure that further reforms take place.

Notes

1 For instance in Germany the detailed principles and procedures of CG of state-owned assets are regulated under the Resolution of the Federal Government of 24 September 2001 (which replaced the Resolution of 24 April 1974). In France, the Act on Companies with State Treasury Participation of 7 July 1983 plays a similar role. In Spain, the counterpart is the Royal Decree no. 5 of 20 June 1995, and in Italy the Decree of the Minister of State Treasury, Budget and Programming of 30 December 1998.

2 Act on Office of State Treasury Minister of 8 August 1996 (Dz.U. 106, item 493) as subsequently amended.

3 Act on Remuneration of Individuals Managing Certain Corporate Organizations of 3 March 2000 (Dz. U. 26/306).

4 In conclusion, the Opening Report alleged an 'unprecedented scale and nature of irregularities and misappropriations that have occurred in the last four years in companies with a State Treasury interest' (p. 46).

5 *MP Bill on Amending the Act on Commercialization and Privatization of State Enterprises*, Sejm form no. 625, 7 June 2002.

6 Regulation of the Council of Ministers of 18 March 2003 on management board members qualification procedure in certain commercial companies, Dz. U. 55/476.

7 The Regulation applies exclusively to companies wholly-owned by the State Treasury established in the process of commercialization. There is, however, a group of important companies (e.g. Nafta Polska S.A.) which were set up by the

State Treasury from scratch, rather than by the process of commercialization of former SOEs.

8 Act on Access to Public Information of 6 September 2001, Dz. U. 112/1198.
9 Regulation no. 10 of the Minister of the State Treasury of 18 April 2004.
10 In the autumn of 2004, opinions were voiced during the meetings of the Parliamentary Commission for Orlen plc, that each of the key players – the President, the PM, the Speaker of Parliament and the Chairman of the governing party – had their 'own man' on the supervisory board of that largest Polish company which has significant, even if minority, state treasury shareholdings.

Part III

Institutional Owners and Relational Finance

5
The Rise and Fall of a Central European Enterprise: The Case of Elektrim*

Piotr Jaworski and Slavo Radosevic

'Elektrim's final product is shares.'

(Elektrim ex-CFO Piotr Mroczkowski,
Global Finance, February 1997, p. 23)

Introduction

During the period of a command economy (that is before 1990), Elektrim operated as one of the largest Polish foreign trade organizations which, during the course of transition, became a conglomerate. Since the transition, Elektrim S.A. has manufactured cables, power, provided telecom services (mobile and fixed), and has been in the process of divesting a host of unrelated businesses. In 2000, Elektrim was the biggest manufacturing private company in Poland in terms of market capitalization and the second largest publicly traded company after TPSA (the national telecom company), with the maximum price of shares at a level of 72.90 Zloty on 20 March 2000. Two years later, this former blue-chip company struggled to survive with the share price reaching a minimum of 1.14 Zloty on 6 June 2002. In 2005, its shares oscillated in the range of 4 to 7 Zloty (inwestycje.elfin.pl and gielda.onet.pl).

Elektrim's case has a wider relevance for understanding the growth and slowdown of enterprises in Central and Eastern Europe. It illustrates the changing pattern of growth of enterprises between the transition and post-transition periods. Elektrim had grown primarily through conglomeration in the early transition period, and subsequently started to focus on a few core areas (telecommunications, cables, energy). The strategic shift to telecommunications has been based on partnerships with foreign firms, and analysing these strategies helps us to understand the key factors behind its problems.

---

* This chapter builds on our previous study on Elektrim (see Radosevic *et al.*, 2001). However, this is not only its updating but what we consider a definite interpretation of Elektrim's evolution and outcomes in the light of its history of the last 15 years.

First, we provide a background for the analysis of Elektrim by pointing to factors that led to the transformation of the Polish ex–foreign trade organizations (FTOs) into conglomerates, of which Elektrim was a good example. We then present the reasons for problems encountered by the firm after ten years of operations in a market environment, and then summarize the current state of affairs. Several analytical issues that are important for understanding the growth and decline of the Central and East European (CEE) enterprises are highlighted in the light of Elektrim's case.

Transformation of FTOs into conglomerates

Elektrim is one of the seven Polish ex-foreign trade organizations (FTOs) that in the transition period transformed themselves into conglomerates. Out of more than 40 FTOs in 1989, around a dozen have managed to survive and grow in the market context including the 'big seven', which include Elektrim, along with Agros Holding, Animex, Mostostal Export, Universal, Rollimpex and Stalexport. Although they are all conglomerates, they differ in the degree to which they are focused, with Mostostal Export and Universal being the least focused.

During the communist era, FTOs were the main intermediaries between foreign markets and domestic producers of export goods, the latter being basically reduced to production units. Moreover, they had a monopoly over international transactions. For example, Elektrim was monopolist in selling electrical equipment and turnkey power systems produced by Polish enterprises. This led to an accumulation of expertise and knowledge about foreign markets as well as about what domestic producers could deliver. Furthermore, the FTOs hired employees who were relatively well-prepared for operations in a free-market environment. Before 1990, economic education was divided according to the division of the socialist economy into five branches: internal trade, organization of production, finance and statistics, theoretical economics and foreign trade. The latter prepared staff for the FTOs and the international market environment, while the other branches were concerned only with the internal economy, teaching mainly socialist economy and management. Moreover, only selected higher-education institutions had foreign trade departments and limits on the numbers of students there were usually four times lower than at other, 'centrally planned' departments. These factors made the graduates of foreign trade departments and subsequent employees of FTOs a kind of 'socialist management elite'.

FTOs also accumulated diverse engineering skills through participation in large turnkey projects in COMECON and Third World countries. With the dismantling of trade barriers in 1990 and the loss of monopoly positions in their respective branches, FTOs found themselves in an ambiguous situation. On the one hand they lost their privileged status of indispensable intermediary, but on the other hand they had accumulated experience in operating in foreign markets and had strong local knowledge of the value and competencies of domestic producers.

Three factors played an important role in the survival of FTOs as well as in their growth and transformation into conglomerates (*Wall Street Journal of Europe*, 1996). First, when the Polish economy opened in the early 1990s they had accumulated foreign currency reserves – a huge advantage when compared to cash-stripped domestic producers at that time. The value of these reserves was greatly increased through strong zloty depreciation. This enabled them to use accumulated foreign currency reserves to buy up many of the firms they represented, as well as to invest into banking.

Second, the seven largest Polish FTOs were floated on the Warsaw Stock Exchange, where share prices rose fast after floatation in 1993 and 1994. This enabled them to get additional cash and bring into their respective groups their traditional suppliers and other companies that were seriously undervalued. In 1995, their shares accounted for a third of the total value of the Polish stockmarket, excluding banks (*The Economist*, 1995).

Third, trading groups flourished thanks to large windfall profits either as a result of being reimbursed overpaid taxes from 1990 or from one-time asset sales.

These three factors explain why certain FTOs have managed to survive and then to grow, especially given ample opportunities to buy cheap assets via privatization. To some extent, they also explain the strategy of transformation into conglomerations: financial resources together with managerial skills were something lacking in the other parts of the former centrally planned economy.

Furthermore, it seems that the nature of the business environment, in particular market uncertainty in the early transition period and the undeveloped market infrastructure, was such that conglomeration was perceived as the optimum strategic option for both the former FTOs as well as the acquired companies. This led companies to diversify in order to cope with the uncertainty of domestic markets. As Mroczkowski, ex-Chief Finance Officer of Elektrim put it, 'diversification gave security' (*Wall Street Journal*, 1996). In addition, the undeveloped financial system, scarce management skills and the generally undeveloped institutional systems of the market economy suggested conglomeration not only as a viable but also as a desirable strategic option. A business analyst, Martin Taylor from Baring Asset Management, London, put it this way: 'Given the choice, I would always choose a pure producer ... But because of the inefficiencies of the Polish economy, there is a place for conglomerates now' (*Wall Street Journal*, 1996).

However, the internal advantages of conglomerates were not sufficient to sustain their growth. In 'the post transition' period (second half of the 1990s) the institutional factors that had driven conglomeration in CEE earlier no longer operated. The advantages of large business groups in terms of easier access to financial capital disappeared. Nor did advising their member firms with regard to exports or the creation of domestic brands offer competitive advantage. The weak financial standing of the former FTOs led to a search for new investors, including foreign, which did not always produce the expected positive results.

In case of relative market insulation the operation as a big group was also easier from the political point of view. The sheer size of the groups enabled easier access to government through preferential status in receiving licences in areas like telecoms, or in the form of 'certification requirements'. In short, they had advantages in nurturing so called 'network capital'. But with the increased openness of the Polish economy and of the financial system as well as the marketing infrastructure development these advantages disappeared. Even as early as 1995, some subsidiaries were able to raise capital just as easily as Elektrim itself (*The Economist*, 1995). With the stabilization of markets and departure from a period of market uncertainty, diversification of lines of businesses became a problem.

Elektrim's management was aware of all these processes and tried to focus on the wider telecommunications industry. But the expertise of its management, which was an asset in the conglomerate period, turned out not to be useful when in-depth industry-specific expertise was needed. The so called generic managers, who were able to coordinate companies as different as food and heavy machinery producers, were not able to manage a specific industry in a deeper manner: general management capabilities turned out to be insufficient for successfully running either highly diversified businesses or a specialised entity in an open and competitive economy.

The strategy of cooperation with foreign investors together with focusing on 'new economy' business resulted in subsequent problems for the company. Especially after the new technologies bubble ended there was a huge slump in share prices of 'digital' companies. This, together with economic slow-down of the Polish economy made Elektrim almost bankrupt.

Elektrim: a history of growth

Elektrim was established in 1948 as a foreign trade organization. Like other FTOs, until 1989 it had a monopoly to trade internationally in its own range of products. The crucial decision for Elektrim after 1989 was to shift from being a trading organization into becoming also a production company. This quick grasp of the need to migrate from trading to manufacturing was seen in retrospect as being very important for Elektrim to be 'a step ahead of the rest of the game' (*Business Central Europe*, 1994). As Elektrim's Chief Finance Officer, Piotr Mroczkowski, explained, 'To stay in business we had to stop being solely an agent. We had to go for vertical integration and get control of producing what we had been selling' (*Global Finance*, 1997). Elektrim entered production mainly by taking over some 25 enterprises in the course of Poland's privatization process for which it paid around $300 m from a strong cash flow in the early 1990s, when assets were inexpensive. It made a profit by selling shares in companies it had bought cheaply from the state, an activity close to that of investment banking. CS First Boston estimates that Elektrim earned 19 million zlotys ($8.37 m), about a fifth of its pre-tax profit, from selling financial assets in 1994 (*The Economist*, 1995). Its assets even included yoghurt factories, milk plants, fruit drinks manufacturers, pig farms and chicken-feed processers (Dawson, 2000).

During this (second) period the main feature of Elektrim's growth was conglomeration. Elektrim bought many of the concerns it had been representing, including most of Poland's cable manufacturers which had been growing due to the expanding domestic market and exports to Germany and elsewhere. At the end of 1993 Elektrim had a stake in 87 companies concentrated in five sectors. Its management wish was to expand, and acquisitions were seen as essential to build market power. As one of its chief executives, Muszynski, explained: 'If you are late on the train the foreign capital will buy in' (*Wall Street Journal*, 1994).

Despite the fact that Elektrim's acquisitions were haphazard, they were largely in five main areas: power generation equipment, electrical machinery and apparatus, cables, lightning equipment and telecommunications. However, it also had assets in agriculture and food processing, in cement and construction and in seven different banks (1995). The underlying strategy behind the conglomeration in the 1990s was 'to use privatization to integrate vertically' and to transform Elektrim into a 'vehicle for acquisitions of core business suppliers' (Piotr Mroczkowski, Elektrim's then Chief Finance Officer; *Wall Street Journal*, 1994). The idea was that Elektrim should operate as a restructuring agent or a 'network organizer' by pursuing a 'hands-on' approach to restructuring newly acquired subsidiaries. In the mid-1990s the strategy was to model Elektrim on Japan's Mitsubishi and Sumitomo groups. Like them, Elektrim planned to spin off shares in subsidiaries to suppliers, creating a corporate network bound by commercial ties (*The Economist*, 1994).

However, this strategy was not followed for long. Instead of building a diversified business group, in 1999 the company entered a third stage which can be described as consolidation and focusing. According to Piotr Czarnowski of Elektrim, this shift was driven by a variety of factors among which the most important were: a lack of transparency of the conglomerate, inefficiencies in the allocation of capital among different businesses, a lack of expertise in many newly acquired business segments, changes triggered by disclosure problems and by investors demanding streamlining and focusing. Its new Chief Executive Officer, Barbara Lundberg, reinforced the strategy cautiously initiated by former CEO Andrzej Skowroński of focusing on three core businesses: telecommunications, power generating equipment and cables, with strong expansion in telecommunications as a starting point. This included take-overs of local operators and acquisitions of shares in telecom companies.

One of the key components of this new strategy was to invest in mobile telecom. But the outcome turned out to be the main reason for dismissing

Skowroński. In 1996, Elektrim secretly agreed to sell a 6.5 per cent stake in PTC (Era GSM) to Kulczyk Holding. The price Elektrim agreed was close to its nominal price and the latter was not made public until the sale was about to take place. This 6.5 per cent was supposed to compensate Kulczyk, a Polish tycoon, for the role he played in talks with the company's other partners. Although not compliant with the rules concerning the stock exchange companies, this transaction and its secrecy was more a result of an informal way of managing the company by Skowroński than a deliberate attempt not to reveal information to investors (Gadomski, 2002). Furthermore, in 1996 investment in mobile telecommunication was a risky business: even American analysts did not foresee a market for this service, which resulted in relative late development of mobile technology in the USA. The business plan for PTC assumed first profits to appear in five years. The situation was completely different at the time when the transaction with Kulczyk was revealed in October 1998, when the shares were already valued at $165 million. Finally, Kulczyk agreed to $25 million in compensation. The PTC case was the immediate reason to dismiss Skowroński, and by demand of international fund managers the President and Deputy President of Elektrim were also forced to resign.

Foreign investors appeared in Elektrim in May 1997, when the firm issued convertible bonds worth 550 million PLN sold by Merrill Lynch on international markets. As we acknowledged earlier, this coincided with growth of the Polish economy and a resulting optimism of international investors. The foreign investors aimed at close control of firms in which they invested: managers who were too independent and 'spoke a different business language' had to be dismissed and new 'MBA language speakers' had to be hired. Moreover, after the Russian crisis investors were afraid of losing money, as in other emerging markets. The fate of Elektrim's CEO was similar to the fate of other FTOs' CEOs:

- In June 1998, the CEO of Impexmetal, Edward Wojtulewicz (57 years old), was dismissed by the main shareholders, the Japanese investment bank Nomura and the American investment fund Templeton, who replaced him with Nomura's employee Jacek D. Krawiec.
- In October 1998, Kredyt Bank PBI dismissed Witold Pereta (63 years old), CEO of Animex and replaced him with Jerzy Milewski
- In October 1998, Kredyt Bank together with Templeton dismissed Grzegorz Tuderek (60 years old) and replaced him with Marek Michałowski (Grzeszak, 1999).

All four CEOs except Skowroński, who was 52, were in their late 50s or early 60s, and had worked for many years for their FTOs. Furthermore, they had restructured their firms in the early years of transformation and brought them to the Warsaw Stock Exchange. All of them were dismissed at the same time, on the initiative of foreign investors.

The dismissal of Skowroński paved the way for the entry of the new CEO, Lundberg. Lundberg was trusted by international investors and her moves were seen as an example of a new kind of managerial practices in the Polish economy. The extent of changes was described by Lundberg's advisor Piotr Czarnowski who stated: 'This is a completely different organisation. There is no other Polish company that has transformed itself in an eight to ten-month time-frame and invested $1.7 bn in one year alone' (*Business Central Europe*, 2000). Speaking the same language as foreign investors, and being educated in Western-style generic management institutions, Lundberg seemed to be the best-suited person to focus the firm's activities.

Barbara Lundberg became the new CEO in February 1999, two months after Andrzej Skowroński resigned. She speeded up consolidation by selling-off 70 of its non-core subsidiaries out of total of 100 in 1999. In accordance with its new focusing strategy, Elektrim was selling-off assets that did not fit its new focus on the telecoms, energy or cable sectors. In June 1999, jointly with Clifton Consulting, Elektrim set up Warsaw Equity Holdings, a holding company in which it has a 15 per cent share, the remainder falling to Clifton Consulting, which was entitled to 20 per cent of the proceeds from the sale of any assets (Dawson, 2000). Elektrim obtained $62.7 m from the transaction and was reduced to 28 firms following the deal (Polish Press Agency, 1999). Subsequently Elektrim sold 15 per cent of its shares in Warsaw Equity Holding.

Elektrim's share ownership of Chemia Polska was reduced to 21.16 per cent of the total votes in February 1998. In 1997 the Dutch group Campina Melkunie acquired Elektrim Food, a specialist in yoghurt and dairy dessert production, for an undisclosed sum. In its heyday Elektrim had an 8 per cent of share of the Polish dairy market, but its companies in this sector were in the red, running at around only half of actual capacity. Interlektra of Luxembourg bought three of Elektrim's motor producing subsidiaries for PLN 58 m ($14.19 m). This comprised PLN 43 m ($10.52 m) for 99.94 per cent of the motor producer Celma, another PLN 9 m ($2.2 mn) for 67.398 per cent of a similar firm, Besel, and a further PLN 6 m ($1.47 m) for 100 per cent of the shares of Elektrim Motor (January 2000). The acquisition of Celma was contingent on Celma's purchase from Elektrim of the holding's 69 per cent stake in Indukta, another electric machinery factory (*Prawo i Gospodarka*, 2000).

Parallel to selling the unrelated businesses, Lundberg initiated a huge process of investment in the telecommunications industry. In the first three months of her reign Elektrim invested more than $1.1 billion and increased its debt by several billion dollars (Gadomski, 2002).

The two-year period 1999–2000 seemed to be the most successful in the company's history. Elektrim aimed to become a telecommunications group, a competitor to TP SA, the national telecom company, and an operator delivering a full range of telecommunications services. It also intended to continue its operations related to the production of complete energy objects and their refurbishment. The plans were to raise the effectiveness of cable companies

Table 5.1   Elektrim's assets, 2000

Business	Electrim's stake in it	Value of stake (Zl m)
Elektrim (holding company)		420
Telecoms		
Elektrim Telekomunikacja	51%	4,805
Fixed line telephony	87%	1,340
Power		
PAK (electricity generation)	38.5%	935
Elektrim Megadex	97.3%	67
Rafako	49.9%	52
Mostostal Warsawa	28.4%	36
Energomontaż Polnoc	37%	31
Cable		
Elektrim Kable	70.5%	788
Others		325
Total		8,798
Total parent debt	2,892	

Source: Radosevic *et al.* (2001), based on Erste Bank, Central European, July/August 2000, p. 26.

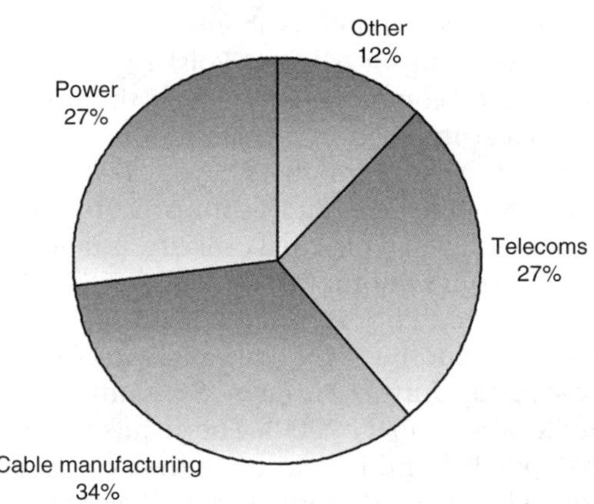

Figure 5.1   Elektrim's consolidated net sales by business segment
Source: Radosevic *et al.* (2001), based on ET *Annual Report*, 2000.

by way of further restructuring but 'without too much investment' (Elektrim, 2000). By 2000, Elektrim's assets became concentrated in telecoms, energy and cables with only 3.7 per cent of assets in other businesses (Table 5.1).

In terms of sales, three major segments had similar shares, with other business amounting to 12 per cent (Figure 5.1).

The growth of Elektrim has been accompanied by strong growth in its market capitalization. Elektrim was the first company listed on the Warsaw

Table 5.2   Elektrim's largest investors, 1999

Institution	Country	$m value held	% of equity
Bank Austria	Austria	79	6.1
Capital International	USA	67	6.9
Emerging markets Growth Fund	Malaysia	66	6.8
Merrill Lynch Mercury Asset Mgmt	United Kingdom	49	5.1
Schroder Investment Mgm (Hong Kong)	China	48	4.9
Barring Asset Management	United Kingdom	35	3.6
Fleming Investment Management	United Kingdom	31	3.2
Schroder Investment Management	United Kingdom	27	2.8
Capital Research & Management	USA	26	2.7
Dresdner Bank Investment Management	Germany	21	2.1
Other large investors		111	12.3

Source: Radosevic *et al.* (2001), based on Carson Group, Central European, July/August 2000, p. 25.

Stock Exchange in 1992, with a share price of 0.35 Polish zloty. In 1996 it was valued at around $620 m (*The Times*, 1996), and by January 1997 the share price had risen to 31 zloty bringing Elektrim's market capitalization to $700 m, and making it the largest non-bank market-capital stock on the Warsaw exchange. In 1999 its market value rose to $912.81 million, and its highest market value amounted to $1.5 billion in March 2000. At that time its shareholders were mainly institutional investors (85%; see Table 5.2).

On the asset side, the structure is presented in Table 5.3. In 2000 it had five major groups of subsidiaries: telecommunications, power, cable manufacturing, internet and others.

The anatomy of failure

However, these were last minutes of the glory. In less than two years from the peak market value, on 19 September 2002 *The Economist* wrote:

> ...privatised Elektrim was the brightest star in the Polish firmament, cherished by patriots who hoped it would be their national champion. In the past week, due in part to the unforeseen consequences of nationalistic 'Poland first' policies, the telecoms and power conglomerate filed for bankruptcy and fired its management for the umpteenth time.

These words were written just after the market value of Elektrim plunged to $23.815 million in March 2002. In December the previous year the company had defaulted on convertible bonds of €440 million. A preliminary and

Table 5.3   Elektrim's major subsidiaries

Telecommunications	*Internet*
ET Telekomunikacja Sp (51%; Vivendi 49%)	VPN – Service Sp (former NASK Service) (85%)
Bresnan International Partners L.P. (100% ET)	
Polska Telefonia Cyfrowa/ERA GSM (51% ET)	
RST El-Net SA (92%)	
Polish Phonesat Sp (93.39%)	
Telefonia Regionalna Sp (99.39%)	
Elektrim Tv-Tel Sp (100%)	
Power:	
Elektrim-Megadex SA (98.41%)	
Rafako SA (49.9%)	
ZE PAK SA (38.46%)	
Elektrim – Volt SA (100%)	
Giełda Energii SA (10%)	

Notes: Elektrim shares in brackets unless stated otherwise; ET = Elektrim Telekomunikacja.
Source: Radosevic *et al.* (2001).

accepted restructuring agreement was cancelled which led to bankruptcy filing in September 2002. The problems were an unintentional result of Lundberg's policity. At that time Lundberg was no longer CEO, she had been dismissed on 15 May 2001. The strategy of stepping into the internet sector had failed; the 'new technology sector' boom disappeared leaving Elektrim with internet firms the majority of which went bankrupt, after being bought earlier by Elektrim for a high price (Elektrim internet site). Also, telecommunication activities did not turn out to be successful. Some of the deals were cancelled as part of a restructuring attempt, but the firm had to pay huge compensations. In general, the assets bought turned out to be overpaid. For example, Brensan International Partners controlling Cable TV operator Aster City was bought for $325 million when Zygmunt Solorz, owner of the first private Polish TV operator 'Polsat' wanted to pay only $170 million. These moves increased the liabilities of Elektrim to almost 6.2 billion PLN in one year (Gadomski, 2002).

This was not the only risky game that Eletrim played under Lundberg's management. The highly indebted company, which had recorded a loss since 1998, played a hazardous corporate game with two international players: German Deutche Telkom (DT) and French Vivendi. Before 1999, DT was seen as the strategic investor in Elektrim. The pearl in the crown of Elektrim's assets, Polska Telefonia Cyfrowa (PTC), Poland's top mobile company, was owned jointly by DT and Elektrim, the latter owning a 51 per cent stake. The Germans, blocked by Polish telecommunications law from owning a majority stake, were in the process of increasing their share of the PTC to 45 per cent. They pushed for control of Elektrim's telecoms subsidiary once the law changed, but Elektrim resisted and the negotiations fell through[1].

In December 1999 the company chose a new strategic partner – Vivendi, which was to invest $1.2 billion in Elektrim Telekomunikacja and receive 49 per cent of the shares. Vivendi (renamed Societe Generals des Eaux, a French company and the world's largest water company) employed 193,000 people, with assets of $43.1 bn and revenues of $28.6 bn at that time (UNCTAD, 1999). In the previous 20 years Vivendi had diversified into telecommunications, media and several other activities. Vivendi was a major shareholder in Cegetel, the number-two telecom company in France, second behind the incumbent France Telecom, offering fixed and mobile telephony as well as internet access. Vivendi streamlined its organization during 1997, disposing of 334 companies in the health, cable television, laundry, restaurant and car-parking sectors. The group consisted of 3,371 companies in December 1998, of which 1,394 were located abroad.

However, Deutsche Telekom claimed the right to 3 per cent of the 15.8 per cent PTC shares purchased by Elektrim in August 1999 from minority share-holders. Also, it claimed it had right of first refusal on some of the shares. It blocked the transfer of Elektrim's stake in PTC to its subsidiary and took the case to court. Elektrim maintained that DT's refusal to agree to the transfer of shares was a violation of the Shareholders Agreement and was damaging to Elektrim as it blocked the restructuring of Elektrim's telecom sector development with Vivendi's support. Elektrim offered a defence to the State Telecom and Postal Inspectors PITIP as to its transfer of shares to PTC, which was challenged in court in August 1999 by DT. Elektrim also announced that it intended to submit a motion against the German firm for irregularities over PTC.

As a result, DT stopped the Vivendi investment, blocked debt financing and threatened to force Elektrim into default on its massive short-term debt payments. For a time, it looked as if the Germans would take over. In order to secure the deal Elektrim had to sell a larger stake. Fortunately for Elektrim, Vivendi stepped in by investing $1.2 bn, including $250 m in cash, to clean up Elektrim's balance sheet. In exchange, the French got a 49 per cent stake in Elektrim Telekomunikacja and, indirectly, ownership of 25 per cent of PTC.

In the meantime, DT failed initially to prove legal credibility to its claims to pre-emptive rights to PTC shares. A Warsaw court dismissed the claim by DT, which argued that, as a shareholder in PTC, it had first refusal right on any shares that existing partners wanted to sell. DT claimed that it had the right to buy any shares on offer up to a ceiling, which would have maintained the existing proportions between the remaining shareholders. Elektrim stated in court that DT did not have the necessary approvals to purchase the additional shares. In response, DT submitted a motion to the Court of Arbitration in Vienna, and Elektrim has since agreed to abide by the Viennese court's decision. The arbitration was part-financed by Vivendi. At stake was Elektrim's key asset: the PTC shares constituted as much as 85 per cent of the parent company's valuation (*Business Central Europe*, 2000).

Subsequently, Vivendi tried to gain control over PTC: by transferring its shares from Elektrim to its subsidiary Elektrim Telekomunikacja (ET) in December 1999[2] together with increasing the share capital of the latter by almost zloty 9 bln ($2.25 bn) to 10 bln zloty ($2.5 bn) (FT.com, 10 June 1999) and taking over a 49 per cent stake in ET. At the same time, Vivendi converted its earlier loan of $615 m into an equity stake in ET. This gave Vivendi control over PTC by holding a 50 per cent stake[3] (*Polish News Bulletin*, 1999). Vivendi guaranteed to increase its investment to over $1.2 bn, which included an initial immediate payment of $150 m and a second payment of $100 m.

However, the battle for control over PTC was far from over. DT increased its 22.5 per cent stake in PTC to 45 per cent by acquiring MediOne International, a subsidiary of the US Media One Group (Dawson, 2000), paying between $1 bn and $1.2 bn for the stake in PTC. In 1999 DT controlled 45 per cent of PTC, fighting against Elektrim via the courts for another 3 per cent (FT.com, 1999).[4]

In December 2001 Elektrim made another U-turn, returning to partnership with DT and signing a letter of intent to sell 51 per cent (and thus strategic and operational control) of its fixed-line and data transmission companies to Deutsche Telekom for $180 million.[5] As a result, Vivendi claimed in its case against Elektrim in the London Court of International Arbitration that relations/ negotiations with Elektrim had reached an deadlock and in accordance made a set of far-reaching demands concerning Elektrim's telecommunications operations, including (1) that Elektrim transfer its shares in VPN Service and Inter-Net Polska to the Elektrim Telekomunikacja joint venture company, (2) that Elektrim discontinue negotiations or any contracting with Deutsche Telekom concerning fixed telephony, (3) that Vivendi is enabled to sell its shares in Elektrim Telekomunikacja to Elektrim for a market price (Rzecz-pospolita 2001).[6,7] The collapse of the partnership between Elektrim and Vivendi was made public in February 2001. Vivendi (1) brought suit in an international arbitrage court in London against Elektrim for breach of the investment agreement from December 1999, and (2) asked a Polish regional court to prevent sale of Elektrim's assets, where the latter would prevent Vivendi from 'undertaking its rights as a majority shareholder' in the joint telecoms holding (*Reuters*, 2001).

Elektrim publicly denied the validity of Vivendi's claims, asserting that Vivendi never availed the procedure for resolving a conflict/impasse between the sides, which would involve consultations between the Directors General of the two companies. Moreover, it claimed that (1) Elektrim was not obli-gated to conduct its Internet operations under the Elektrim Telekomunikacja umbrella; (2) that Vivendi conducted 'in bad faith lengthy negotiations con-cerning the acquisition of a stake in Elektrim S.A.'s fixed-line businesses for more than 12 months although it was obliged to present a serious proposal in this respect on or before 14 February 2000';[8] and (3) that it would be in the interests of the involved sides to attempt to resolve the impasse using the provisions in the Investment Agreement before initiating the share-sellback process (Elektrim, 2001).

This corporate game was played in the period when the Polish economy slowed down, a disadvantage for Elektrim which was far more capital-constrained than its foreign partners. After 7 per cent growth, a time of near stagnation came at the beginning of the new millennium. This adversely affected the construction sector on which the firm was relying, and was accompanied by the mentioned earlier crash of the 'new economy' internet market. The strategy of high debt financing together with the involvement in legal dispute with stronger international partners was very risky even in times of economic prosperity, but turned to become disastrous under the economic slowdown. The mixture of a negative net profit of -1.2 billion PLN with assets of almost 15 billion PLN and almost 11 billion PLN of liabilities for 2000 (Table 5.4) under the slowing-down economy resulted in big financial troubles. In *The Economist's* words:

> By the time it came to its senses and realised that it had to relinquish majority control of PTC in order to stay afloat, the telecoms boom had turned to bust, while its two jilted partners, Vivendi and Deutsche Telekom, had their own problems to attend to. (*The Economist*, 2002)

Elektrim's financial situation was negatively affected by Lundberg's moves, in June 1999, when Elektrim sold convertible bonds worth €430 million. Under an actual share price of 40 zloty, the option price was 64 zloty. The move was presented as a way of financial restructuring hoping that the bonds would be converted into shares. Unfortunately, after the end of the telecommunications boom the prices of Elektrim shares were much lower and those bonds were claimed at the end of 2001, which became a direct reason for the bankruptcy claim.

The rescue

2002 was very a very difficult year for the firm: Elektrim became almost bankrupt and changed CEO several times. Waldemar Siwak was nominated in May 2001 as Lundberg's successor, and was replaced in February 2002 by Dariusz Krawiec. In April 2002 Maciej Radziwiłł became the new CEO only to be replaced in September 2002 by Wojciech Janczyk. The latter was finally replaced in May 2003 by Piotr Nurowski, who has occupied this post until the time of writing this chapter.

In order to rescue the firm, Elektrim Kable, Port Praski and some smaller entities were sold for 100 million PLN. These fund together with €491 million

Table 5.4 Elektrim's annual reports, 2000–05 (current PLN)

	2000	2001	2002	2003	2004	2005*
Net earnings	5,565,319	3,625,985	2,487,411	2,243,439	1,921,797	406,148
Operational profit	−278,665	−481,685	−160,897	−14,119	19,085	100,128
Gross profit	−1,201,722	−538,014	−616,482	−439,552	790,610	1,637
Net profit	−1,078,041	−462,547	−699,437	−344,139	816,598	−9,592
Net flows	−567,827	624,946	−432,549	80,929	−107,952	−47,769
operational activity	432,587	781,046	−127,309	−89,656	−113,194	24,478
investment activity	−17,780	717,984	−122,133	−83,730	5,191	−22,236
financial activity	−982,634	−874,084	−183,107	254,315	51	−50,011
Assets	14,910,962	7,574,164	6,325,481	6,062,422	5,771,268	5,655,216
Liabilities and reserves	10,677,420	5,587,904	5,323,239	5,392,491	4,255,980	4,235,559
Long-term liabilities	5,759,136	231,024	1,998,776	2,538,454	464,635	832,368
Short-term liabilities	3,383,133	3,380,896	1,527,686	1,435,048	3,078,199	3,403,191
Own capital	1,050,461	639,267	−73,643	−426,399	453,759	1,419,657
Share capital	83,770	83,770	83,770	83,770	83,770	83,770
Number of shares	83,770	83,770	83,770	83,770	83,770	83,770
Book value per share	12.54	7.63	−0.88	−5.09	5.42	16.95
Earning per share	**−12.87**	**−5.52**	**−8.35**	**−4.11**	**9.75**	**−0.12**

*First quarter
Source: gielda.onet.pl

Table 5.5   Elektrim's major disinvestments, 2002–04

Date	Seller	Company sold	Buyer	Value
19.02.2002	Elektrim S.A.	Elektrim Kable S.A.		$110 million
25.12.2002	Elektrim	Aster Polska	Consortium of Hicks	€110 million
	Telekomunikacja	Warszawskie Sieci Kablowe RTK Autocom Autorom ZTP S.A.	Muse Tate & Furst, Emerging Markets Partnership and Argus Capital Partners	
27.02.2003	Elektrim Telekomunikacja	Telefonia Polska Zachód Elektrim TV-Tel	EVL Poland	PLN73 million
30.06.2003	Elektrim Telekomunikacja	EL-Net El	BRE Bank	
28.01.2004	Elektrim S.A.	Mostostal Warszawa SA		
15.07.2004	Elektrim S.A.	DM Penetrator	DM Penetrator S.A., In the name of third parties	65,600 shares for 1.52 PLN each

Source: Elektrim's announcements at gielda.onet.pl

paid by Vivendi for the equity in Elektrim Telekomunikacja were used for repaying the majority of the creditors but not the owners of the convertible bonds. The latter claimed their money back in December 2000 and were offered repayment of only 60 per cent (Gadomski, 2002). The offer was refused and a subsequent claim for bankruptcy was filed in January 2001. However, in October 2002 Elektrim reached a restructuring agreement worth $503million providing for exchange defaulted bonds for new bonds maturing at the end of 2005 and repayment of $54.2 million by June 2003 (*Business Eastern Europe*, 2002).

Between 2000 and 2001 Elektrim's assets were halved from almost 15 billion PLN to 7.5 billion PLN. This was also accompanied by the halving of its liabilities from almost 11 billion PLN to little more than 5.5 billion (Table 5.4). This trend continued after 2001 at a slower pace and finally resulted in focusing only on two sectors in 2005: mobile telecommunications and power (see Table 5.6). Due to the huge asset sell-out shown in Table 5.5, combined with the bankruptcies of the internet companies, the structure of the company became much simpler. Paradoxically, because of the troubles, the company now focused mainly on its initial area of expertise: power. Elektrim was rescued, but at the cost of a considerable downsizing.

The ownership situation of the 'pearl in the crown', PTC, was also not simple, and its ownership structure was not stable. According to the Economist Intelligence Unit (2005):

> Elektrim is seeking to dispose of its share in mobile operator PTC. However, Elektrim's PTC shareholding is held jointly with Vivendi (France), and the two firms have so far not been able to agree mutually acceptable terms with Deutsche Telekom, which currently holds the other 49% of PTC. PTC itself is eastern Europe's largest mobile operator; it had about 7.5 m customers in mid-2004, and generated net profits of PLN347m in the first half of 2004.

In 2003, Deutsche Telecom offered €1.1 bn for ET's stake in PTC, but the deal fell through when Vivendi and Elektrim could not agree on how to divide the cash (*Business Eastern Europe*, 23 August 2004). In December 2004, the Arbitration Court in Vienna decided that 48% of PTC did not belong to Elektrim Telekomunikacja but to Elektrim itself. This was subsequently approved by the Polish court in February 2005 and, as a result, Elektrim itself became 51 per cent owner of PTC. This led to Vivendi claiming €2.2 billion from DT in the Paris Commercial Court in May as a compensation for earlier investment in Elektrim Telekomunikacja. In addition, Vivendi asked for the shares of PAK owned by Elektrim Telekomunikacja, as compensation in the legal procedure in July 2005, but they were transferred to Inwestycje Polskie and moved out of Elektrim control. Furthermore, at the end of June 2005, Elektrim called DT to sell 45 per cent of PTC as a fulfilment of an earlier agreement, but on the other hand in July 2005 Elektrim was banned from selling its 48 per cent stake by a Warsaw court.

The PAK company (power generation) was another major project. At the beginning of 2005, Elektrim possessed almost 42 per cent in the venture while the Polish State Treasury and 50 per cent. In the privatization agreement Elektrim was required to build a new electric block Pątnów II. Elektrim invested €210 million in PAK but there were problems with securing finance of €350 million for completion of the project, for which Elektrim was blamed and the State Treasury asked the arbitration court to cancel the privatization agreement in March 2003. Finally, one month later, an amicable settlement was reached and construction was restarted. Finance was provided by a consortium that consisted of Canadian banks and the EBRD (€227 million to be paid back in 15 years), the National Environmental Fund (226 million PLN, which is €50 million) and one of the Polsat Group Companies (€90 million) whose contribution was treated as own resources of Elektrim. The project should be completed in 2007. However, on 16 June 2005 Elektrim transferred the majority of its shares to Embud, its daughter company, as compensation for the credit provided to PAK by Embud two years earlier. Then, on 2 August 2005 the Embud shares were transferred to Inwestycje Polskie (IP) controlled by Mr Solorz, at present a major shareholder of Elektrim. Therefore, by late

Table 5.6 Elektrim's main investors, 2003 and 2005 (% of equity)

Investor	March 2003	July 2005
PAI Media SA (Former Polsat Media SA)	9.55%	34.83%
Vivendi Universal SA	10.04%	15.04%
TCF Sp. z o.o.	8.08%	8.08%
Schroder Investment Management Ltd.	4.43%	4.43%
Merrill Lynch & Co. Inc	4.16%	–
BRE Bank SA	20.31%	–
Zbigniew Jakubas, Multico and Multico – Press	7.61%	–
Others	35.64%	37.62%

Source: gielda.onet.pl

2005 IP effectively owned 40 per cent of PAK through Embud, and Elektrim lost its control over the venture.

PAK's problems had a chain effect on another Elektrim company: Megadex. Troubles started with problems in the Pątnów II construction, and Megadex was a main executor of the project. Because of the payment problems, the company accumulated debts of 53 million PLN, almost twice the capital of the firm, owed to the Treasury and did not pay several other building constructors. In February 2002 the Treasury won a preliminary court battle for 53 million PLN, but the company appealed. On the other hand the agreement to continue the construction of Pątnów II excluded Megadex from the game, and the Canadian company SNC Lavalin was hired as a main executor. The future of Megadex does not look promising as of 2005.

There was also consolidation on the investors' side. From 10 main players in 1999, through seven in 2003, Elektrim ended up with only four, with one strategic investor PAI Media (controlled by Solarz) owning a little more than a third (see Table 5.6).

Polsat Media started to increase the equity holdings in Elektrim in February 2003. First it bought 9.55% (from a Mr Jakubas), then more in August and November the same year, and then in June 2004 (respectively an additional 9.81%, 5.5%, 3.05% and 5.73%) becoming the main investor in the Elektrim.

Analytical issues

Elektrim belongs to a group of large domestically controlled CEE enterprises that operated in the socialist period and which have managed to survive in the free market era. Elektrim, a foreign trade organization during the socialist period, tried to expand in the transition period and failed. We should ask why this blue-chip became almost bankrupt and whether this fate was unavoidable.

Here we highlight analytical issues that link Elektrim's case to the broader literature on corporate and industrial change, related to the CEE region in particular. We want to raise several analytically and theoretically relevant questions which are based on the case study of Elektrim.

The management

Elektrim entered the new era after transformation of 1989 relatively well-equipped with managerial skills. Of course these were not managerial skills earned in a free-market environment, but on the other hand its staff were trained at the foreign trade faculties of Polish economic schools and had earned some experience in practical foreign trade operations as noted earlier. The president Andrzej Skowroński, who led the firm in the times of change, had earned very good experience in the East (two years in the Moscow office) as well as trading with the West. In Elektrim since 1978, he also knew the company very well. His education was formally concluded with a PhD in International Economic Relations.

The situation was characteristic also for other CEOs of other Polish FTOs as well as for their employees. In an economy which was autarkic to some extent, and with domestic enterprises being only production units with no intent to market their products (Smith, 2000), the knowledge of an FTO's management could result in competitive advantage, a strategic resource that could be combined with other assets to enhance value. Such 'transactions' took the form of acquisitions of domestic enterprises as the FTOs were one of few entities which had financial resources inherited from the time of the centrally planned economy. Elektrim's knowledge of the Polish manufacturing companies that it worked with helped it to circumvent informational problems associated with the efficiency of take-overs. Also, the management of Elektrim encompassed general management expertise with capabilities that were relatively scarce in the transition years in Poland. Finally, its preferential access to bureaucracy and policy-makers, especially important in telecoms, gave it great advantages over independent firms.

From the outside, the initial transformation of Elektrim might seem comparable to establishing a company like Mitsubishi, Sumitomo on Mitsui – Japanese industrial groups led by trading companies (former *zaibatsu*). However, the business history of Elektrim suggests it did not want to operate as a network organizer or the core of a new industrial group where individual diversified firms would find significant advantages in exploiting intra-group externalities in cheaper finance, secure demand and supply, and so on. In many respects the frenzy of acquisitions from the early-1990s suggest that Elektrim behaved like some other CEE tycoons who put the opportunity to 'build empires' over the profitability of individual operations or over the exploitation of synergies among intra-group firms.

There is a literature that suggests that in emerging markets or economies with undeveloped market institutions, business groups like Elektrim may have significant advantages over focused enterprises (Khanna and Palepu, 1997, 1999). The advantages of industrial groups have also been analysed in economies with developed market institutions (Kester, 1992; Encaoua and Jacquemin, 1982). The underlying factors behind the growth of diversified business groups are in multi-market power, related resources, informational imperfections, entrepreneurial scarcity and policy distortions in the emerging market environment (Ghemawat and Khanna, 1998; Khanna and Palepu, 1997). These factors have played an important part in explaining Russian industrial financial groups (Petkoski, 1997). The case of Elektrim suggests that some of the factors that work in favour of such groups are relevant in explaining its initial growth. The grouping of unrelated businesses has helped Elektrim to gain market power and improve access to outside capital. Moreover, to help finance its growth, Elektrim moved into banking; it founded a medium-sized commercial bank and owned stakes of up to 11 per cent in four others. However, most of these were too small to be of much use.

The beginning of the 1990s in Poland were times of fast and uncertain changes and the post-transformational recession. Foreign investor involvement in the Polish economy remained small as it was perceived as unstable and not secure enough for regular transactions and allowed only for minor speculative inflows. That implied a firm like Elektrim faced little competition when it was bidding for underpriced privatized assets. However, since 1993 the Polish economy returned to growth, regaining its 1989 GDP level in 1996 and continuing in fast growth of more than 5 per cent annually. This attracted foreign investors to this emerging economy and the inflow of FDI increased considerably.

There were also changes in domestic management. Firms and their managers learned how to operate in the domestic as well as in foreign markets, which stripped Elektrim of its main competitive advantage.

The changes in management observed in the Polish economy were also bound with the new generation of middle-level managers educated in the Polish economic schools after 1989. They started their careers in the FTOs, introducing to some extent a new management culture. However, these changes were not fully accommodated by the 'old' managers, even those who had been accustomed to the foreign trade practices before 1989. The best example of such problems was the Elektrim case of PTC and Kulczyk described earlier.

The shift from conglomeration to focusing was a sign that, as we have pointed out, many of these advantages did not operate any more in the Polish economy. Companies were able to access capital under similar terms as a large business group, markets for management skills had developed and the market environment became more stable. However, Lundberg's aggressive strategy was only possible because of the high trust provided to her by foreign investors and a subsequent lack of willingness to admit that this confidence was a costly mistake, leading to the bankruptcy. Lundberg', supreme had been shaped in venture capital institutions, especially foreign, and was not well-suited for the conditions of a big Polish enterprise in need of focusing its activities.

Subsequent CEOs (see Table 5.7) were educated in the free-market environment in Poland or abroad. They were relatively young with supreme with

Table 5.7   A Elektrim's CEOs, 1987–2005

President	Period	Age*	Education	Experience
Andrzej Skowroński	1987–Dec. 1998	40	MSc Szczecin Technical University PhD in International Economic Relations	Until 1978 academic career From 1978 in Elektrim including 2 years in a representative office in Moscow (1985–87)
Barbara Lundberg	Feb. 1999–May 2001	46	Wharton School, Pennsylvania University Jackson College, Tufts University.	1977–83 Exxon Enterprises then McGraw-Hill; 1983–86 Alan Patricof Associates, Inc.; 1986–90 Kidder Peabody Co., Inc.; 1990 Polish-American Enterprise Fund; second half of '90: Enterprise Investors
Waldemar Siwak	May 2001–Feb. 2002	31	MA in Banking and Finance Warsaw School of Economics	1991–96 dealer in Polish Financial Institutions; 1996–2000 International Financial Institutions in London:Carnegie; Emerging Markets, Peregrine Securities and ABN AMRO Equities (UK); Since 2000, ABN AMRO Securities (Polska) S.A
Dariusz Jacek Krawiec	Feb. 2002–Apr. 2002	35	MA in Economics and Organisation of Foreign Trade Poznan Economics University (1992)	Before 1997 dealer in Bank Pekao SA and than consultant at Ernst & Young and Price Waterhouse; 1997–98 Nomura International plc London; 1998–2002 CEO Impexmetal
Maciej Radziwiłł	Apr. 2002–Sep. 2002	41	MA in Sociology MA in Marketing and Management Warsaw University MBA Illinois University at University of Warsaw	1987–90 Assistant Professor in the Institute of Sociology of Warsaw University; 1990–91 International Privatization and Financial Markets Development Fund; 1991–93 NBS Bewe Rogerson; 1993–94 Creditanstalt Securities SA; 1994–95 Credit Suisse First Boston (Polska) Sp. z o.o;

				1995–98 Union Bank of Switzerland; 1998–2002 CEO Cresco Finacial Advisors Sp. z o.o.
Wojciech Janczyk	Sep. 2002–May 2003	38	MSc King's College MBA Imperial College	1985–87 L.E.K. Partnership; 1987–89 OC&C Ltd; 1989–91 director of Corporate Finance Department in Swiss Bank Corporation London; 1991–2001 BMF SA; 2001–02 Vice Minister of Infrastructure
Piotr Nurowski	May 2003 up till time of writing	57	LLB Warsaw University	1973–80 President of Polish Association of Light Athletics; 1981–91 Ministry of Foreign Affairs; 1981–84, First Secretary of Embassy in Moscow; 1984–86 Department of Asia and Pacific and Australia; 1986–91 Councillor of Embassy in Rabat, Morocco; 1991–92 PZ SOLPOL

*At the time of becoming CEO.
Sources:　Elektrim's announcements at gielda.pl and Polityka Dzial Kadr

international investors, such as Karwiec who was designated as CEO by Nomura to Impexmetal. Their role was to rescue the company and avoid bankruptcy. This task was accomplished by Wojciech Jańczyk, for example, who was sent to Elektrim by the BRE Bank. From a managerial perspective, we can say that as well as being a graduate of London University he also gained his experience in the Polish environment working for the public as well as for the private sector. His nomination also marked the return to a more active role of Polish shareholders and a withdrawal of foreign investment funds.

The clear mark of the next era was the nomination of Piotr Nurowski as CEO by the main Polish strategic investor Polsat Media, owned by Polish businessman Zygmunt Solorz, also the owner of the private television Polsat. The new CEO was well-established in the old socialist period, working for the Ministry of Foreign Affairs, as well as in the new free market period working for Solorz. To the same extent we can compare his experience to Skorowński's but with an additional 15 years of free-market training (Mizerski, 2005).

Thus, the stabilization period coincides with the return of Polish strategic investors and focusing on the initial area of expertise – energy. Here, PTC could be treated as an asset, although frozen by the legal dispute as of 2005, which could potentially finance the main area – energy. However, the action of transferring PAK out of Elektrim in late 2005, mentioned before, could suggest that Elektrim still faces bankruptcy and partition, as the strategy of the Polish dominant owners is unclear, with some best assets being transferred out of the firm.

The current situation (Figure 5.2) is similar to the other former FTO – Impexmetal, which concentrated again on its initial area: metallurgy. In 2005 it was bought by the internal investor Boryszew Group owned by Roman Karkosik. The new owner delegated his manager Sławomir Masiuk for the post of new CEO with the task of restructuring the holding. The Boryszew-Impexmetal group is to concentrate on packaging through its two pillars: Boryszew as a provider of plastic components and Impexmetal as a provider of aluminium components. However, at the time of writing this firm is much more stable, while the fate of Elektrim is very uncertain.

International investors

The institutional framework features strongly in determining the modes of growth of enterprises. Within this perspective it is useful to distinguish between three basic modes of growth in any enterprise: generic expansion; mergers and acquisitions; and networks (alliances) (see Peng and Heath, 1996). Undercapitalized enterprises with limited management capabilities have difficulty in growing through generic expansion. Among the top companies in CEE, there were only few new private firms in the 1990s and early 2000s. Mergers and acquisitions were limited to foreign investors who had funds for take-overs, and to domestic companies like Elektrim. The difficulties that Elektrim had to overcome to grow independently have been confirmed through its difficulty

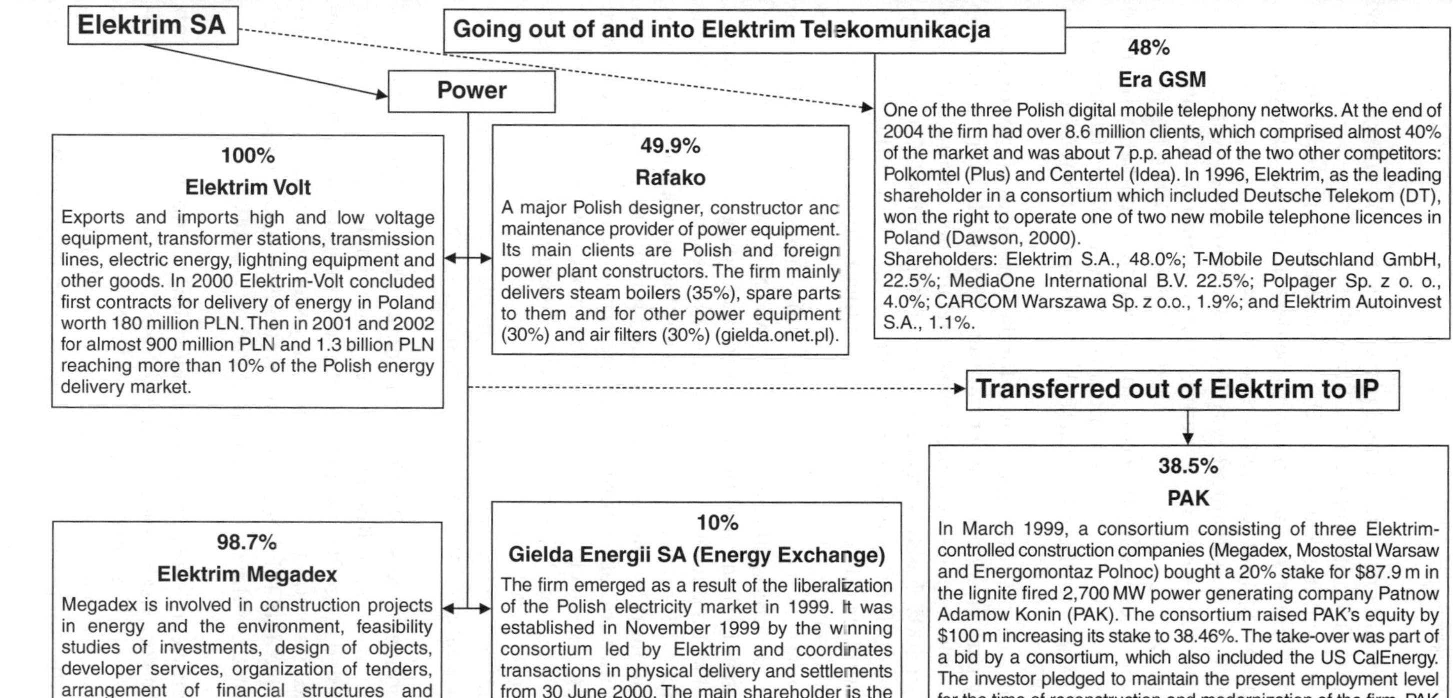

Figure 5.2 Elektrim's structure by the middle of 2005

in remaining a sustainable independent player rejecting the take-over of key assets by Deutsche Telecom and later on Vivendi.

Unfortunately, handling relations with two strong international investors with contradictory interests turned out to be devastating for Elektrim. The management problems that resulted were analysed in the previous section. As regards finance, the joint venture with Vivendi could have given Elektrim access to much needed capital and expertise in the telecommunication sector, but instead it provoked a long-lasting legal battle with Deutsche Telekom. Even Elektrim licences giving it access to the telecom market, which the company hoped to trade for access to finance and technology, turned to be illusory in the situation where it became the battleground between the two big external players.

This legal struggle is an immediate reason for the difficulties of the company. Its only healthy part, energy, was either transferred to another entity (PAK) or suffered from knock-down effects which in fact undermined all future activities (Megadex). As of 2005, Elektrim seems to be a hostage of its PTC ownership and its only reason for existence may be the unresolved conflict between Deutsche Telkom, Vivendi and Mr Solorz, all of them struggling to get independent control over the whole PTC.

The cases of alliances in CEECs (Radosevic, 2004) suggest that the balance between generic expansion, alliances (networks) and M&A as modes of growth, reflects differences in firms' abilities to control technology, access to market and finance. Elektrim's access to the domestic market enabled it to trade it for access to capital. But this opportunity was lost because of the risky expansion strategy followed by the wrongly designed international game plan. If we take a look into the other former FTO, we can conclude that there were possibilities to grow effectively, either at a slower pace using only domestic capital (Impexmetal); or choosing one strategic investor and selling its access to market (the case of Animex).

However, the underlying most important problem for Elektrim was the lack of a strong strategic investor in the expansion phase:

> Moreover, unlike owners with a vested interest in maximizing profits, professional managers gain little from direct profit maximization. They will not be interested in profit maximization per se or the maximization of shareholder value as an end in itself. Rather, they seek to maximize their own power, prestige and affluence. Such motivations are more closely aligned with the growth of the firm. (Dunn and Pressman, 2005)

Yet, as we can clearly see in the case of Elektrim, an independent growth strategy may be very risky, especially if it focuses on new technology industries which may follow an initial boom and bust cycle. The management of Elektrim was not controlled well enough by any shareholders with a clear long-term vision of the company's future. Therefore, the main role was played by management. Their visions were not coherent and often changed completely: from wide diversification to selective focusing together with huge investment. From a strategic perspective, large block shareholders may not allow for a poor strategy, such as diversification, to evolve into poor performance, therefore decreasing the magnitude of restructuring (Gibbs, 1993; Hoskisson *et al.*, 1994). On should stress, however, that in the case of Russia, Filatotchev *et al.* (2001) argue that 'large-block shareholding is negatively associated with the firm's investment and performance, and this relationship does not depend on the identity of controlling shareholders'. The difference results from the fact that unlike Poland, in the latter case we see an environment which does not adequately protect minority shareholders creating very different incentives for dominant stakeholders.

Thomsen and Petersen (2000) argue that institutional investors, who are relatively wealthy, have a strong preference for portfolio management and diversification. This could be in line with the initial period of activity of Lundberg and the support she had from the side of financial investors making her CEO. The story of Elektrim also supports another point they make, namely that corporate owners are likely to emphasize business trans actions and growth instead. The initial period of Skowronski as CEO and the final period of Nurowski may serve as example.

We can also notice one connection with resource-dependence theory stating that not all outside directors may have a positive impact on a firm's performance. Peng (2004) suggests 'that only affiliated (mostly institutional) directors play a positive role ... In contrast, non-affiliated (mostly individual) investors have no influence on performance ... only resource-rich outsiders such as institutional directors are likely to contribute to firm performance, and that resource-poor outsiders such as individual directors, despite their presumed incentive to influence management per agency theory logic, may be unable to contribute.' In the case of Elektrim, Barbara Lundberg and Piotr Nurowski could be seen as examples of this theory. Table 5.8 summarizes Elektrim's evolution.

The fate of Elektrim is still undecided as of late 2005. As we have seen, at the time of writing, paradoxically, the main reason of its continuing existence is the complex nexus of ownership disputes, in particular over the PTC equity it controls. The question is whether it is enough to survive and for how long this situation would last? Although the firm is still on the market, its days seem to be numbered.

It also seems that this fate was not unavoidable. Other former FTOs chose different strategies and now have good prospects for future development. The problem of Elektrim resulted from a combination of wrong managerial strategies, which arguably resulted from the lack of a strategic investor who could have influenced the firm's management. This, together with market difficulties, has resulted in a situation which does not provide much hope for the future. The deadlock, which keeps Elektrim alive, could be easily ended with

Table 5.8   Elektrim's evolution – development dimensions

	Stage 1 *Foreign trade* *organization* *1945–90*	*Stage 2* *Production/trade* *holding* *(1990–97)*	*Stage 3* *Aggressive* *growth* *1998–2001*	*Stage 4* *Rescue* *2002–03*	*Stage 5* *Stabilization* *2003–05*
Management	Old socialist; Polish	Foreign trade graduates accustomed to free market environment; Polish	Internationally educated; foreign	Internationally educated; Polish	Old Polish but trained in the new business environment
Owners with main influence	State	State and private internal	International financial institutions	International financial institutions with increasing role of Polish investors	Polish investors and International investors (specialized holdings)
Main functional area	Trading	Production	Infrastructure	Undecided	Infrastructure
Business strategy	Exclusive intermediation	Opportunistic conglomeration	Diversified specialization	Assets sale	Narrow specialization
Relations between key stakeholders	Role-exclusivity in foreign trade	Implicit sponsorship of stockmarket manoeuvrings	Emerging conflict	Conflict	Conflict resolution

International relations	Russian connection	Buffering by state/ limited foreign ownership	Majority diversified foreign ownership; emerging conflict	Conflict	Inherited conflict
Corporate governance	State ownership	Commercialization/ some state ownership	Fully private; number of key owners (8–10)	Fully private; number of key owners (5–7)	Fully private – number of key owners (4)
Organizational structure	Unitary organization	Holding	Multi-divisional corporation	Holding	Holding
Primary objectives	Intermediating deals; Bargaining over the plan and resources with the state administration	Building financial management skills; Building internal governance mechanisms in select business areas; strategy; cables (initial specialization); and telecom (ERA GSM – initial diversification)	Telecoms (fixed, cellular, internet); energy; centralizing business/ investment strategy; profit-centre creation; narrowing of the portfolio; alliance-building and financing projects	Survival	Energy; mobile telecommunications

Source: Authors', except stages 1 and 2 which are partly based on Radosevic *et al.* (2001).

the agreement of the main actors: two international investors – Vivendi plus Deutsche Telkom – and one domestic – Solorz. With the agreement in place, Elektrim's assets would be divided and Elektrim itself could cease to exist.

Postscript

At the time of preparation of this chapter, spring 2006, Elektrim still existed. PTC shares were transferred here and there: first to Mega Investments and then back to Elektrim Telekomunikacja due to the court order settling the complaint of DT. However, the management board established by Mega Investments does not allow the DT-nominated 'old-new' board to carry out their responsibilities. On the other hand, DT covers the current operational costs of PTC, what is declared illegal by the Mega Investment Board. DT also sued Elektrim Investments and PTC to transfer 48 per cent of the disputed shares at the International Arbitration Panel in Vienna. The broad dispute still involves the same three parties – Vicendi and DT, plus Mr Solorz – and is far from resolving.

Notes

1 In Feb. 1999, Elektrim disclosed that it had signed a preliminary agreement with DT in October 1998 whereby DT would acquire a 26 per cent stake in El-Net. On 19 May 1999 Elektrim announced it had broken off talks with DT about the potential purchase by the Germans.

2 47.99 per cent of the shares of PTC were transferred.

3 As part of this deal, Elektrim has sold Vivendi 50 per cent in Carcom Warsaw SA that holds 1.9 per cent of PTC. After the capital raising operations and sale of Carcom shares in Elektrim, Elektrim and Vivendi hold 50 per cent each of the nominal capital and voting rights at Carcom's shareholders' meeting.

4 DT is also present in the two Hungarian mobile phone operators Wester Radiotelefon and Westel 900, which at 58 per cent has the largest market share in Hungary.

5 These companies are RST El-Net SA, Telefonia Regionalna Ltd., Elektrim Tv-Tel Ltd, Internet Polska Ltd., VPN Service Ltd and Polish Phonesat Ltd.

6 As defined in the Investment Contract, this would involve each partner selecting an investment bank who would undertake a valuation of the shares involved, which would then be the purchase price for Elektrim.

7 Vivendi's appeal in the Polish regional court was made primarily to keep Elektrim from taking any actions on the sale of shares to Deutsche Telekom before the process in the London Court could be completed. The Polish court has denied Vivendi's appeal.

8 Moreover, Elektrim has gone further and claimed the following with regard to the fixed telephony operations: 'Vivendi has recently attempted in unauthorized fashion to block the important cooperation agreements between Aster City Cable and El-Net, which constitutes an unjustified attempt at limiting the ability of Elektrim to conduct business in the area of fixed telephony. The Investment Agreement clearly foresees the possibility of cooperation and market-based contracting between companies from the Elektrim Telekomunikacja group and with other companies affiliated with Elektrim, including Aster City and El-Net' (Elektrim press release, 'Stanowisko Elektrima SA w sprawie Umowy Inwestycyjnej z Vivendi', 25 February 2001).

6
Financial Performance and Knowledge Management in Capital Groups: Privatized versus New Private Businesses

Jan Chadam and Zbigniew Pastuszak

Introduction

The aim of this chapter is to present the findings of research focused on the financial performance of groups of companies in Poland. The formation of these groups of companies follows directly from the systemic transformation implemented in Poland after 1989. This was the transition period from a 'command and control' economy to a market economy. The issue is all the more significant, as the groups of companies became a widespread phenomenon. As many as 307 groups of companies can be found amongst the top 2,000 Polish companies. They account for nearly a third of the turnover of the entire category and in 2003 their total sales revenues amounted to some €75.8 billion (€1 = Zł4) against €246.3 billion generated by this entire category of businesses (*Rzeczpospolita*, November 2004). In 2003, the turnover of the groups of companies was up 18.7 per cent on an annual basis, compared to a 12.7 per cent increase for the whole category.

In this chapter, the financial performance of groups of companies is evaluated in the context of the factors underlying the origins of those organizations and the management systems employed by them, including knowledge management procedures. The term *knowledge management* is understood as a process that enables identification, selection, organization, dissemination and transfer of important information among the individual members of the group of companies. The process involves effective problem-solving, dynamic learning as well as strategic planning and decision-making (Gupta, Iyer and Aronson, 2000). As indicated by the findings of our research, these processes significantly affect the level of financial performance achieved by groups of companies.

The majority of Polish groups of companies emerged in the process of restructuring of the former state-owned enterprises. Parent companies saw these processes as a way of trimming down their operations, mainly by reducing auxiliary functions not directly connected with the core business. Consequently, the emerging subsidiaries had no clear-cut development strategies (Chadam, 2002). Instead of the expected improvement in effectiveness, the groups oftentimes saw fixed costs increase as a result of additional overheads, infrastructure costs, overlapping of some positions and unnecessary rivalry among the group's subsidiaries. Not at all infrequently, subsidiaries treated their mother company as the main provider of orders, at the same time expecting to secure higher prices on deals with the parent than the rates prevailing in the market. All this may suggest that the bulk of Polish groups of companies were established as part of a fad, rather than as a result of genuine needs created by the market. Another important facet of those organizations was a relatively strong parent organization and weak subsidiaries, both in terms of their market offering and financial standing.

Our research is an attempt at an objective evaluation of the financial performance of groups of companies. Extending the well-known studies presented among others by Megginson, Nash and Van Randenborgh (1994), Megginson and Netter (2001), Nwankwo (1996), Perotti and von Thadden (2005), Pistor, Raiser and Gelfer (2000) and Stephen and Backhaus (2003), our analyses reach beyond individual companies and focus on processes that took place in groups of companies, while retaining due consideration for ownership transformations.

As the first stage of this research, financial results were assessed in terms of the two key paths of formation of groups of companies in Poland: via expansion of newly established private companies (*de novo*) and restructuring of state-owned enterprises (SOEs). Simultaneously, we focus on the application of the knowledge management systems in these two groups of companies; consequently, we attempt to determine the co-variation between the integrated knowledge management systems and the financial results is these two types of groups of companies. Research shows (for example Becker, 2000; Mambula and Sawyer, 2004; or Simatupang, Wright and Sridharan, 2002) that the application of integrated procedures in knowledge management systems in enterprises and its relations with contracting parties contributes to increased market activity, which, in effect, translates into better financial results.

The purpose of the second stage of our research was to indicate the direction of the development process of Polish groups of companies in terms of the contribution of group members (parent companies and subsidiaries) to the reported financial performance. The need for this second stage was evident from the conclusions drawn at the first stage of research, that is the observation that the ultimate economic performance of groups of companies is driven by both the results of the parent company and by the all other members of the group. And given the current weakness of subsidiaries in Polish groups of companies, one could even claim that positive changes in the operation of groups of companies is mostly dependent on the capacity of the subsidiaries to improve their contribution to the overall financial performance of the group.

Origins of groups of companies in Poland

As already mentioned, the formation of groups of companies followed the transformation from the command to a market economy. In practice, a state-owned enterprise would be transformed into a commercial company (commercialization) wholly-owned by the State Treasury and subsequently different parts of its assets would be hived off from it to set up commercial subsidiary companies. With the intermediary phase (that is, commercialization) in place, the manner of handling privatization was somewhat different from the so-called 'direct' methods described in the literature. However, the results obtained were usually those intended, as shown by various authors (such as Megginson and Netter, 2001; Frydman *et al.*, 2000; Mickiewicz and Bałtowski, 2003; Hanousek and Kocenda, 2003).

According to numerous studies (such as Chadam, 2003a; Frydman, Hessel and Rapaczynski, 2000; Hanousek and Kocenda, 2003; Marangos, 2005) groups of companies established as a result of equity/assets restructuring (spinning-off subsidiaries) aimed at improved effectiveness mainly by improving the operations of the smaller units and by creating a transparent business structure (Figure 6.1). This leads to the establishment of a rational organizational structure with no room for activities that do not relate directly to the core business. While the efficiency of management increases, the costs of operation are carefully controlled. The companies were more flexible and the decision-making

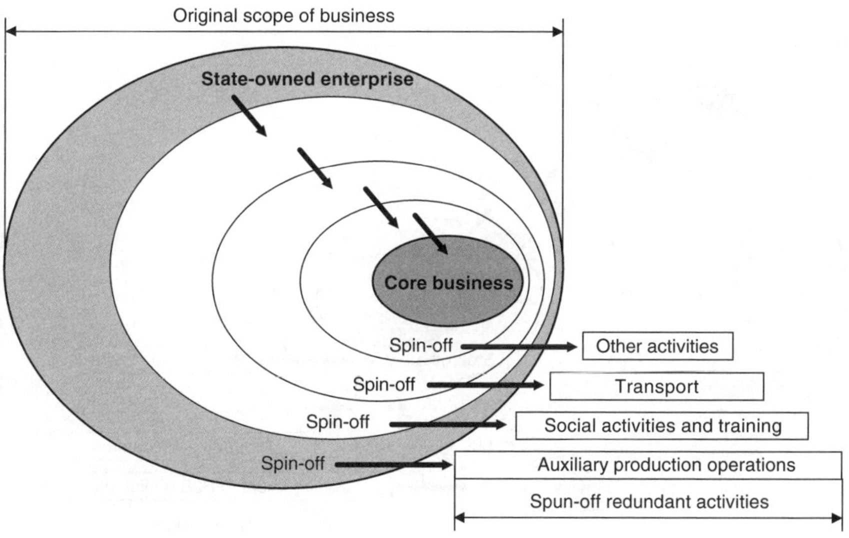

Figure 6.1   Establishment of groups of companies by state-owned enterprise (SOE) restructuring

process took far less time (Becker, 2000; Chadam, 2003a, 2003b; Nelson and Tylor, 1995; Simatupang, Wright and Sridharan, 2002). The gradual privatization of the individual subsidiaries was also an important factor, for example by merger with a strategic investors.

In parallel development, the economic changes taking place after 1990 resulted also in the formation of many smaller groups of companies originating with the private enterprises set up already in the market economy which – by a natural process of investing profits – expanded the scope of their business and market presence. Encouraged by market success, those companies invested their profits into new activities often jointly with newly found strategic or financial partners. Generally, the size of these equity projects was smaller than in the first group, that is of the ones set up on the basis of large former state-owned enterprises.

The two types of groups of companies were founded on the same legal basis, while the reasons and grounds for their establishment varied. Summing up, it needs stressing that groups of companies established as a result of transformation of former state-owned enterprises typically went through a contraction of the scope of their operations, as a result of restructuring. Successively – depending on the size of the enterprise and the scope of its operations – certain activities were hived off to set up new subsidiary companies. Auxiliary processes, outside of the core business of the parent company, were almost always spun off. In this way, new companies emerged engaging in transport, overhaul

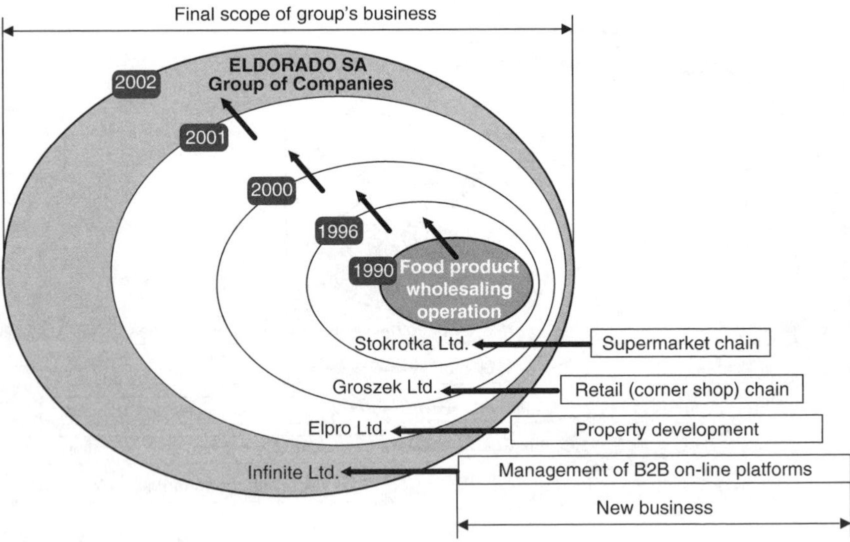

Figure 6.2   Establishment of Eldorado S.A. group of companies

and maintenance, social activities, construction, machine and equipment maintenance, tools production, and so on.

In contrast, the other path involves the process of capital concentration resulting from the 'organic' growth of the business. Business start-ups, business acquisitions or take-overs were typically a reflection of a coherent business development strategy. They usually complemented the core business of the parent company and were set up by investing profits in new areas of business, albeit by no means unrelated to the core business of the group. One of the analysed company cases (ELDORADO SA – Figure 6.2) shows how a parent company operating in wholesale distribution of food products developed a groups of companies supplementing its core business by setting up new entities with a view to develop a retail chain and integrate buyers within a system of electronic data interchange (EDI). As a result, specialized subsidiaries (organized as limited liability companies) were set up, pursuing the objectives of the group.

Knowledge-management and effectiveness of groups of companies

Management is a process of planning, empowering and evaluating performance of teams of people working towards a common goal (Stanton, Etzel and Walker, 1994). These efforts are undertaken in various areas in which the business operates (such as logistics, production, marketing and sales, maintenance, R&D, HRM, infrastructure), described in detail by Porter (1985). The aim of these activities is to achieve the intended market outcomes, translating directly into the economic and financial performance of the business. Improving financial performance and competitiveness were also the key objectives underlying the establishment of groups of companies. The operation of groups of companies in their market environment, similarly to individual businesses, is subject to various forces reflecting constant changes in both the external environment and in the company (group of companies) itself. Those organizations had to learn to be flexible in response to change and to develop strong features of a learning organization.

The main resource of a learning organization is its knowledge; and the effective use of knowledge to serve the purposes of the organization is determined by the existence of an effective system of knowledge management at the level of the entire organization. Regardless of the internal organization of a group of companies and the type of products offered, the effective knowledge management system creates value and enhance a competitive edge by collecting, transmitting and applying knowledge acquired during interactions with the customer (Tiwana, 2001). Two particular processes that have been observed are labelled 'externalization' and 'combination' (Nonaka and Takeuchi, 1995). Both contribute towards improving the flow of information inside the group and consequently enhance the performance of its basic business functions. In addition, effective knowledge management in multiple organizations requires paying special attention to strategy, organizational culture and technology – the principal constituents of the knowledge management system (Heck and Rogger, 2004; Hussain, Lucas and Asif Ali, 2004). The process has been shown to be based on four basic functions (Frappaolo, 1998): identification of internal sources of knowledge (*cognition*), internal processing of knowledge (*internalization*), transfer outside (*externalization*) and acting as an intermediary in exchanging it with the environment (*intermediation*). An effective knowledge management strategy has to be coherent throughout the entire groups of companies and supported by the appropriate technology and organizational culture. In that case, it facilitates generation of the relevant knowledge by each member of the group, offering it in the right form to other members of the group. It also enables identification of the best sources of procuring knowledge in a specific area of operation (Becker, 2000; Chaston and Mangels, 2000; Humphreys, Shiu and Chan, 2001).

It is highly likely that the initial conditions (such as original ownership – SOEs versus *de novo* companies, profile of business activity conducted before 1990 or well-developed organizational structures which covered a wide range of auxiliary processes) play a significant role in the subsequent development and operation of a knowledge management system within a group and in consequence affect its economic performance. Once established, multiple organizations had to reinvent common goals, scope and manner of operation. As a result, they require an effective group knowledge management system (*know-why, know-what, know-how*), based on coherent procedures and applications, facilitating effective knowledge management at various levels of the organizational structure and in the different areas of business (Yim, Kim, Kim and Kwahk, 2004). The knowledge management system has to include all levels of management decision-making, that is strategic, operational and tactical (Biloslavo, 2004), and in effect determines the quality of economic relations of the group of companies with its external environment. As indicated by earlier Polish research (Bałtowski, 2003; Wawrzyniak, 2003), the establishment of a group of companies with a strong parent company, as a rule, resulted in the unification of the internal processes and an intensive flow of knowledge among members of the group, related to the internal organization, technical solutions and market procedures employed. The process, however, was not limited to a passive acceptance of all solutions of the parent company by subsidiaries, but involved a multi-directional flow of best solutions among all member companies, as well as between the group as such and its business environment. Thanks to that, a sequence of events typical of the Knowledge Life-Cycle Model (Leitch and Rosen, 2001) involving (Wielinga, Sandberg and Schreiber, 1997) knowledge selection, development, distribution, retention and consolidation was observed, which consequently becomes decisive in multiple organizations demonstrating strong features of learning organizations.

A learning organization constantly develops its knowledge, improving its value. The development occurs as a result of changes in the company's environment as well as internal changes (Slater and Narver, 1995). Thus, knowledge is built in a continuous process of learning on the part of the organization and its workforce, it is collected in human minds and IT systems, appropriately stored and updated. Knowledge is created in the organization in response to the needs and expectations relating to its use. The knowledge resource evolves with staff meetings, R&D efforts, marketing research (Shipley, Hooley, Beracs, Fonfara and Kolos, 1995), innovation, improvement of market offering, engagement of experts, innovation transfer, and so on (Wiig, 1995), as well as during structural changes occurring within the group of companies as the number of its corporate members is increased or reduced.

The features observed in network organizations, which operate in broad regional, national, European and global markets (Ching, Holsapple and Whinston, 1996) may also be found in a group of companies operating in a selected market as a multiple organization. In the latter case, as a rule, the parent company is usually the integrating agent for the network (group of companies), acting as the core of the organization and contributing most to the appreciation of the group's value and the development of synergy (Hargadon and Sutton, 2000). A factor that directly affects the achievement of synergy, and – as a result – the good financial performance of the group, is an intensive transfer of knowledge among members of the group of companies as they actively cooperate implementing all the internal processes and responding to changes in the tumultuous environment (Figure 6.3).

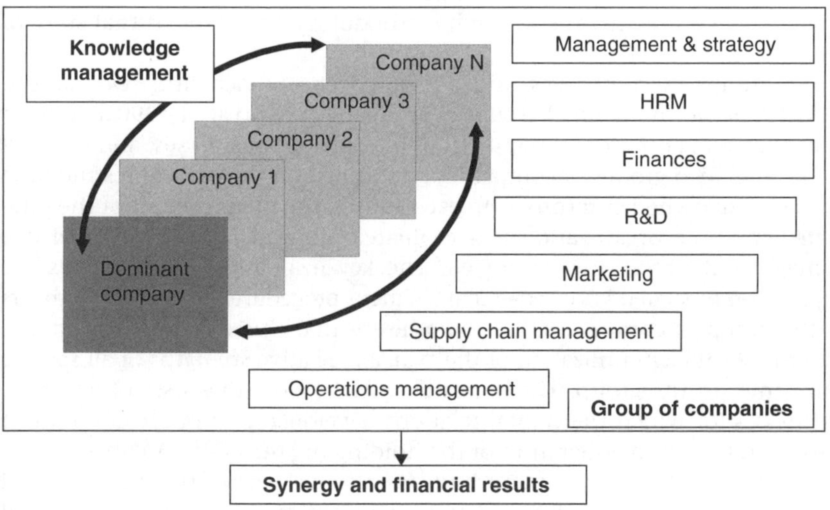

Figure 6.3   Knowledge management and synergy

In effect, integrated multiple organizations represent a specific business structure, which is capable of achieving synergies thanks to the cooperation of its constituent parts in the individual areas of operations. The sources of potential synergies refer also to the aspects of the knowledge management, which involve discovery and management of a varied knowledge of individuals, teams and organizations, in a way that helps to improve their effectiveness (Nonaka, 1994). The synergies therefore have their specific economic dimension translating into the financial performance of the entire group of companies. The findings of research addressing this issue with reference to the origins of the development of groups of companies in Poland are presented in the following sections of this chapter.

Knowledge management procedures and financial performance of groups of companies in Poland

Research methodology

As already mentioned, the first stage of our research focused on the effect of the initial conditions on the subsequent development and operation of groups of companies in Poland. These factors strongly affected the management of groups of companies, knowledge transfer system applied and, ultimately, the financial performance of the organizations. Our research covered smaller groups of companies. The sample included 17 groups of companies, which consisted of 61 individual companies (parent and subsidiary) and comprised the full population of groups of companies operating in one region of Poland. The results obtained for the period from 2000 to 2003 were analysed, and Figure 6.4 presents the research methodology employed at that stage of research.

The groups of companies under review were divided into two subsets. Subset A (*de novo*) included groups of companies set up after 1990 as a result of capital concentration and growth of new private businesses, and subset B (SOEs) included groups of companies established on the basis of restructured former state-owned enterprises. In each subset, the management of the integrated multiple organization was evaluated along the lines of knowledge management procedures employed. The key evaluation criterion was the application of shared knowledge management procedures among all members of the group of companies. We hypothesize that this characteristic should lead to the efficient utilization of the available relative strengths of all specific companies in the group. The opposite extreme would be a set of 'random' businesses for which the capital relations developed do not affect (or affect only marginally) the operation of the holding organization. A coherent system of knowledge management built for all members of the group should help to achieve the objectives of the integrated multiple organization and lead to the gradual improvement of its financial performance.

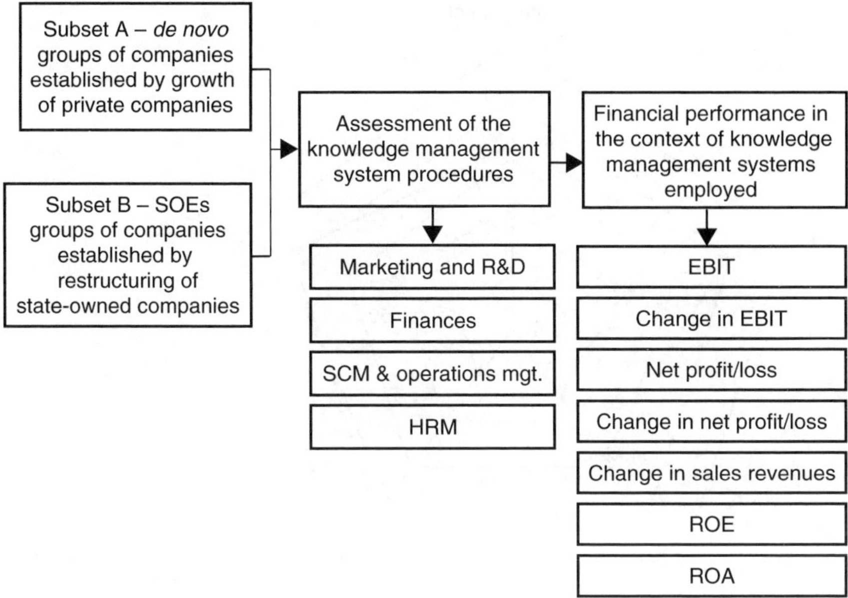

Figure 6.4   Research methodology

Summary of research findings

Figure 6.5 presents a summary of our research findings related to the integration of knowledge management procedures in the individual functional areas of the groups of companies under review. The ratio indicates the proportion of groups of companies implementing knowledge management procedures in an organized manner throughout the group for all its members (Chadam, 2003a).

It is apparent that the level of integration of the management function in those groups of companies that were established through the restructuring of the former state-owned enterprises is much more limited. The groups of companies developed by concentration of capital and growth of private businesses demonstrate a much higher ratio of the application of knowledge management procedures and internal integration of the group's members. Therefore, it is the latter organizations that may expect to reap additional benefits from the operation as parts of groups of companies. The summary picture of the information and decision-making area is based on the shared knowledge management efforts in strategic planning, quality management, group's activity monitoring, implementation and application of IT systems and other activities supporting management processes. The superior performance in financial activities of the group stems from a better organization of loan procedures, guarantees, mutual settlements and debt and financial

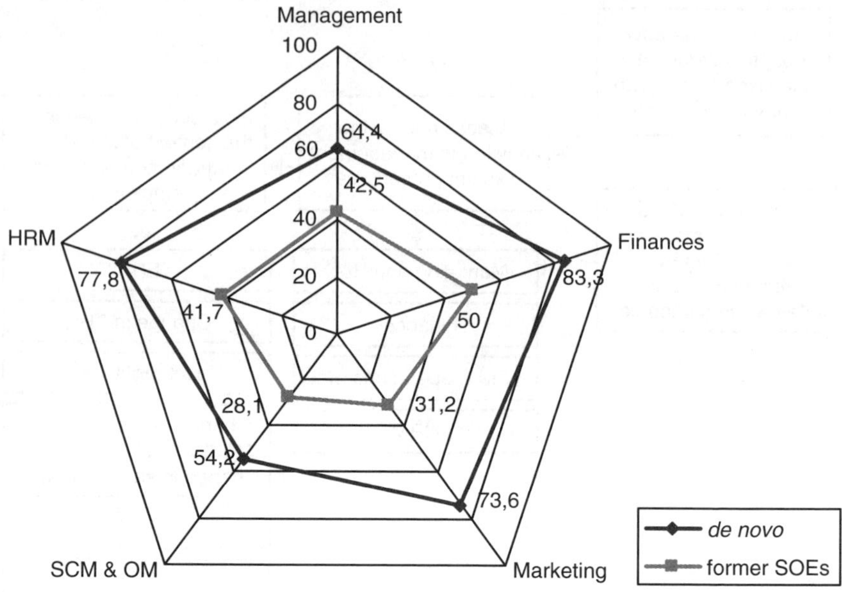

Figure 6.5 Implementation of knowledge management procedures (% of former SOEs and *de novo* firms)

surplus management throughout the group of companies. Very clear dispar-ities are also visible in the common marketing policy and group develop-ment. In particular, this applies to the standardization of offers and to the overall presentation of the group, to common price and promotional policies, to a common trade network, to use of market research shared throughout the group, to common product development and to R&D efforts. As far as operations management and SCM go, the research has demonstrated the propensity towards building a common network of suppliers, cooperation inside the group and utilization of the group's production capacity, technol-ogy development and environment protection efforts. The situation is simi-lar in the area of a common personnel policy for the entire group, reflected in a common pay and incentive policy, common skills development activities and transfer of staff among members of the group.

Table 6.1 presents the differences in selected financial performance measures between the two subsets of integrated multiple organizations. An analysis of performance as reflected by EBIT and net profit, pattern of change of these indicators over time and changes in sales revenues provides some interesting insights into the differences in the outcomes of operations of groups of com-panies in both subsets.

Table 6.1   Analysis of financial performance in companies, former SOEs versus *de novo* (%, *t*-tests)

Description	No. of companies available for comparison			% share of companies with a specified result		
	Total	De novo	*Former SOEs*	*Total*	De novo	*Former SOEs*
1 [EBIT/sales] Number of companies with positive result	45	24	21	73.77	85.71	63.64

De novo versus former SOEs, *t*-test, $\alpha = 0.05$, df $= 27$, critical value ± 2.052; $t = +2.840$; hypothesis H_0 (no difference) = FALSE (also significant for $\alpha = 0.01$, critical value ± 2.771)

Description	Total	De novo	Former SOEs	Total	De novo	Former SOEs
2 [net profit] Number of companies with positive net profit	43	23	20	70.49	82.14	60.61

De novo versus former SOEs, *t*-test, $\alpha = 0.05$, df $= 27$, critical value ± 2.052; $t = +2.489$; hypothesis H_0 (no difference) = FALSE (also significant for $\alpha = 0.01$, critical value ± 2.771)

Description	Total	De novo	Former SOEs	Total	De novo	Former SOEs
3 [change in EBIT] Number of companies with positive change in EBIT	37	18	19	60.66	64.29	57.58

De novo versus former SOEs, *t*-test, $\alpha = 0.05$, df $= 27$, critical value ± 2.052; $t = +0.565$; hypothesis H_0 (no difference) = CANNOT REJECT

Description	Total	De novo	Former SOEs	Total	De novo	Former SOEs
4 [change in net profit/loss] Number of companies with positive change in net profit/loss	33	18	15	54.10	64.29	45.45

De novo versus former SOEs, *t*-test, $\alpha = 0.05$, df $= 27$, critical value ± 2.052; $t = +1.587$; hypothesis H_0 (no difference) = CANNOT REJECT

Description	Total	De novo	Former SOEs	Total	De novo	Former SOEs
5 [change in sales revenues] Number of companies with positive change in sales revenues	36	22	14	59.02	78.57	42.42

De novo versus former SOEs, *t*-test, $\alpha = 0.05$, df $= 27$, critical value ± 2.052; $t = +3.833$; hypothesis H_0 (no difference) = FALSE (also significant for $\alpha = 0.01$, critical value ± 2.771)

In the set of businesses under review, nearly 74 per cent of companies reported a positive EBIT and 70 per cent reported positive net profit. In terms of EBIT, 86 per cent of companies from the *de novo* set generated a profit and only 14 per cent sustained a loss. In the former SOE set, positive EBIT was reported by 64 per cent of companies, while 36 per cent incurred a loss. And so in terms of the basic profitability measures, the performance of *de novo* companies is superior ($t = +2.840$; significant for $\alpha = 0.01$) than in the former SOE set, which includes companies established in the process of restructuring. The pattern is similar for net profit/loss. Among *de novo* companies, 64 per cent reported a positive change in EBIT (profit up or loss down), with 58 per cent of former SOEs set reported an improvement in this area ($t = +2.489$, significant for $\alpha = 0.05$). A positive change in net profit/loss was reported by the same percentage of *de novo* companies as in the case of EBIT change, whereas in former SOEs, a positive change was reported by 46 per cent of companies.

Although *t*-tests on change in the value of EBIT and on the net profit change did not constitute the basis to refute the hypotheses H_0; the superior efficiency of *de novo* companies is confirmed by the test on changes in sales revenues ($t = +3.833$). A positive change in sales revenues was reported by 79 per cent of *de novo* companies and by only 42 per cent of SOEs – which is the most significant difference amongst all those analysed. The findings indicate that *de novo* companies develop more vigorously than their former SOE counterparts. The findings described above are closely related to the analysis focusing on the use of the human factor, with a much higher level of workforce productivity among the *de novo* companies (not reported here, see: Chadam, 2003b). It should also be added that while *de novo* groups of companies are mainly engaged in trade and services (56%), SOEs groups are active in production (61%). This feature is a reflection of underdeveloped services and trade in centrally-planned economies, with the new groups of companies filling in a gap in the market that the new economic realities have created.

It should also be underlined that the additional studies we carried out on *de novo* companies indicate that they focus their business activity on sectors in which investment risk is estimated at a low level (that is, sector growth prospects are good or very good). The companies from the groups of companies classified under the former SOE set function in sectors with a smaller growth potential and greater risk factor. It follows that these companies will have smaller chances to attract investors and financial partners for their investment projects (Chadam, 2003b).

The final conclusion from this section is that the pattern of differences in financial performance closely matches the one we observe for joint knowledge management systems. Capital groups of new private companies are characterized both by more integrated knowledge-management systems and better financial performance.

Operation of groups of companies and contribution of group members to a group's financial performance

Research methodology concerning internal factors of performance

The research outlined above confirmed that the protracted distortions inherited from the centrally-planned economy had a major impact on the operation of Polish groups of companies and their financial performance. It should also be noted that among the groups of companies under review, in 1991 subsidiaries accounted for 19 per cent of the total sales revenues and for a meagre 16 per cent of EBIT. Thus, assuming no major distortions in financial reporting, we may confirm our earlier observation that the typical picture of the group is the presence of a relatively large and strong parent company and weak subsidiaries. In the case of groups of companies, which developed through restructuring, the decisive factor was the initial process of group organization outlined earlier. Here, subsidiaries were set up on the basis of the parent's assets. With the arrival of the market economy, many of such assets became either redundant or their utility for conducting a core business diminished significantly. Once hived off from the integrated organizational structure, the new entities found themselves in a quite competitive market. In the case of groups of companies set up by concentration of capital and growth of new private businesses, the subsidiaries established were start-ups. But this also meant that they were weaker from the parent companies establishing them. While observing these organizations in the late 1990s, one could have an impression that some of the parent companies would be better off without subsidiaries, which simply provided an additional burden to them. All these findings encouraged us to undertake research focusing on the current situation of Polish groups of companies, with a special emphasis on the assessment of the contribution of the individual members of the group (parent company, subsidiaries) to the performance of the entire organization. This second stage of research was conducted in 2004 and it covered groups of companies whose parents are quoted on the Warsaw Stock Exchange. The principal aim of the research was to determine the development direction of Polish groups of companies in terms of the participation of the group's members in the overall financial performance. An objective assessment of this sort, based on official financial data, could help address the claim that was sometimes voiced, according to which Polish groups of companies were part of a fad of developing multiple organizations, rather than a response to genuine market needs. Figure 6.6 presents the scope of stage 2 of research.

The research relied on consolidated financial statements of groups of companies and financial statements of parent companies. The analysis covered 108 financial statements of groups of companies for 2001 and 2002, and 104 financial statements of groups of companies for 2003 (banks and investment funds were excluded from the analysis).

Research findings

The analysis of sales revenues generated by groups of companies in 2001–03 (Table 6.2) demonstrates that parent companies of Polish multiple organizations continue to be the main driving force of their respective groups (parents account for nearly 70% of revenues). Yet, the value of sales revenues of the other group members is on the rise. In the period under review, sales revenues of other group members as a percentage of group's revenues went up from 28

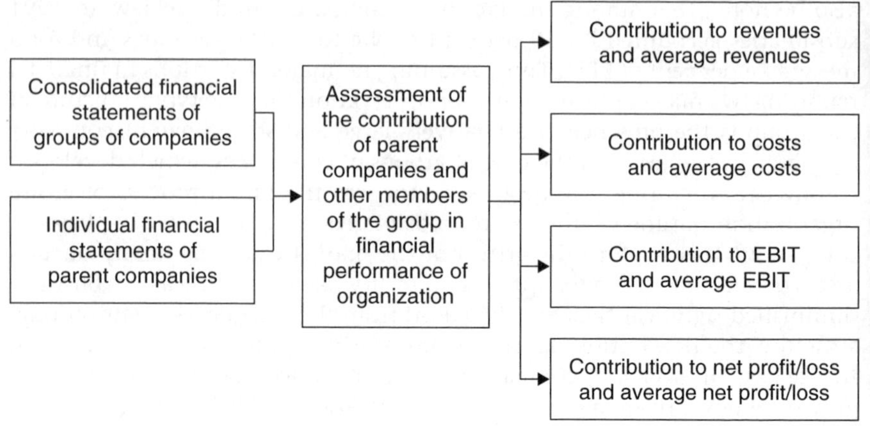

Figure 6.6   Scope of stage 2 of research

Table 6.2   Percentage share of subsidiaries in revenues and expenditures of groups of companies, 2001–03

	Year	No. of groups	Sales revenues in € millions			AC as %		
			PC	*AC*	*Total*	*Revenues*	*Costs*	*Difference*
1	2001	108	13,239	5,242	18,480	28.36	28.52	(0.16)
2	2002	108	13,255	4,975	18,230	27.29	26.75	0.54
3	2003	104	13,664	6,876	20,539	33.48	32.66	0.82

per cent to over 33 per cent. In 2002, out of 108 groups of companies under review, 48 (that is 44%) reported improvement in sales revenues, including 45 (42%) parent companies ('PC') and 60 (56%) other (affiliated) companies ('AC'). In 2003, when the research covered 104 groups, sales revenues went up in 61 groups (65%), including 61 PCs (59%) and 61 ACs (59%). Thus, sales revenues were up in the majority of groups of companies under review, to a significant extent thanks to the improved standing of the subsidiaries.

A comparison of the costs of operations (sum of costs of products, goods and materials sold, selling expense and overheads) of ACs as a proportion of the group costs with the contribution of ACs to sales revenue generation demonstrates that in 2001 ACs accounted for a larger proportion of costs than sales revenues. This means that the business of affiliated companies was less effective than that of their parents. Starting from 2002, the difference between the revenue percentage contribution and the cost percentage contribution is positive, which means that the subsidiaries of groups of companies under review

Table 6.3   Financial performance of groups of companies, 2001–03

Year	No. of groups	EBIT in € millions			As %		EBIT > 0		Net profit/loss > 0	
		PC	AC	Total	PC	AC	No. of AC	As %	No. of AC	As %
1	2001	108	274	58	332	82	18	57	53	44	41
2	2002	108	386	177	563	69	31	74	69	50	46
3	2003	104	531	273	804	66	34	79	76	57	55

improved their financial performance. The EBIT analysis for 2001–03 shows an increasing contribution of ACs to EBIT generation in the groups of companies under review. In 2001–03, subsidiary contribution to group EBIT was up from 18 per cent to 34 per cent. This means that year after year subsidiary EBIT improved as did their contribution to group EBIT.

The growing contribution of ACs to EBIT is demonstrated by the number of groups of companies in which ACs generate positive profits (Table 6.3). The number of such groups in 2001–03 increased from 53 per cent to 76 per cent. And so there is a growing number of groups of companies in which affiliated companies report EBIT improvement. The percentage of groups of companies in which subsidiaries generated a net profit improved from 41 per cent in 2001 to 55 per cent in 2003. The improved net profit of subsidiaries proved a valuable contribution to the groups' net result both in 2002 and 2003. In that period, the subsidiaries under review reported a significant improvement of financial performance, as reflected in both better net results in the groups and improved contributions of these groups to the positive change of the group net result. One should also emphasize that as our sample relates to the quoted companies, the financial reports we rely upon remain under close scrutiny of independent auditors, and therefore we may have some confidence that the reported differences are more than just a reflection of the manipulation of accounts by the controlling stakeholders.

Discussion and conclusions

Groups of companies, which were set up in Poland after 1990, are a very interesting and significant facet of the systemic transformation. We have discussed both the process of formation and the current performance of these organizations. In the majority of management areas, groups of companies established as a result of restructuring of former state-owned enterprises lack satisfactory integration of activities covering all members of the group. By the same token, processes of identification, selection, organization, dissemination and transfer of important information and expertise among the individual members of a multiple organization do not rely on procedures that could ensure their highest effectiveness. In contrast, groups of companies which evolved by 'organic' growth and by concentration of capital demonstrate much better integration of knowledge management processes. It is these groups that can expect to reap additional benefits accruing to integrated multiple organizations. This conclusion is confirmed by the financial performance of these groups. Their results are much better in the category of new private groups of companies applying knowledge management procedures. *De novo* organizations developed by growth of new private businesses in the period of market economy. They operate in more attractive industries, their management is more effective, including knowledge management inside the group of companies, and they set up new subsidiaries with a view to pursuing the overall strategy of the group. *De novo* companies achieved significantly better financial results than those of SOEs, as confirmed in the observations of Frydman, Hessel and Rapaczynski (2000). It is worth bearing in mind at this point that we have not analysed the changes that occurred in the SOEs under analysis immediately preceding their privatization (as did, for instance, Bozec and Breton, 2003). We have focused on financial results and business undertakings which characterize their activity once restructuring processes were over and groups of companies from the former SOE set were established.

Our second stage of research has helped to formulate a number of interesting conclusions on the contribution of subsidiaries to the operation of Polish groups of companies:

1 The percentage of groups of companies whose subsidiaries are improving their contribution to the group's sales revenues was found to grow.
2 The value of revenues generated by affiliates as a percentage of total revenues of groups of companies under review is on the increase.
3 The difference between the contribution of affiliates to the group sales revenues and to its operating costs was found to be increasing.
4 The contribution of subsidiaries to the generation of the group EBIT is improving. In addition, the high rate of positive EBIT changes in subsidiaries, much higher than in parent companies, and the growing number of groups of companies in which subsidiaries generate positive EBIT changes all demonstrate a positive impact of subsidiaries on EBIT reported by the groups.
5 The pattern is similar for net profit/loss with a positive impact of subsidiaries demonstrated by the growing number of groups of companies in which subsidiaries generate a net profit. In addition, year after year the percentage of groups in which subsidiaries report an improvement of net profit/ loss is higher and higher, thus enhancing the effectiveness of the groups themselves.

Thus, it has been demonstrated that the viability and growth of the groups of companies under review is no longer driven solely by parent companies, but that the other members become more and more of a factor. This is indicated by both the growing contribution of subsidiaries to sales revenues of the groups as well as the improving positive impact affiliates have on the individual items of the profit and loss account, including EBIT and net profit/loss of these organizations.

Our study indicates that *de novo* companies, which are not encumbered by the experience of state enterprises, demonstrate greater flexibility and effectiveness. Their financial results and management procedures may, in fact, lead to the diffusion of information (Perotti and von Thadden, 2000) and increased interest of potential investors (Berglöf and von Thadden, 1999).

7
Sources of Capital and Structures of Influence: Banks in the Russian Corporate Network

Ilya Okhmatovskiy

Introduction

Studies about corporate networks in the United States, Canada, Western Europe and Japan pay significant attention to the role of banks in corporate networks of those countries (Mariolis, 1975; Mintz and Schwartz, 1985; Stokman *et al.*, 1985; Carroll, 1986; Gerlach, 1992). Recently a number of systematic studies of corporate networks in developing economies of Asia and transitional economies of Central and Eastern Europe have appeared (Vedres, 2000; Zang, 2000; Peng *et al.*, 2001; Chung, 2004; Pahor *et al.*, 2004). Many researchers emphasize the importance of interorganizational networks in developing and transitional economies (Hamilton, 1996; Grabher and Stark, 1997; Rona-Tas, 1998; McDermott, 2002) and the research methodology of corporate network analysis provides useful tools for studying interorganizational networks. The role of banks in these economies is an especially interesting topic since banks can play a key role in economic development (Gerschenkron, 1962; Aoki and Kim, 1995), but it is not clear to what extent theories traditionally associated with the analysis of banks in corporate networks of developed economies can be useful in the analysis of corporate networks in developing and transitional economies.

Researchers who study corporate networks in developing and transitional economies often introduce new theoretical models using concepts such as recombinant property (Stark, 1996) or nested hierarchies (Chang, 1999) to explain specific features of these corporate networks. This situation leaves us wondering whether extensive theoretical debates among researchers who studied corporate networks in the United States and Western Europe and the role of banks in these networks have any relevance for the analysis of corporate networks in developing and transitional economies.

This chapter addresses this question by analysing whether theories that have been used to explain positions of banks in the corporate networks of developed economies are consistent with the findings about the role of banks in the Russian economy and whether these theories may be helpful in explaining the position of banks in the Russian corporate network. This analysis not only helps us better understand intercorporate relations in less-developed economies, but may also lead to the development of the existing theories since it may result in a specification of the boundary conditions for these theories or may require a modification of these theories when they are applied in different contexts.

I start with a review of theories that have been developed to explain positions of banks in networks created by ownership and directorship ties among the largest corporations. After describing data and methods, I present some general empirical findings about the position of banks in the Russian corporate network, and I proceed with a discussion whether interpretations based on the reviewed theories are consistent with the empirical evidence about banks in the Russian corporate network. From this discussion I draw a conclusion as to how predictions of the existing theories should be modified to fit the context of the Russian economy. I then return to my data to test the predictions about network positions of banks that reflect the conditions of financial dependence typical for Russian banks. I conclude with a summary and prospects for future research.

Banks in national corporate networks: an overview of theories

Several theories about the role of banks in capitalist economies provide different interpretations of the empirical findings on the interlocks between banks and other firms. We review the key insights below.

Finance capital theory and bank control theory

Finance capital theory and bank control theory emphasize close relations between banks and industrial companies as well as the leading role of banks in these relations. Both of these theories have their roots in the writings of Rudolf Hilferding, who described the cartelization trend in the late nineteenth century: 'As a result of cartelization, therefore, the relations between the banks and industry become still closer, and at the same time the banks acquire an increasing control over the capital invested in industry' (Hilferding, 1981 [1910]: 224).

Subsequent scholarly debates demonstrated a divergence between theorists who emphasize the importance of a merger between bank capital and industry capital in the form of finance capital and theorists who emphasize the leading role of banks in close bank–industry relations (Scott, 1985). The former interpretation of Hilferding's tenets is usually referred to as finance capital theory and the latter as bank control theory.

According to finance capital theory, banks initiate the creation of groups (described as 'empires' or 'spheres of influence') that include industrial companies. These groups are usually created around banks that play important coordinating functions. Finance capital theory also emphasizes the integration of banks into these groups: 'Although banks, insurance companies and other credit-granting companies take on a particularly important role in systematic capital mobilization, these companies at the same time become parts of diversified enterprises, spanning the banking, industrial and commercial sectors' (Scott, 1985: 6–7). As a result, actions of individual organizations affiliated with a group are likely to be dictated by group interests since industrial and bank interests merge and cannot be separated. Financial capital freely flows between banks and industrial companies to those organizations that promise higher returns on investments. Even though Hilferding (1910) referred primarily to the merger of banking and industrial capital within Germany, other finance capital theorists identified 'spheres of influence' in other countries including the United States (for example Menshikov, 1969).

In contrast, according to bank control theory, the relations between banks and industrial companies are characterized primarily by industrial companies' dependence on banks; banks are relatively autonomous from industrial firms they are affiliated with. Banks have interests distinct from the interests of industrial enterprises under their control, and the groups of banks and industrial enterprises are not perceived as decision-making agents that pursue group interests.

Bank control theory suggests that banks occupy the position of dominance in corporate networks because they have discretion in extending loans to industrial companies and because they often have voting rights of shareholders of these companies as owners or trustees of owners (Kotz, 1978). Banks often monitor industrial companies by putting their representatives on boards of these companies. These directors represent banks' interests when strategies of industrial companies are determined during board meetings.

Germany has often been referred to as an example of banks' dominance over industrial enterprises, and a similar situation is observed in some other countries of continental Europe where bank loans are the primary source of financing for industrial enterprises (Windolf, 2002). Several authors have argued that banks have significant control over industrial corporations in the United States (Fitch and Oppenheimer, 1970; Kotz, 1978), but this view is debated since the empirical evidence of direct control of banks over American industrial corporations is equivocal.

Bank hegemony theory

The most elaborated account of bank hegemony (or finance hegemony) theory was presented by Mintz and Schwartz (1985). They differentiate between the strategic control through directives given from dominant to subordinate actors, and the hegemony conditions when dominant actors create structural constraints that limit the range of choices available to subordinate actors. Banks may create such structural constraints for industrial firms because banks control the distribution of financial capital in the economy. Financial capital is a resource that has a universal value since it can be easily transformed into other resources. Even though banks also depend on their borrowers, this dependence is asymmetric since banks easily obtain control when financial capital in the economy is scarce while industrial companies are not likely to control banks even when financial capital is abundant. Mintz and Schwartz (1985) also discuss 'secondary' conditions that buttress banks' power: cooperation among banks, readiness to assume risks that other investors would not take, possibilities of a direct intervention in the management of banks' clients, and so on.

Mintz and Schwartz (1985) argue that interlocking directorates serve primarily as communication channels and banks invite representatives of industrial firms as directors in order to collect information about potential borrowers in various industries of the economy.[1] This interpretation suggests that the relations between organizational power and the directionality of interlocks are exactly opposite to what has been described in bank control theory: powerful organizations are likely to receive rather than send directors.

The cooptation model

The concept of cooptation gained recognition in organization theory after Selznick's influential account of TVA's strategy to absorb potentially disruptive groups into its formal structure (Selznick, 1949). Thompson and McEwen (1958) described interlocks created by banks' representatives sitting on the board of a corporation as a cooptation strategy used by the corporation to cope with its environment.

The cooptation model was systematically developed and applied to various types of interorganizational relations by Pfeffer, Aldrich, Salancik and others (Pfeffer and Salancik, 1978; Aldrich, 1979).[2] The cooptation model is based on the idea of resource dependence introduced in exchange theory: A's power over B is a function of B's dependence on resources controlled by A (Emerson, 1962). The cooptation model brings in the concept of uncertainty by suggesting that B's major concern is to minimize the uncertainty associated with B's dependence on A in getting necessary resources. This uncertainty is minimized by building close relations with A that ensure a continuous supply of the needed resources.

The application of the cooptation model to the context of interlocking directorates suggests that a corporation could invite representatives of organizations that control needed resources to serve as directors. The idea is that a participation in the governance of a corporation will change the attitude of these organizations towards the corporation since organizations that have some control over the corporation are less likely to take actions that have negative consequences for 'their' corporation. By surrendering some degree of control over the corporation to these organizations, owners or managers of this corporation hope to create a favourable attitude of these organizations towards the corporation.

Following this logic, industrial companies that depend on banks as sources of loans should co-opt representatives of banks to their boards. A number of empirical studies demonstrated that, indeed, corporations with higher level of indebtedness are more likely to have representatives of banks on their boards (Pfeffer, 1972; Burt, 1983; Mizruchi and Stearns, 1988). The problem is that these findings are consistent not only with the cooptation model, but also with the model of bank control suggesting that banks insist on having their representatives on boards as means of monitoring. Many researchers allow for the possibility that interlocks between banks and industrial companies serve simultaneously the functions of cooptation and monitoring (Mizruchi, 1996: 276).

In the following analysis of the Russian corporate network I evaluate the applicability of each theory described in this section. The question is whether theories developed to explain network positions of banks in developed economies can be used to explain the position of banks in the Russian corporate network.

Methods

My analysis is based primarily on archival data, but the collection of archival data was preceded by several interviews with executives and board members of Russian banks. I conducted interviews in five banks to find out how directors are elected to the board, whom they represent, and what role directors play in determining strategies of these banks. I asked my interviewees to compare boards in their banks with boards in other banks they were well informed about. The interviews were not used to collect specific information about particular banks, but rather to obtain a general understanding of the functioning of boards in Russian banks.

Sample

The rankings of the largest Russian companies are published by several information agencies. Among the most prominent are AKM, Expert and Kommersant. The rankings of industrial companies and banks are usually compiled separately. Industrial companies are compared on the basis of the information about total sales or market value. For my analysis I have selected 100 industrial companies with largest total sales on the basis of AKM and Expert rankings.[3] Sales data is more comprehensive than market value data and the choice of sales-based ranking is consistent with the prior research on national corporate networks (Stokman *et al.*, 1985). My sample excludes companies with 100 per cent state ownership registered as 'unitary state enterprises' because they do not have boards of directors. I also had to exclude from my sample several companies where the functioning of boards was terminated because these companies filed bankruptcy. Besides data on the 100 largest industrial companies I have collected data on the 60 largest Russian banks selected on the basis of total assets (as published by Expert). The 160 largest corporations were sampled twice – in 1998 and in 2001.

Data and measures

The data on board composition of industrial companies is obtained from quarterly reports and reports on issues of securities filed by these companies in accordance with the requirements of the Federal Commission on Securities

Markets. Information from these reports is publicly available and can be obtained directly from the Federal Commission on Securities Markets or through information agencies. The data on banks, including the information about executives and directors of banks, is obtained from quarterly reports that the Central Bank of Russia makes publicly available and from annual reports found on websites of some banks. For the sample of the largest banks in 2001 I have recorded information about household deposits, corporate deposits, foreign credits and total assets. I also have coded business group affiliation, state ownership and ownership by other firms in my sample for these banks.[4]

In my analysis I use two types of measures: network characteristics and attributes of nodes represented by the 160 firms in my sample. The network characteristics were calculated from the initial affiliation matrix using UCINET. The results of a regression analysis reported in this paper were obtained using STATA.

Terminology

This analysis continues a long tradition of studying interlocking directorates (see Mizruchi, 1996 for a review). Researchers in this area have developed a terminology to describe different types of interlocking directorates, but this terminology is not standard and uniform. According to Mizruchi, 'an interlocking directorate occurs when a person affiliated with one organization sits on the board of directors of another organization' (1996: 271). In this chapter I consider interlocking directorates as ties that connect organizations. I concentrate on one type of interorganizational ties and further in the text I often refer to interorganizational ties through interlocking directorates simply as 'ties' or 'interlocks'. There are two major types of interlocking directorates: one created when an officer of firm A sits on the board of firm B, and another created when someone who is not an officer of firm A or firm B sits on boards of both firms. In the former case I say that there is a 'directional' tie from firm A to firm B: firm A sends this tie and firm B receives this tie. In the latter case there is a 'non-directional' tie between firms A and B (see also Scott, 1985, on the importance of differentiating directional and non-directional interlocks).

Banks in the Russian corporate network

Access to financial capital is a necessary condition for rapid economic development. Historical studies demonstrate that banks as providers of financial capital played an important role in the economic development of Germany and Japan (Gerschenkron, 1962; Teranishi, 1995). Some researchers suggest that banks may also play a key role in economic development of transitional economies. Banks are perceived as an alternative to financial markets that function poorly in transitional economies since weak institutions of corporate governance do not provide investors with means of proper monitoring (Aoki, 1995). A number of researchers have emphasized the importance of interorganizational networks in transitional economies (Grabher and Stark, 1997; Rona-Tas, 1998; McDermott,

2002) and we may expect that the role played by banks in transitional economies will be reflected in their position in interorganizational networks.

Research about corporate governance in Russian corporations has concentrated on the relations among owners and on the relations between owners and 'entrenched' managers (Estrin and Wright, 1999; Filatotchev *et al.*, 2001; Dolgopyatova, 2002; McCarthy and Puffer, 2003). There are few quantitative studies that look at boards of directors in Russia. Existing studies of boards are based on surveys and provide information about average board composition and about a typical agenda of board meetings (Bureau of Economic Analysis, 2001; Russian Institute of Directors, 2004). From these studies we know that boards of Russian corporations consist mainly of managers-insiders and outside directors representing other corporations. Similar to boards typical for other transitional economies, the outside directors in Russian corporations often represent major shareholders (Radygin *et al.*, 2004). Besides management and large shareholders, directors may represent other parties concerned with the operations of a bank: federal or regional governments, important business partners, and others (Lane, 2003). Large corporations listed on stock exchanges make efforts to improve the quality of corporate governance and invite independent directors to their boards (Russian Institute of Directors, 2004), but in practice independent directors do not have much influence (Radygin *et al.*, 2004).

Executives of other firms constitute the largest group of outside directors on boards of Russian banks. According to the president of one bank where I conducted interviews, 'The presence of people from other organizations on the board of a bank is not a coincidence. This tells about special, sometimes rather complex, relations between a bank and these organizations' (Interviews, 2003).

Executives of other corporations are rarely invited to boards of Russian banks as knowledgeable experts who may provide information useful in making strategic decisions. Usually they represent on the board interests of those organizations where they occupy executive positions. Often these organizations are major shareholders of a bank that have enough votes to put their representatives on the board. Executives of other firms on the board of a bank also frequently represent important clients, who may or may not be shareholders of a bank. According to my interviewees, banks often establish closer relations with important clients by offering these clients to become shareholders, but they also may invite representatives of clients on the board even if they do not hold shares in these banks.

Representatives of other organizations are often restricted in their voting during board meetings by instructions they receive from their 'home' organizations. If these directors change their primary affiliation, they are substituted by other directors representing the same organization (Interviews, 2003).

All interviewees agreed that the presence of an executive of a large corporation on the board of a bank suggests that this corporation has some concerns about the bank as its shareholder or its business partner. The presence of such directors on the board of a bank can be taken as an indicator that corporations sending these directors have a say in making important decisions regarding the bank's strategy.

Network position of Russian banks in 2001

The first distinct characteristic of the network position of Russian banks is that they send relatively few directional ties. On average in my sample each bank sends 0.63 ties while each industrial company sends 1.56 ties. Table 7.1 lists companies with the highest numbers of sent directional ties. There are only four banks in this table and none of them sends more than four ties. Since two companies may be connected by more than one tie, it is important to have information not only about the number of ties sent by a firm, but also about the number of ties sent to different firms. Table 7.2 demonstrates that only two banks send directional ties to three or more other firms.

Even though banks send relatively few directional ties, they are well-connected with other companies in my sample through received directional ties and through non-directional ties. On average, each bank receives slightly more directional ties (1.25) than each industrial company (1.19). Banks also have slightly more non-directional ties with other firms in the sample: each bank on average has 1.57 non-directional ties while each industrial company has 1.42 non-directional ties. Among firms with the highest number of received ties and non-directional ties, there are many banks. Table 7.2 demonstrates that

Table 7.1   Russian companies that send the highest number of directional ties, 2001

Company	Number of sent ties	Industry
Gazprom	22	Oil & gas
Severstal	14	Ferrous metallurgy
Sibur	13	Chemical & petrochemical
Lukoil	12	Oil & gas
Tatneft	12	Oil & gas
Sibneft	11	Oil & gas
EES	9	Electro-energy
UGMK	7	Non-ferrous metallurgy
Surgutneftegaz	6	Oil & gas
TNK	6	Oil & gas
VSMPO	5	Ferrous metallurgy
Yukos	5	Oil & gas
Alrosa	4	Diamonds and precious metals
CB Avtobank	4	Banking
Nornikel	4	Non-ferrous metallurgy
Bashneft	3	Oil & gas
CB Vneshtorgbank	3	Banking
CB Mosnarbank	3	Banking
CB Rosbank	3	Banking

Note: Names of banks start with CB (for a commercial bank) and are given in bold type.

Table 7.2   Firms that send or receive directional ties from three or more other firms, 2001

Firms that receive directional ties from 3 or more other firms		Firms that send directional ties to 3 or more other firms	
CB Ak Bars	Banking	Gazprom	Oil & gas
Sidanko	Oil & gas	EES	Electro-energy
CB DIB	Banking	Severstal	Ferrous metallurgy
CB Menatep SPb	Banking	Lukoil	Oil & gas
Achinski GOK	Non-ferrous metallurgy	Tatneft	Oil & gas
CB Inkasbank	Banking	Sibneft	Oil & gas
CB Rosbank	Banking	Sibur	Chemical/petrochemical
CB Bashkredit	Banking	TNK	Oil & gas
		Yukos	Oil & gas
		CB Avtobank	Banking
		Nornikel	Non-ferrous metallurgy
		CB Mosnarbank	Banking

Table 7.3   Directional interlocks between financial and industrial companies in different countries

	RUS 2001	G 1993	UK 1993	F 1997	S 1995	N 1995	US 1997
Proportion of all financials-industrials directional ties sent by financials, %	27.0	73.9	40.4	69.9	45.9	50.3	43.3
Sent by financials / received by financials	0.36	2.83	0.68	2.32	0.85	1.01	0.76

Notes: Ratios for Western Europe and the USA are calculated on the basis of information provided in Windolf (2002: 32). Country codes: RUS = Russia, G = Germany, F = France, S = Switzerland, N = Netherlands.

banks prevail among firms that receive directional ties from three or more firms in the sample.

A high ratio of received directional ties to sent directional ties that we find for Russian banks is especially striking in comparison with the analogous ratios calculated for European countries and the United States (Table 7.3). Most directional ties between financial companies and industrial companies in Germany and France are sent by financial companies and received by industrial companies. In Britain, the United States and Switzerland most directional ties between financial and industrial companies are sent from industrial companies to financial companies. It is also the case in Russia, but the proportion of directional ties sent from financial to industrial companies is even lower in

Table 7.4   Twenty firms with highest Bonacich centrality and betweenness centrality, 2001

Company	Bonacich centrality	Company	Betweenness centrality
TNK	57.26	**CB RBR**	1547.46
CB RBR	55.65	Lukoil	1438.30
Lukoil	51.30	Gazprom	1201.71
CB Rosselhozbank	47.72	**CB Menatep SPb**	1015.83
Rosneft	43.12	**CB DIB**	1007.95
SIDANKO	29.27	EES	876.98
CB Alfa-Bank	29.21	Rosneft	829.51
CB Sberbank	24.08	TNK	683.76
CB Vneshtorgbank	23.71	**CB PSB**	672.00
Vimpel-Com	22.37	**CB Vneshtorgbank**	665.83
CB Mosnarbank	19.29	**CB Zenit**	606.16
Aeroflot	19.28	Sibneft	557.86
Nornikel	18.96	**CB NRB**	551.40
SUAL	17.10	**CB Eurofinans**	505.75
CB Zenit	16.18	Nornikel	394.85
CB DIB	12.55	**CB Rosbank**	387.41
CB Petrokommerts	12.38	**CB Sberbank**	352.95
CB Nikoil	12.30	**CB Petrokommerts**	338.46
CB Rosbank	11.99	Sibur	318.98
Slavneft	11.23	Slavneft	298.36

Note: Names of banks are given in bold type.

Russia: less than one-third of all directional ties between financials and industrials are sent by financial companies.

A number of banks occupy 'strategic' positions in the Russian corporate network – they have connections with other well-connected firms and with firms that do not have immediate ties between them. The centrality measure suggested by Bonacich (1972) takes into account not only the number of ties that connect a focal firm with other firms, but also weights the importance of these connections by centrality scores of these other firms (Wasserman and Faust, 1994). Betweenness centrality indicates how often a focal firm is located between other firms in the network (more precisely, how often a focal firm occurs on a shortest path between pairs of other firms in the network). Table 7.4 demonstrates that 11 out of 20 firms with highest Bonacich centrality and betweenness centrality are banks. Since Russian banks send relatively few ties, their high centrality is due mostly to received ties and non-directional ties with other firms in the sample.

Centrality of banks in national corporate networks is a common finding across many countries (Stokman *et al.*, 1985; Windolf, 2002). In some countries this centrality is due mostly to a large number of directional ties sent by banks (Germany and France); in other countries it is due primarily to a large number of non-directional ties and directional ties received by banks (Russia and the United States). In order to provide an adequate interpretation to the network position of Russian banks, we need to look at the role of banks in the Russian economy.

Banks and the distribution of financial capital in the Russian economy

Table 7.1 demonstrates that oil & gas companies send significantly more directional ties than firms from other industries. Oil & gas companies have significant power because they have access to a crucial resource – financial capital. Oil, oil products, and gas constitute more than one-half of the total value of Russian exports. Revenues of firms from extracting industries represent the major source of financial capital for the Russian economy (including the Russian government that collects most taxes from exporters of oil and gas). A substantial number of firms striving for financial capital found themselves dependent on large oil & gas companies: many of them were eventually acquired by oil & gas companies or became effectively controlled by these companies.

If firms that have access to financial capital are influential and send their executives to boards of other firms, why do Russian banks tend to receive rather than send directorship ties? Under conditions of scarce financial capital, banks with access to household savings could be very influential players in this under-capitalized economy. But Russian banks find themselves in special circumstances because only a small proportion of household savings in Russia is kept in commercial banks. The history of high inflation and bank failures during the 1990s is the reason why many Russians prefer to convert their ruble savings into hard currency and keep it at home (Spicer and Pyle, 2002). A majority of those who decide to deposit their savings go to state-owned Sberbank that accumulates more than 70 per cent of all household deposits. The reason for the near-monopolistic position of Sberbank is that in the absence of a deposit insurance system for private banks (currently being introduced), the Russian government guaranteed the safety of deposits in Sberbank. Other banks in Russia attract a relatively low amount of household deposits and have to look for other sources of capital. Most commercial banks rely on industrial companies as their major sources of funds.[5] Banks do not have much discretion in using this capital, because these funds come from a very limited number of industrial corporations that, in exchange for these funds, require the right to monitor and even determine how these funds are used (Gnezditskaia, 2003). Sometimes banks have one major sponsor or client, as in the case of 'pocket' banks of the largest industrial companies (Johnson, 2000). Other banks achieve more autonomy by balancing their dependence on several companies that supply them with financial resources.

Privately owned Russian banks not only failed to attract household deposits, but they also play a limited role as creditors of industrial companies. The role of Russian banks as sources of external funds for industrial companies is limited primarily to providing short-term loans. Most industrial companies rely on internal sources to generate funds necessary for investments. In 2001 only 3 per cent of investments made by industrial companies were financed by bank loans (Mizobata, 2003). The proportion of total bank lending to GDP in Russia is very low (20% in 2001) and it would be even lower if we did not count state-owned Sberbank and Vneshtorgank that have largest industrial credit portfolios (Tompson, 2003: 73).

Russian banks used to be much more influential before the financial crisis of August 1998 since they had access to other sources of capital. In the early 1990s banks could obtain cheap loans from the Central Bank of Russia and lend these funds to other enterprises at much higher interest rates. In the early 1990s the rate of inflation was very high and banks earned high profits in speculations with hard currencies. Close affiliations of some banks with the Russian government brought them lucrative government accounts. During this early transitional period banks were involved in financial schemes used to channel state funds and funds of large corporations to personal accounts of state officials and managers of these corporations. Thus, Russian banks played an important role in the process of 'informal' privatization and were also able to profit from arbitrage in inefficient financial markets of the early 1990s.[6] Speculative profits permitted large banks to become main bidders during the privatization of large enterprises in the mid-1990s. Several large banks provided loans to the Russian government in exchange for shares of the largest enterprises in oil, non-ferrous metals and some other strategic industries. These large banks also cheaply acquired nearly bankrupt enterprises that had already been privatized. As a result, several financial-industrial groups were formed around such large banks as Oneksimbank, Menatep, Rossijski Kredit, and so on. (Brent, 2003).

Large banks were also able to attract significant amounts of capital from foreign investors, since many foreign investors were reluctant to deal with non-transparent Russian enterprises directly and Russian banks often served as intermediaries to channel funds from foreign banks and investors to industrial companies in Russia. Foreign investors also used Russian banks as intermediaries and partners for operations in the Russian securities markets; in particular, they signed futures contracts with Russian banks to hedge against the risk of ruble devaluation.

Large banks were major players and beneficiaries in the market for government bonds. Interest rates for these bonds were very high and many banks chose to invest most of their assets in these bonds. Such investments brought very high profits until August 1998 when the government debt was frozen and the ruble was devaluated.

The financial crisis of August 1998 hit Russian banks very hard and such sources of capital as foreign loans and high profits from investments in government bonds dried up after the crisis. This financial crisis eliminated a number of large banks that used to be founders and coordinating centres of several important financial-industrial groups. Since then, banks yielded leading positions

Table 7.5   Companies that sent the highest number of directional ties, 1998

Company	Number of sent ties	Industry	Banks that became insolvent and were liquidated after August 1998 crisis
Gazprom	25	Oil & gas	
CB_Rossijski_Kredit	12	Banking	Liquidated
Yukos	10	Oil & gas	
CB_Oneksim	9	Banking	Liquidated
Severstal	8	Ferrous metallurgy	
CB_PSB	6	Banking	
CB_Sberbank	5	Banking	
CB_Mosbiznesbank	4	Banking	Liquidated
TNK	4	Oil & gas	
CB_AkBars	3	Banking	
CB_Menatep	3	Banking	Liquidated
CB_Mezhkombank	3	Banking	Liquidated
CB_MFK	3	Banking	
CB_Uralsib	3	Banking	
CB_Vneshtorgbank	3	Banking	
EES	3	Electro-energy	
Rostelekom	3	Telecom	
Tatneft	3	Oil & gas	

in the Russian economy to companies that generated financial capital by exporting natural resources (Tompson, 2003).

Changes in the role played by banks in the Russian economy are reflected in the differences between network positions of banks in 1998 and in 2001. The analysis of interlocking directorates among the 160 largest firms in 1998 demonstrates that banks enjoyed a much more dominant position in the Russian corporate network before the financial crisis. In 1998 each of the 60 largest banks sent on average 1.13 ties (compared to 0.63 in 2001). Among firms that sent 3 or more directional ties in 2001 there were only four banks with maximum of 4 ties sent by Avtobank (Table 7.1). In 1998, 11 banks sent 3 or more directional ties with Oneksimbank and Rossijski Kredit sending 9 and 12 directional ties respectively. Oneksimbank, Rossijski Kredit and several other banks found among those that sent most directional ties in 1998 went bankrupt in the aftermath of the financial crisis in August 1998 (Table 7.5).

Since the early days of the economic transition, Russian banks did not serve the traditional function of financial intermediaries typical for banks in developed economies. The rise of banks in Western Europe and in the United States during the period of industrialization was due to their ability to accumulate private investments and fund large industrial projects with this capital (Scott, 1997). The rise of banks in the Russian economy during the period of reforms was due to the high profitability of financial speculations in inefficient markets.

The failure of the Russian government to collect taxes during this period explains why it was so receptive to lobbying by banks that supplied the government with funds necessary to sustain liquidity (Tompson, 2003). While providing Russian banks with multiple benefits, this role was inherently unstable. As speculative sources of financial capital disappeared and the financial standing of the government and industrial companies improved, the network position of banks changed dramatically. The fact that Russian banks failed to assume the role of financial intermediaries differentiates them from banks in developed economies and is crucial for interpreting the position of banks in the Russian corporate network as of 2001.

Interpretation of banks' position in the Russian corporate network

We may notice similarities between positions of banks in the Russian corporate network and in the American corporate network. Table 7.3 demonstrates that more directional ties are sent from industrial companies to banks than from banks to industrial companies in both Russia and the United States. Mizruchi and Bunting (1981) argued that an index suggested by Bonacich (1972) is the most adequate for identifying central actors in the network and demonstrated that among American firms with high Bonacich centrality there are many banks. Similarly, Table 7.4 shows a high proportion of banks among Russian corporations with the highest Bonacich centrality. Therefore, in both national corporate networks banks are among most central corporations and their centrality is due primarily to a large number of interlocks created by executives of other firms sitting on boards of banks.

The similarity of network positions of Russian and American banks should not be taken as an indication that they enjoy similar influence in national economies. All theories about the position of banks in the American corporate network describe large banks as very influential players in the American economy. This description is consistent with the empirical evidence (Mintz and Schwartz, 1985). In contrast, the description of Russian banks in the previous section demonstrates that they failed to assume the role of intermediaries that redistribute financial capital in the economy. As a result, they lacked a stable basis for influence and as soon as speculative sources of income disappeared banks lost their influence in the Russian economy.

The similarity of network positions between American banks that play the role of coordinating centres and Russian banks that serve as treasurers for large industrial corporations can be explained by the different meaning of interlocks among large corporations in Russia and in the United States. According to bank hegemony theory, a large number of directional ties received by banks indicate power or prestige of banks since executives of the largest non-financial corporations are ready to accept invitations to boards of these banks. This interpretation relies on the view of interlocks as communication channels created when banks invite knowledgeable executives from selected industries as directors. And, indeed, in the United States directors are usually invited rather than 'placed' on the board. The ownership of large American corporations is very diffused and CEOs of these corporations to a large extent determined who would be appointed to the board (Lorsch and MacIver, 1989). Directors are invited as experts who are supposed to act in the best interests of the corporation that invited them rather than in the interests of corporations where they have full-time positions. These practices determine the meaning of interlocks in the modern American corporate network.

Interlocking directorates in the Russian corporate network have a different meaning because directors of large Russian corporations are selected differently. In Russia, directors are 'placed' on the board and they represent the interests of organizations that sent them to the board. My interviews confirmed that directional ties among large Russian corporations reflect the relations of influence, and firms that send directional ties have influence over firms that receive these ties. This interpretation is consistent with the above-mentioned evidence that powerful oil & gas companies send many but receive few directional ties. A significant number of directional ties received by Russian banks does not reflect their prestige and influence; on the contrary, this network position should be interpreted as an indicator of the subordinate role played by banks in the Russian economy. In the next section I test hypotheses that directly relate the number of directional ties received by banks with their dependence on financial resources provided by industrial companies.

According to bank control theory, the main source of bank control is the discretion that banks have in extending loans and managing shares of industrial corporations as trustees of owners-beneficiaries (Fitch and Oppenheimer, 1970; Kotz, 1978). Industrial companies are dependent on banks because the latter act as financial intermediaries by transforming household deposits into industrial loans and by acting as trustees for investors who deposited their shares with trust departments of banks. In the relations between banks and industrial companies in Russia the asymmetry of dependence is reversed, because Russian banks failed to become true financial intermediaries between investors and industrial firms looking for financial capital. Earlier, I argued that industrial corporations rather than households represent the primary source of financial capital for Russian banks. Mintz and Schwartz (1985) argued that while banks have significant power over industrial companies as suppliers of capital, households do not have such power over banks since there are many of them and their actions are not coordinated. Russian banks do not enjoy similar independence since they often obtain a lion's share of their financial resources from a small number of industrial corporations. The nature of control relations described by bank control theory is very similar to the relations we find between banks and industrial companies in Russia, but in the modern Russian corporate network the directionality of control relations is reversed. During the early period of 'market reforms' a number of banks were able to accumulate financial capital from sources other than traditional banking operations of taking deposits and providing loans (see the previous section). These resources were used to obtain control over industrial enterprises, but after the financial crisis of 1998 it became obvious that the locus of control had shifted: industrial corporations (especially, exporters of oil and gas) generated financial resources while banks served as treasurers for these corporations (Brent, 2003). In order to capture the current distribution of control among the largest banks and industrial companies in Russia, bank control theory should be modified into 'oil & gas control' theory.

A similar modification is required to adapt finance capital theory to the realities of the Russian corporate network in 2001. Consistent with finance capital theory, it is difficult to distinguish banking and industrial capitals in the Russian economy. The merger of banking and industrial capitals was institutionalized in the form of financial-industrial groups that emerged in Russia in the mid-1990s (Pappe, 2000; Brent, 2003). In accordance with finance capital theory, Russian banks played a leading role in the formation of financial-industrial groups as evidenced by their active participation in the loans-for-shares privatization auctions (Johnson, 2000). While financial operations were bringing high profits, banks dominated many of these business groups; but over time, the industrial components of these groups were increasing in their importance with bank executives changing positions to become top managers in extracting companies. After the financial crisis in August 1998, industrial enterprises assumed leading roles in virtually all financial-industrial groups.[7] In 2001 we do find the integration of banking capital and industrial capital described by finance capital theory, but industrial companies rather than banks play the leading role in this process and act as coordinating centres in financial-industrial groups.

Studies based on the cooptation model traditionally tested a hypothesis that under the conditions of dependence on banks as sources of financial capital, industrial companies are likely to invite representatives of banks as board members (Pfeffer and Salancik, 1978; Pennings, 1980). But taking into account the distribution of financial resources in the Russian economy, we may expect that, in accordance with the cooptation model, banks will co-opt to their boards the representatives of large extracting companies. The observed pattern of directional interlocks is consistent with this prediction, but our knowledge about the meaning of directional ties in the Russian corporate network suggests that often these ties reflect control rather than cooptation relations. For example, it is very common for large shareholders of the firm to have their representatives on the board and we can hardly interpret such ties as 'cooptation' interlocks since under the conditions of concentrated ownership board members are usually selected by large shareholders. In relations with other influential stakeholders, a bank may also not have much choice but to allow representatives of these stakeholders to sit on the board. This situation is more adequately described in terms of control and monitoring than in terms of cooptation. At the same time, I do not rule out a possibility that in some cases directors are co-opted; for example, it is often the case with representatives of regional governments. A bank may also co-opt an industrial company by inviting it to become a co-owner of the bank. The resulting relations between the industrial company and the bank have both control and cooptation components.

The resource-dependence logic underlies not only the cooptation model, but also bank control theory. After describing 'influence' interlocks created by banks that actively pursue their interests through board representation, Mizruchi argues:

> there is nothing in this view which is inconsistent with the idea that possession of crucial resources enables a corporation to better cope with its environment. In fact, it is precisely the bank's control over a particular resource (in this case loan capital) which confers power upon it. (1982: 43)

This interpretation of interlocks among American corporations in the beginning of the twentieth century can also be applied to interlocks among Russian corporations a century later, but the directionality of interlocks in the Russian corporate network is reversed due to the reversed relations of resource dependence.

Our analysis demonstrates that the interpretation of the network position of banks suggested by bank hegemony theory is not adequate in the analysis of the Russian corporate network. The logic of bank control, financial capital and cooptation theories can be applied in the analysis of the Russian corporate network, but predictions of these theories should be modified to reflect a specific role played by banks in the Russian economy. In the next section I formulate and test predictions that relate network positions of Russian banks with their reliance on different sources of financial capital.

Financial dependence of Russian banks: a test of hypotheses

In this section I consider the sources of financial capital available to Russian banks and the patterns of dependence associated with these sources of capital. I use empirical data about deposits and credits obtained by banks to test whether banks' reliance on various sources of capital is associated with a number of received directional ties. While dependence-based hypotheses often did not find empirical support in the analysis of interlocks with banks in the United States (for example Pennings, 1980), this may reflect the fact that a significant portion of interlocks in the American corporate network is not associated with the relations of resource dependence (Zajac, 1988). The above discussion of the meaning of interlocks suggests that executives of large Russian corporations are rarely invited to boards as independent experts and hence we may expect to find stronger support for dependence-based hypotheses in the Russian corporate network than did studies of the modern American corporate network.

Financial capital is a scarce resource in the Russian economy and we can expect that firms that control financial resources will send executives to boards of corporations that rely on these resources. Russian banks depend on industrial companies as the primary sources of funds (in the form of deposits, accounts or contributions to equity capital) and we may expect that industrial corporations that provide banks with financial resources send their representatives to boards of these banks. A large proportion of corporate deposits in liabilities of a bank demonstrates its high dependence on non-financial companies that make these deposits. Correspondingly, we may expect that banks with a high proportion of corporate deposits are likely to receive more directional ties than banks with a small proportion of corporate deposits.

> **Hypothesis 1**: Banks with a large proportion of corporate deposits in their liabilities receive more directional ties than banks with a small proportion of corporate deposits.

On the other hand, I expect that banks with a large proportion of household deposits will be less dependent on other firms as sources of funds. Correspondingly, banks with a large proportion of household deposits in their liabilities should receive fewer directional ties created by executives of large firms on boards of these banks.

> **Hypothesis 2**: Banks with a large proportion of household deposits in their liabilities receive fewer directional ties than banks with a small proportion of household deposits.

Foreign credits represent another important source of funds for Russian banks. Bankers quickly realized that foreign credits are relatively cheap and they can make significant profits by borrowing money abroad and investing this money in highly profitable projects in Russia. Not surprisingly, many of these projects also had high risks. Difficulties in estimating risks of these projects explain why foreign investors preferred to use Russian banks as intermediate borrowers. Access to foreign credits makes banks less dependent on other Russian firms as sources of capital. Correspondingly, we can expect that banks with a significant proportion of foreign credits in their liabilities receive fewer directional ties.

> **Hypothesis 3**: Banks with a large proportion of foreign credits in their liabilities receive fewer directional ties than banks with a small proportion of foreign credits.

To test these hypotheses I have obtained data on the structure of liabilities for banks in my sample. As a dependent variable I use the number of directional ties received by each bank. Independent variables include the proportion of household deposits, corporate deposits and foreign credits in the liabilities of each bank. I also use several control variables: size measured as a logarithm of the total amount of assets, a number of ownership ties created if other firms in my sample are found among owners of a bank, capitalization measured as a ratio of equity capital to total liabilities, a dummy variable for state-owned banks, and a dummy variable for banks affiliated with business groups. Descriptive statistics and bivariate correlations for all variables are presented in Table 7.6. On average for my sample, household deposits, corporate deposits and foreign credits constitute 9 per cent, 37 per cent, and 14 per cent of total liabilities, respectively. Together with equity capital these variables on average account for 76 per cent of total liabilities. Other liabilities such as inter-bank loans, funds received from the government and so on, taken together, comprise on average 24 per cent of total liabilities. This residual category of liabilities is not correlated with the number of received ties and I use 'other liabilities' as an omitted variable in my analysis.

Since the dependent variable is a count of received ties and since the mean and standard deviation for this variable are similar, I use the Poisson regression (Rice, 1995). The results of the regression analysis are summarized in Table 7.7. We can see that size, state ownership and capitalization have insignificant effects on the number of received ties. In some models business group affiliation has a significant positive effect on the number of received ties – banks affiliated with business groups receive more ties from other firms in the sample than 'independent' banks. It is not surprising that the ownership variable is significant in all models since banks partially owned by other firms from my sample often have directors representing these firms, but many interlocks do not have underlying ownership relations. There is a high correlation between ownership and business group affiliation, but these control variables have low correlations with independent variables.

Two of three independent variables appear to be significant: the proportion of corporate deposits has a positive effect on the number of received ties and the proportion of foreign credits has a negative effect. While hypotheses 1 and 3 are supported, hypothesis 2 about the proportion of household deposits does not find empirical support. The lack of support for hypothesis 2 is consistent with the observation that household deposits constitute a relatively small portion of total liabilities in most banks.

I have also run models with sent ties and non-directional ties as dependent variables. None of the independent variables is significant in predicting the number of ties sent by banks to other firms in my sample. In the model with the number of non-directional ties as a dependent variable, only a proportion of foreign credits in liabilities is statistically significant. Banks with a large proportion of foreign credits in their liabilities share less directors with other firms in the sample. This finding reflects a general orientation of these banks towards foreign partners and a lack of interest in developing close ties with Russian corporations at the administrative level. Models with sent and non-directional ties demonstrate that dependence on corporate deposits is associated only with

Table 7.6 Descriptive statistics and correlations for the sample of Russian banks

		Mean	S.D.	Min	Max	1	2	3	4	5	6	7	8
1.	Total assets (log)	16.58	1.04	15.03	20.47								
2.	Business group bank	.22	.42	0	1.00	.13							
3.	State bank	.10	.30	0	1.00	.20	−.18						
4.	Ownership	.25	.51	0	2.00	.19	.54**	−.06					
5.	Equity capital/ total liabilities	.16	.08	.02	.38	−.12	.25	.22	.06				
6.	Household deposits/ total liabilities	.09	.10	0	.63	.38**	−.06	.12	−.11	−.29*			
7.	Corporate deposits/ total liabilities	.37	.19	.01	.93	.08	.07	−.25	.14	−.36**	.06		
8.	Foreign credits/ total liabilities	.14	.17	0	.67	−.04	−.23	−.05	−.14	.09	−.17	−.18	
9.	Number of received directional ties	1.25	1.6	0	5.00	.20	.50**	−.12	.63**	−.03	.09	.32*	−.34**

* $p < .05$; ** $p < .01$

Table 7.7   Summary of regression analysis results (dependent variable: number of received ties)

Independent variables	Model 1	Model 2	Model 3	Model 4	Model 5
Total assets	.11	.06	.09	.14	.06
Business group bank	.64*	.63*	.57	.25	.26
State bank	−.45	−.78	−.36	−.58	−.88
Ownership	.77**	.85**	.79**	.79**	.90**
Equity capital	−1.79	−1.18	.76	−.50	2.65
Household deposits		2.35			3.05
Corporate deposits			1.93**		1.90*
Foreign credits				−4.16**	−2.77*
Log likelihood	−79.24	−77.88	−75.84	−73.55	−70.52
Pseudo R^2	.21	.22	.24	.26	.29
LR chi^2	41.46	44.17	48.24	52.83	58.88
N	57	57	57	57	57

* $p < .05$; ** $p < .01$

the number of received ties. This finding provides additional justification to our focus on directional ties and supports the claim that in the Russian corporate network interlocks are directed from firms that have resources to firms that need resources.

In this study I have demonstrated the association between financial dependence and the existence of interlocks, but since my analysis is cross-sectional I cannot prove causality. Therefore, along with more traditional resource-dependence interpretation where interlocks are created as a response to the conditions of dependence, we should allow a possibility that the existence of interlocks leads to more reliance on financial resources from such related firms (Mizruchi and Stearns, 1994) The reality may be even more complex than these two simple alternatives: even if a researcher can demonstrate that the existence of interlocks precedes some business transactions between interlocked firms, it is possible that interlocks were created to facilitate these transactions (Mizruchi, 1996: 291).

The important finding of this analysis is that the correspondence exists between ties received by Russian banks and their reliance on corporate deposits. The most prominent characteristic of the network position of Russian banks is a relatively high number of received directional ties. A significant portion of the variation in the number of received ties can be explained by the reliance on different sources of financial capital. The empirical support of hypotheses 1 and 3 provides additional evidence that patterns of interlocks in the Russian corporate network are not random as would be the case if directorship positions were purely nominal or if directors were selected just on the basis of familiarity with executives or owners of the firm. The empirical support of these hypotheses demonstrates that the resource dependence logic can be used to explain patterns of directional interlocks in the Russian corporate network if predictions based on this logic take into account the specific role played by banks in the Russian economy and the specific meaning of interlocks in the Russian corporate network. Earlier I suggested that directional interlocks among large Russian corporations can be interpreted as indicators of intercorporate influence. The finding that the patterns of interlocks are associated with the dependence on financial resources supports this interpretation since the relations of resource dependence provide a basis for the relations of influence (Emerson, 1962).

Conclusion

This chapter provides a description and interpretation of the position of banks in the Russian corporate network. I have analysed whether different theories that were developed to explain positions of banks in corporate networks of developed economies can be used to explain the position of banks in the Russian corporate network. While some of these theories are inconsistent with the empirical evidence about interlocks among Russian corporations, the resource-dependence logic underlying other theories may provide a basis for explaining the patterns of interlocks in the Russian corporate network. The resource-dependence logic plays out differently in the Russian corporate network because banks play a different role in the Russian economy. Rather than acting as intermediaries that transform household savings into industrial loans, Russian banks became dependent on large industrial companies as sources of financial capital. Correspondingly, the relations between banks and industrial companies described by bank control theory are reversed since in Russia control is exercised primarily by producers and exporters of raw materials. Consistent with finance capital theory, we do find a merger of banking and industrial capitals in the form of financial-industrial groups, but currently industrial companies rather than banks act as coordinating centres of these groups. Finally, patterns of interlocks between banks and industrial companies may to some extent reflect cooptation efforts, but in contrast with the original account of the relations between banks and industrial companies by Pfeffer and Salancik (1978), Russian banks have more reasons to co-opt the representatives of industrial companies than vice versa.

This study has several limitations that future research is expected to overcome. First, I have concentrated on interorganizational ties created by interlocking directorates, and the analysis of the Russian corporate network would be enriched by adding data on other types of ties among firms. Second, it would be desirable to trace the relations with important non-corporate economic actors such as federal and regional governments. Finally, this study demonstrates the importance of business-group affiliations for network positions of Russian banks. A promising direction for future research would be to combine the methods of network analysis with a rich qualitative description of business groups in Russia.

Notes

1   See also Davis and Mizruchi (1999), who argue that as banks' need for information about industrial borrowers diminishes, the number of representatives from industrials on boards of banks also decreases.
2   Burt's theory of structural constraints (Burt, 1983) represents a variation of the cooptation model that goes beyond dependencies between individual organizations and looks at the constraints created in inter-industry relations.
3   There were some discrepancies between Expert and AKM rankings because some companies were excluded from Expert or AKM rankings for different reasons (e.g. Expert ranking did not include companies from transport, electrical energy, and telecom industries). There were also some discrepancies due to the differences in counting some firms as separate companies or as subsidiaries of other firms. I tried to create the most comprehensive list of 100 largest industrial companies, but if several companies were integrated into one business holding (that filed aggregated financial reports), I included in my sample only a head company of this holding (e.g. Yukos or Lukoil).
4   Business group affiliation of banks was coded on the basis of information about integrated business groups published by the business magazine *Delovie Ludi*.
5   Table 7.6 demonstrates that on average for my sample of the 60 largest Russian banks, household deposits and corporate deposits constitute 9% and 37% of total liabilities, respectively.
6   Many banks accumulated their initial capital by arbitrage in inefficient commodities markets acting as *de facto* trading companies in the late 1980s–early 1990s (Hellman, 1993).
7   Even at the moment when these extracting companies were acquired by the leaders of large Russian banks, the 'real' value of these companies exceeded the amount of assets controlled by the acquiring banks. A special agreement with the Russian government permitted relatively small (by world standards) banks to obtain control over extracting companies that were among the largest in the world by the amount of confirmed reserves of oil, gas and nonferrous metals (Pappe, 2000).

8
'Private Benefits of Control' and Debt Financing*

Igor Filatotchev and Tomasz Mickiewicz

Introduction

There is a substantial body of research in financial economics and strategic management literatures that links the pattern and amount of stock ownership with managerial behaviour, and, eventually, with corporate performance (Shleifer and Vishny 1997; Jensen and Warner, 1988). A fast-growing literature on the optimal ownership structures of firms depending on the levels of 'private benefits of control' (for example Almeida and Wolfenzon 2005; Bennedsen and Wolfenzon, 2000; Grossman and Hart, 1988; Harris and Raviv, 1990; see also Holderness and Sheehan, 1988; Short, 1994) has extended governance research beyond the conventional US/UK environment and has recently become a focal point of theoretical and policy debates (Bebchuk, 1994; Filatotchev *et al.*, 2001; La Porta *et al.*, 1998, 2000; Modigliani and Perotti, 1997).

This research is particularly important for countries with relatively low protection of minority investors and where potential for expropriation of minority shareholders by the controlling shareholders is extensive. This expropriation may take various forms, such as misappropriation of investment resources, inflated cost of administration, related-party transactions, use of transfer pricing, assets stripping and other forms of 'tunnelling' of financial resources, assets and revenue from the firms (see La Porta *et al.*, 1998, for an extensive discussion). As a result, the primary agency problem in such an environment is not the failure of professional managers to satisfy the objectives of diffused shareholders, but rather the expropriation of minority shareholders by the large-block shareholders (La Porta *et al.*, 1999b; Shleifer and Vishny, 1997). This opportunistic behaviour would deter outside equity investment and negatively affect the firm's value (Jensen and Meckling, 1976; La Porta *et al.*, 1998; Wruck, 1989). Thus, inadequate legislative and enforcement frameworks may hamper the development of equity markets and may account for the

---

*This research was financed by the European Union ACE-Phare project P98-1048-R.

relative weight of intermediated credit as compared with direct equity financing (LaPorta *et al.*, 1997; Modigliani and Perotti, 1997).

A number of authors suggest that in an environment of low protection of minority shareholders, fixed-claim holders may provide an effective counterbalance to opportunistic behaviour of concentrated owners of cash-flow rights (Hart, 1995b; Jensen, 1986). Debt can provide a hard mechanism in the sense of the need to meet interest payments and bankruptcy procedures, which can be invoked when there is a failure to meet such payments. Banks and other debt-holders may specialize in post-lending monitoring, alleviating problems of the post-contractual opportunism (Boot and Thakor, 1997a and 1997b). This monitoring is part of bank–corporate relationships involving regular information provision, face-to-face meetings, flexible interpretation of covenant breaches, and so on (Holland, 1994; Myers and Majluf, 1984). Finally, institutional theorists suggest that close relationships between banks and industrial enterprises in emerging market economies with relatively underdeveloped capital markets provide enterprises with reliable access to funds for expansion (Khanna and Palepu, 2000). More specifically, 'institutional voids' theory argues that the development of bank-centred industrial groups in emerging markets may compensate for market and legal imperfections that increases the transaction costs of external funding.

However, despite these considerable research advances, the theory of optimal ownership structure depending on the levels of 'private benefits of control' still has a number of conceptual and empirical gaps that require further analysis.

First, the main bulk of studies within the 'law and economics' framework have focused on equity financing, and governance roles of fixed-claim holders and their relationships with dominant shareholders received less attention. While, empirical evidence from developed and emerging market economies indicate that banks may be less then efficient in dealing with the opportunism of managers and controlling owners (Peek and Rosengren, 2005; Tian, 2005; Andersen *et al.*, 2003; Chang, 2003; Chang and Hong, 2000), this chapter makes one step further, offering a novel and simple way of modelling the performance implications of *collusion* between banks and controlling shareholders in the firm.

Second, previous studies are mainly concerned with *ex post* expropriation of minority shareholders by large-block shareowners, that is an expropriation before pro rata distribution of profits on investment. However, opportunistic dominant owners may attempt *ex ante* misappropriation of investment resources before selecting an investment project, and this chapter explores in detail the economic consequences of this type of opportunism.[1]

The chapter is organized as follows. In the next section we provide a review of literature that addresses the effects of 'private benefits of control' on a firm's investment decisions and performance. In the second section, we discuss issues related to concentrated ownership and debt finance within the framework of a simple theoretical model. In the following section we discuss the bank–firm relationship in the context of business groups, and analyse the implications of a possible collusion between fixed-claim holders and concentrated owners of cash-flow rights in terms of 'crowding-out' of entrepreneurial firms from the market of debt financing. To illustrate our arguments, we provide evidence from emerging and transition economies, Russia in particular. Finally, we discuss policy implications and limitations of our study.

Theoretical framework and literature review

Previous research has recognized several possible governance roles for large-block shareholders, some of which are likely to be value-enhancing while others are likely to have negative effects (see Morck *et al.*, 1998; Shleifer and Vishny, 1997, for an extensive discussion).

Both strategy and agency perspectives traditionally focus on analysis of the possible incentive effects associated with concentrated share ownership. Jensen and Meckling (1976), for example, explain how the increase in entrepreneur/manager's cash flow rights constrains the consumption of perquisites and thus produces a positive effect on corporate valuation. Further research suggests that large-block outside ownership may also be an effective counterbalance to managerial opportunism. Companies may have large undiversified shareholders that play a critical leadership and monitoring role. They have both the incentives and the means to restrain the self-serving behaviour of managers (Maug, 1998; McConnel and Servaes, 1990; Zeckhauser and Pound, 1990).

Some researchers, however, have indicated that concentrated shareholding may create entrenchment effects in addition to incentives effects (McConnell and Servaes, 1990; Mikkelson and Partch, 1989; Morck *et al.*, 1988), and, instead of imposing an efficient monitoring and control on managerial discretion, large-block shareholders may produce their own set of agency costs (Pound, 1988; Roe, 1990). Building on this research, a number of authors point out that ownership concentration *per se* may be value-destroying when majority shareholders have the chance to realize private benefits of control at the expense of minority shareholders (Bebchuk, 1994; Stiglitz, 1985), especially when legal protection of minority shareholders is weak. This may be facilitated by specific governance arrangements, like differential voting rights and ownership pyramids (Grossman and Hart, 1988; Harris and Raviv, 1990; La Porta *et al.*, 1998; Almeida and Wolfenzon, 2005), and may take various forms ranging from cash-flow appropriation to asset-stripping through the use of cross-shareholdings and pyramids (La Porta *et al.*, 1998; Almeida and Wolfenzon, 2005).

Therefore, economic effects of concentrated ownership are ambiguous, and they depend on an interplay of factors that effect incentives and entrenchment motives of the dominant owners. On one hand, the willingness of controlling shareholders to expropriate minority investors may be constrained by financial incentives linked with equity ownership by controlling shareholders that enhances their interest in non-distortionary distribution of dividends (Shleifer and Wolfenzon, 2002). On the other hand, when costs of expropriation such as legal manoeuvring, setting up pyramids, risk of prosecution and so on are low due to inadequate legal and regulatory regimes, the entrenchment effect of ownership concentration may prevail leading to higher extraction of benefits (see La Porta *et al.*, 1999b and 2000; Filatotchev *et al.*, 2001, for a discussion).

Other things equal, whether the negative effect of ownership concentration dominates the positive one depends not only on the firm's idiosyncratic characteristics (for example the level of diversity, control systems, and so on), but also on the legal and regulatory environments in a particular country (Doidge *et al.*, 2004). In countries with low legal protection of minority shareholders, one should expect more frequent cases of minority shareholder abuse (La Porta *et al.*, 2000; Filatotchev *et al.*, 2001; La Porta *et al.*, 1999a). As a consequence, equity markets are both larger in terms of the level of capitalization to the GNP and 'deeper' in terms of the development of market infrastructure, in countries with good legal protection of minority shareholders (La Porta *et al.*, 1997, 1999a). Elsewhere, firms have to rely more extensively on retained profits and bank loans as the main means of financing their investment projects (Modigliani and Perotti, 1997; Rajan and Zingales, 1995).

Building on this framework, some researchers suggest that in case of a weak legal and regulatory framework and the large relative weight of intermediated credit to direct equity financing, the relationship governance of either the Japanese or German models may substitute for open capital markets of the US/UK type (Berglöf and Perotti, 1994; Gilson and Roe, 1993; Hoskisson *et al.*, 2004). A number of authors raise the issue of the governance role of debt and debtholders (Hart, 1995b; Jensen, 1986; Both and Deli, 1999; Myers and Majluf, 1984). The literature on financial system architecture puts stress on the monitoring functions of banks, which 'deter borrowers from investing in bad projects' (Boot and Thakor, 1997a: 154). More generally, Hart (2001) and Dewatripont and Tirole (1994) show that there is a complementarity between debt and equity in terms of corporate governance functions.

These aspects of an integrated system of monitoring by banks in the West, may be more important in restraining block-holders' opportunism and enhancing performance than a simple reliance on default. Banks may develop intimate and well-informed relationship with company executives, which facilitate provision of funds for company expansion (Franks and Mayer 1997). This process is particularly suited to the contingency where the firm's activities are opaque to outsiders, either because of high technical complexity (as evidenced, for example, by high levels of R&D expenditure, see Zeckhauser and Pound, 1990; Roe, 1997), or when the firm is crucially dependent upon idiosyncratic personal relationships with clients or suppliers, thus hampering active monitoring by outside investors.

More recent research highlights the role of bank-centred, diversified corporate groups in emerging market economies (see chapter by Okhmatovskiy in this volume). These groups may serve the function of creating a private capital market, where smaller firms have access to finance inside the group (Almeida and Wolfenzon, 2005). Modigliani and Perotti (1997) and Perotti and Gelfer (2001) suggest that the ability of a holding company or 'in-house' bank to capture the benefits from control ensures a steady supply of financing. These groups may also develop long-term relations with lenders to attenuate the risk of moral hazard. Empirical evidence indicates that firms associated with financial *keiretsus* in Japan or South Korean *chaebols* are not as credit-constrained in their investment choices as independent firms (Berglöf and Perotti, 1994; Chang, 2003; Chang and Hong, 2000). Khanna and Palepu's (2000) 'institutional voids' theory suggests that the development of diversified groups in emerging markets may be a response to market and legal imperfections that increase the transaction costs of external funding. More recent studies suggest that monitoring and control associated with relationship banking may help to restrain entrenchment and opportunism of dominant owners, in particular in family controlled, and publicly listed firms (Filatotchev *et al.*, 2005).

Although they provide firms with ready access to funds for expansion, relationship investors have been criticized for personal involvement with executives in failing companies, where 'rescue packages' are the norm (Macey and Miller, 1997). In particular, Harris and Raviv (1990) provide evidence that German banks are reluctant to discipline managers in client companies, especially when they are linked to these companies through a system of cross-shareholding. Banks with board seats and/or shares in a firm have been seen to protect their investments by advocating massive internal cash transfers within German firms into hidden reserves that can be used to smooth declining firm income in a crisis. Even more serious problems have been documented for Japan, where bankruptcies of insolvent companies are delayed by inefficient allocation of credit (Peek and Rosengren, 2005). This amounts to banks forming a coalition with managers to keep down dividends payable to outside shareholders (Baums, 1993).

In addition, there is growing evidence that bank holdings distort investment decisions. For example, Thomas and Waring (1999) report that investment decisions in large, bank-controlled firms in Japan and Germany are influenced more by liquidity considerations than by expected investment returns, as is the case in the USA. Problems with restructuring of South Korean *chaebols* can be used as an example of banks putting good money after bad in a situation when managers are encouraged by family block-holders to spend investment finance on value-destroying diversification projects (Taniura, 1993). Evidence from transition economies such as Russia suggests that banks provide weak governance effects in terms of constraining discretion of controlling shareholders (see chapter by Okhmatovskiy in this volume). Wright *et al.* (2003) attribute this to a possible collusion between banks and incumbent managers who may try to obtain private benefits of control at the expense of minority shareholders. These benefits are ranging from the direct misappropriation of loans by managers to diverting of debt finance to other companies controlled by managers.

Therefore, there is ambiguity concerning the corporate governance effects of fixed-claim holders. While the typical argument is that monitoring offered by banks may prevent the post-contractual opportunism of controlling shareholders, we argue that stronger direct monitoring combined with the threat of bankruptcy sanction enables collusion between banks and controlling stakeholders in firms. This collusion has value-destroying effects since banks may allow extraction of private rents by controlling shareholders, while protecting their interests and being compensated by the higher cost of finance paid by the firm, and, ultimately, by minority shareholders.

To help our understanding of the specific mechanism of this collusion, the next section develops an optimization model which clarifies the main incentive-entrenchment trade-offs faced by the controlling shareholder and the providers of fixed-claim finance. The main objective of this model is to provide an explicit and simple framework outlining various contingency factors that may lead to poor governance and value-destroying strategic decisions. It helps to clarify links between the amount of fixed-claim finance raised, *ex ante* extraction of private benefits and the investment outcomes. By comparing the case of private-benefit extraction with the benchmark case of the entrepreneurial firm, this model also provides a useful framework for an evaluation of efficiency implications and more general structural effects of block-holders' opportunism.

The model

As our benchmark, we consider an entrepreneurial firm that has valuable investment opportunities and no (little) internal financial resources. The firm's investment expenditures I are financed by a perpetuity $L = I$,[2] which will pay an (exogenous) real interest i, where $0 < i < 1$. Both finance and investment relate to period zero. In all future periods, the firm will produce a net revenue $I^\beta - iL$, where β is a productivity parameter, and $0 < \beta < 1$ because of diminishing returns to investment.

The entrepreneur maximizes the net present value of his/her cash flow:

$$\underset{L}{Max}\, V = \int_0^\infty (L^\beta - iL)e^{-rt}\, dt = \frac{L^\beta}{r} - \frac{iL}{r} \tag{8.1}$$

where r is a subjective discount rate, $0 < r < 1$.

The optimum amount of investment is determined by:

$$I^* = L^* = \left(\frac{\beta}{i}\right)^{1/(1-\beta)} \tag{8.2}$$

It is clear that the level of investment (and borrowing) is negatively affected by the prevailing interest rate (i), and positively affected by productivity (β). This investment project generates positive net revenue that is appropriated by the owner-entrepreneur.

Now, let us consider a joint-stock company with a dominant shareholder who owns a percentage of voting shares, λ, where $0 \leqslant \lambda \leqslant 1$. In an environment of low protection of minority shareholders' rights, the dominant shareholder is able to extract the control premium s, and we define s as the share of the fixed-claim finance L that can be appropriated before investment I ($0 \leqslant s \leqslant L$). The specific characteristics of these 'private benefits of control' s may vary with the identity of the dominant owner. If corporate control remains with employees, these benefits are consumed as wage income or the employee welfare provisions (Filatotchev *et al.*, 1996). Managers may misappropriate part of loan finance (L) to inflate administration cost, maximize their perks, or use various 'tunnelling' schemes to re-direct loans to outside companies under their control. The same relates to outside owners. For example, family owners may consider the firm as a source of their personal wealth, and they may divert externally provided finance to satisfy family members demands such as high levels of individual compensation (Filatotchev *et al.*, 2005). What is important is that all these actions will decrease the net present value of the firm. In this case, I is no longer equal to L ($I = L - s$).

However, the expropriation of minority shareholders may be costly, since the controlling shareholder has to engage in legal manoeuvring to divert finance, such as setting up intermediary companies, facing legal challenges, taking risks of being fined, and so on. Therefore, the net private benefits of control are given by $s - c(s)$, where an expropriation cost function $c(s)$ has the following properties:

$$c_s(s) > 0, \qquad c_{ss}(s) > 0, \qquad c(0) = 0$$

If $c(s) = 0$ for all s, we have a completely inefficient legal system. The opposite case is where the expropriation cost is high. If $c(s) \geqslant s$ for all s, the extraction of private benefits of control is no longer an attractive opportunity and we are back to the benchmark case of the entrepreneurial firm.

In a general case, the firm solves the following optimization problem:

$$\underset{L,s}{\text{Max}} \; \varphi = s - c(s) + \lambda V = s - c(s) + \lambda \int_0^\infty [(L-s)^\beta - iL]e^{-rt}\, dt = s - c(s) + \frac{\lambda(L-s)^\beta}{r} - \frac{\lambda iL}{r}$$

$$(8.3)$$

subject to constraint: $iL - (L-s)^\beta \leqslant 0$

The Kuhn–Tucker conditions for a maximum become:

$$\frac{\lambda\beta(L-s)^{\beta-1}}{r} - \frac{\lambda i}{r} - \mu i + \mu\beta(L-s)^{\beta-1} = 0 \qquad\qquad (8.3a)$$

$$-\frac{\lambda\beta(L-s)^{\beta-1}}{r}+1-c_s(s)-\mu\beta(L-s)^{\beta-1}=0 \tag{8.3b}$$

$$\mu[iL-(L-s)^{\beta}]=0 \tag{8.3c}$$

$$iL-(L-s)^{\beta}\leq 0 \tag{8.3d}$$

The positive expropriation costs create a trade-off between (net) private benefits of control and profits (shared with minority shareholders). As a result, it is likely that the non-negative profit constraint is not binding ($\mu=0$), and for this case we obtain an equilibrium solution for s:

$$c_s(s^*)=1-\frac{\lambda i}{r} \tag{8.4}$$

The left-hand side represents the marginal cost of present consumption of the private benefits of control. The right-hand side represents the marginal benefits of switching consumption from future periods to the present. This enables important comparative statics results. In particular, the extraction of private benefits of control decreases with ownership concentration, since:

$$s^*_\lambda=-\frac{i}{rc_{ss}(s^*)}<0 \tag{8.5}$$

This is a counterpart of the Jensen and Meckling (1976) analysis of the incentive effect of concentrated entrepreneurial ownership on the consumption of perquisites (see Shleifer and Wolfenzon, 2002, for a detailed discussion). Similarly, the private benefits of control are lower when interest rate is high, as it makes expropriation relatively more expensive in terms of future financial costs:

$$s^*_i=-\frac{\lambda}{rc_{ss}(s^*)}<0 \tag{8.6}$$

This expression sheds a new light on the economic effects of relationship banking in economies where minority shareholders are open to abuses by controlling owners. In situations when the dominant owner has close relationship with banks or when the dominant shareholder and provider of finance are the same institution, one may expect a reduction in cost of finance i. However, this reduction will be accompanied by an increase in inefficiency and expropriation of minority shareholders.[3] We will return to the implications of this finding in the discussion section.

As our model shows, a higher (subjective) discount rate results in higher benefits of control since:

$$s_r^* = -\frac{\lambda i}{r^2 c_{ss}(s^*)} > 0 \tag{8.7}$$

This result is also important, as the subjective discount rate may differ with both the owner's perception of risk in the environment and with the identity of owners. The first effect is well-illustrated by the chapter by Kuznetsov *et al.* in this volume. An exemplification of the second effect may relate to the difference between insiders (employee- and manager-owners) as opposed to outside investors.[4] An increase in opportunism associated with insider ownership is well-documented in previous research with respect to equity finance (for example Blanchard and Aghion, 1996; Filatotchev *et al.*, 1996; Frydman *et al.*, 1996; Morck *et al.*, 1988), and our model suggests that this may be a more general phenomenon.

Using equation (8.4) we can obtain the optimal level of finance from the point of view of the dominant owner:

$$L^{**} = \left(\frac{\beta}{i}\right)^{\frac{1}{1-\beta}} + s^* = I^* + s^* \tag{8.8}$$

This equation clearly demonstrates that the firm will choose the same investment project I^* as the entrepreneurial firm. However, it is in the interests of the dominant owner to increase the volume of finance beyond the investment needs in order to obtain private benefits of control at the expense of net profits, which s/he has otherwise to share with the minority shareholders. It means that a smaller proportion of debt funding is (efficiently) invested, as compared to the benchmark model, that is:

$$L^{**} > L^* \quad \text{and therefore} \quad \frac{I^{*\beta}}{L^{**}} < \frac{I^{*\beta}}{L^*} \tag{8.9}$$

These arguments may have important implications on both micro- and macro-economic levels in countries where banks are involved in a complex web of relationships with industrial firms, and where the interests of minority shareholders are not adequately protected. As our model shows, the economic return on debt financing in the firm with an opportunistic dominant owner is lower then in the entrepreneurial firm. This research framework may shed new lights on economic effects of the relationship banking, in particular within financial-industrial groups in emerging markets. In addition, the dominant owner's attempts to increase the volume of finance beyond the investment needs in order to obtain private benefits of control may lead to structural problems in countries with underdeveloped capital markets and limited financial resources available to firms. In the next section we use our conceptual framework to reevaluate recent trends of firm- and industry-level developments in transition economies.

Discussion and empirical evidence

Unlike previous research that focused on equity financing, we suggest that the dominant owner 'control premium' can be obtained even when the firm relies on intermediated forms of funding, or in fact, may be even more likely in the latter case. Moreover, it appears that the ownership concentration effects do not depend on the identity of the large-block shareholder. These findings are consistent with the proposition that at a high level of concentration the distinction between insiders and outsiders becomes blurred, and blockholders may have strong incentives to divert resources in ways that make them better off, at the expense of other shareholders (Wruck, 1989). Our research, however, suggests that the extent of the expropriation may be contingent on a decision-making horizon of the controlling shareholders, and the insiders' short-termism contributes to opportunistic behaviour. More specifically, an ability of the dominant shareholder to extract *ex ante* private benefits is followed by a less-efficient use of financial resources compared to an entrepreneurial firm as clearly indicated by the inequality (8.9). At the same time, a diversion of financial resources to private use is accompanied by relative higher payments to the fixed-claim holders (that is, $iL^{**} > iL^{*}$) that represents a direct transfer of wealth from the minority shareholders and depresses the firm's value. As long as debt is regularly serviced, this expropriation is carried out with 'silent approval' by the fixed-claim holders who turn a blind eye to the opportunistic behaviour of a dominant shareholder. In a Modigliani–Miller framework, the value of a share is the discounted value of the stream of its pro rata dividends; the method of financing and allocation of control being irrelevant. Our results demonstrate that fixed-claim holders may (implicitly) collude with large-block shareholder who is able to extract a 'control premium' at expense of minority shareholders, with subsequent detrimental effects in terms of the firm's value.

Thus, our model shows that governance roles of debt may not be as straightforward as previous research suggests (Aghion and Bolton 1992; Berglöf, 1990; Klein *et al.*, 1978; Jensen, 1986; Myers and Majluf, 1984), in particular when dominant shareholders have enough power to extract *ex ante* benefits of control. Although ownership concentration creates substantial agency costs for minority shareholders, the opportunistic behaviour of controlling owners is not restricted by debtholders, as long as the firm does not default on its debt servicing payments. This bodes well for most recent research that has questioned the ability and incentives of providers of intermediated finance, and banks in particular, to monitor and interfere with the firm-level strategic and operating decisions (Holland, 1994). For example, banks may collude with controlling parties concerning preferences for profit retention over distributing dividends (Baums, 1993). High retention reduces the risk that the company will default on its outstanding debt (this problem has been discussed with respect to German banks in Nunnenkamp, 1996). In addition, research on the roles of banks in transition economies suggests that over-exposure of financial institutions to loans to large enterprises created a 'systemic failure' when banks and managers were trying to obtain rents at expense of shareholders (Saunders and Sommariva, 1993).

A closely related issue is the analysis of governance roles of 'relationship investors' within bank-centred, diversified corporate groups. This analysis has become particularly important in the context of those emerging market economies where financial markets are characterized by a lack of adequate disclosure and weak corporate governance (see McGee in this volume). Within the framework of the 'institutional void' theory, Khanna and Palepu (2000) suggest that relatively high transaction costs imply that the enterprise can often be better off as part of a large diversified business group. This group may effectively internalise ineffective markets, including capital markets, in particular when the group members are associated with a main bank through the web of cross-shareholding (La Porta *et al.*, 1997; Macey and Miller, 1997; Modigliani and Perotti, 1997). In addition to the reduction of finance costs, banks-shareholders may provide other services that may be vital to the firm, in particular when it is experiencing financial distress. For example, Berglöf (1990) emphasizes the role of commercial banks as reorganization specialists in those systems with pronounced alliance groups. However, the role of banks as shareholders provides obvious incentives for banks to behave opportunistically as a result of their multiple roles and access to information: banks may handle the accounts of companies and thus be intimately aware of their cash-flow positions, while at the same time offering their services as investment brokers, management consultants and agents in corporate finance, seeking funds for the company abroad. While these multiple roles offer significant economies of scope, other shareholders may be disadvantaged, as bank-shareholders may have too much influence within the firm (Coffee, 1991). And, in a more general perspective, it is not the balance of power between banks and non-financial corporations, but the potential of opportunistic behaviour at cost of non-related minority shareholders that matters. In this respect, a system where non-financial corporations have very strong influence on banks, not *vice versa* (see Okhmatovskiy in this volume), may produce similar outcomes.

Our model provides a clear illustration to these arguments. Let us assume that the 'relationship' bank provides a loan L to the firm at preferential interest rate $i' < i$. From equation (8.8) it follows that this reduction in the costs of finance will be accompanied by an increase in investment I^*, in line with the 'institutional void' theory. However, as (8.6) clearly indicates, a reduction in i will lead to an increase in private benefits of control s^*. Moreover, if the fixed-claim holder is at the same time a dominant shareholder, as it usually happens within bank-centred business groups, then s/he has a direct incentive to expropriate minority shareholders by diverting part of L to his/her private use.

Without effective 'firewalls' between lending and investment departments, a bank with a shareholding in a client firm may have less incentive to monitor the firm's investment decisions (Dittus and Prowse, 1996), and this would reduce the costs of expropriation $c(s)$. As a result, relational banking may increase expropriation of minority shareholders.

Our research may help to re-assess recent evidence associated with rapid development of financial-industrial groups (FIGs) in transition economies. A particularly characteristic exemplification of this trend is the oil & gas and telecommunication industries in Russia, which are dominated by holding companies such as Gazprom, Sibneft, Tyumen Oil Company (TNK) and Yukos (before it found itself on a collision course with the Russian government). These companies are fixing the borders of their empires through intra-holding consolidations, mergers and single-share swaps. They are also characterized by concentrated ownership. Moreover, outside shareholders in each of them have suffered a dilution of their holdings, at different stages and to various degrees. As a result, many industries in Russia have also experienced a rapid development of FIGs, which very often are actively trying to fend off pressure for their members to restructure, and sometimes become simply a vehicle for creating pyramidal ownership structures. La Porta *et al.* (1999a) and Almeida and Wolfenzon (2005) suggest that these structures can be used by controlling shareholders to make existing shareholders pay the costs, but not share all the benefits, of new ventures. Perotti and Gelfer (2001) provide empirical evidence from Russia that suggests that, although members of FIGs have easier access to investment finance, the extent of their restructuring and performance is lower that non-group firms. Our conceptual framework may help to provide further explanations to these findings.

In addition, the model's findings may have implications for the analysis of structural imbalances in transition economies on a sectoral level. More specifically, a possible collusion between the dominant owners and providers of debt (or a passive acceptance by debt-holders the fact that the dominant owner is abusing its power at expense of minority shareholders) can also create serious resource constraints for the development of entrepreneurial firms (see also the chapter by Mickiewicz in this volume). Let us assume that both the entrepreneurial firm and the joint-stock firm with a dominant owner have the same investment opportunity, I^*, but the credit available to them is limited to $2L^*$. Even if we assume that the credit rating of both firms is the same, the *relationship* bank would consider lending to the affiliated joint-stock firm as a priority. However, this firm will borrow $L^{**} > L^*$, since the dominant shareholder wants to extract the control premium from the loan. As a result, the entrepreneurial firm would end up with a lesser amount of finance that is not sufficient to fund its investment project. Effectively, it is 'crowded-out' from the financial market by its counterpart. Our model directly links the extent of crowding out to the scale of the expropriation of minority shareholders in the environment where their interests are not protected by legal or reputational considerations.

The lack of funding is a particularly serious disadvantage for the emergence and growth of *de novo* firms in emerging market economies, for which internal funds are limited and external finance is, therefore, essential. The results of a set of enterprise surveys conducted by the World Bank in Hungary, the Czech and Slovak republics, Poland and Russia investigating the obstacles faced by small and medium enterprises (SMEs) suggest that credit constraints constitute one of the main barriers to growth of SMEs (Pissarides, 1999). As Table 8.1 indicates, the entrepreneurial sector accounts for a relatively small share of GDP in a vast majority of transition economies, and in the former Soviet Union in

Table 8.1   The legal environment and the development of the entrepreneurial sector

Country	Size of entrepreneurial sector, 1997 (% of GDP)	Cost of loan financing, 1996[a]	Legal transition indicator: financial regulations 1998[b]
Central Eastern Europe and Baltic States			
Albania	50	n/a	2- (1.7)
Bulgaria	40	27	3 (3.0)
Croatia	45	n/a	3 (3.0)
Czech Republic	30	7.2	3 (3.0)
Estonia	50	−3	3 (3.0)
Hungary	45	9.7	4 (4.0)
Latvia	50	4	3 (3.0)
Lithuania	40	9.3	3- (2.7)
Macedonia	40	n/a	2 (2.0)
Poland	50	3.1	4- (3.7)
Romania	35	31.2	3- (2.7)
Slovakia	25	10.2	3- (2.7)
Slovenia	45	15.1	3 (3.0)
Commonwealth of Independent States			
Armenia	35	n/a	2 (2.0)
Azerbaijan	25	n/a	2- (1.7)
Belarus	10	35	1 (1.0)
Georgia	25	n/a	1 (1.0)
Kazakhstan	20	n/a	2 (2.0)
Kyrgyzstan	35	n/a	2 (2.0)
Moldova	20	34	2 (2.0)
Russia	20	27	3- (2.7)
Tajikistan	15	n/a	1 (1.0)
Turkmenistan	15	n/a	1 (1.0)
Ukraine	30	25	2 (2.0)
Uzbekistan	30	n/a	2- (1.7)

Notes: [a] The cost of lending is calculated as the difference between the market lending rate to SMEs and consumer price inflation. [b] Numbers in brackets represent our mapping of the EBRD indicators into numbers.
Sources: The measure of financial regulation quality taken from EBRD (1999a), Table 2.2.2. The size of the 'enterpreneurial sector' taken from Johnson *et al.* (1997), Appendix 3. Data on cost of loan financing from Pissarides (1999).

particular. This table also shows that entrepreneurial firms suffer from penalizing real rates of interest on loan finance compared to their larger counterparts. Similarly, results presented by Mickiewicz in this volume demonstrate that the role of new entrepreneurial firms differ significantly among the transition economies.

In our model, the extent of the crowding-out effect directly depends on the costs of expropriation of minority shareholders, the latter being predominantly determined by the legal and competitive environment in a particular country (Doidge *et al.*, 2004; Filatotchev *et al.*, 2001; La Porta *et al.*, 2000; see also McGee in this volume). Therefore, the quality of the legal system may impact not only on the development of equity markets, as has been indicated in previous research; it should also affect the development of the entrepreneurial firms. Figure 8.1 clearly supports this assumption by showing strong and significant correlation between the size of the entrepreneurial sector in various transition economies and the 'legal transition indicators (financial regulations)' developed by the EBRD. Countries with the least developed and most volatile legal environment, such as Belarus, Central Asian countries and Caucasian republics, have relatively small entrepreneurial sectors compared to Poland and the Baltic states. Russia and Ukraine are somewhere in between. Although the governments of these two countries have introduced a comprehensive set of laws regulating firms and financial markets, there are widespread problems with law enforcement, and this fact is reflected in the EBRD indicators (EBRD, 1999a).

Obviously, there may be other factors affecting the development of the entrepreneurial sector in a transition economy. In particular, Johnson *et al.*

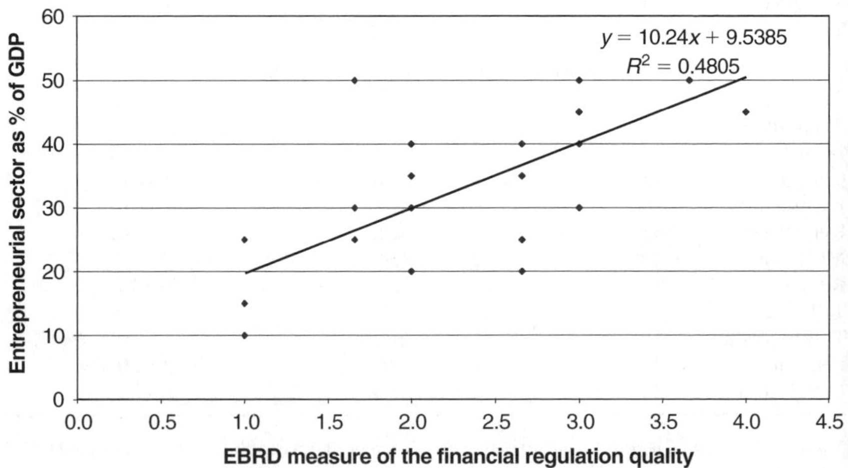

Figure 8.1   The quality of financial regulations and the size of the entrepreneurial sector in GDP.

(1997) argue that new entrepreneurs face a choice between operating in official or unofficial sectors, and inadequate legal protection creates incentives to move into the 'shadow economy'. Without denying these arguments, we suggest that there also may be an important indirect role of governance factors, since a distorted legal environment creates incentives for banks to collude with dominant owners in the large-size firms and to overextend finance to this sector at expense of entrepreneurial firms.

Policy implications

Our analysis leads to one obvious policy recommendation, that is to improve the legal environment in countries with a low protection of minority shareholders so as to make their expropriation more difficult (La Porta *et al.*, 1999a; OECD, 1999a; Hay *et al.*, 1996). The quality and evolution of corporate governance regulations is analysed in detail by McGee in this volume.

However, La Porta *et al.* (1999a) indicate that controlling shareholders generally do not support the legal reform that would enhance minority rights, and typically lobby against it. Protracted and slow reforms imply that the probability of abuses of minority shareholders in the future remain high. In many developing and emerging market economies, political links between enterprises, especially large holding companies, banks and all levels of the state are still very strong, and a deliberately inadequate legislative framework may also be a result of rent-seeking behaviour of politicians who have strong formal and informal relations with powerful shareholders (Modigliani and Perotti, 1997). More recently, the Russian authorities orchestrated the dismantling of oil group Yukos and the transfer of its assets to the state-controlled Rossneft (see Adachi in this volume). At the same time, state ownership in the largest Russian business group, Gazprom, has been increased to 51 per cent (see Adachi in this volume). If the Russian authorities are to follow the OECD guidelines, legal and regulatory reforms would need to be considerably more radical in nature, and address not only corporate governance problems but also such issues as competition policy, taxation, accounting standards, and so on. In addition to the equity markets, 'good corporate governance' rules should also include providers of debt, in particular when they are involved in a web of cross-share ownership with client firms. Similarly, recent evidence from China (Tian, 2005) suggests that ownership and finance architectures based on networks of firms with significant state shareholdings and state banks offering fixed-claim finance may result in particularly inefficient outcomes.

Limitations

Because of the simplified nature of our model, this chapter has not addressed several important issues that might be pursued in future research. First, we have treated ownership concentration as exogenous and do not address the issue of what affects ownership concentration for a given firm. A number of authors have suggested that firm characteristics such as size, industry, location and so on may determine its ownership structure (Demsetz and Lehn, 1985; Jensen and Warner, 1988; Demsetz and Villalonga, 2001; Bishop *et al.*, 2002). In other words, a firm's ownership structure is an equilibrium response to an individual firm's operating characteristics and its competitive environment, and parameter λ may be endogenous. Still, an application of the exogenous case as in our simple model is justified by the characteristics of many emerging markets where conditions are transient; that is, far from an equilibrium, the distribution of share ownership may be a result of 'non-equivalent' transfers of ownership titles through various privatization schemes, and markets for corporate control are not working efficiently (Mickiewicz and Bałtowski, 2003; see also the chapters by Andreff and by Mickiewicz in this volume).

Second, equity ownership does not necessarily equate with control of the firm (see Short, 1994, for a comprehensive survey of the relevant literature). Therefore, on both a theoretical and empirical level it is very important to learn how concentrated shareholders may develop an ability to extract the control premium, and what channels of influence they normally use (on the latter theme, see Okhmatovskiy in this volume). In this regard, the evidence coming from emerging market economies is still sketchy and incomplete, and both the investment community and regulatory authorities might benefit from research in this area.

Conclusions

Despite its limitations, this study lends further support for the case of strong regulatory and capital market institutions and effective enforcement of 'good corporate governance' rules, especially concerning the protection of minority shareholders. So far, most studies of corporate governance problems have focused on issues related to the consequences of opportunistic behaviour of insiders and their opposition to outside control. Our research shows that the protection of minority shareholders from blockholders' opportunism is as important for enterprise restructuring and development of an efficient system of corporate governance as protection against entrenched management. More importantly, we extend this conclusion to the environment where debt finance is predominant and equity finance plays a minor role. We have demonstrated that in such an environment, fixed-claim finance, instead of alleviating the agency problems, may lead to (implicit) collusion between dominant owners and financial institutions and to efficiency distortions.

Notes

1   So far, an *ex ante* misappropriation of investment funds and a possible collusion between fixed claim holders and controlling shareholders have been analysed in the context of 'looting' (Akerlof and Romer 1993; Cull *et al.*, 2002). This framework

describes an expropriation of ultimate providers of funds such as bank depositors, the government, etc., which eventually leads to a firm's bankruptcy.

2   We model finance this way for the sake of simplicity. It can be interpreted as an issue of a bond with a fixed yield and indefinite maturity (i.e. perpetuity). Another interpretation is that the finance for the investment project is raised through a new line of credit (say, where investment relates to the working capital necessary to initiate new operations). However, the model can be easily expanded to a situation when the firm obtains a term loan.

3   Tian (2005) provides empirical evidence from China that supports these arguments.

4   Recent empirical evidence consistent with this effect is provided in Faleye *et al.* (2005).

Part IV

Concentrated Ownership and Performance

9
Ownership Structure and Corporate Governance in Russian Firms

*Andrei Kuznetsov, Olga Kuznetsova and Rostislav Kapelyushnikov**

Introduction

Historically, all (post-)industrialized countries of the world have been accumulating experience in organizing, running and controlling corporations over a long period of time. As a result a variety of national systems of corporate governance has evolved. All of them represent a set of processes, customs, policies, laws and institutions affecting the way a corporation is directed, administered and controlled. In Russia the formation of the modern system of corporate governance has not followed this evolutionary pattern. In fact, it had emerged in the course of a profound institutional revolution of the early 1990s, which had as its core element the restoration of private property. As a result, the history of corporate governance in the country is not only short but is also punctuated by dramatic transformations: events, which elsewhere might have taken decades to unfold, have been compressed in time under the pressure of fast and sweeping reforms.

In modern society the system of corporate governance is responsible for reassuring individual investors that the money they invest in a public company will be handled with due care by the management of the company, so that the interests of investors are protected. Seen in this perspective, corporate governance presents itself as one of the fundamental institutes of modern Western democracy, acting as a guarantor of sustainable economic growth (Sullivan, 2003). The situation is different in Russia. More than ten years in the making, the Russian system of corporate governance remains a controversial construct as far as its conceptual foundations, features, efficiency and future are concerned. There is a sizable gap between the real assets of firms and market capitalization,[1] indicating that corporate governance is not a well-established institution and investors are preoccupied with the safety of their money.

---

*The authors acknowledge the contribution of Natalia Demina to the preparation of the statistical materials used in this chapter.

The importance of corporate governance, and market institutions in general, was not fully appreciated during the early stages of market reforms. As a result, corporations were to cope with incomplete institutional settings and the extreme politicization of economic policy-making; economic efficiency has been slow to materialize. It took a better part of the 1990s for both academics and politicians to appreciate the centrality of the institutional aspects of reforms and identify corporate governance as one of the central elements responsible for the success of transition (Stiglitz, 2002).

In this chapter we will be looking at the forces that have determined the development, shape and performance of the system of corporate governance in Russia in the period following the collapse of communism, in an attempt to evaluate the strengths and weaknesses of the national system of corporate governance in Russia in the context of post-communist reforms and identify those crucial issues that need to be addressed in order to increase the effectiveness of this system. Our analysis is based on a variety of sources. Original data come mostly from the regular microeconomic surveys organized by the Russian Economic Barometer (REB), an independent research centre located in Moscow. REB's respondents are executive managers of 500 industrial enterprises, 300 agricultural firms and 150 banks in almost all regions of Russia. From 1995, every two years REB conduct specialized surveys dedicated to the issues of ownership and corporate governance, effectively covering the period from the completion of the Mass Privatization Programme upto the present. Usually, the studies of corporate governance in Russia focus on the so-called 'blue chip' firms, a rather small group of super-large firms operating in oil extraction and other lucrative industries. By contrast, REB respondents represent the hard core of Russian firms, average in size and every other respect, that enjoy no exclusivity but remain the backbone of the national economy. Utilizing this data-set we supplement our discussion of corporate governance in Russia with new results on the link between the concentration of ownership and performance. We find that both ownership concentration and insider ownership (the latter: more ambiguously) affect performance negatively. We link the results to our institutional analysis.

Corporate governance and a national context

Western practice offers more than one proven model of corporate governance, each of which has emerged as a result of an evolutionary process in response to the requirements of a particular national environment (Potthof, 1996; La Porta *et al.*, 1997). A recent discussion on comparative advantages of various models (Hart, 1995a; De Jong, 1997; Milgrom and Roberts, 1992; Shleifer and Vishny, 1997; Yoshimori, 1995) has nominated no clear winner. Every system has its pros and cons but, as Moerland (1995) infers, it is impossible to say that one system is better than another on theoretical grounds as the optimization of economic organization leaves room for multiple configurations. This claim is echoed by Rozman (2000) who, having compared Anglo-Saxon and Germanic systems, reaches a conclusion that both systems are logical and in harmony within themselves despite being different.

The fact that national systems of corporate governance are products of historical circumstances, that is that they have been influenced by cultural, political and socio-economic factors specific to age and nation, has important consequences for countries like Russia in which the progress of capitalism was interrupted with a period when the economy was based on public property and central planning. Reformers tried to catch up by transplanting foreign (Anglo-American in the case of Russia) models of corporate law, but this did not bring the expected results. Whilst it is possible to try and import conceptual and statutory underpinnings of corporate governance wholesale from the West, it is not possible to recreate the circumstances under which they have emerged. Attempts to transfer best practices inevitably create a number of immediate and long-term problems related to adaptation and interpretation of utilisable concepts.[2] In Russia the elements of corporate governance that were set in place during and immediately after privatization were rather artificial constructs implanted by the state which at that time was under the control of political forces who saw it as their priority to change the economic landscape of the country in such a radical way that the restoration of the Soviet regime would become impossible. Consequently arrangements regarding corporate governance were not the product of an evolutionary process prioritizing efficiency, but rather the implementation of a certain political agenda. What followed was that these elements were soon found coexisting and sometimes in competition with other elements that were emerging out of the everyday practice of corporate relations as they were evolving in the national economy. The conflict between the norms and rules imposed from above and the motivation of the economic agents has been increasingly identified as a determining factor of the development of corporate governance practice in Russia (Yakovlev, 2004). Considering the depth and breadth of changes through which the Russian economy and political system have been going since the beginning of 1990s, this conflict is a reflection of some extreme pressures to which the institutional system in the country has found itself exposed. This pressure is vividly illustrated by the design, speed, scale and the manner of implementation of privatization, which was very unique and, not surprisingly, its impact on society and economy was profound and various.

The allocation of property

During 1992–2003, over 141,500 enterprises were privatized, of which 31,200 became joint-stock companies (Goskomstat, 2003). From the point of view of its impact on corporate governance Russian privatization had one definitive feature – it concentrated the majority of corporate shares in the hands of insiders: managers and workers.[3] The ownership structure that originally emerged was far from equilibrium; the authors of privatization saw the speed and breadth of the chosen model of privatization as its main advantage and hoped that market forces would soon urge a more efficient redistribution of ownership through a secondary market (Chubais and Vishnevskaya, 1993). Yet the bias in the allocation of shares has remained a feature of the Russian corporate system ever since privatization: according to data collected by the Russian Economic Barometer (REB), as late as 2003 insiders remained the largest group of shareholders, controlling 47 per cent of all outstanding shares. This does not mean, though, that the configuration of shareholding had remained unaltered during this period. In reality, it experienced some sharp and pronounced changes. Data by REB indicate that as much as 15 per cent of shares were changing hands between the shareholders (managers v. workers; insiders v. outsiders) in a typical Russian firm every year between 1995 and 2003. The redistribution of shares proceeded according to the following pattern: ownership shifted from workers to managers; from insiders to outsiders; and from the state to private owners (Table 9.1). Top managers have come out as the biggest winners, having secured possession on average of 31 per cent of all shares. According to REB data, already by 2003 in an average industrial firm the managers had accumulated more shares than the rest of employees, whose original share was over 44 per cent; by 2007 they are expected to control 40 per cent of all shares against 14 per cent held by other employees.

The participation of outsiders has also increased, although not as much as could have been expected. Currently, according to REB, outsiders on average control 41 per cent of the capital of a typical firm, which is about as much as controlled by insiders. The important, feature of the emerging ownership structure is that the majority of outsiders are industrial firms and individuals. The share of banks, financial companies and investment funds

Table 9.1   Ownership allocation within Russian firms based on REB survey results

	1995	1997	1999	2001	2003	2005	2007 (forecast)
Insiders, total	54.8	52.1	46.2	48.2	46.2	46.6	54.0
Managers	11.2	15.1	14.7	21.0	25.6	31.5	40.0
Employees	43.6	37.0	31.5	27.2	21.0	15.1	14.0
Outsiders, total	35.2	38.8	42.4	39.7	44.8	41.0	40.1
Non-financial outsiders, total	25.9	28.5	32.0	32.4	35.6	33.5	29.3
individual investors	10.9	13.9	18.5	21.1	20.1	18.0	15.0
other firms	15.0	14.6	13.5	11.3	15.5	15.5	14.3
Financial outsiders, total	9.3	10.3	10.4	7.3	9.2	7.5	9.8
The state	9.1	7.4	7.1	7.9	4.3	7.3	4.1
Other shareholders	0.9	1.7	4.3	4.2	4.9	5.2	2.8
Total	100	100	100	100	100	100	100
Number of firms	136	135	156	154	104	108	71

remains stable and low at about 10 per cent. Foreign participation is also very low: only one in nine firms has shareholders from abroad. When there is a stake owned by a foreign party it tends to be rather high at the average figure of 43 per cent of the authorized stock (Dolgopiatova, 2004). We will be investigating possible explanations for these structural peculiarities later on, but first we need to highlight the impact that the Russian model of privatization has had on some aspects of corporate governance in the country.

Corporate governance and the national business environment

Privatization had transferred state-owned enterprises into joint-stock companies almost overnight, which had multiple consequences at different levels. To begin with, new corporations inherited the operational profile, the structure of assets and employment from their predecessors, state-owned enterprises. Among other things this meant that some of these corporations were extremely artificial entities from the point of view of market efficiency. By contrast to market-driven buy-outs, in Russia 'buy-outs' were imposed on insiders by the government whether or not there were resources to make new firms viable. In fact, many companies were doomed from the outset. Commonly for the insiders becoming owners was not so much the issue of increasing efficiency and returns as preserving their employment and income in an adverse and uncertain environment.

Ownership transformation coincided with a period of a profound economic crisis in the country, which had as its most notable manifestations demonetization and barterization of the economy. This had a long-lasting impact on corporate governance by diluting the strength of monetary signals and incentives, and distorting their message. It was very difficult for both shareholders and investors to make a distinction between well-managed firms and badly managed firms on the basis of their financial accounts, to determine the value of shares or identify the investment potential of individual corporations. Open market competition for financial resources was unfeasible and the investment markets were extremely depressed.

These circumstances created incentives for substituting networking and other informal arrangements for the market. Managers had to rely on successful networking as they sought to compensate the poor performance of formal institutions with arrangements based on personal contacts. The role of networks was controversial. On the one hand, informal relations provided means to create zones of trust within the general environment of distrust, thus reducing transaction costs. On the other hand, in the context of economic crises and weak institutional arrangements, networking often pursued the goal of conspiring against outsiders and avoiding legal control over financial and other transactions, rather than getting better knowledge of business partners and their needs (Radaev, 1998).

The striving of business networks to resolve 'problems' internally often created costs for the society in the form of poor disclosure of information, price fixing, tax evasion and so on. Together with other consequences of privatization, the proliferation of informal networks affects the character of market relations in the country. The atmosphere was charged with the sensation of abounding opportunities for quick and easy enrichment due to the corporate control vacuum that was left by the dismantling of the socialist state. A direct outcome of these ambiguous circumstances was disregard to generally recognized behavioural rules designed to induce collaborative conduct in the modern society. As the moral standards of business deteriorated, the criminalization of the economy intensified.

New points of reference required

The distinctive realities of the Russian business environment of the post-privatization period makes it ill-suited to scrutinize the corporate sphere in the country exclusively or predominantly in terms and within the framework of conceptions developed with mature market economies in mind, or using the latter as the point of reference. The singularity of the Russian case begins to reveal itself already at the fundamental level of relations between managers and investors in joint-stock companies. To begin with, in the Russian context shareholders are not necessarily the same as investors as property rights were mostly appropriated through a give-away distribution rather than bought or sold. The privatization process had some similarities with insider buy-outs, but in fact was radically different as the acquisition of property by insiders in the course of mandatory privatization represented an entirely peculiar type of action in terms of motivation, objectives and rationale and therefore was utterly unlike anything ever assumed by standard corporate governance models (Kuznetsov and Kuznetsova, 2003).

Corporate governance also had to account to the fact that barterization, weak financial markets, rampant inflation, criminalization of economy seriously undermined the impact of standard financial instruments of control whilst at the same time forcing both investors and managers to develop aversion to long-term financial and business commitments. Overall, the specificities of the post-privatization era signified that the newly-created shareholders were lacking, in terms of accepted theory, some central characteristics that were necessary to regard them as the primary constituent of the firm. Traditionally shareholders are singled out as most likely to behave towards a corporation as 'responsible owners' because of a combination of economic risk and remuneration associated with tying up certain assets in a particular type of investment that they experience (McAlister *et al.*, 2003). This assumption, however, does not really work in Russia. Privatization favoured, at least formally, one particular group of the population, the employees and managers of state owned enterprises: once privatization was completed, only half of firms had shareholders-outsiders who in total owned no more than 10 per cent of all outstanding shares. Even in the early 2000s, as we demonstrated earlier, managers and workers remained the largest groups of shareholders.[4] Individually the majority of shareholders are in possession of only an insignificant block of shares. By acquiring then they did not take any additional risk, but equally the prospect of remuneration was quite illusory considering the economic situation in the country. Throughout the post-privatization period shareholding did not bring any real benefits to most share-holders as shares had low liquidity and dividends were not paid. On top of that the capital market was not functioning well. As a consequence the necessary prerequisites for 'responsible' behaviour were missing and small shareholders-insiders were motivated more by their interests as stakeholders-employees, that is in maintaining the viability of their organizations, then as investors-shareholders. Shareholders-outsiders were involved even less because they soon found that, post-privatization, small blocks of shares were almost worthless (Kuznetsov and Kuznetsova, 2001; Atanasov, 2002; Dolgopiatova, 2004).

Thus, the bulk of shareholders in Russia obtained ownership rights without injecting any capital of their own and had few incentives and few opportunities to exercise their property rights. This not only creates conceptual difficulties for corporate governance modelling,[5] but, more importantly, has some serious practical implications. According to some estimates, nearly 70 per cent of property has been left without effective ownership control by genuine owners.[6] The capital market as the backbone of the mechanism of ownership control was and still is quite weak. Of hundreds of tradable stocks, only about 30 large issues see some trading. With little or no activity in most issues, the disciplinary function of the securities markets is next to paralyzed.

Managerial capitalism?

Although there is a link between the general apathy of small shareholders and the circumstances under which they acquired their shares, the fact that there has been no mechanism in place on which they can rely for exercising and defending their rights of ownership is even more consequential. As our analysis of the business environment has demonstrated, the capital market struggles to fulfil most of its functions like providing information and incentives based on the economic performance of firms or supporting shareholders' rights of exit as a measure disciplining managers. Any campaign to restraint managers (a proxy fight, for example) would require resources and persistence that most of shareholders cannot afford and is hampered by the lack of a supportive legal environment.

The task of a system of corporate governance is to create trust based on control between investors and people who run corporations. No system anywhere in the world is perfect, but the level of *de facto* protection that the Russian system offers to shareholders is exceptionally low. Consequently, in the Russian context there is an essential practical distinction between being a largest and a dominant shareholder. Presumably, in market economies with a mature and sophisticated institutional set-up this distinction is irrelevant because domination is based on exercising ownership rights according to the principle 'one share-one vote' (DeMarzo, 1993). Under the Anglo-Saxon system a stake as low as 3–5 per cent can give its owner considerable power; under the continental system, concentration of ownership is higher and as result the stake has to be close to 50 per cent to give noticeable influence to a shareholder. In Russia poor legal protection of shareholder rights, lack of disclosure about the business operations or finances of corporations, the underdeveloped state of the security market and a weak shareholder culture signify that holding even very large blocks of shares may result in little or no effective control over the firm.[7] The same conditions favour people who are privy to the firm's management decisions. This category includes primarily senior managers, who have an important advantage because they consolidate the power of shareholding with the power of decision-making. As a result, domination can be achieved by simple if unscrupulous means exploiting the fact that other categories of shareholders cannot accurately monitor the day-to-day performance of the firm.

Privatization has put senior managers in an exceptionally strong position *vis-à-vis* employees and outsiders. From the outset their control of the firms was far in excess of their share of ownership. As pre-privatization incumbents they enjoyed privileged access to information, admission to important networks and, at least initially, support of the labour force. Later they developed special tactics designed to maintain and reinforce their position. These include, for example, keeping share registries locked up in their offices; keeping more than one registry; changing entries into the registry at will; threatening to fire workers who sell shares to outsiders; misleading 'undesirable' shareholders about dates and venues of the shareholders' general meetings; refusing to register share purchases by outsiders; declining to recognize board directors properly elected by minority shareowners, and so on. These tactics bring results thanks to a low level of corporate transparency as well as of effective law enforcement.

At the end of the day, however, it was the institutional environment that had the decisive impact on the behaviour of managers. In the economy stricken with shortage of safe long-term financial opportunities and inadequate legal framework, managers were tempted to use corporate resources for illegal personal enrichment without excessive risk of prosecution in the absence of sufficient low-risk investment opportunities to motivate them to invest via their businesses instead. In big firms the most popular scheme of managerial enrichment involves the creation of a number of small affiliated firms, which are put in charge of the cash flows of the big firm. This makes the control of cash flows extremely complicated and allows the organizers of the scheme to transfer money into their personal accounts either directly or through off-shore companies and various sham firms. The scale of capital flight indicates that the uncertainty of the institutional environment is a key factor affecting these strategies. Alternatively, instead of being channeled abroad, the resources could be used by senior managers for increasing their own block of shares and preventing other parties from accumulating more shares. Eventually, the combination

Table 9.2   Ownership concentration within Russian firms based on REB survey results

	1999	2001	2003	2005
The proportion of firms in which	%	%	%	%
the largest shareholder holds				
fewer than 10% of shares	21	16	9	2
10–25% of shares	28	33	35	15
25–50% of shares	26	26	30	32
more than 50% of shares	25	25	26	51
Total	100	100	100	100
Average stake of the largest shareholder	32.9	34.5	37.2	51.8
Average stake of the second largest shareholder	–	–	17.2	20.3

of give-away privatization and underdeveloped institutions has brought about a situation in which, in the majority of joint-stock companies, the function of manager and the function of dominant owner became united.

Statistics are not too helpful in validating this fact. The secretive nature of the Russian corporate world makes it very difficult to quantify the structure of ownership. Within the sample covered by REB surveys the proportion of firms that have their senior manager as the largest shareholder increased from 24 per cent to 39 per cent in 1999–2005. It is also typical that the stake of the largest shareholder continues to grow (currently on average it exceeds 40 per cent of authorized capital, see Table 9.2). According to expert evaluation based on in-depth empirical studies, senior management is in control of no less than 50 per cent of firms because many shareholders-outsiders are just a façade for managers (Dolgopiatova, 2001; Sizov, 2004). The standard problem of corporate governance, therefore, is transformed: it is no longer a conflict between managers and owners, but rather a conflict between different categories of owners of which one has advantages because of its position within the firm. Consequently, Russian corporations acquire many features of manager-owned firms.

Pros and cons

Because we attribute so much attention to the position of top managers in the Russian system of corporate governance it is necessary to highlight one important issue. As we demonstrated earlier, the composition of corporate ownership in the country has not been stagnant. A considerable volume of shares has moved between the people who received their shares as members of working collectives during mass privatization and those who bought or received these shares from original owners at a later stage. Some of the latter have managed to consolidate their acquisitions into blocks that allowed them to dislodge the old 'red director' and step into his place. According to our estimates, in 2005, among firms controlled by top managers as a group, 44 per cent were controlled by their former 'red directors' whilst 56 per cent were controlled by the teams who arrived after privatization. Among firms in which the CEO was the largest shareholder the proportion was 36 per cent and 64 per cent. In other words, today it would be wrong to attribute to the term 'insider control' the retrograde undertone it used to have in the early days of market reforms. Nonetheless, although 'new' insiders may be different from the 'old guard' in many respects, there is at least one thing that they have in common: apart from the group of super-rich oligarchs both old and new owners seek to reinforce their control based on shareholding with control associated with a senior managerial position.

Some researchers find this feature of the Russian system of corporate governance, that is that the controlling owners have to occupy senior management positions in the firm because this is the only way to protect their controlling rights and make a real impact on the running of the firm, so important that they propose a new descriptive term for it – for example, 'entrepreneurial system', in which 'there is no separation of ownership and control' (Konstantinov *et al.*, 2002). Although this particular effort to produce a new keyword does not really convince, as it runs against the well-established meaning of the term 'entrepreneur', it indicates that there is growing realization that the situation with the protection of ownership rights in Russia has had a profound effect on corporate governance in the country.

In most countries of the world companies with concentrated ownership grew and developed as family firms, often from entrepreneurial origins. In Russia, in which private property of industrial assets has its origins in mass voucher privatization, large firms neither originated with some innovative ideas of the founder-owners, nor could they become a family affair. Instead, shares are usually concentrated in the hands of two to seven individuals tied with informal links and a common background. Taking the key from the term 'family' firm, we may call them 'comradeship' or 'companionship' firms (Kapelyushnikov, 2002). Indeed, the owners of such firms have usually been associated together for long time. Often they already knew each other professionally before market reforms started, taking their first steps as businessmen together and now owning comparable stakes in the firm. This model of ownership may be found in the most successful Russian companies.

Link between concentration and performance

Conceptually, a system of corporate governance based on the concentration of ownership in the hands of senior managers has its pros and cons in term of efficiency. On the negative side, high ownership stakes facilitate managerial strategies aimed at wealth and value-skimming transfers at the expense of small shareholders. This is usually the aspect that raises the gravest concern of foreign experts and advisers. They justly point out that the very rationale for public corporation, that is to provide business with investment resources, is defeated when minority shareholders are neglected. There has been pressure on the Russian government to introduce and promote the principles of good corporate governance developed by the OECD (2002a). In 2002 a government body, the Russian Federal Securities and Exchange Commission, introduced the voluntary Code of Corporate Behaviour founded on these principles. Field studies demonstrate that the larger firms were more inclined to implement the Code (Guriev *et al.*, 2003; see also McGee in this volume). This may be attributed to the fact that large firms are more likely to be interested in tapping the open financial markets than smaller firms. In particular, Russian corporations that seek to attract financial resources from foreign and international markets may be seen making an effort to comply with the Code and other international standards such as those of the USA. Accordingly, they comply with Generally Accepted Accounting Principles (GAAP) or International Accounting Standards (IAS), depending on which financial markets they are targeting. Generally speaking however, the majority of firms do not feel pressure to abide by the letter or spirit of the 2002 Code of Corporate Behaviour. Conceptually, this and similar codes implicitly have the assumption of a liberal and efficient market at their core, not applicable in the Russian case. It is enough to mention that the 2005 Index of Economic Freedom by the *Wall Street Journal*, which may be construed as an indirect measure of the maturity and efficiency of the market in various countries of the world, positions Russia in the 'mostly unfree' category (*Wall Street Journal*, 12 January 2005).

On the other hand, there are also arguments in favour of encouraging managers to maintain an ownership stake in their company. Jensen and Meckling (1976) famously argue that the most important agency conflict could arise from the fact that as a manager's ownership stake falls, his incentive to search out new profitable investment opportunities decreases. Russian conditions demand some modification of this approach, but the conclusions run in a parallel direction. Investors cannot rely on published accounts to make an informed decision; the level of trust in business relations is very low (Fox and Heller, 1999). As was demonstrated earlier, a weak performance of formal institutions increases the role of informal institutions, and under such circumstances the involvement of managers as shareholders may be seen by financial investors as an assurance of long-term commitment on the part of managers and may make raising capital easier.

Data accumulated by the REB may be employed to corroborate conceptual assumptions, and statistical analysis based on both pooled estimations (OLS and logit) and simple panel individual effects models reveals two important relationships. First, there is statistically significant and negative correlation between the size of the stake owned by the largest shareholder and the breadth of investment in the firm (Table 9.3). Second, there is a statistically significant and negative correlation between the size of the stake owned by the largest shareholder and such parameters of the firm as capacity utilization and profitability (Table 9.4).

Table 9.3   The impact of ownership on investment activities of the firm; based on REB survey results, 1999–2003 (panel data)

	Pooled OLS	RE	FE
Ownership variables			
CON	−0.54 (3.09)*	−0.52 (2.82)*	−0.31 (0.90)
INS	0.53 (0.06)	−0.47 (0.05)	−11.88 (0.84)
FIN	3.54 (0.31)	−0.49 (0.04)	−20.81 (1.17)
STATE	7.43 (0.53)	5.86 (0.40)	−7.53 (0.31)
Constant	−167.91 (0.74)	−196.87 (0.79)	−84.43 (0.65)
No. of observations	157	157	157
Hausman test		4.2	
R^2	0.16	0.23	0.11

Notes: The absolute values of *t*-statistics are in parentheses.* denotes significant at 1% level. CON = percentage of equity held by the first largest shareholder; INS = dummy variable for holding the first single block of shares by insiders; FIN = dummy variable for holding the first single block of shares by financial outsiders; STATE = dummy variable for holding the first single block of shares by state. The reference category is enterprises, in which the largest block of shares is held by insiders.
Controls: order-book level (as per cent of the previous year); size (number of employees); age (calendar year of the enterprise foundation); dummies for the survey dates; industry dummies regional dummies.
OLS = ordinary-least-squares regression; RE = random effects model; FE = fixed effects model.

These findings, in our opinion, reflect the insecurity of dominant shareholders, including top managers. They may be well-practiced in expropriating smaller shareholders, but they are aware that the size of the holding gives no immunity against raiders. It is worth reiterating here that the legal system offers inadequate protection of legitimate owners, even if they hold majority stakes. In the West, hostile takeovers are feasible when shares of the target company are widely available and easily purchased. In Russia, hostile takeovers rely on the abuse of the rights of shareholders and the exploitation of legalistic hitches and corruption in the judicial system.[8] Therefore it might be the case that the incumbent owners are reluctant to see their firms as long-term commitments in spite of large ownership stakes. On the other hand, concentrated ownership facilitates wealth transfers from the company, and as a result they use their position to drain resources out of the firm. Insiders routinely loot companies, dilute the shares of outsiders, fail to pay dividends and mistreat shareholders in other ways because they feel threatened by the general instability and uncertainty regarding property rights, inheritance rights, contract law, judicial protection, personal safety, and so on. The results in Table 9.4 demonstrate that *both* a high concentration ratio and the insiders' share may affect performance negatively, albeit the second result is more ambiguous.

The negative correlation between concentration of ownership, insiders' ownership and some major economic parameters of the firm established by our analysis of the REB data, if representative of a more general trend, gives grounds

Table 9.4 The impact of ownership on the firm's performance; based on REB survey results, 1999–2003 (panel data)

| | *Dependant variables* | | | | | | | | |
| | *Capacity utilization rate* | | | *Profit margin* | | | *Binary variable profit/loss* | | |
	Pooled OLS	*RE*	*FE*	*Pooled OLS*	*RE*	*FE*	*Pooled Logit*	*RE Logit*	*FE Logit*
Ownership variables									
CON	−0.19	−0.20	−0.21	−0.08	−0.18	−0.26	−0.02	−0.03	−0.09
	(2.32)*	(2.44)**	(1.92)[+]	(0.88)	(2.42)**	(2.78)**	(2.06)*	(2.04)*	
(1.95)*									
INS	−5.22	−7.70	−8.60	−2.00	−0.22	2.60	0.60	0.51	−0.49
	(1.25)	(2.02)*	(1.96)*	(0.51)	(0.07)	(0.71)	(1.36)	(0.81)	(0.40)
FIN	−0.81	0.73	5.08	0.08	0.86	−0.82	0.27	−0.36	−0.96
	(0.15)	(0.15)	(0.90)	(0.01)	(0.12)	(0.09)	(0.47)	(0.42)	(0.59)
STATE	1.95	1.29	−1.62	−0.59	1.95	3.25	−0.37	−0.01	39.08
	(0.30)	(0.20)	(0.20)	(0.06)	(0.27)	(0.41)	(0.55)	(0.01)	(0.00)
Constant	202.93	217.15	−122.67	−24.19	−10.73	36.28	−3.23	−1.21	
	(1.95)*	(1.65)[+]	(2.97)**	(0.14)	(0.04)	(0.82)	(0.29)	(0.07)	
No. of observations	169	169	169	54	54	54	163	163	65
Hausman test		27.2**			5.5				
R^2 (Pseudo R^2 for Logit)	0.48	0.46	0.19	0.14	0.11	0.01	0.14	0.17	0.40

Notes: The absolute values of *t*-statistics are in parentheses. [+]denotes significant at 10 per cent level; *significant at 5 per cent level; **significant at 1% level. CON = percentage of equity held by the first largest shareholder; INS = dummy variable for holding the first single block of shares by insiders; FIN = dummy variable for holding the first single block of shares by financial outsiders; STATE = dummy variable for holding the first single block of shares by state. The reference category is enterprises in which the largest block of shares is held by insiders.
Controls: order-book level (as per cent of the previous year); size (number of employees); age (calendar year of the enterprise foundation); dummies for the survey dates; industry dummies regional dummies.
OLS = ordinary-least-squares regression; RE = random effects model; FE = fixed effects model.

for concern. In this chapter we have identified two tendencies in the Russian corporate sector, both of which are related to the same cause. The poor state of the institutional framework puts a pressure on large shareholders to keep increasing their stake, and as a result their control over the firm increases. However, the same institutional constraints make this category of shareholders feel insecure about the future of their investment, which undermines their commitment to the firm they own/control and encourages to use the higher stakes as means to tunnel wealth out of companies. Evidently, these are the signs of an unhealthy situation that may endanger long-term restructuring and growth of the Russian economy.

The jury is still out

The Russian system of corporate governance in its present form bears all the signs of an *ad hoc* construct. It is not illogical to assume that in a pursue of wealth maximization the current generation of directors-owners, as Western managers-owners before them, will eventually embrace the necessity to delegate executive functions to more competent managers than themselves and will either focus on strategic ownership and/or diversify their assets. This choice will be the choice of self-interest and self-preservation. In the current environment, though, the same instincts prevent managers giving up direct control over the firm and its assets and seeing the companies as long-term investments. Therefore, the progress of corporate governance towards a more conventional model is unrealistic without changes in the political, social and economic realities of Russia in the first place. In other words, the current system of corporate governance is another yet manifestation of the inadequate state of the institutional infrastructure in the country. The paradox is that certain behavioural patterns and business arrangements in Russia bring rewards although they should be a ticket to failure in a market economy as contradicting its rules and institutions. It this context the idiosyncratic behaviour of economic agents determined to bypass the 'legal' market economy is in fact a rational reaction to the uncertainty and challenges caused by institutional distortions. The high perceived cost of acting legally is a fundamental impediment to the progress in corporate governance along the lines suggested by the OECD code of corporate governance.[9]

There is a growing consensus that the shortage of market-type responses in Russia has the frailty of market-based incentives as its cause. The present institutional arrangements reflect the drawbacks and weaknesses associated with a period of systemic change such as domination of short-term interests, poor access to business information, lack of trust, collapse of traditional business ties and parallel existence of incompatible business cultures. The state as an active force in creating an institutional set-up had been weakened and reticent during this period. However, it is evident that the makeshift arrangements have reached the limits of their efficiency and have become a barrier to further development as they fail to provide a solid and cost-effective foundation for market transactions. The path for further modernization of corporate governance in Russia is the path of a comprehensive modernization of the institutional framework as a whole.

Notes

1   At its peak before the 1998 collapse, the total stockmarket capitalization of all Russian industry only reached about $130 billion – less than Intel Corp (Fox and Heller, 1999).
2   As indirect evidence of difficulties in attempts to introduce best practices one can consider the fact that experts count up to 1,500 laws and regulations related to corporate governance rules and norms in Russia (Dolgopiatova, 2004).
3   Large stakes were initially retained by the state, but the state has never played a notable independent role as a shareholder (Kuznetsova and Kuznetsov, 1999).
4   A feature of the Russian corporate scene is that ownership of the largest resources exporting firms is concentrated in the hands of the handful of so-called oligarchs who exploited their special relations with the top state bureaucracy. They came into possession of their original stakes through the notorious loans-for-shares tenders held by the Russian government in mid-1990s. Later they consolidated their control through diluting shares of the state and minority owners.
5   For example, the standard definition of corporate governance as the ways in which suppliers of finance to corporations assure themselves of getting a return on their investment proves wanting.
6   'Investitsionnaya politika v Rossii', *Nezavisimaya Gazeta*, 26 August 1997, p. 2.
7   As some foreign investors have learnt to their own cost. See contribution by Adachi in this volume.
8   One of the common tricks is to obtain a judicial decision that bans the current owners of the firm from using their right to vote in the shareholders' general meeting or take a position on the board of directors. Another ploy is to make the court requisition the registry of shareholders, the only legal proof of ownership, and then replace it with an alternative registry with a different composition of shareholders (Sizov, 2004). One notorious incident involved Krasnoyarsk Aluminum, which deleted from its share register a 20 per cent stake held by the British Trans World Group, effectively wiping out its holding (Mileusnic, 1996).
9   Interviews with managers of companies importing white goods into Russia, the sector where the presence of 'grey' practices is very noticeable, revealed in 2001 that the choice between 'grey,' semi-legal schemes and fully legal procedures was entirely determined by considerations of comparative cost (Radaev, 2002).

10
Ownership Concentration and Corporate Performance: Evidence from Poland

Maria Aluchna

Since 1989, Poland has been on its way out from a centrally planned to a market economy, introducing nation-wide reforms of it social and economic system. The most essential component of reform refers to the ownership structure of Polish companies (Frydman and Rapaczynski, 1995), and has been introduced at two levels. The first comprises the privatization of the formerly state-owned enterprises accomplished either by the sale to strategic domestic or foreign investors, by the sale to insiders or, in the case of companies covered by the mass privatization programmes, by the transfer of control to investment funds representing interests of private individuals (Mickiewicz and Bałtowski, 2003). The second level refers to the removal of entry barriers for the newly founded non-state-owned companies (Jackson *et al.*, 2005). While the second of these reforms turned-out to be a success (see also the contribution by Andreff in this volume), the first was extremely complex, protracted and difficult to implement.

The ownership structure should not be viewed as the transition goal *per se*, or at least not as a sufficient condition of microeconomic efficiency. The reform process should aim at the development of sound governance mechanisms (Frydman and Rapaczynski, 1995) since only a new institutional order supporting investors' rights may lead to value-maximization and provide a framework for further growth and development.

This chapter concentrates on the analysis of the ownership structure of Polish public companies listed on the Warsaw Stock Exchange. It traces the characteristics of the ownership structure of the sample companies and provides some insights into the question of the efficiency of ownership structure, investigating the links between ownership concentration, shareholders' identities and corporate performance. The results reveal significant and growing ownership concentration of Polish companies as well as a strong involvement of strategic foreign and domestic investors in their ownership structure. The position of insiders remains stable although not significantly strong. Interestingly, the findings show that the effect of ownership concentration is positive only if the latter reflects the strong position of more than one shareholder.

The chapter is organized as follows. The next section presents a review of the literature on the ownership structure of companies, comparing the cases of developed and transition economies. The characteristics and efficiency of the ownership structures in transition economies are then explored, before presenting the methodology and research hypotheses. Descriptive statistics and empirical tests on the ownership structure and corporate performance of 130 non-financial public companies listed on the Warsaw Stock Exchange are then presented, and the results and research limitations are discussed in the final section.

Ownership structure and corporate governance

Theoretical framework

Ownership structure, in particular the degree of ownership concentration and shareholders' identity, is perceived as a decisive aspect affecting corporate performance. The agency theory (Jensen and Meckling, 1976; Fama and Jensen, 1983a, Fama and Jensen, 1983b) perceives the company as a nexus of contracts between various actors, and corporate activity implies cooperation between these parties. Some of them act as principals delegating different tasks for their agents to execute. The theory assumes that the principals and agents focus on individual goals and since they differ in terms of possibilities of risk diversification and activity horizons, the interests of one party may not always be aligned with those of the others. As a result, agents may show a tendency towards opportunistic behaviour (opportunities for which are created due to informational asymmetries), acting at the expense of their principals. Thus, shareholders, who in the case of public corporations are the residual claimants, use different control mechanisms to discipline managers or reduce conflicts between owners and, in result, improve efficiency.

From the wider perspective, the ownership structure of corporations is a key characteristic of the economic system in a given country. It is closely tied with the financial system, as the structure of corporate finance and the structure of corporate ownership are highly correlated. In addition, the incentives in principal–agent relations are shaped by the law system and by other aspects of the regulatory framework.

Ownership concentration

While concentrated ownership is a feature of most of economies, with only a few examples of dispersed ownership mainly in Anglo-Saxon legal-origin systems (La Porta *et al.*, 1999a), analysis of the agency problems of dispersed ownership and the meaning of the monitoring and disciplinary role of the major shareholder has dominated research in the corporate governance literature.

There are two modes of ownership concentration. First is the case of concentration of shares as in the case of the one share = one vote rule. In the second case the concentration of votes is carried through preferred stock (Halpern, 2000), popular for example in German corporations, and leads to pyramidal structures (albeit, the latter may exist without the preferred stock mechanism; see Almeida and Wolfenzon, 2005; Morck and Steier, 2005; Walter, 2000; Boehmer, 1999; La Porta *et al.*, 1999a). In this second case, there are no ownership barriers but control barriers (Prevezer and Ricketts, 1994). The deviation from the one share-one vote rule makes sense if the private benefits of control are high, which happens in countries with worse shareholder protection (Grossman and Hart, 1988; Harris and Raviv, 1988).

Concentrated ownership may be the solution to agency problems and free-raider problems that result from dispersed ownership and lead to higher profitability when the dominating owners are active, but do not abuse their position (Neun and Santerre, 1986; Holderness and Sheehan, 1988), being a second-best solution when market/external mechanisms are not working well (Morck and Steier, 2005).

However, the dominant shareholder (via his/her representatives on the board) may assure decisions favouring him/her at the cost of minority shareholders (Fama and Jensen, 1983a); that is may expropriate minority shareholders through tunnelling or compensation policies (Stulz, 1988). The dominant shareholders may also be passive (Shleifer and Vishny, 1986) or can be locked in – the large stake does not allow for voting by feet since it results in a decline in prices and smaller gains. Recent research on ownership structure by Kirchmaier and Grant (2005) demonstrates significant differences among European countries. It reveals that ownership structures in Europe are not consistent with value-maximization principles, and proves best performance in the case of dispersed ownership of sample companies; concentrated ownership is ranked second best, whereas legal control (that is, the case of one dominant shareholder with more than a 50% stake) is shown to be inefficient.

Ownership characteristics and performance

Another stream of research shows that the growing role of institutional investors (II) has become a characteristic feature of corporate ownership in developed economies. The stake of institutional investors rose from 15.9 per cent in 1965 to 30 per cent in 1986 (Brickley *et al.*, 1988) and to nearly 50 per cent in the late 1990s (Useem, 1996; Johnson and Greening, 1999). Today it is estimated that institutional investors own 70 per cent of shares of companies listed on the London Stock Exchange, and 60 per cent of shares of companies listed in the USA (Steele, 2005). In 1950, 6 per cent, of funds were allocated in stocks and 56 per cent in bonds, whereas in 1989 it was 40 per cent and 30 per cent respectively (Parthiban and Kochhar, 1996). At the same time, institutional investors are perceived as enhancing efficient governance due to their economies of scale and diversification (Faccio and Lasfer, 2000) and skills and knowledge (Monks and Minow, 1994; Brickley *et al.*, 1988). They are able to monitor management (Shleifer and Vishny,

1997), and the evidence shows that institutional investors tend to limit managers' manipulation of profits (Chung *et al.*, 2002). Among institutional investors, pension funds appear to play an important role (Del Guercio and Hawkins, 1999; Faccio and Lasfer, 2000; Woidtke, 2002). On the other hand, banks involved in the ownership are more willing to undertake corporate restructuring and salvation (Gilson, 1996). However, the monitoring function of institutional investors remains a relatively controversial issue since much research indicates that they are just the next level of the agency relation chain (Blair, 1995; Romano, 1994 as quoted in Faccio and Lasfer, 2000) and they do not necessarily become efficient monitors due to business interdependency or the capital or personal interlocks. Thus, the issue of the impact of institutional investors on corporate performance remains blurred. While some researchers have found positive results of II influence on the firm's value (Parthiban and Kochhar, 1996; Brickley *et al.*, 1998; McConnell and Servaes, 1990; Black, 1998; Woitdke, 2002), other research indicates that II may have a negative impact (Gilian and Starks, 2000); while yet other findings show no influence at all (Demsetz and Lehn, 1985; Craswell *et al.*, 1997; Faccio and Lasfer, 2000; Singh and Davidson, 2001). The results are clearly context specific and influenced by the relationships and interdependence of business interests between institutional investors and companies (Parthiban and Rahul, 1996). Institutional investors face some limitations in exerting their decision rights – their decisions may be limited with business or capital ties, may be restricted by legal regulations or may be constrained by information processing capacities (for example CalPERS invested its assess in several thousands of companies).

Another research stream in the corporate governance literature investigates the importance and role of managerial ownership. Managerial ownership may mitigate agency problems (Jensen and Meckling, 1976; Morck *et al.*, 2000; Ang *et al.*, 2000; Singh and Davidson, 2001), although it causes offsetting costs. Research also shows positive results of management buy-outs (MBO) (Smith, 1990). Some research on managerial ownership and performance indicates a non-linear U-shaped relationship between managerial ownership and corporate performance (Morck *et al.*, 1988; McConnell and Servaes, 1990; Chen *et al.*, 1993), while in a few other cases no significant influence has been detected (Craswell *et al.*, 1997; Himmelberg *et al.*, 1999).

Ownership structure in transition economies

Ownership concentration[1]

Most of the research on the ownership structure in transition economies relates to the link between the identity of owners and performance (see next section), and research on the effects of concentration still remains relatively scarce. However, significant ownership concentration is the most dominant feature of the emerging governance structure of transition economies. Ownership concentration is the common result of the privatization policies and is still increasing after privatization, at least in some countries in the region (Olsson and Alasheyeva, 2000; see also Kusnetsov *et al.* in this volume). The analyses of the concentrated ownership structure in transition countries focus on some negative effects. Ownership concentration may lead to value distracting practices by the dominant shareholder and the abuse of minority investors' rights. Controlling shareholders may have no incentive to increase the firm's value since they realize benefits elsewhere, which results in an absence of new minority investors (Pajuste, 2002).

While the dominant shareholder would on average exert a negative effect on the company, this result is context-specific, namely it depends on the country and the dominant shareholder's identity. For instance in Poland, having a privatization investment fund (NIF) as a controlling shareholder is associated with negative effects (Grosfeld and Tressel, 2001), whereas in the Czech Republic ownership concentration is associated with better performance as long as a strategic investor other than an investment fund represents this concentration (Weiss and Nikitin, 1998). On the other hand, research by Claessens and Djankov (1999) shows that foreign and non-bank-sponsored-funds ownership is associated with higher profitability.

For Poland, Grosfeld and Tressel (2001) found that firms with relatively dispersed ownership enjoyed productivity growth of 2.27 per cent above the average; firms with intermediate levels of ownership concentration faced a decrease of productivity growth of 3.9 per cent below the average; whereas firms with a high concentration level experienced productivity growth of 2.9 per cent above the average.

In general, negative effects of ownership concentration related to the potential extraction of private benefits may be counterbalanced by the positive strategic role of the dominant owners, who may stimulate restructuring (Commander *et al.*, 1999); these authors point out that the boost of productivity and corporate restructuring takes place under the condition of (1) hard budget constraint being imposed on the company and (2) market competition. The results are, however, far from robust, since the ownership concentration of investment funds in the privatized Czech companies was not associated with higher performance (ibid.). Thus the issue appears to be controversial.

Ownership and performance

Moreover the identity of owners becomes a decisive variable affecting performance – research stresses the positive role of outside investors and argues for limiting the position of insiders such as those behaving opportunistically (Frydman *et al.*, 1999). Outsider-owned privatized firms noted significantly higher annual revenue growth than either state or insider-owned firms, whereas no significant difference was found for cost performance. Other research shows that privatization to foreigners and blockholders is more productive than privatization to insiders (Estrin, 2002; Djankov and Murrell, 2002). There are significant differences in growth rates between private and state firms, the former estimated to be higher by between 5.4 per cent and 8.7 per cent, confirming evidence of the positive influence of the privatization process. Some authors, however, are a bit sceptical as to the positive effects of the privatization process pointing out that usually the best and most likely to survive companies were chosen for privatization (Estrin, 2001). In addition, the positive effect of privatization on performance may be concentrated within three to six years after privatization (Mickiewicz *et al.*, 2005). On the other hand, some authors suggest that some degree of insider ownership may be unavoidable, as a form of compensation without which the insiders in state enterprises may block privatization (Blanchard and Aghion, 1996).

The wide surveys of the empirical literature on enterprise restructuring and privatization in transition point out the following (Djankov and Murrell, 2002; Megginson and Netter, 2001):

- private as opposed to public ownership is associated with better performance – privatization leads to corporate restructuring and results in higher productivity and profitability;
- increased competition and hard budget constrains improve with performance (this refer to Central Europe, not to CIS where increased competition was detrimental to companies);
- foreign ownership increases the post-privatization performance;
- ownership concentration in the hands of outsiders is associated with significantly greater performance;
- results on the role of investment funds are mixed – some research shows performance improvement in companies with IF stakes, other research does not reveal such results (see Megginson and Netter, 2001);
- privatization to workers does not enhance the corporate restructuring and performance;
- results on MBOs show that a strong position of managers (incumbent managers) is not associated with restructuring and better performance, although the results are context-specific and differ among cases – researchers stress the importance of incentives and new executive teams.

The analysis of ownership characteristics and the efficiency of ownership structure in the case of transition economies requires at least a short discussion on the reforms of the financial and legal system. La Porta *et al.* (1999a) drew attention to the importance of legal regulation and shareholder protection for the development of the capital market and access to external finance. The development of a capital market is a crucial issue in transition economies as companies going public protect investors better and gain facilitated access to finance; benefits which should exceed the cost of disclosure and other requirements (see also chapter by Köke and Schröder in this volume). Pistor *et al.* (2000) discussed the effectiveness of legal institutions and the law on books from the perspective of shareholder and creditor rights in transition economies. Pistor (2001) analyses shareholder property rights, investor protection and stock exchange trading rules, and shows, consistently with previous research, that investor protection rules referring to minority protection and disclosure requirements are more important for capital market development that other criteria. A comparison of the Polish and Czech stockmarkets (Glaeser *et al.*, 2001; Coffee, 1998; Köke and Schröder in this volume) reveals that the listing requirements as well as effective supervision over the stockmarket were important for external finance. Relatively strict securities law, disclosure requirements as well as legal enforcement by specialized regulators (external and independent SEC) led to the development of the Warsaw Stock Exchange and the avoidance of company delisting and major value expropriation, which was the case of the Prague Stock Exchange (Glaeser *et al.*, 2001).

Poland

The ownership structure in Poland is highly diversified. Despite transition reforms, the state still possesses shares in almost every second-largest industrial company, approximately 3,000 enterprises, among which are many of the largest (Kozarzewski, 2002; OECD, 2002b; see also chapter by Bałtowski and Mickiewicz in this volume). Some of them operate as state-owned, whereas others were commercialized with a 100 per cent state stake. In some cases the state is not able to sell shares, even though willing to do so, since 50 per cent of the enterprises with state ownership of more than 20 per cent of shares are unprofitable (typically, having at the same time a strategic investor who often has a controlling block of shares).

The analysis of non-state companies reveals different characteristics. Ownership of companies privatized after 1989 or newly set up is highly concentrated in the hands of either foreign institutional or domestic (both institutional and individual) investors (Dzierżanowski and Tamowicz, 2004). The picture appears to be only slightly different in public companies listed on the Warsaw Stock Exchange. Research based on data covering the period 1991–2000 also reveals a significant concentration of ownership and control: the biggest shareholders hold more than a 50 per cent stake in 75 per cent of companies, and in fact a more than 75 per cent stake in 27 per cent of the companies. The median size of the biggest voting block is estimated as either 33 per cent (Grosfeld and Tressel, 2001) or 39.5 per cent (Dzieżanowski and Tamowicz, 2002), and for the second blockholder it amounts to 10.4 per cent (Dzieżanowski and Tamowicz, 2000). More strikingly, the ownership concentration has been still growing in the late 1990s – the average stake in the hands of the largest shareholder rose from 54.2 per cent at the beginning of 1998, to 55.7 per cent in 1999 and to 59.1 per cent in 2000, whereas the average stake of the five largest shareholders rose from 78.2 per cent to 78.7 per cent and 80.7 per cent respectively[2] (Kozarzewski, 2002). Ownership concentration tends to be smaller in the sample of new and privatized firms, although these companies are characterized by relatively stronger CEO positions in terms of ownership stake. Although most of the privatization methods in Poland included employees, the rate of insiders' ownership is no longer substantial and is decreasing, and in the case of the biggest companies their role is marginal (Kozarzewski, 2002). Hence, neither individuals nor employees tend to be the authors of the significant concentration of ownership of Polish public listed companies.[3] Foreign and domestic institutional investors appear to be the most dominant shareholders and their position is growing, and what is more, companies with foreign investors tend to be more concentrated than the rest. This is consistent with the findings of Konings (2001) who shows that out of 10 per cent of companies with foreign participation in 1997 the average fraction of shares owned by foreign investors in Poland was esti-mated at 73 per cent and was significantly higher than for Bulgaria (61 per cent) and Romania (59 per cent). An additional important reason for the dominance of foreign ownership refers to the advantage the foreign owners enjoyed at the time of privatization having easier access to finance compared to domestic players. This argument combined with relatively low privatiza-tion prices led to a build-up of large stakes driven by the expected ratio of the privatization price to future earnings (as discussed in Bishop *et al.*, 2002).

Among foreign investors and domestic institutions, the most significant role is played by the funds, financial institutions and industrial companies. NIFs' stake accounts for 10–16 per cent. Banks tend not to be heavily involved in equity ownership of the companies – they own a 15.6 per cent average stake in ownership structure (Dzieżanowski and Tamowicz, 2000) and posses shares in 11 companies out of 84 analysed in another empirical survey, with only one case of a controlling stake (Kozarzewski, 2002). Bank involvement tends to increase in cases of leverage-led restructuring (Grosfeld and Tressel, 2001). There is little to suggest that other institutional investors would get involved in ownership and active governance of Polish companies. Although the position of pension funds (Szczurek, 2002; chapter by Zalewska in this volume) and insurance companies (Pye, 2000) is increasing, their role is limited by the small size of the capital market and hence the risk of a 'bubble' as well as constrains on voting rights.

Methodology

Data

The data on ownership structure and performance were collected from annual financial reports from the Polish Securities and Exchange Commission. Data on stock prices were taken from the internet database of Bank Ochrony Środowiska (Environment Bank). The research sample covered 130 non-financial companies listed on the Warsaw Stock Exchange, on the main and regulated markets one six years (1997–2002).

Table 10.1   Sample companies according to WSE sector classification

Sector	Number of companies
Construction	28
Chemicals	14
Wood processing	6
Machinery	15
Trade	10
IT and telecommunication	13
Textiles	8
Construction materials	6
Media	3
Iron	11
Food and beverages	16
Total	130

The sample companies were classified according to the Warsaw Stock Exchange (WSE) sectors classification, and the breakdown is presented in Table 10.1.

Data from before 1997 are not included in the analysis due to significant turbulence of the environment, noisiness and insufficient information. The quality of information improved substantially over the analysed period. Standard SPSS software was used for the statistical analysis.

Research hypotheses

The hypotheses presented below refer to Frydman *et al.* (1999), Kozarzewski (2002), Dzierżanowski and Tamowicz (2002) on the ownership characteristics of Polish public-listed companies and to Grosfeld and Tressel (2001) on the governance structure of Polish corporations tied to corporate performance.

We focus on the characteristics of the ownership structure and the relations between the ownership structure and corporate performance. Consistent with the literature, we hypothesize a curvilinear relationship between ownership concentration and performance. We expect worse corporate performance to be associated with higher insider/CEO stakes in ownership, whereas better performance should be observed with higher supervisory board member stakes in ownership. It is also expected that companies with foreign investors and newly established companies would perform better.

Dependent variables

Dependent variables reflect the performance of the analysed corporations. A proxy for Tobin's Q (market value/book value) as well as the accounting indicators (ROA, ROE, ROS, net profit per employee and operational return; all in percentages) were taken as performance variables. Based on the data, the average values of indicators were computed for our period of analysis (6 years). Although use of the indices of the average values may restrict the analysis and may weaken the observed relations, it lowers the variance and allows the tracking of some tendencies in the longer period. The given ownership structure would not result in performance changes within, for instance, one year.

All the indicators were sector-adjusted and standardized according to the following equation:

$$\text{Standardized indicator} = \frac{\begin{array}{c}\text{(individual mean of the indicator for} \\ \text{6-year period} - \text{sectoral} \\ \text{mean indicator for 6-year period)}\end{array}}{\text{standard deviation for 6-year period}}$$

where 'indicator' refers to the proxy for Tobin's Q, ROE, ROA, ROS, operational return, net profit per employee and the stock price.

Independent variables

Independent variables refer to the characteristics of the ownership structure and describe the degree of ownership concentration as well as the shareholders' identities in the sample companies. All variables indicating ownership concentration assume 5 per cent votes as the starting point, since the ownership structure disclosed in the financial annual reports of sample companies do not cover shareholders who own less than 5 per cent (shareholders are obliged to disclose their stakes if they own 5 per cent or more). All percentages describing the stakes refer to the percentage of **votes**, not **shares**, since as noted below almost half of the sample companies use preferred shares. The stakes were summed in cases of marriage, personal or business agreement and capital dependence for all the shareholder types. The independent variables are as follows:

1   nominal indicator for one share = one vote rule (1 for one share = one vote rule, 0 otherwise);
2   the free-flow indicator – stands for the stakes owned by shareholders with stakes less than 5 per cent votes each;
3   the stake of the dominant shareholder – the percentage of votes held by the dominant shareholder;
4   the stake of the second biggest shareholder – the percentage of votes held by the second shareholder;
5   the identity of the dominant shareholder – (1) domestic company, (2) foreign company, (3) financial institution, (4) the state, (5) for newly established companies, (6) those companies with significant changes in dominant shareholder;
6   the stake of the three biggest shareholders – the percentage of votes held by the three biggest shareholders;

7   the stake of the five biggest shareholders – the percentage of votes held by the three biggest shareholders;

8   *HH* indicator – Herfindahl–Hirschman indicator illustrating the ownership concentration described as the sum of quadratic votes stakes of all *n* shareholders accordingly to the following equation:

$$HH = \Sigma_{i=1} \, u_i^2$$

where u_i = vote stake of *i* shareholder;

9   the number of shareholders – the number of all shareholders with stakes exceeding 5 per cent votes;

10   the stake of the management board members – the percentage of votes held by top management team members;

11   the stake of the supervisory board members – the percentage of votes held by the supervisory board members;

12   the stake of the employees – the percentage of votes held by employees;

13   the stake of the banks – the percentage of votes held by banks;

14   the stake of the pension funds – the percentage of votes held by the pension funds;

15   the stake of the insurance companies – the percentage of votes held by the insurance companies;

16   the total stake of the financial institutions – the percentage of votes held by the financial institutions.

The indicators were identified over six years. For the purposes of statistical analysis the values of the variables from the beginning of the period were taken into account to avoid a serious endogeneity problem (see Bishop *et al.*, 2002, for a similar approach).

Descriptive statistics

Ownership concentration

We focus on the following concentration indicators: the number of shareholders, the *HH* indicator, the stake of the dominant shareholder, the stake of the second biggest shareholder, the total stake of the three biggest shareholders and the total stake of the three biggest shareholders. The descriptive statistics based on the average values, constructed as described above are presented in Table 10.2.

In addition, in Table 10.3 we present evidence of a growing ownership concentration as shown by the indicators of the stake of the dominant shareholder, and the total stake of the three and five biggest shareholders. The average stake of the dominant shareholder is growing between 1997–2001 and accounts for 40.6 per cent at the end of 2002. Additionally, the ownership concentration with respect to the stake of the three and five biggest shareholders reveals an

Table 10.2   Descriptive statistics: ownership concentration indices

Concentration index/statistics	Mean	Median	Standard deviation
Number of shareholders (above 5%)	3.97	3.00	9.55
HH indicator	0.19	0.14	0.19
Dispersed ownership (share of free flow)	43.19	43.00	24.98
Stake of the dominant shareholder	33.76	32.00	20.45
Stake of the second biggest shareholder	13.36	13.00	9.39
Stake of three biggest shareholders	52.05	51.00	24.69
Stake of five biggest shareholders	53.38	57.00	24.98

Table 10.3   Characteristics of ownership structure of Polish companies, 1997–2002, average values (median) [SD]

Index	1997	1998	1999	2000	2001	2002
No of shareholders (above 5%)	3.03 (3) [0.5]	3.2 (3) [1.89]	3.2 (3) [1.95]	3.2 (3) [1.95]	3.27 (3) [1 73]	3.47 (3) [2.49]
One share = one vote	0.61 (1) [0.5]	0.56 (1) [0.5]	0.56 (1) [0.5]	0.55 (1) [0.5]	0.56 (1) [0.5]	0.56 (1) [0.5]
Free float	43.19 (43) [24.98]	43.9 (43) [23.16]	39.85 (38) [21.65]	37.64 (37) [19.26]	33.53 (34.5) [18.34]	33.13 (33) [19.65]
Stake of the dominant shareholder	33.76 (32) [20.45]	33.4 (29) [21.06]	36.33 (32) [21.8]	37.84 (33) [21.4]	41.69 (37) [22.08]	40.64 (34) [22.65]
Stake of the second biggest shareholder	13.36 (13) [9.39]	12.67 (12) [9.08]	12.98 (13) [8.85]	13.34 (13) [9.15]	13.27 (13) [8.69]	13.02 (12) [8.94]
Stake of the three biggest shareholders	52.05 (51) [24.6]	51.22 (52) [22.41]	54.24 (55) [20.76]	56.23 (56) [19.47]	60.12 (59.5) [19.13]	58.9 (58.5) [20.44]
Stake of the five biggest shareholders	56.39 (57) [24.69]	55.44 (57) [22.47]	58.84 (60.5) [20.88]	60.67 (61.5) [18.71]	64.78 (65) [18.28]	64.64 (65) [19.13]

upward trend. The biggest shareholders together own on average 59 per cent of votes whereas the average stake of the five biggest shareholders is approximately 65 per cent. The ownership concentration reveals the upward trend over the years 1997–2001, although in 2002 the concentration decreases slightly. 56 per cent of the analysed companies comply with the one share, one vote role, which correspond to 44 per cent of the companies using preferred shares.

There are companies that reveal a stake of the biggest shareholder above 50 per cent or even 75 per cent of votes. Apparently, such a situation affects the liquidity of the stockmarket.

In general, the results indicate a substantial and growing ownership concentration over the analysed period. The concentration calculated by the stake of the dominant shareholder as well by the stake of the three and five biggest shareholders increases. The voting stake of the dominant shareholder rose from 34 per cent in 1997 to almost 41 per cent in 2002, whereas the position of the three biggest shareholders increased from 52 per cent in 1997 to 59 per cent of votes in 2002. At the same time, the free float calculated as the stake held by shareholders who own less than 5 per cent fell from 43 per cent in 1997 to merely 33 per cent in 2002. These results are consistent with other analyses (Grosfeld and Tresel, 2002; Kozarzewski, 2002; Dzierżanowski and Tamowicz, 2002; Olsson and Alasheyeva, 2000). It is worth noting that 40.6 per cent is the effective control without legal control. An interesting reference to these finding is presented by Kirchmaier and Grant (2005) in their analysis of European ownership patterns. They distinguish three levels of the ownership concentration – legal control (over 50 per cent stake), *de facto* control (when the shareholder breaches the mandatory bid threshold) and dispersed ownership. Their analysis indicates the dominance of legal control (over 50 per cent stake) in France, Germany, Spain and Italy (with significant presence of banks in widely held companies). Only UK companies are characterized by dispersed ownership. Clearly, ownership of shares on the Polish stockmarket is converging towards the model observed in continental EU countries.

Owners' identity

The characteristics of the identity of the dominant shareholder of the sample companies are presented in Table 10.4.

As shown in the table, foreign and domestic companies are the dominant shareholders in 23 per cent and 22 per cent of the sample companies, respectively. As the result of many privatization schemes the presence and involvement of foreign companies in the ownership structure reveals a strong upward trend over the analysed period. The data reveal the decrease of involvement of National Investment Funds (NIF) as the result of the sales of their stakes to strategic investors and in consequence their withdrawal from the companies covered by the mass privatization programme. The presence of individual investors decreases over the research period, whereas the involvement of insiders remains at the same stable level. Managers and employees are the dominant shareholders in almost 15 per cent and almost 14 per cent of the sample companies respectively.

The table shows the growing presence of foreign and domestic companies that together controlled approximately 45 per cent of the sample companies in 2002. The analysis also reveals the decrease of financial institutions in the

Table 10.4 Identity of the dominant shareholder in Polish companies (% of companies with a given type of dominant shareholder, 1997–2002)

Shareholder's identity	1997	1998	1999	2000	2001	2002
Domestic company	13.8	13.8	18.5	20	20.8	22.3
Foreign company	7.7	8.5	13.1	16.9	22.3	23.1
Bank	6.2	11.5	10	6.9	7.7	7.7
Insurance company	0	1.5	0	0	0	1.5
NIF	10	13.1	12.3	9.2	6.2	5.4
Individual	10	10	6.2	4.6	5.4	3.1
Manager	11.5	11.5	14.6	16.9	16.9	14.6
Employees	11.5	13.8	12.3	14.6	12.3	13.8
Investment fund	1.5	1.5	0.8	0.8	0.8	0
Pension fund	0	0	0	0	0	0
Cross shareholding	0	0.8	0.8	2.3	2.3	2.3
State	8.5	5.4	5.4	6.2	3.8	4.6

ownership structure. Insiders and individual investors controlled 31.5 per cent of the sample companies in 2002. Additionally, state involvement in the ownership structure of Polish listed companies shows a downwards trend as the result of the ongoing privatization processes.

Table 10.5 presents the total stakes owned by different shareholders groups. It reveals trends with respect to the presence and the role of different shareholder groups in Polish listed companies. The role of financial institutions seems to decline; at the end of 2002 they owned less than 13 per cent of votes in all sample companies. Surprisingly, banks own merely 5 per cent of votes. However, in line with the pension system reform and substantial funds allocation by the pension funds, the involvement of these institutions on the ownership structure is growing – from 0 per cent in 1997 and 1998 to more than 2 per cent of votes in 2002. Additionally, the stakes owned by the supervisory board members increase over the period 1997–2002 reaching 10 per cent of votes of all sample companies, whereas the involvement of managers remains stable and accounts for about 5 per cent of votes. The total involvement of employees is marginal.

Econometric results

Correlations

In order to test the hypothesis on the link between ownership concentration and performance, Pearson's correlation was carried out as a preliminary method. Table 10.6 presents the Pearson's correlation results of indicators describing ownership concentration and corporate performance of the sample companies.

The results do not deliver strong evidence on the relationship between ownership concentration measures and corporate performance. As shown in the table, the dominance of the biggest shareholder is negatively related to

Table 10.5 Stakes owned by different shareholders groups, average values (median) [SD]

Shareholder's identity	1997	1998	1999	2000	2001	2002
Members of the management board	8.49 (0) [19.76]	8.6 (0.2) [17.91]	8.03 (0.2) [15.72]	8.38 (0.075) [16.82]	7.47 (0.025) [15.59]	7.4 (0.025) [15.55]
Members of the supervisory board	5.41 (0) [13.48]	6.32 (0) [14.47]	7.6 (0) [16.32]	8.84 (0) [16.91]	9.48 (0) [17.89]	9.56 (0) [17.9]
Employees	2.09 (0) [9.88]	1.23 (0) [7.53]	0.7 (0) [5]	0.52 (0) [4.77]	0.52 (0) [4.77]	0.29 (0) [2.85]
Banks	4.12 (0) [9.69]	6.58 (0) [10.53]	5.23 (0) [10.18]	5.16 (0) [10.25]	4.97 (0) [10.38]	4.99 (0) [10.23]
Insurance companies	0.33 (0) [1.96]	0.99 (0) [3.05]	1.4 (0) [4.88]	1.18 (0) [6.09]	0.43 (0) [1.88]	0.53 (0) [2.41]
Other financial	12.21 (0) [19.47]	10.95 (0) [16.41]	8.17 (0) [15.41]	6.26 (0) [13.32]	6.46 (0) [14.23]	5.07 (0) [13.18]
Pension funds	0 (0) [0]	0 (0) [0]	0.18 (0) [2.06]	0.24 (0) [1.47]	1.67 (0) [5.95]	2.05 (0) [5.1]
Financial total	15.74 (7) [0.64]	18.52 (14) [18.68]	15.09 (10) [17.69]	12.88 (7) [16.85]	13.41 (6) [17.94]	12.75 (6) [16.99]

performance measured by return on sales ($r = -0.18$; $p < 0.1$) and income per employee ($r = -0.2$; $p < 0.05$). The results indicate a positive relationship between concentration exerted by more than one shareholder and performance – the stake of the three biggest shareholders correlates with operational return ($r = 0.18$; $p < 0.1$) and the stake of the five biggest shareholders also correlates with operational return ($r = 0.197$; $p < 0.05$). The stake of the second biggest shareholder reveals a positive relationship with operational return ($r = 0.34$; $p < 0.001$), but a negative relationship with return on equity ($r = -0.017$; $p < 0.1$). The stake of dispersed ownership correlates negatively with operational return ($r = -0.2$; $p < 0.05$). In conclusion, all the above mentioned statistics refer to accounting indicators, and it is interesting to notice that the strongest correlations are observed for the case of the profitability measure based on (sectorally adjusted) operational income, which is not affected directly by costs of finance and is most closely related to overall productivity. However, there are no statistically significant results related to

Table 10.6   Results of Pearson's correlation for ownership and performance variables

Variable	Number of observations[a]	ROE	ROA	ROS	OPERAT. RETURN	INCOME Per EMPL	PROXY FOR Q
HH indicator	106/100	−.029	.021	−.158	.089	−.155	.101
Number of shareholders	106/100	−.003	.015	.005	.067	.013	−.024
Biggest shareholder	106/100	−.018	−.098	−.190(†)	.027	−.202(*)	.114
Second biggest shareholder	101/97	−.171(†)	.056	.054	.335(***)	.009	.149
3 shareholders total	106/100	−.106	−.042	−.123	.175 (†)	−.164	.157
5 shareholders total	106/100	−.090	−.014	−.113	.197(*)	−.118	.160
Dispersed ownership	106/100	.095	.008	.092	−.193(*)	.113	−.177(†)

[a] First figure relates to the number of observations for five financial indicators, the second to the number of observations for Tobin's Q. $†p < 0.1$; $*p < 0.05$; $***p < 0.001$

the proxy for Tobin's Q. This could be explained by problems with the denominator: historical book values may not be good proxies for the value of assets in the transition context.

Although the analysis does not deliver strong results about ownership concentration and corporate performance, some of the outcomes can suggest a positive role of concentration. The concentration of the three and five biggest shareholders proves to be positive and relates to better performance. However, the stronger position of the biggest shareholder leads to poor performance indices what may suggest the detrimental effects of a dominant owner realizing his/her own interest at the cost of other shareholders. The role of the second biggest shareholder is rather positive although the results are mixed. Dispersed ownership correlated with worse economic results for the sample companies proves consistent with previous research (see surveys by Megginson and Netter, 2001; Djankov and Murrell, 2002).

Regression

In order to test the relationship between ownership structure and performance, a regression analysis was carried out. The analysis focused on the following concentration indicators: the number of shareholders, the *HH* indicator, the stake of the dominant shareholder, the stake of the second biggest shareholder, the total stake of the three biggest shareholders and the total stake of the five biggest shareholders. The analysis on the accounting measures such as ROA, ROE, ROS, Tobin's Q and ownership characteristics does not prove to be statistically significant. Statistically significant results were indicated only in the regression with the operational return and these outcomes are presented in Table 10.7. As argued above, the operational return may be taken as a good proxy for performance, and that may be the underlying reason for the more significant results.

As seen in Table 10.7, the stake of the second biggest shareholder is positively associated with the operational return of the sample companies. This finding is consistent with the correlation results and may indicate that the presence and stronger position of the second biggest shareholder may balance the negative results of the dominant owner who may realize his/her own interest acting at the cost of other shareholders. Therefore, the stake of the second biggest shareholder who may deliver some monitoring and control proves to be positive and is related to better performance.

Additional regression analysis was conducted in order to test whether the relationship between the stake of the second biggest shareholder and the operational return of the sample companies remains statistically significant when we control for the main shareholder identity. The six categories of ownership identity were taken into account: variables for the stake of financial shareholders, foreign companies, domestic companies, the state, insiders as well as private individuals (not insiders). A regression based on the ownership identity variables alone was insignificant ($F(7,93) = 0.66$; $p > 0.05$; $R^2 = 0.05$). Only when the predictors based on ownership concentration (the stake of the biggest shareholder, the stake of the second biggest shareholder) were entered into the regression model in the second step, did the model become significant ($F(9,91) = 1.98$; $p = 0.05$). As presented in Table 10.8, the regression analysis

Table 10.7   OLS regression results; dependent variable: operational return

	B	*Beta*	t
Biggest shareholder	0.000	0.006	0.62
Second biggest shareholder	0.035	0.335	3.54**
Constant	−0.5		−3.13**
Adj R^2		0.11	

Note: ** $p < 0.01$

Table 10.8   OLS regression results; dependent variable: operational return; controlling for ownership identity

	B	*Beta*	t
Biggest shareholder	0.002	0.071	0.576
Second biggest shareholder	0.036	3.562	3.56***
Const.	−0.4		−0.039
Adj R^2		0.16	

Note: *** $p < 0.001$

confirms that the relationship between the stake of the second biggest share-holder and the operational return of the sample companies remains statistically significant even when we control for ownership identity.

Listing method

We also performed additional tests based on the distinction between privatized and new private companies (see also chapter by Mickiewicz in this volume). Accordingly, the sample companies were divided into two groups: listed during the privatization process and newly founded companies listed on the stock exchange. Since these two groups were unequal in size, the U Mann Whitney non-parametric test was used. The results are presented in Figure 10.1.

The analysis reveals that the origin of companies differentiates corporate performance estimated by operational return ($U = 1152$; $p < 0.01$) and return on assets ($U = 1358$; $p = 0.06$). As shown in Figure 10.1, the newly founded companies perform better that the privatized (that is, formerly state owned) companies. The newly established companies are significantly more efficient by all the variables based on accounting data. This finding is consistent with the opinion that the privatization and restructuring of the

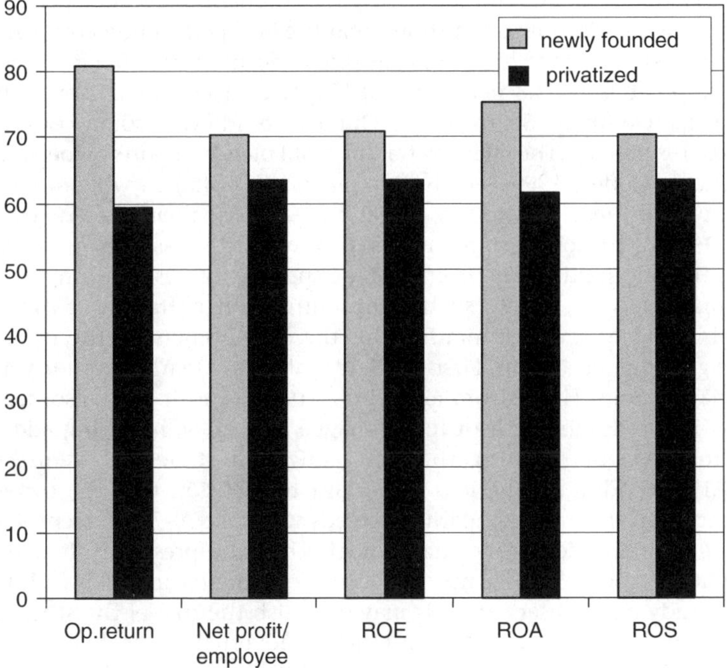

Figure 10.1   Origin of companies and performance

former SOEs is a long and costly process, and the new private sector is a driving force of corporate performance. It also mirrors Chadam and Pastuszak's results reported in this volume.

Further discussion

Research results

The analysis reveals significant ownership concentration in Polish listed companies, consistent with the results of other researchers (see Grosfeld and Tresel, 2002, and Dzierżanowski and Tamowicz, 2002). The dominant shareholder holds on average a 41 per cent state of votes, whereas the three biggest shareholders control almost 60 per cent of the votes. Ownership concentration seems to at least to some extent result from the privatization schemes favouring the sale of the company to a strategic investor. Second, ownership concentration corresponds to the continental Europe ownership patterns (Carlin and Mayer, 2000), since – for listed companies – Poland still reveals a medium ownership concentration compared to other countries such as Austria, Italy or Spain. The latest analysis carried out by Kirchmaeir and Grant (2005) indicates the dominance of legal control (over 50 per cent stake) for listed companies in France, Germany, Spain and Italy. Only UK companies reveal dispersed ownership. However their research shows that the best performing companies are characterized not by the highest ownership concentration, but either by block ownership between 33.3 per cent and 50 per cent (France) or by dispersed ownership (Germany, Spain, Italy). Our results indicate some convergence towards this pattern. The civil law tradition of Poland supports ownership concentrations (Coffee, 1999; see also McGee in this volume), which may result from investors' reactions to weak legal protection of their interests (La Porta *et al.*, 1999a). Although some analyses show positive aspects of ownership concentration, particularly from the perspective of restructuring schemes (Commander *et al.*, 1999), such a substantial concentration of ownership may also lead to severe limitations for the development of the Polish corporate governance system. First of all, it limits stockmarket liquidity and its information role (Holmstrom and Tirole, 1993), and it may also deter the motivation and behaviour of top managers as well as incurring additional costs for investors limiting their diversification strategies (Demsetz and Lehn, 1985). Additionally, it is important to mention that the ownership concentration in some companies exceeds the stake of 75 per cent votes in the hands of the dominant shareholder. Thus the presence of such companies at the stock exchange may be severely questioned and their withdrawals have already been observed. This may diminish the role of the stockmarket as the source for capital and as an efficient governance mechanism. It also affects the information role of the stockmarket. On the other hand, the rapid development of the Warsaw Stock Exchange should also be noted – in 2004 the

Polish stockmarket was ranked second (after the LSE) in terms of new listings and the trend continued in 2005 (see also discussion by Köke and Schröder in this volume). Research shows that the dominant shareholders' presence deflates stock prices (Pajuste, 2002), since they realize private benefits of control (Grossman and Hart, 1986).

Moreover, the results indicate that the ownership concentration of listed companies is substantial and was growing over the analysed period of six years. Concentration calculated by the stake of the dominant shareholder as well by the stake of the three and five biggest shareholders increases. The stake of the dominant shareholder rose from 34 per cent in 1997 to almost 41 per cent in 2002, in terms of votes, whereas the position of the three biggest shareholders increased from 52 per cent in 1997 to 59 per cent of votes in 2002. At the same time the free float calculated as the stake held by shareholders who own less than 5 per cent fell from 43 per cent in 1997 to merely 33 per cent in 2002. All the research on the ownership concentration is consistent with previous analyses (Grosfeld and Tresel, 2002; Kozarzewski, 2002; Dzierżanowski and Tamowicz, 2002; Olsson and Alasheyeva, 2000; see also chapters by Mickiewicz and by Andreff in this volume).

Our analysis also focuses on aspects of shareholders' identity. The research reveals substantial involvement of institutional investors, particularly the increase of the stakes of foreign investors and the decrease for financial institutions in the ownership structure. This corresponds with the withdrawal of 'structural' intermediaries in the privatization and the restructuring processes. The decreasing presence of national investment funds is observed since the funds withdraw after the company's sale to the strategic industry-based investors. Banks' stakes are very small (consistent with Kozarzewski, 2002, and Mickiewicz in this volume). Insiders or other individuals are the dominant shareholders in approximately of one-third of sample companies although their stakes are – on average – not substantial. For the listed companies, the involvement of employees is marginal. Moreover, for newly founded companies the founders tend to withdraw from the top management teams to the supervisory board, shifting from management to supervision functions.

The analysis focuses on the efficiency of the ownership structure as the governance mechanisms in Polish listed companies. It reveals negative relations of dispersed ownership calculated as stakes smaller that 5 per cent (which are not obliged to be disclosed) and corporate performance. Pearson's correlations indicate that companies with dispersed ownership were performing worse between 1997 and 2002. Consistent with this finding our analysis shows a positive relationship of the ownership concentration measured by the stake of the three and the five biggest shareholders for performance indices. This finding is consistent with previous research of companies in transition economies (see the reviews by Megginson and Netter, 2001; Djankov and Murrell, 2002).

The analysis shows, however, that ownership concentration is positive for Polish companies under certain conditions. The position of the second biggest shareholder is important, and the results suggest that the ownership concentration is positive only if the biggest shareholder does not dominate the company. As the regression analysis indicates, the role of the second biggest shareholder appears to be crucial. Owning a significant stake, the second biggest shareholder can monitor the dominant shareholder, may outweigh his/her impact on the company, and exert a monitoring role leading to better performance of the company. The relation remains statistically significant even when the shareholder identity is controlled for. Therefore ownership concentration may be turned into value-destroying practices of dominant shareholders if they hold large stakes, have full control over the company and are not monitored by strong minority blockholders. This finding is confirmed by the examples of companies controlled by dominant shareholders, whose value-destroying strategies (transfer pricing, share-diluting) were challenged by strong minority shareholders, pension funds in particular (Stomil Olsztyn, Bank Śląski).

Finally, the analysis as regards company origins was tested in order to identify any differences between newly founded and privatized enterprises. It reveals that newly founded companies perform better that the privatized formerly state-owned companies; the newly established companies are significantly more efficient as calculated by all the dependent variables based on accounting data. This finding is consistent with Chadam and Pastuszak findings, reported in this volume, and generally with the research that stresses the performance-enhancing role of new entry (see also Mickiewicz in this volume).

Limitations

Limitations of the research methodology should be mentioned. Despite substantial improvement in the disclosure of the data referring to performance as well as the control structure, the high standards of the developed countries have not yet been achieved (see McGee in this volume). Some information is still not disclosed, and some financial reports, mostly from earlier years however, have missing data. The accounting and stockmarket data that were used for estimation of the performance indicators reveal significant noisiness, and the short period of six years taken for the analysis is also a limitation for research interpretation.

Notes

1   For economies in transition, the application of a wider theoretical perspective that includes conflicts between managers and employees as well as between dominant and minority shareholders is suggested (Pistor, 2003). From the perspective of this broader agency theory, corporate governance is related to various control mechanisms that limit the conflicts between different actors in the company.

2   The same trends are observed for Baltic countries and Slovakia (Olsson and Alasheyeva, 2000).

3   Some other research, however, finds evidence for large insider ownership (Jelic *et al.*, 2001).

Part V

Stockmarket Finance and Corporate Governance Rules

11

Home Bias and Stockmarket Development: The Polish Experience*

Anna Zalewska

Introduction

Over 40 developing countries have engaged in significant reform of their pension structures since the 1980s. In Central and Eastern Europe (CEE) and central Asia alone, 14 countries have introduced voluntary and compulsory saving schemes that operate in addition to the preexisting (often simultaneously reformed) pay-as-you-go (PAYG) systems. Poland is one of the countries that have already implemented pension reforms along these lines. Under the slogan 'security via diversity' the Polish authorities have restructured the existing defined-contribution PAYG system (first pillar) and introduced two additional segments, one based on compulsory contributions (second pillar) and one based on voluntarily contributions (third pillar). To compliment the introduction of the compulsory pillar, 21 private pension funds were created and started to collect and invest money of future pensioners.[1] However, the commitment to diversification as a method of securing the efficient allocation of collected contributions did not stretch as far as one might expect. The Polish authorities have imposed restrictions on the assets that the pension funds could use in their portfolio allocation decisions and the capital markets that they are free to invest in. In particular, they have put strong limits on how much money could be invested on international markets (max. 5 per cent) and have effectively restricted the pension funds to invest on the domestic market only. In this way, diversification and, hence, security of investments have not been fully implemented. This chapter is concerned with the general issue of home bias and stockmarket development and uses the Polish experience as a case study.[2] I discuss the main arguments for portfolio diversification, some of the main side effects that emerge from locking significant amounts of money on underdeveloped

* The chapter was prepared for and presented at the Finance and Corporate Governance Conference, UCL, London. I would like to thank participants of my seminar at the National Bank of Poland for interesting comments and suggestions.

equity markets, and assess some problems that can already be observed on the Polish capital market as a result of the 'enforced' home bias.

Approximately 800 million people, or one-third of the total world labour force, are covered by publicly managed pension schemes. Of this, 80 per cent is covered by mandatory publicly managed defined-benefits, of which nearly 50 per cent are PAYG schemes and over 30 per cent are partially funded schemes. The remaining contributors are covered by a mix of public and privately funded defined-benefit and defined-contribution schemes. The three-tier system (consisting of a government guaranteed PAYG part, a compulsory scheme that obliges workers to save via contributions in purpose-created pension funds, and the third, a voluntary component) has been widely proposed and implemented. In particular, the World Bank has been one of the biggest and most important propagators and sponsors of the three-pillar system.

The tendency to focus on the increasing body of pensioners seems more present in middle-income countries. In 1981, with the support of the World Bank, Chile started to restructure its pension systems believing that the reforms would benefit both pensioners and economic systems.[3] Both hopes and stakes were high. Since then nine more countries in Latin America have implemented laws introducing mandatory savings, and two more have passed relevant laws necessary to implement reforms. The World Bank sees pension reform as the way to fight poverty, regulate the workforce, improve governments' finances, stimulate the development of financial markets and institutions and, in consequence, boost economic growth.[4] More recently the post-communist countries of Central and Eastern Europe (CEE) have stepped on to the path of pension reform. Over the last decade 14 countries started to restructure pension systems of which 10 have implemented new structures. Using the Latin American reform as a pattern, compulsory and voluntary pension schemes were created and pension funds started to operate. However, the most recent assessment of the Latin American pension reform shows rather disappointing results (see for example Indermit, Packard and Yermo, 2005).[5] This raises serious worries whether the chosen methods are appropriate and about the future performance of pension reform.

When we consider the pension reforms in post-communist counties, the benchmark of success has an extra dimension. Pensioners' welfare and government spending were not the only anticipated beneficiaries. Pension reform and, in particular the creation of pension funds as big institutional investors, has been seen as an integral part of the reform of the financial system.

The importance of financial market development makes the CEE experience very different from the Latin America experience. When pension funds started to operate in countries like Chile or Argentina, the equity and bond markets of those countries were relatively sizable and provided some opportunity for investment. In contrast, when the first pension funds of the post-communist countries started to invest (for example in Hungary, the Czech Republic), their domestic equity and bond markets were still very small and highly underdeveloped. Obviously, this brought serious limitations to the investment opportunities for pension funds in general and, in particular, on their ability to diversify portfolios.

Some common characteristics can be identified when comparing the investment practices of the pension funds operating in CEE. First, most, if not all, pension funds' monies tend to be invested at home. Second, most of the monies have been located in government bonds, and the remainder has been mostly invested in local shares. Such an allocation cannot be good for the funds and pensioners who rightly expect a decent return on their savings. Moreover, it may not be good for the markets themselves since they are not big enough to efficiently allocate substantial cash inflows.

In the light of the above, an assessment of the pension reform experience is extremely important both to better understand the drivers behind the current unsatisfactory position of the pension market, and to learn lessons from the mistakes that have been made so far. This has relevance for countries that have decades of experience and feel disappointed with their situation, those who have just started to implement reforms and those whose pension reforms are still in an embryonic form.

The performance of pension reforms can be assessed from several perspectives. First, the low level of contributors as a ratio of the labour force (for example less that 20 per cent in many Latin American countries) suggests that the reforms have not succeeded in securing an income in old age for a vast majority of the population. Second, the recent experience of Argentina clearly shows that even those who are covered by the compulsory pension schemes may not be able to secure their retirement income. Argentina's default on government bonds has deeply affected the portfolios of pension funds that had heavily invested in government securities. Recent developments on the Russian pension market also clearly demonstrate that a strategy of investment in government bonds may not be as safe as Russian investors may have thought when they made a decision to leave their savings in the national pension fund managed by the state-owned Vneshekonombank. Thanks to high oil and gas prices on international markets the Russian government does not have much need to issue new debt and, hence, burden itself with obligations to pay high interest on it. Therefore, the current yield of about 7 per cent does not cover the two-digit inflation and as a result pensioners' savings do not earn a positive real rate of return. Third, it is not obvious that pension funds stimulate development of the local financial sectors and are a driving force for financial and economic development and integration across borders.

In this chapter I abstract from the issue of incentives for employers and employees to increase participation rates and the related social issues, such as how to deal with unfulfilled obligations (for example the deficits in pension funds portfolios). Instead, I concentrate on the link between home bias (that is, the strong tendency of pension funds to invest on domestic markets), the profitability of such investments and the development of financial markets. I expand on the well-documented view in the financial literature that home bias has a negative impact on portfolio performance by claiming that home bias may also be harmful for the development of markets where it occurs. To illustrate the point I discuss the case of the Polish pension funds' investment practices. I document the weak performance of pension funds' equity investments and argue that the enforced home bias is responsible for the situation. In particular, the very limited diversification opportunities faced by pension funds are partly responsible for the situation and may result in even weaker performance in the future. The findings support the view that enforced home bias has a negative impact on the local stockmarket development, on the performance of pension funds, and on the whole of pension reform. The findings suggest that borders should be opened to capital flows.

The chapter is organized as follows. In the next section I outline the basic arguments for portfolio diversification and provide some evidence on its practical effect. The existing literature on the impact of pension funds on market development is then summarized, and data from the Warsaw Stock Exchange interpreted. A final section closes with conclusions.

Diversification in theory and practice

The idea of locking funds on domestic markets contrasts sharply with the financial principles of efficient asset allocation stemming from Markowitz portfolio theory. When investment opportunities are limited to a group of highly correlated assets (that is, assets that are characterized by high sensitivity to the same factor or factors), investors become vulnerable to potentially adverse market conditions. Assuming that an investor's main objective is to maximize return for a given level of risk (or minimize risk for a given level of return), she or he benefits from diversification when less than perfectly correlated assets are included in the portfolio.

The reduction in risk that arises through the inclusion of low correlated assets in a portfolio is illustrated in Figure 11.1, which shows the level of risk for portfolios of assets that are characterized by different levels of correlation. Here, risk is represented by standard deviation and the portfolios contain up to 30 assets. The fact that a portfolio consists of many assets does not imply that there are any diversification benefits. The top line represents the risk of an (equally weighted) portfolio that is constructed using assets with the pair-wise correlation coefficient of 0.8, and shows that the initial reduction of risk achieved from including, say, three assets does not improve when more assets are put in the portfolio. The standard deviation of the portfolio remains nearly unaltered whether 10 or 30 stocks are included. The diversification benefits kick in when the correlation between assets is low. For instance, the bottom line that represents risk of a portfolio based on uncorrelated assets (the correlation coefficient is equal to zero). The standard deviation of the

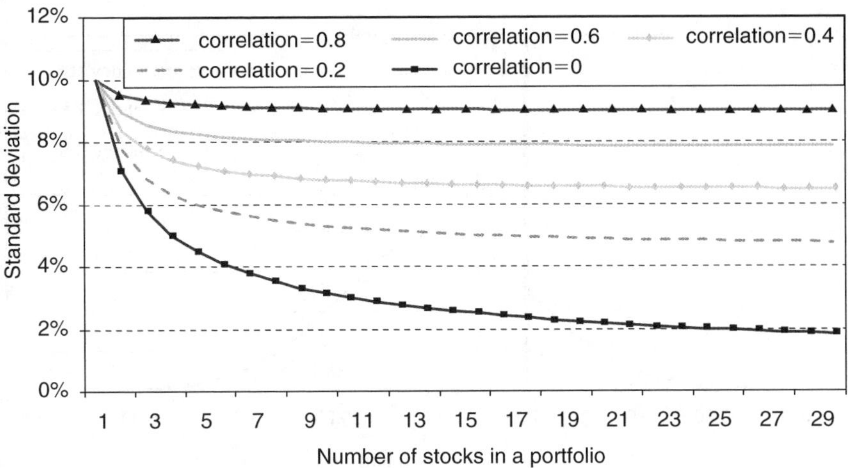

Figure 11.1   Impact of different correlation levels of stocks included in a portfolio on a portfolio's risk

portfolio consisting of uncorrelated assets drops from the initial 10 per cent level (the standard deviation of every individual asset) to less than 2 per cent when 30 assets are included. This is equivalent to more than an 80 per cent risk reduction. It is important to note, that this reduction in risk does not affect the expected return in this sense that the expected return on each portfolio for every level of correlation is the same; that is, although the standard deviations of the portfolios differ and depend on the size of correlation between assets, the mean values of the portfolio are the same for each number of assets included.

To highlight the benefits of diversification, Figure 11.2 shows that the effect of high volatility on the probability of losing money increases substantially when portfolio risk increases. If we assume that the expected average return on a portfolio is 8 per cent, then the probability of not earning a positive return is 21.2 per cent, 14.3 per cent and 5.5 per cent when the standard deviation is 10 per cent, 7.5 per cent and 5 per cent respectively. Therefore, in this example a twofold decrease in standard deviation results in nearly a quadrupled decrease in the probability of not making any money at all.

Therefore, making the 'right' diversification, rather than simply including many (highly correlated) assets in a portfolio, is vital to minimize portfolio risk and the likelihood of losing money. However, in practice there is no simple and unique answer to what the 'right' portfolio is. This is partly because the choice of assets for a diversified portfolio is based on expectations on the future performance of assets that, by definition, are not known with certainty

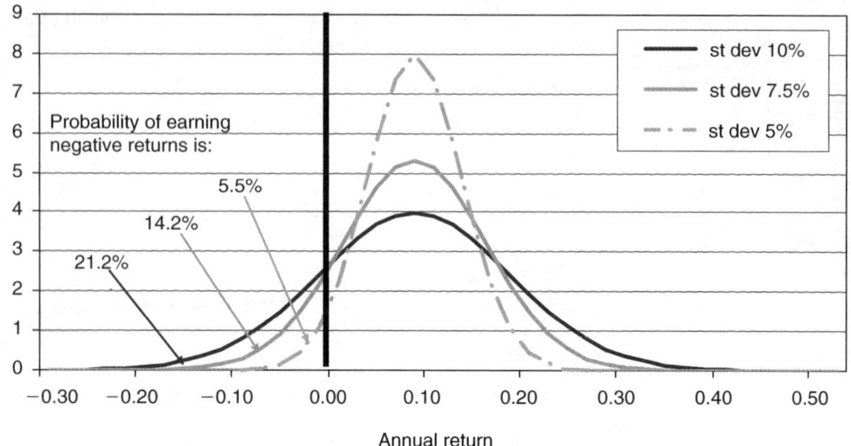

Figure 11.2　Return distribution and probability of losing money

at the time of the portfolio creation. Moreover, despite the common assumption that investors have homogeneous preferences, investors have indeed different characteristics (for example attitudes to risk exposure, or time-horizon of investment). Transactions costs also restrict optimal allocation.

The first, systematic approach to the problem of the optimal portfolio selection was offered by Tobin (1958) who postulated the idea of the efficient portfolio; that is, a uniquely defined portfolio held by all investors, consisting of all assets available on the market (the mutual fund theorem). The efficient portfolio guarantees the optimal allocation of assets in the sense that in the absence of transactions costs it offers the lowest exposure to risk for the highest return (determined by the risk-free rate of return available on the market).

However, this idea of holding a unique portfolio by all investors contrasts with the advice of financial planners. Asset managers and financial planners differ sharply in their advice on asset allocation to clients. The individual differences stem, for example, from the fact that different investors have different degrees of risk-aversion. For instance, in addition to differences in personal taste and the amount of money that investors are ready to gamble, such factors as the investors' age and, somewhat related to this, the investment horizon are strong determinants of the selection choice.

Bodie (2001) suggests that as long as age is the determining factor of the asset allocation, the general rule of thumb should be that the percentage invested in equities should be 100 minus the investor's age. More explicitly, a person 30 years old should invest 70 per cent in equities, whereas a person of 60 years of age should reduce the equity exposure to 40 per cent.

Campbell and Viceira (2002) also argue that the optimal portfolio of long-term investors may be quite different from that of short-term investors. The long-horizon analysis assigns a far more important role of bonds in the optimal portfolio. Although cash (that is, the money market) and T-bills are assumed to be risk-free in traditional financial analysis, they are risky, or even very risky, when a long-horizon investment is considered. Their long-term risk stems from the fact that when a long-horizon is under consideration, the money or T-bill investments must be rolled over at uncertain future interest rates. Long-term bonds with low inflation uncertainty, or better still, inflation-indexed bonds are much safer for a long-term investor. Campbell and Viceira (2002) also show that in the absence of complete financial markets (highly likely in the case of emerging markets) the time-varying nature of volatility of stock returns warrants a reduction in stocks (estimated to be around 10 per cent for the US data, presumably more for an emerging market). Finally, they show that while it is optimal for a young person to hold more stocks (an argument consistent with Bodie, 2001), this advice has to be nuanced when investors have insecure jobs and/or are close to subsistence levels of consumption (this argument might also strongly apply to emerging markets). Canner, Mankiw and Weil (1997) show that in the period 1926–92 the optimal portfolio on the US market should hold bonds and stocks in a ratio 1:3.

Therefore, the question of what is the 'right' decomposition of assets in a portfolio is far from having a unique answer. This ambiguity is particularly troublesome when portfolios of pension funds are discussed. This is because, although pension funds are definitively long-term investors, they manage portfolios of very diversified groups of clients. While many young contributors may be quite happy to invest in more risky assets, older contributors and those already receiving their pensions may find portfolios dominated by risky assets unacceptable.

This problem of different preferences may be particularly relevant to newly created funds (like those in the CEE) that have a relatively high proportion of young contributors. This suggests that 'young' pension funds may be more equity oriented to match the preferences of the relatively young group of contributors. However, emerging markets are prone to higher inflationary pressures and economic instabilities that result in higher unemployment swings and this factor may bend the choice of the portfolio allocation towards bonds.

Bonds or stocks?

In contrast to the financial literature, which emphasizes the benefits of diversification, several economists (particularly those associated with the actuarial industry) argue that pension payments are bond-like in nature, and therefore pension funds should not take risks with the sponsoring company's shareholders' funds. In the light of this, they suggest that pension funds should invest heavily, or even completely, in government (domestic) bonds (see for example Bodie, 1995; Exley, Mehta and Smith, 1997; Gold, 2001; Bader and Gold, 2003). This, they argue, would also help governments finance their national debt (again an appealing argument for emerging markets). However, even if such investment strategies fulfil a 'patriotic' duty towards financing government debt, it does not make the investment safer or even profitable enough to cover pension funds' liabilities, which should be the primary objective of funds' managers. In addition, such investment policies are a clear violation of the generic idea behind pension reform and the creation of a compulsory saving pillar that is separated from the centralized PAYG scheme. This is because, if government debt is the primary asset of allocation, pensioners' wealth directly depends on the government 'generosity', that is the size of a premium on government bonds. If for some reason the government keeps such interest rates low, or even negative in real terms as it is currently in Russia, compulsory saving for retirement is more like a time-bomb than a long-term solution to pension deficit.

Moreover, if a smooth transfer of contributions between pension funds' clients and the government is the main responsibility of pension fund managers, then the high fees that managers typically receive as the reward for their asset allocation skills are not justifiable. In addition, the concentration on government debt as the investment asset does not rationalise social and fiscal cost related to the creation and management of compulsory pension funds. In fact, there is no need to have pension funds, and one central organization, similar or even the same as the one that is responsible for PAYG contributions and pension payments should be sufficient.

Moreover, despite the common belief to the contrary, bond investments are not safe, especially on emerging markets. For example, the prolonged Argentinean recession and the final default on government bonds in August 2003 present a strong argument against investing in (local) bonds.[6] Elsewhere, the financial and economic distress experienced by Brazil in the 1980s and early 1990s clearly shows that a guaranteed high demand for government bonds (especially those that are inflation-indexed) may loosen government's discipline on monetary and fiscal policy and spiral inflation.

Heavy investment in government bonds can be troublesome on developed markets, too. The enforced bond bias that took place in the UK after the collapse of the Maxwell Pension Fund in 1992 resulted in a lower rate of return on pension fund investments.[7] However, more recent statistics show that the problem arising from low yields is far from over. The stockmarkets' fall in 2000–03 had a large impact on pension fund portfolios and appears to convince pension fund managers that bonds rather than equities are a better match for the long-term liabilities of pension funds. This view has resulted in an increase in the demand for bonds with bond holdings rising from 16 per cent to 22 per cent in recent years. The effect is that bond yields have tumbled and the pension fund deficit has grown to £35 billion.[8]

Therefore, are stocks an alternative investment despite their inherent high risk? On average stocks do offer a higher expected return (to compensate for their higher risk), but one must remember that the expected equity risk premium that attracts investors may not be realized. MaCurdy and Shoven (2001) show that 25 per cent of time equity investments underperform 20-year inflation-indexed bonds yielding 3.5 per cent in real terms. Crashes on equity markets do happen, and they are not exclusively an emerging market phenomenon (for example the 2000–01 correction that shook developed markets and ended the period of the high-tech boom is a good example).

In the case of emerging markets, and especially those of CEE, an additional problem with extensive equity investment can stem from the fact that domestic markets offer very limited investment opportunities. The lack of stocks that a prudent fund manager would be willing to invest in, that is stocks big enough, liquid enough and about which information is reliable and available, can be a major obstacle. For instance in Peru, although there are 202 listed stocks, only nine are large and liquid enough to be included in the S&P/IFC index. These nine comprise 94 per cent of the volume traded in the country's stock exchange. On the Prague Stock Exchange and the Budapest Stock Exchange there are alltogether 55 and 54 listed stocks respectively (end of 2004). The Warsaw Stock Exchange, with 230 stocks, is definitively one of the biggest and most developed stock exchanges of the CEE region, however only 25 of the listings have been included in the S&P/FCI index. Eight of these stocks are from the banking sector, five are chemicals and four are construction firms. The remaining companies are from the media, gas & oil, and high-tech sectors. Such narrow sector divisions indicate that, not only are there very few stocks that a big institutional investor might be willing to invest in, but also the returns on these companies may be highly correlated. This indicates that diversification opportunities are limited. To illustrate the case, Table 11.1 shows correlation coefficients calculated for the sector indices that companies included in the S&P/FCI index come from (that is, banking, chemical, constructions, gas & oil, telecoms & media, and software & computers). The correlations are calculated for monthly returns over the period 2001–04. it is apparent, that with correlation coefficients as these presented in Table 11.1 reduction of risk resulting from investing in the biggest companies listed on the Warsaw Stock Exchange is weak.

The scarcity of stocks available on emerging markets contrasts with the abundance of government bonds available on these markets. Local authorities often use pension funds' assets as an easy way to finance government debt (again, Argentina's case should be a warning against such practices). This 'patriotic support' can be enforced by direct or indirect restrictions on the portfolio allocation of pension funds.

Table 11.1   Correlation coefficients of the Warsaw Stock Exchange selected sector indices, 2001–04

Sector indices	Banks	Chemicals	Construction	Gas & oil	Telecom & media	Software & computers
Banks	1					
Chemicals	0.54	1				
Construction	0.61	0.52	1			
Gas & oil	0.69	0.66	0.61	1		
Telecom & media	0.70	0.71	0.56	0.80	1	
Software & computers	0.63	0.73	0.57	0.73	0.79	1

Note: Statistics are based on monthly observations.
Source: Own calculations based on data available from DataStream.

In summary, investment in equities alone or bonds alone does not automatically guarantee success especially when domestic assets only are included in a portfolio. It has been shown that risk is lower and there is a lower probability of losing money when a portfolio is built on low-correlated assets. Therefore, investment must be open to international markets that offer a broader range of low correlated assets.

Investment in practice

Some developed countries have advanced private pension schemes with significant foreign investments in their portfolios. For example, in the Netherlands foreign assets can be up to 70 per cent of pension fund portfolios (this includes within-EU investments). In the case of the UK and Japan, foreign assets constitute about 23–24 per cent of portfolios. Similar figures are recorded for Chilean funds. However, such high figures are not general for either developed or emerging markets. In Germany and France, where pension reforms have proved difficult to implement, only 10 per cent of the operating pension funds' assets are allocated on international markets. In the case of emerging markets, even those with compulsory pension schemes, international assets are only a small proportion of total assets included in pension funds' portfolios. For instance, in Argentina and Peru the foreign assets are below 9 per cent, and 7 per cent respectively. In the post-communist countries of CEE these ratios are close or even equal to zero.

The lack of international diversification is striking since the small scale of local equity markets means that most of the collected contributions have to be invested in local, predominantly government bonds. Iglesias (2002) reports that 83.4 per cent of El Salvador' pension funds assets are invested in domestic bonds. Analogous figures for Bolivia and Uruguay are 73.5 per cent and 57.6 per cent respectively. In the case of CEE countries, high ratios are also observed. For instance, in Hungary and the Czech Republic 76–78 per cent and 84 per cent of pension funds' assets under management are invested in local T-bonds. In Poland the proportion of bond investment reached 60 per cent in 2004. With T-bills added the ratio was 64 per cent. This is particularly important given that the size of the Polish public debt exceeds 50 per cent of GDP (EBRD, 2004).

Russia is also an interesting case. Although the Russian pension system reformers displayed a very positive attitude towards international investments for non-governmental pension funds, governmental organizations are restricted to investing in governments bonds only.[9] This might not be a serious limitation if pension savings were more or less evenly distributed among governmental and non-governmental funds. However, since 'the decision to set low requirements for asset managers – both domestic and foreign – is seen as a result of fierce lobbying by Russia's powerful financial groups in the highest echelons of the government",[10] ordinary Russian have chosen not to move their savings to newly created pension funds, but stay with a default fund managed by the state-owned Vneshekonombank. As a result $5 billion of savings have been invested in government bonds that offer a rate of interest far below the inflation rate.[11]

Overall the statistics indicate strong domestic bias and tendency to invest in bonds. The domestic bias is partly the result of inefficient markets (that is, lack of information on foreign assets, restrictions to trade, and so on), but mostly it is enforced by authorities in an attempt to boost the development of local markets.[12] The bias towards bond investment often results from investment regulations faced by pension funds. It may, however, also reflect the fact that there are not enough equities available on domestic markets that fund managers are able and willing to invest in.

Restrictions on pension funds' international investments are quite common. For example, German, Italian and Canadian funds must not invest more than 20 per cent of their assets abroad. The UK and US regulations are somewhat more liberal as funds must apply a 'prudential rule' to the size of international investments. In the case of emerging markets restrictions are typically much stronger. For instance, Polish pension funds can invest no more than 5 per cent abroad, in Peru 8 per cent, and in Argentina 10 per cent. Brazilian funds are restricted to invest all their money at home. Chilean authorities are more liberal, allowing up to 30 per cent of money to be allocated in foreign assets. However, this was not always the case; in the early 1980s, when the funds started to operate, they were restricted to invest all their money in domestic fixed-income securities.

Taking into account the limited domestic investment opportunities of (emerging) markets, it is striking that local authorities impose such restrictions on the funds. It is even more surprising that the World Bank, which promotes and stands by pension reform programmes, has not exercised stronger powers to change these 'xenophobic' attitudes. If the World Bank is such an advocate of international diversification, as James (1996), for example claims, then more efforts should be made to stop local governments from locking pensioners' money on domestic markets.

Since it is obvious that such restrictions do not help funds to improve their performance, enforced home bias could be justified if and only if it resulted in other broader benefits. Given that one of the expected consequences of pension reform is the improvement and further development of domestic financial structures and institutions, the decision to lock funds on local markets could be justified if such improvements and efficiency gains have been actually taking place. As the next sections show, this is not the case.

Home bias and financial market development

In theory, financial institutions should stimulate economic growth as they increase the rate of savings/investment and improve the efficient allocation of funds (for example, see the endogenous growth models of Lucas, 1988, and Roemer, 1989). However, empirical research indicates a less straightforward relationship, with deviations from the theoretical predictions being particularly prevalent in developing markets. Emerging markets exhibit inefficiencies at various levels of market organization and operation, resulting in dramatic departures from 'friction-less market' theoretical assumptions.

In the early 1980s, when the World Bank started to champion the idea of pension reform via the introduction of a three-pillar system, it was argued that the creation of big institutional investors would lead to financial market deepening. In particular, it was argued that strong institutional investors (that is, pension funds) would enforce prudence and transparency of market structures and operations leading to physical and operational development of local markets. As a market's efficiency improved, more companies could be expected to go public, which would result in more capital coming on the market. This would improve market liquidity, which in turn would improve market efficiency. In addition, corporate governance of listed (and indirectly non-listed) companies would grow stronger.

The evidence, however, suggests that the introduction of pension funds as dominant investors does not have an ambiguously positive impact on market development and performance. While there is relatively strong evidence that fixed-income security markets grew (as a result of the heavy investments in government bonds), it is not obvious that these markets became more efficient. Although Roldos (2004) concludes that private pension funds in Latin America and CEE have a positive impact on the development of local bond markets, he stresses some problems with liquidity. Liquidity, or rather its lack, can be a serious problem, indeed. For example, when in 1985 Chilean pension funds gained permission to include equities in their portfolios, they found it excessively difficult to close their fixed-income position. As the result, their asset allocation changed only slowly (Srinivas, Whitehouse and Yermo, 2000).

Other problems can also emerge. For instance, Abdel-Motaal (2002) reports that in early 2003 a spread between external (swapped to pesos through cross-currency swaps) and local bonds in Mexico was around 300 basis points. The difference was mainly caused by regulations preventing local pension funds from investing abroad.[13] Similarly in Peru, Brady bonds paid higher spreads than local corporate bonds, owing to the fact that pension funds could invest only up to 5 per cent of the portfolio in sovereign external debt versus 40 per cent in corporate bonds. The Argentinean experience is yet another case of growing market inefficiencies. Although as the result of the government policy the size of the bond market had experienced steady growth, the efficiency of pricing and allocation of funds was highly questionable.

Arguments supporting the view that pension funds can have a negative impact on equity market development can also be found in the financial literature. For instance, Singh (1996) strongly criticizes the World Bank for enforcing the placement of contractual savings on underdeveloped financial markets as a part of the pension reform programme. He warns against fund misallocation and its negative impact on economic growth. He provides evidence that, in contrast to the common belief, emerging equity markets had increased less in value in the late 1980s, that is after pension funds started to invest in local equities, than they had increased in the early 1980s. The Chilean market, despite being a commonly quoted example of pension reform success, underperforms in many indicators when compared with the other 11 emerging stockmarkets discussed in the paper. Zalewska (2005) gives a systematic analysis of the development of an emerging stockmarket facing the pressure of growing pension funds. The paper documents the underperformance of the Warsaw Stock Exchange as compared with the other seven emerging CEE markets operating in the post-communist countries that joined the EU in May 2004. Zalewska (2005) shows that nearly all performance measures commonly applied to assess stockmarket performance are worse for the Polish market since 2002, that is since pension funds operating in Poland started to dominate the local market (this theme will be further developed in the next section).

Several authors stress that a significant initial level of market development is a necessary precondition for pension funds' investments to have a positive impact of on market development. For instance, Impravido, Musalem and Vittas (2003) emphasize that such a precondition is particularly important in the case of small countries that cannot fully exploit economies of scale and scope in the provision of financial services. The authors warn that in such countries the financial sectors are too small to create competition and liquidity. The markets tend to be poorly regulated and burdened with high transaction costs.

In addition, several authors stress the role of foreign investors in stimulating market development. Frenkel and Menkhoff (2004) point out that the correlation between foreign investors and market development may not be positive. They argue that foreign (less informed) investors may have a strong negative impact on the relative position of local investors as 'they are likely to amplify occurring imbalances or even trigger financial shocks'. To avoid, or at least to minimize, such situations the authors propose that local investors should be encouraged to internationally diversify their portfolios. That is, not only should foreign capital come to a developing country, but also a developing country's capital should be invested on international markets.[14] Such 'exchange' would create more balance on an emerging market and a healthier coexistence of different players.

Although Holtzmann (1999, 2000) defends the multi-pillar system sponsored by the World Bank as the solution that achieves diversification of risk, offers higher rates of return and accelerates market development, he points out that it does not solve all the problems, and in fact, its 'total effects are likely to be limited' if various political and economic preconditions are not in place. These preconditions include a reasonably developed financial market and a reduction in home bias.

All in all, there are several voices in the financial literature that argue that domestic bias is not unconditionally positively correlated with market development. Intensive investments of domestic institutional investors, such as pension funds, do not automatically impact positively on market development. Indeed, if investments are overwhelming relative to what a market can (efficiently) absorb, they may, in fact, hamper market development. To illustrate the case, the Warsaw Stock Exchange (WSE) is analysed in the next section.

The Polish experience

In 1999, when the Polish pension funds started to operate, the Warsaw Stock Exchange (WSE) was comparatively large. While small compared with the main world markets, it was big compared to the other emerging markets of CEE. For instance, at the end of 1999 the stockmarket capitalization of the WSE was just below $30 bn, that is about 1 per cent of the capitalization of the U.K. companies listed on the London Stock Exchange (£1,820.08bn or $2,939.97 bn). At the same time, the WSE was twice as big as the neighbouring markets in the Czech Republic and Hungary (with market capitalizations of about $13.5bn, and $16.7bn, respectively) and ten times as big as the Riga Stock Exchange (with capitalization of $0.3bn). The following years resulted in further growth of the WSE, both in terms of the number of companies and capitalization.[15] Table 11.2 presents some basic statistics on the WSE growth and the size of pension funds' assets and equity investments. Capitalization of the WSE was over $68 bn at the end of 2004. Although the capitalization was more than twice that recorded for 1999, it was still small compared with the capitalization of the developed markets. The biggest company on the

Table 11.2   Selected statistics of the WSE (end of year figures)

	1999	2000	2001	2002	2003	2004
No of listed companies	221	225	230	216	203	230
Equity market capitalization (bnPlz)	123.41	130.09	103.37	110.57	167.72	291.69
Equity market capitalization (bn$)	29.84	31.48	25.94	29.02	44.91	68.64
Equity market capitalization, %GDP	19.9	18.1	13.7	14.3	17.3	24.3*
Capitalization of 10 biggest companies as % of market capitalization	69.5	66.4	66.3	71.2	54.4	37.7
No of companies with capitalization > 500 mln$	13	14	15	14	16	21
% growth of market capitalization		5.4	−20.5	6.9	51.7	73.9

* based on EBRD estimates of GDP

Table 11.3   Selected statistics of OFEs' equity investments (NIFs included)

	1999	2000	2001	2002	2003	2004
Amount of OFEs assets under management (bnPlz)	2.21	9.92	19.41	31.56	45.44	62.63
Equity investments (bn Plz)	0.64	3.23	5.38	8.62	14.42	20.99
Equity investment as a % of all investment	0.30	0.35	0.29	0.28	0.33	0.34
No of companies included in the OEFs portfolios	97	117	120	106	103	143
No of companies included in the OEFs portfolios as % of all listed equities	43.9	52.0	52.2	49.1	50.7	62.2
No of companies selected by more than half of the operating OFEs	22	23	23	25	35	43
% growth of equity investment		401.9	66.5	60.1	67.3	45.6

London Stock Exchange (BP, with the market capitalization of £110bn or $211bn) was over three times as big as the total equity quoted on the WSE.

It is clear from Table 11.3 that the pension fund assets under management grew fast (although since 1999 the number of listed companies has increased slowly). The pension funds, however, have only a limited choice of assets for their portfolios. Although, there are over 200 stocks listed on the market, only 25 of them have been included in the S&P/FCI index, and these 25 contribute to about 75 per cent of market capitalization. However, OFEs (that is, the Polish abbreviation for pension funds) have been broader in their choice.[16] As Table 11.2 shows, almost from the beginning of their operation the portfolios of the pension funds include shares issued by more than 100 companies. This amounts to about 50 per cent of all listed shares, with the ratio growing to 61.5 per cent in 2004. These figures suggest that pension funds may indeed face difficulties in choosing stocks for the portfolios.

The pension funds face tight restrictions on the proportion of their assets that can be invested in equities and the proportion of shares of listed companies that they can invest in. For instance, no more than 40 per cent of total assets may be invested in publicly quoted shares although an additional 10 per cent can go to the NIF shares.[17] Within this, up to 10 per cent of total assets may be invested on parallel and free markets on the WSE with a maximum 5 per cent invested on the free market; up to 10 per cent of the total assets may be invested in shares quoted on the regulated over-the-counter market and shares not publicly quoted but admitted for public trade. In total each individual pension fund cannot hold more than 10 per cent of the shares of a company. Pension funds are not allowed to invest in securities issued by its owning company, the company managing the pension fund or any entity associated with these shareholders.

The statistics presented in Table 11.3 show not only that the choice of stocks is limited, but the stocks chosen are often chosen by several funds. About 30 per cent of all selected companies are common to more than half of the operating funds. Indeed, as many as five companies are common to all the OFEs. These are the biggest companies on the market and contribute to as much as 33.8 per cent of OFE's portfolios. Those stocks that are chosen by at least half of the operating pension funds contribute to nearly 62 per cent of the pension funds' portfolios (see Table 11.5 for more details). This suggests that risk/return characteristics of the OFE's portfolios are very similar across funds.[18] Given the cost of running a fund and the small size of the market, this raises the question of what the benefit is of having as many as 17 separate funds.

It is important to point out that the fact that a company is only included in the portfolios of a few funds does not in itself necessarily mean that they are less 'good'. The fact that few funds have bought particular shares may be the result of the limited number of shares available on the market. The free float of some companies is very small. Even if only a small number of funds buy shares within the allowed limits, these purchases can completely exhaust the freely floating shares for some companies. For instance, although only one fund (Pocztylion) invested in shares of Centrozap, it owned nearly 100 per cent of the company's free-float.[19] Table 11.4 presents, for selected companies, the percentage of free float taken over by pension funds and the number of pension funds that have invested in a particular company. The companies presented are chosen from the group of companies in which less than half of the pension funds have invested. The statistics are as of the end of December 2002.

Table 11.4   Percentage of free float acquired by pension funds for selected 'less popular' companies, December 2002

Company	% of free float acquired by OFEs	No of OFEs investing in shares	Company	% of free float acquired by OFEs	No of OFEs investing in shares
Bauma	40.98	2	Mostostal Warszawa	36.25	2
Centrozap	98.58	1	Novita	96.31	3
Cersanit	39.10	7	Permedia	68.33	3
CSS	46.15	3	Polfa Kutno	28.28	1
Eldorado	34.16	4	Polgrafia	72.25	4
Emax	72.30	5	Stomil	54.99	7
Farmacol	40.24	7	Talex	55.50	5
Grajewo	76.24	3	Telmax	30.33	2
Groclin	59.42	4	Tras Tychy S.A.	88.72	5
Krosno	46.40	4	TUE	88.21	2
Lentex	39.95	6	Wilbo	35.52	5
Mennica	38.93	2	Zywiec	56.80	6

Source: Economic Update, Bank Austria Creditanstalt, www.ca-ib.com

In contrast, Table 11.5 shows statistics on the acquisition of the free float for companies that attract the most pension funds; these companies are among the biggest on the market. The table also shows weights allocated to each of the companies in the total portfolio of pension funds and in three indexes: WIG 20 (based on the 20 biggest and most liquid companies), WIG (based on approximately the 100 biggest, and the international Morgan and Stanley MSCI index. It is apparent that the two biggest companies on the market (TP S.A. and PKN Orlen) are heavily weighted in the pension funds' portfolios. Together with Bank PEKAO (also overinvested as compared with the composition of the WIG index), these three biggest companies on the market constitute 38.4 per cent of the pension funds' portfolios. In addition, the correlation of the share price movement of these 'dominant' companies is high. In 2002 the correlation of the TP S.A. returns with the PKN Orlen returns was 60.3 per cent, and with Bank PEKAO returns 57.1 per cent.[20] PKN Orlen and Bank PEKAO returns were correlated at 42.5 per cent. A year later, 2003, the corresponding correlation coefficients were 63.2 per cent, 57.1 per cent and 55.9 per cent. These statistics alone show that diversification of pension funds portfolios is not really in place.

This does not mean, however, that the OFEs do not search for new investment opportunities. The limited number of existing listings has turned the pension funds' attention towards newcomers to the market and new listings are very popular with the funds. The financial literature, however, is very consistent in reporting long-term underperformance of IPOs. New listings, although underpriced when placed on a market, tend to provide investors

Table 11.5   OFEs' stakes in the most commonly chosen companies and their weights in leading indices

Company	OFEs' portfolios	WIG20 index	WIG index	MSCI	Free float of the stock (%)	OFEs' holdings as % of free float	No of OFEs investing in shares
	% proportion in						
TP S.A.	13.9	12.7	9.9	20.2	19.89	33.6	17
PKN Orlen	13.4	12.8	9.8	20.2	50.49	30.6	17
Bank PEKAO	11.1	14.6	10.2	24.4	34.50	17.6	16
BPH PBK	6.1	10.0	7.0	10.0	28.92	23.2	14
BZ WBK	3.6	6.1	3.0	0.0	29.53	20.2	15
ING BSK	2.9	0.0	2.4	0.0	12.23	40.2	9
Prokom	2.8	6.4	4.5	4.1	46.62	30.0	17
BRE	2.0	4.4	2.0	3.4	50.00	16.7	11
Swiecie	2.0	2.5	5.0	1.9	18.52	49.1	9
Kredyt Bank	1.8	0.0	1.1	0.0	20.30	34.3	12
KGHM	1.4	7.9	7.3	6.6	35.67	12.0	14
Computerland	0.5	1.9	1.6	1.4	74.92	8.9	17
Agora	0.4	5.7	3.7	3.7	53.00	2.5	17
Total	61.9	85	67.5	95.9			

Sources: Schroder Salomon Smith Barney/Dom Maklerski Banku Handlowego SA, 2003; KNUiFE Yearly Reports.

with lower returns than 'established' stocks in the three–five-year period (see for example Loughran and Ritter, 1995, 2000, 2002; Ritter and Welch, 2002). Therefore, if pension funds are safe players and tend to keep passive portfolios, the tendency to include big proportions of new listings is surprising. However, this is exactly what is observed on the WSE. For instance, all five companies that went public in 2002 became a part of OFEs' portfolios. Six companies that went public in 2003 were also acquired by the pension funds. In 2004, out of 36 new listings, 31 became a part of at least one pension fund portfolio and as many as 17 of these stocks attracted at least six out of 15 operating funds.

The performance of these new purchases is rather unimpressive. In total, the whole group of 314 new offerings chosen by the pension funds in 2004 lost on average 2.7 per cent per invested Polish zloty (counting from the first quotation price to the closing price recorded on 31 December 2004; more details can be found in Table 11.6). If only the most popular 17 new offerings are taken into account, then the average return is 2.47 per cent, heavily affected by the 66 per cent return earned on shares of Inter Cars S.A. (which, if excluded brings the average down to −1.51 per cent). It is interesting to note that the pension funds successfully managed to avoid the IPO with the most dramatic decline in share price value (that is, Capital Partners whose share price dropped by 70 per cent). However, it remains unclear whether it

Table 11.6   Returns of the 2004 IPOs (since the first listing)

Company	No of purchasing OFEs	Return (%)	Company	No of purchasing OFEs	Return (%)
Artman S.A.	3	−57.1	Inter Cars S.A.	9	66.2
ATM Grupa S.A.	7	14.2	IVAX Corporation	6	−14.5
ATM S.A.	6	1.3	JC AUTO S.A.	9	−1.6
Borsodchem RT.	8	−6.3	Koelner S.A.	7	6.2
Broker FM S.A.	6	−11.5	MOL Magiar Olaj- ES Gazipari RT.	2	0.2
Capital Partners S.A.	0	−70	PBG S.A.	7	21.3
CCC S.A.	3	−4	PEKAES S.A.	7	−10.7
Ceramika Nowa Gala S.A.	6	8	Polcolorit S.A.	3	−3.2
Comp. Rzeszow S.A.	10	−10.7	PKO Bank Polski S.A.	14	13.5
DGA S.A.	2	−2.3	Praterm S.A.	3	0
Drozapol-Profil S.A.	1	24.3	PTSZ Plast-Box S.A.	6	−28.4
Elstar Oils S.A.	4	3.7	SWISSMED Centrum Zdrowia S.A.	2	−26.1
FAM – Technika Odlewnicza S.A.	3	16.9	Techmex S.A.	11	−19.5
Firma Chemiczna Dwory S.A.	9	7.4	Torfarm S.A.	5	−1.6
Globe Trade Centre S.A.	12	7.1	TVN S.A.	5	10.4
Hygienika S.A.	2	−49.1	Wydawnictwa Szkolne i Pedag. S.A.	0	−5.8

Sources: WSE *Fact Book 2005* and KNUiFE.

was good understanding of the market that protected the OFEs from the investment, or it was the lack of their interest in the company that pushed the price down. In the case of other big losers (Artman S.A. and Hygienika with share price declines of −57.1 per cent and −49.1 per cent respectively) the pension funds were not that skilled and have included them in the portfolios. For comparator purposes it should be mentioned that the average performance of all the companies listed on the WSE was 55 per cent in 2004. In the light of this the choice of new listings is rather surprising.

In Zalewska (2005) I show that over time the performance of the pension funds' portfolios has became very much index-like. The early overperformance of the OFEs' portfolios relative to the WIG market index has vanished over time, and since 2002 the pension funds' portfolios have 'almost become' the WIG index. Figure 11.1 shows that the story is more pessimistic. As the funds target big companies heavily represented in the market index, their weighted portfolios can indeed look very much like the WIG, but in general the choice of the assets is less than impressive. Figure 11.3 presents yearly returns for the three groups of assets in the period 1997–2004.[21] The first bar, named 'included', represents the average (equally weighted) return

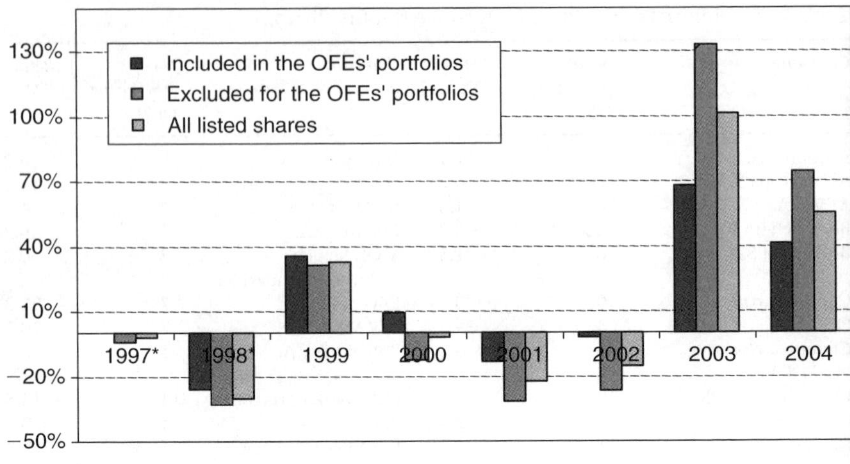

Figure 11.3   Average yearly returns on companies listed on the WSE

on companies that have been reported to be included in the portfolios of at least one OFE at the end of every calendar year. The second bar is the average return on companies that are 'excluded' from the OFEs portfolios at the end of a corresponding calendar year. The last bar is the average return for the market. Since the pension funds' first investment took place in 1999, two additional averages for 1997 and 1998 are presented for comparator purposes. In the case of these two years the 'included' bars are the average returns calculated for these companies that were selected by the OFEs in 1999 and were listed in 1997 and 1998 respectively. In other words the 1997 and 1998 included bars measure the post-market performance of the 'first choice' companies as of 1999. The excluded bars are the averages of the returns of the remaining companies listed on the market in these years.

It is clear that the initial choice of assets, at least as measured by returns, is quite good. The selected companies, on average, performed better than those excluded, and the equally weighted market averages. However, the figures for 2003 and 2004 are not that impressive. The included stocks perform worse than those excluded and worse than the total market. The difference between the groups is also large. These differences are also statistically significant. Table 11.7 shows the means of both included and excluded groups, t-statistics and corresponding probabilities of accepting the null-hypothesis that the two groups come from the same population. Tests with the assumption of different variances in the groups are performed; different variances in the two populations are assumed to control for the fact that companies

Table 11.7   Results of *t*-tests that a group of companies included and excluded from the OFEs' portfolios come from populations with the same mean

Year	Average yearly return		t-stats	Probability (2 tail)
	'Included' stocks	'Excluded' stocks		
2004	0.414	0.746	−2.620	0.009
2003	0.679	1.328	−3.081	0.002
2002	−0.023	−0.266	3.754	0.000
2001	−0.135	−0.314	3.854	0.000
2000	0.094	−0.127	3.334	0.001
1999	0.355	0.310	0.611	0.542
1998*	0.005	−0.040	0.393	0.695
1997*	−0.259	−0.333	1.359	0.176

Note: The statistics are based on yearly observations.

included in the portfolios may be less risky than companies excluded from the portfolios.

First, it is interesting to note that the initial performance of the stocks selected in 1999 and those not selected are not statistically different in 1999 and the two preceding years. However, the quality of the choice seems to be confirmed by the superior performance of the included companies in 2000–02. The average return for the selected group (there are very few variations in the selections from year to year) suggests that the managers have made good investment decisions. The superior performance of the included stocks over the excluded stocks is confirmed at the 1 per cent level. Unfortunately, the pattern is reversed in 2003 and 2004. The included stocks' average is statistically significantly lower than the average of the excluded stocks at the 1 per cent level.[22] Combined with the results presented in Zalewska (2005), it can be concluded that the portfolios of the OFE's have 'lost their bloom' over the last two years. The fact, that the portfolios resemble the WIG market index is because the compositions of the portfolios and of the market index are very similar, and are dominated by the shares of just a few companies. However, in general, shares included in the portfolios perform much worse than those shares that have not been selected.

One might try to speculate further on the cause of the reversal in pattern. Although, the pension funds started to operate in 1999, the major investments took place in the next few years (see Table 11.3). The portfolios of the OFEs were rather well-established from the very beginning, and in this sense once shares were selected and purchased they stayed in the portfolio for the following years. New purchases tended to concentrate on enlarging stakes in companies already acquired and shares of new listings. Very few existing companies whose shares were not selected as 'the first choice' were included in the portfolios later. Such a strategy might first push the prices of acquired shares up and subsequently contribute to their relative stagnation. In contrast, the opposite process may be observed for the excluded companies. If this is true, it might mean that the OFEs are not as good at picking the right stocks as they are in creating fads.

To complete this brief discussion of the Polish experience I look at the correlation between how many funds include a stock in their portfolios and returns on these stocks. To do so I construct a 'popularity indicator' that for a given company is calculated as a ratio of the number of OFEs that have reported holding the company in their portfolios at the end of a calendar year to the number of pension funds operating at that time. That is, if a stock is included in none of the OFE's portfolios, then its popularity indicator is set to zero. On the other hand, if it is included in, say, the portfolios of all the 15 pension funds operating in December 2004, then for 2004 the popularity indicator is one. Figure 11.4 shows that although the period of the pension funds operation is short, three distinct periods are apparent. Years 1999–2000 are characterized by the statistically insignificant correlations. The next two years, 2001–02, show that the popularity indicator is positively and statistically significantly (at the 5 per cent and 1 per cent levels, respectively) with the yearly returns on stocks. However, in 2003 and 2004 the pattern gets reversed and the more 'popular' a stock is, the worse its market performance is. Both 2003 and 2004 correlation coefficients are negative and highly statistically significant.

The relatively poor performance of the OFEs' equity portfolios is a matter of fact but it is hard to blame pension fund managers for such outcomes

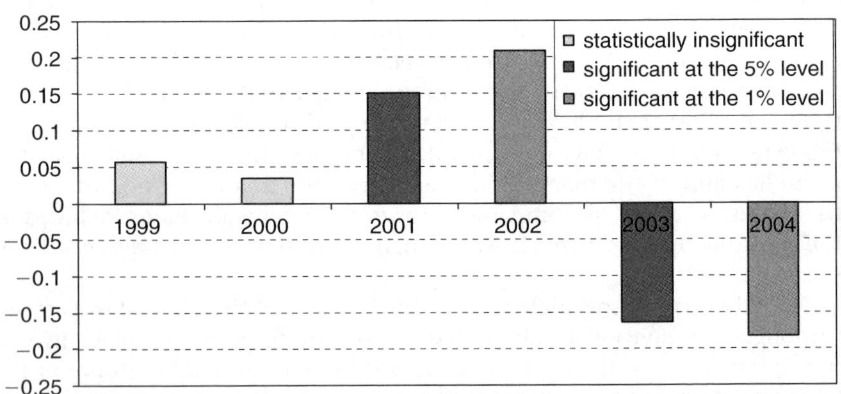

Figure 11.4   Correlation between the popularity indicator defined as a ratio of the number of OFEs choosing a stock to the number of OFEs operating (as of 31 December for each year) and the yearly rate of return on the stock

since their investment opportunities are restricted to a narrow selection of domestic assets. The underperformance, to a large extent, is the result of the enforced home bias and the inability to diversify pension funds' portfolios within the domestically available assets. This lack of diversification, however, is the effect of policies passed by the local authorities. Such policies could be justified if the potential pensioners that contribute to the pension funds' portfolios were rewarded in other ways, that is risking their life savings for higher goals. For instance, if the injection of vast amounts of money could help the local market to develop faster, one might argue that it would be the right policy. A more developed market could lead to a more efficient allocation of recourses and result in faster economic growth. The initial loss of some funds would be compensated with better market conditions, improvement in quality of life, or maybe even more generous payments within the PAYG system. Unfortunately, it does not seem to be the case.

Figure 11.5 gives yet another assessment of the performance of the WSE, by showing its performance relative to the emerging stockmarkets operating in CEE. It plots the two main indexes of the WSE, that is WIG and WIG20, and the average of the main stockmarket indices of the other seven post-communist countries that joined the EU in May 2004 (referred to as CEE-EU). The seven stockmarkets operating in the post-communist countries that are currently in the EU are chosen to create a diversified but consistent group of comparators. Values of the indices are presented in US$ terms and are normalized to 100 at the beginning of the period presented,

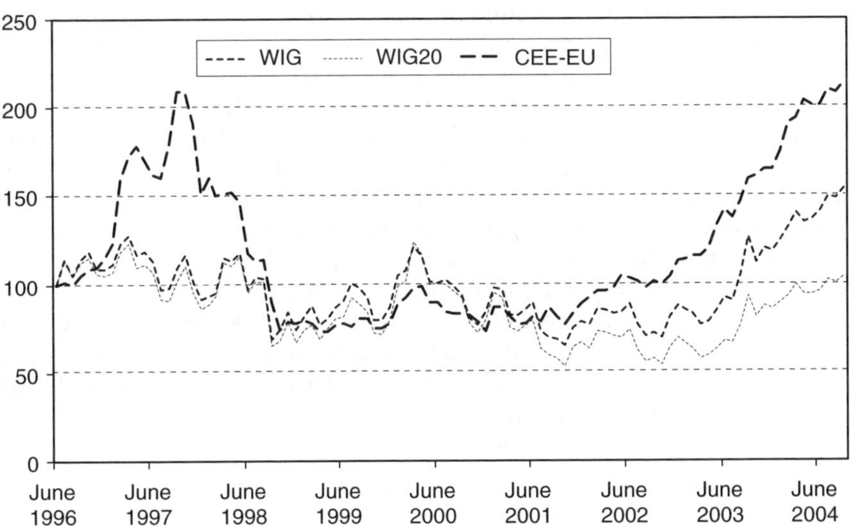

Figure 11.5   Comparison of the performance of stockmarket indices in US$ terms

that is in June 1996 (when the indices from the Baltic states start being provided by DataStream). The period is also chosen to give an overview of the relative market performance before the Polish pension funds started to operate.[23]

It is clear that the WSE performs better only in the period from 1999 to the first half of 2001, that is in the period when the first investments of the pension funds took place. It is reasonable to conjecture that as the general public might find it difficult to guess what stocks would be selected and what not, as Figure 11.4 indicates, the expectations of the market to the increasing demand for shares pushed prices up. The pressure was strong enough to place the WSE in a privileged position in relation to the other CEE emerging stockmarkets. However, this was a short-lived phenomenon; this is the only period when the WSE outperforms the comparators. Since 2002 the situation on the WSE stabilizes. The pension funds, although still investing large amounts of money in equities, target the very same companies they have initially chosen. If additional companies enlarge the pension funds' portfolios, they are mainly new offerings. Those companies that were not trusted and not selected when the first selection process took place are still unwanted, although, as Figure 11.3 shows, in the most recent period they are the leading performers in the market.

The development of the WSE in the period 1996–2004 is studied in detail in Zalewska (2005). Using different measures of market development I show that the WSE does not perform better than the comparator stockmarkets operating in the post-communist countries that joined the EU in 2004. I also show that the comparative performance of the WSE has been in decline since 2002, that is since the pension funds became the dominant players on the market. Therefore, the argument that the home bias helps the market to develop in the long run does not find support in empirical evidence.

The situation on the market appears unhealthy and suggests that intervention to remove the restrictions may be necessary. However, since stakes in selected companies are large, it will be excessively difficult for the pension funds to liquidate their long positions in these shares. At the time of entry the OFEs did not have any serious competitors, and others that might have counted were crowded out. If the pension funds grow further and remain such dominant players in the market, this will distort prices further, cause more severe illiquidity on the market and, in consequence, deter other investors. Although, the cost of exiting may be high at present, it will rise even further if the pension funds do not change their investment strategies. The costs can only rise, and will, finally, have to be faced both by the funds (that is, pensioners) and the market.

Conclusions

Polish pension reforms, designed along World Bank lines, have been based on three pillars with the mandatory saving scheme being the most important.

To manage compulsory contributions, pension funds have been created. Due to the restrictions imposed on investments and, in particular, restrictions on international investments, a large proportion of the pension funds' assets under management have been located in local equities. These share purchases have changed the investor decomposition of the Warsaw Stock Exchange making the pension funds the most important players. However, despite general expectations that these institutional investors would have a positive impact on the development of the stockmarket, the investment policies of the pension funds have had a negative impact on the market and on the value of the pension funds' portfolios. Within the group of selected stocks two subgroups are clearly distinguishable: stocks with high capitalization and stocks with low capitalization. High capitalization stocks are often chosen by several, if not all or almost all, pension funds. These investments constitute over 60 per cent of the pension funds' equity investments. Low capitalization stocks are chosen by very few funds, but these investments gobble up most of the free-float of these companies. Since adjustments within the pension funds' portfolios have been small, the pension funds contribute to the creation of fads and a decline in market liquidity. This results in weak performance of the pension funds' equity investments, and if significant changes are not introduced to loosen up restrictions on international investments, even weaker performance, both of the pension funds' equity portfolios and the Warsaw Stock Exchange, can be expected in the future.

In this chapter I have argued that the emerging markets domestic-market-oriented investment policy can be bad both for investors and for the development of the local stockmarket. Since portfolios of pension funds are not sufficiently diversified, they are exposed to high risk and suffer from low returns. At the same time, the hunger of pension funds for new shares negatively impacts stockmarket development.

Notes

1   Currently only 15 funds operate. The reduction in the number of operating pension funds was a part of a consolidation programme aiming to strengthen the pension market.
2   See Zalewska (2005) for a detailed statistical analysis of the Polish experience.
3   The reform designers, led by Milton Friedman, are sometimes referred to as the 'Chicago Boys'.
4   *Averting the Old Age Crisis: Policy to Protect the Old and Promote Growth*, 1994, World Bank.
5   The World Bank report of 2005 is also critical about the success of pension reform implementation. However, the main criticism seems to concentrate on a weak penetration of the implemented schemes and an insufficient coverage of the old-age population (*The Economist*, 'Second thoughts on the third age', 17 February 2005).
6   In fact, the pressure of the Argentinean government on pension funds increased in October 2001. It was argued that pension funds' bond investments were a part of the economy rescue plan. First, the government enforced pension funds to

invest in government bonds. Next, it requested that all bondholders had to swap government bonds with interest rate as high as 26% for new securities with a 7% return.

7   The Bank of England *Quarterly Review Market and Operation* (May 1999) reports 'The combination of strong and rather price-insensitive demand (largely from pension funds) with limited supply, has pushed real yields down, perhaps more than in the conventional gilt market'.

8   See, for example, an article by P. Inman and L. Elliott, 'Overheated gilt markets burning pension funds', *Guardian*, 20 January 2006.

9   In 2003 the funds were not allowed to invest on international markets at all, but in 2004–05 an upper limit for international investments was set at 5%. The plan is that this limit will increase to 10% in 2006–07, to 15% in 2008–09, and to 20% after 2010.

10   *Financial Times*, 8 September 2003, 'Russia fears on pension managers'.

11   The *St Petersburg Times*, Issue 1126(92), 29 November 2005, 'Stalled pension reform threatens bond market' by G. Bryanski.

12   A recent study by Aguila (2005) show that the expectations of achieving higher saving rates may also be incorrect. Her study of the Mexican case shows that saving rates decreased rather than increased as the result of pension reform and the introduction of the compulsory saving schemes.

13   This phenomenon has been also mentioned by IMF (2004).

14   Roldos (2004) also postulates 'a gradual but decisive loosening of restrictions on equity and foreign investments'. He argues that locking assets on a local market may lead to price distortions, bubbles and concentration of risk. Impravido *et al.* (2003) also warn that new policies 'should not be constructed as an argument for maintaining a closed capital account and to prohibit pension funds from investing overseas'. Restricting capital flows may lead to mispricing of domestic assets.

15   However, Zalewska (2005) shows that the market growth was not that impressive when compared with other emerging markets of CEE.

16   The abbreviation 'OFEs' comes from the Polish name for pension funds – Otwarte Fundusze Emerytalne.

17   NIF (National Investment Funds) have been created as the result of mass privatization.

18   Data as of the end of 2003.

19   The company was delisted in on 1 September 2003.

20   The statistics are based on daily observations.

21   The statistics are based on data reported by the WSE.

22   These results are also significant at the 1% level when 1-tail tests are performed.

23   Very similar graphs have been obtained for other currency denominations (£ and €), and when excess returns over the bank deposit rates were used.

12
The Contribution of CEE Capital Markets to Corporate Finance

Jens Köke and Michael Schröder

Introduction

The securities exchanges of Central and Eastern Europe (CEE) are relatively small but fast growing emerging markets. The largest market among them – the Warsaw Stock Exchange – is comparable in size and market turnover to the smallest Western European exchange – the Vienna Stock Exchange. But most of the other CEE stock exchanges such as Tallinn, Riga or Bratislava are still relatively small and belong to the smallest exchanges in the world. Taken as a whole, the CEE stockmarkets account for no more than 0.4 per cent (= US\$ 148.4 billion) of the world stockmarket capitalization in 2004. Taken together, they are also smaller than the energy sector-driven Russian stockmarkets, for which the comparative figures are 0.6 per cent and US\$ 354.8 billion correspondingly.

In this study we concentrate on the current status and possible future developments of CEE capital markets and, in particular, on their contribution to financing the private sector. The next section provides a detailed assessment of the current status of CEE capital markets. We analyse the major characteristics of stock and bond markets as well as the market for derivatives and investigate the role of institutional investors, which is a particularly important group of investors with regard to the development of financial markets. Section 3 evaluates the role of CEE capital markets for corporate finance. The sources of finance of all CEE companies are then analysed, before investigating in detail the sources of finance of Polish non-financial companies listed at the Warsaw Stock Exchange using firm-level data. As a result of this section we can evaluate the use of publicly issued instruments (stocks and bonds) for corporate finance. A final section concludes.

Current status of CEE securities markets

To assess the current stage of development of CEE securities markets (stocks, bonds and derivatives), we look at these markets from various perspectives and compare them with selected Western European markets.

Stockmarkets

Table 12.1 gives an overview of important characteristics of CEE stock and bond markets for the year 2004 and compares these markets to selected Western European exchanges and to the Russian stock exchanges. The table shows that the CEE stock exchanges are still relatively small in absolute terms. Only the Warsaw Stock Exchange (WSE) is comparable to the smallest Western European exchange – the Vienna Stock Exchange. But the market capitalization of almost all CEE stock exchanges has increased significantly over the last four years. For example, the market capitalization of the three large stock exchanges (Warsaw, Prague, and Budapest) has more than doubled since the year 2000. The importance of the CEE stock exchanges has also improved in relative terms. With the only exception of Lithuania the ratio of market capitalization to GDP has increased significantly, and has even reached the levels of some Western European exchanges. Thus, the gap between the relative importance of Eastern and Western European exchanges for their local economy seems to have diminished considerably. One may also note that the Russian capital market experienced even more spectacular growth in recent years, following the demand for energy-related assets (Table 12.2).

Another important characteristic of stockmarkets is liquidity, which is often measured as the ratio of market turnover to market capitalization (Table 12.1, column 5). This ratio tells how often the total value of stocks is turned over on average during a year. A high ratio indicates that the market is relatively liquid. This is particularly important for institutional investors with usually large order sizes. With the exceptions of Austria and Greece many Western European stockmarkets have a turnover ratio of 75 per cent to 180 per cent. Most of the CEE stock exchanges still exhibit very low turnover ratios, and over recent years the relative trading volume has even decreased. Although the economic relevance of these markets has improved, the degree of trading activity seems to be relatively low compared to western exchanges.

Examining the recent development of CEE stockmarkets in terms of listed domestic companies provides another perspective (Table 12.2). The number of stocks listed at the Warsaw Stock Exchange increased continuously until 2000 and then remained stable at a relatively high level. In contrast, in the Czech Republic, Hungary and the Slovak Republic the numbers of listed firms decreased more or less strongly, as the early IPOs resulted from privatizations and some of these companies were withdrawn from the market, not being replaced by new IPOs. A similar pattern can be found with regard to market capitalization. But in the run-up to the EU membership the stock prices have begun to increase significantly. Thus, the higher ratio of market capitalization to GDP is to a large part due to a higher valuation of CEE stocks. Since the number of listed firms did not increase, it is therefore doubtful whether CEE stockmarkets really increased in importance for the financing of private companies. This development may be contrasted with the Russian market,

Table 12.1   Major characteristics of CEE stock and bond markets, 2004

| | Stock markets (domestic companies) | | | | | Bond markets capitalization in US$bn (in % of GDP) |
| | Market capitalization | | | Market turnover[b] | | |
	US$bn	Thereof: foreign investment[a]	In % of GDP	US$bn	In % of capitalization	
Czech Rep.	26.9	34.8%	25.1%	20.2 (TSV)	75.1%	19.5 (18.3%)
Estonia	5.6	17.0%	50.5%	0.9 (TSV)	15.9%	0.04 (0.3%)
Hungary	28.6	39.9%	28.7%	13.4 (TSV)	46.9%	39.3 (39.4%)
Latvia	2.0	7.2%	15.1%	0.2 (REV)	8.2%	0.9 (0.4%)
Lithuania	1.7	10.1%	7.6%	0.5 (TSV)	28.8%	0.39 (3.5%) (2000)
Poland	71.5	18.3%	29.9%	16.3 (TSV)	22.8%	76.2 (31.8%)
Slovak Rep.	2.4	19.8% (2003)	5.8%	0.8 (TSV)	31.3%	2.2 (7.0%) (2000)
Slovenia	9.7	2.6% (2002)	30.1%	1.5 (TSV)	15.2%	6.3 (19.6%)
Russia	206.4	32.9%	44.4%	109.4	53.0%	n/a
Austria	87.8	51.5%	30.1%	24.2 (TSV)	27.6%	229.3 (78.5%)
Germany	1,194.5	34.4%	44.4%	1,541.1 (TSV)	129%	2,076.5 (108.9) (1999)
Greece	121.9	23.3%	59.4%	44.4 (TSV)	36.4%	214.6 (104.5%)
UK	2,865.2	35.6%	135.4%	5,169.0 (REV)	180.4%	2,532.2 (119.7%)

Notes: [a]Foreign investment = international investment position, liabilities, equity securities (*International Financial Statistics*, IMF, February 2006 issue, line 79 ld; accessed online on 26 Feb 2006) as % of stock market capitalization. [b]TSV counts only transactions which pass through the trading system or the trading's floor, REV counts all transactions under supervision by the market authority (off- and on-market). REV figures are not directly comparable to TSV figures and are usually much larger by construction.

Sources: IMF, national central banks, International Federation of Stock Exchanges (FIBV), national stock exchanges, EBRD. For Russia: MICEX, RTS and Moscow Stock Exchange jointly.

Table 12.2   Development of stockmarkets (number of listed companies, capitalization)

	1996	1998	2000	2002	2004
Number of domestic companies listed					
Czech Republic	82	92	57	44	33
Hungary[a]	44	53	58	48	46
Poland[a]	83	198	225	216	225
Slovak Republic[b]	14	10	7	11	8
Russia (MICEX only)[c]	0	18	38	97	132
Market capitalization (in % of GDP)					
Czech Republic	26.7%	19.3%	19.2%	13.7%	25.1%
Hungary	12.2%	29.4%	26.1%	20.1%	28.7%
Poland	6.2%	13.0%	18.9%	15.1%	29.9%
Slovak Republic	6.4%	3.2%	2.3%	3.8%	5.8%
Russia (MICEX + RTS + MSE)	9.7%	16.9%	15.3%	36.6%	44.4%

Notes: Statistics for market capitalization and trading volume exclude stocks traded in the unregulated free market. The data include only domestic companies. [a] The data for Poland and Hungary include also the regulated free market. [b] The data for the Slovak Republic include the official market only. [c] For Russia: number of listed securities on regulated market. Data include MICEX stock exchange only (the trade volume in stocks on MICEX stock exchange was 2,138 bln roubles in 2003, as compared to 228 bln roubles on RTS for the same year).
Sources: International Federation of Stock Exchanges (FIBV), national stock exchanges, EBRD.

where the dynamic increase in market capitalization was driven by both the increase in value of shares and the number of companies quoted.

The analysis of foreign demand for CEE assets gives an indication for the attractiveness of CEE stockmarkets for foreign investors. Column 2 of Table 12.1 measures the value of stockmarket capitalization that is held by foreigners. These figures are calculated using the international investment position in equity securities which are documented in the *International Financial Statistics* (IMF, line 79 ldd). They measure the total value of foreign equity holdings at the end of the year relative to the total stockmarket capitalization. As some equity holdings are part of foreign direct investments, the foreign equity holdings may to some degree underestimate the true holdings by foreigners. Two CEE countries – the Czech Republic and Hungary – exhibit a foreign investment ratio that is comparable to Western countries. For Poland, foreign stock holdings are significantly lower but still much higher than in Latvia, Lithuania and Slovenia – the latter market being the least internationalized. Taking the foreign investment ratio as an indicator of the attractiveness of CEE stockmarkets, we find that those CEE countries are attractive to foreigners for which liquidity and market capitalization are comparably high. Over the last years the investment position of foreign investors increased significantly which may have been induced by the (expected) EU membership.

Figures on the inflow of portfolio capital (for stocks and bonds) broadly confirm this result (Table 12.3). Other reasons might be the institutional

Table 12.3   The structure of foreign capital inflows, US$ billions, average of 1995–2004

	Equities	*Bonds*	*Portfolio investment (% of GDP)*	*Other investment*	*FDI (% of GDP)*
Czech Rep.[a]	0.6	0.4	1.0 (1.6%)	1.9	4.1 (6.5%)
Estonia	0.1	0.2	0.3 (3.9%)	0.4	0.4 (6.8%)
Hungary	0.4	1.4	1.8 (2.7%)	1.2	3.5 (6.6%)
Latvia	0.01	0.1	0.1 (0.9%)	0.9	0.4 (4.7%)
Lithuania	0.02	0.2	0.2 (1.7%)	0.6	0.4 (3.6%)
Poland	0.4	2.3	2.7 (1.4%)	0.6	5.6 (3.3%)
Slovak Rep.[b]	0.02	0.3	0.3 (1.7%)	0.8	1.1 (4.6%)
Slovenia	0.02	0.2	0.2 (1.0%)	0.9	0.4 (1.8%)
Russia	6.8	4.1	10.9 (0.6%)	15.8	11.5 (0.6%)

Notes: FDI = foreign direct investment.
Sources: *International Financial Statistics*, IMF, calculated from lines 79lb–79lf. [a]Czech Rep.: average of the period 1995–2003. [b]Slovak Rep.: not available for 2001 and 2004.

development of the securities markets and the protection of property rights (see Garibaldi *et al.*, 2001).

Overall, the CEE stockmarkets are still underdeveloped and economically less important compared to Western stockmarkets. The markets in the Czech Republic, Hungary and Poland are the best developed markets among the CEE countries, and these three markets also have a market liquidity that is comparable to Western European stockmarkets. The least developed CEE markets are those of the Slovak Republic, Latvia and Lithuania. Although the stock price upswing of the last years increased the ratio of market capitalization to GDP significantly, the decline in the number of listed companies shows that most CEE stockmarkets still did not gain much in importance with regard to financing private companies. Only the Warsaw Stock Exchange is a notable exception, since the strong growth in stock prices over the last few years has also led to an increase in the number of newly listed companies at this exchange.

Bond markets

To examine the size of bond markets, we first look at total capitalization (last column of Table 12.1). These figures should be interpreted with caution because a large part – in some cases even the majority – of bonds are traded over the counter (OTC). Typically, OTC-traded bonds are included neither in capitalization nor in turnover figures of bond markets. Therefore, Table 12.1 gives only an approximate picture.

We find that the CEE bond markets are – in absolute and relative size – small compared to Western European bond markets. With the exception of Poland, Hungary and the Slovak Republic, the bond markets are even much smaller than the CEE stockmarkets, but this can probably be explained by the large amount of OTC trade. Nevertheless, the bond markets of Poland,

Hungary, the Czech Republic and the Slovak Republic increased significantly over time, both in absolute and relative terms.

A different approach to examining the importance of CEE debt markets is the analysis of all debt securities outstanding. This approach has the advantage that not only publicly traded securities are examined, and that it can distinguish between domestic and international debt securities. According to the definition of the Bank for International Settlements, *domestic debt securities* are bonds issued by local issuers in local currency. *International debt securities* are (a) bonds issued by local residents in the domestic or international market, denominated in foreign currency, or (b) bonds issued by international issuers (corporations or other institutions such as the EBRD or the EIB) issuing in domestic markets, denominated in local or foreign currency.

Table 12.4 shows the amount of outstanding domestic and international debt securities as of December 2004. The Czech Republic has – relative to GDP – the largest domestic debt market, measured in terms of total outstanding debt securities (61.3% of GDP) and Poland ranks second (40.1%). In absolute terms, the Polish market for domestic debt securities is the largest with $95.9 billion in 2004. This result suggests that the OTC market in Poland is indeed significant. Compared to major Western economies these markets are nevertheless less important. We also find that the markets for corporate non-financial bonds are insignificant with the exception of the Czech market. However, corporate bond markets are also underdeveloped in most of the Western countries considered here, with the notable exceptions of Spain (domestic debt) and the UK (international debt).

Regarding international debt securities, the debt markets are relatively small compared to Western Europe. In addition, the largest fraction of these

Table 12.4   Outstanding debt securities (% of GDP), December 2004 by type of security

	Domestic securities			International securities		
	Financial	*Corporate*	*Total[a]*	*Financial*	*Corporate*	*Total[a]*
Czech Republic	3.7%	4.0%	61.3%	n.a.	n.a.	n.a.
Hungary	3.9%	0.1%	32.9%	1.1%	n.a.	15.9%
Poland	n.a	n.a	40.1%	2.4%	0.2%	9.8%
Slovak Republic	n.a	n.a	n.a.	1.0%	1.7%	10.2%
Germany	33.4%	4.9%	82.6%	76.1%	3.5%	86.6%
Spain	24.0%	18.5%	87.9%	50.2%	2.8%	58.5%
United Kingdom	15.8%	1.5%	49.2%	55.9%	10.3%	66.3%
Austria	34.4%	6.7%	77.4%	40.1%	3.9%	69.5%

Notes: [a] *Total* outstanding debt securities volume encompasses *financial* debt securities, *corporate* debt securities as well as *public* debt securities. The last category is omitted from this table.
n.a. = not available.
Sources: Bank for International Settlements, National Bank of Hungary, DB Research.

international debt securities is issued by the public sector, thus contributing little to corporate finance.

In sum, the CEE bond markets are generally still small compared to Western markets. In particular, the markets for corporate debt securities are underdeveloped. Only in the Czech Republic is there a significant and active primary market for domestic corporate debt securities.

Derivatives markets

Budapest and Warsaw are currently the only CEE exchanges offering derivatives for trading. Prague obtained permission to organize derivatives trading in August 2001, but trade in derivatives has not yet started (as of mid-2006). In this section we give a brief overview of the derivatives markets in Hungary and Poland, regarding the type of securities, trading value and some remarks on the markets' recent historical development.

The Budapest Stock Exchange started trading futures contracts in April 1995: index futures on the BUX, the main stock index in Budapest, interest futures with terms between three months and three years, as well as currency futures on the US dollar, the euro, the Japanese yen, the British pound and the Swiss franc. Since 1998, trading in derivatives on individual stocks has also been possible. The futures contracts' maximum maturity is 12 months, and for the BUX future it is 21 months.

The Warsaw Stock Exchange (WSE) started trading derivatives in January 1998: index futures on the WIG20, the main stock index in Warsaw, interest futures as well as currency futures on the US dollar and the euro. In August 2000, an index future on the TechWIG, the stockmarket segment for young high-tech firms, was added, and since January 2001 futures on individual stocks have been available. Since February 2002 there has also been trade in futures on the MIDWIG, the medium-cap stock index of the WSE. The futures contracts' maximum maturity is nine months, and for the individual stocks it is three months.

Additionally, there are standardized options market in Budapest and Warsaw. The Hungarian market started in February 2000, but trade in options on the BUX future, on single stocks and on currencies is still very low. For example, in 2004 the turnover in all types of options amounted to only 0.6 per cent of the turnover in futures and the total number of transactions during this year was only 19, compared to about 176,000 in futures.

In September 2003 the Warsaw Stock Exchange introduced trade in options on the WIG20 index, and at the end of 2004, 18 series of put and call options were available for trading. In Warsaw, there is also an OTC market for warrants on stocks, indices and bonds; at the end of 2004, 29 series of warrants were available. However, trading in these warrants is almost negligible.

Table 12.5 gives a brief summary of the recent historical turnover volume for futures. We find that both in Hungary and in Poland futures trading shows a jump-start, increasing exponentially after the introduction of derivatives

Table 12.5   Turnover value of futures trading (in US$ million)

	1996	1998	2000	2002	2004
Hungary					
BUX	322.0	8,313.2	3,126.1	954.7	2,240.7
Currencies	731.2	4,542.7	101.1	286.9	3,999.6
Stocks	–	239.5	1,563.5	2,028.4	4,873.2
Interest Rates	197.7	591.5	6.6	0	4.25
Poland					
WIG20	–	0.2	9,041.6	18,379.6	30,548.0
Currencies	–	–	129.51	117.8	68.0
Stocks	–	–	0.0	325.5	521.3

Sources: Budapest Stock Exchange, Warsaw Stock Exchange.

trading. However, futures trading on the BUX peaked in 1998 and since then has declined steadily. In contrast, futures trading on the WIG20 has continued to increase in volume since its introduction in 1998, reaching a value of US$ 30.5bn in 2004. This compares to US$ 2.2bn for futures trading on the BUX.

Similarly, in Budapest the trading value on interest derivative products sharply declined after 1998, and since 2002 trading in interest futures even came almost to a halt. One reason for this decline is probably the improvement in macroeconomic conditions and stabilizing interest rates. In contrast, the performance of futures contracts with a single underlying stock looks encouraging as its turnover value continuously increased and significantly exceeds the turnover value of the BUX futures contracts. Regarding currency futures the trading volume increased strongly in 2004 in Hungary after some years of very low turnover. In contrast, trading in currency futures is almost negligible at the Warsaw Stock Exchange.

Overall, the derivatives markets of CEE countries, as far as they exist, appear to be quite active with regard to futures. Currently, in Poland the market for stock index futures is the most active in terms of trading volume; the markets for futures on currencies and individual stocks are much smaller. In Hungary, active trading takes place in the markets for index futures, futures on individual stocks and currency futures.

Institutional investors

For Western capital markets, assets under management of institutional investors (such as mutual funds, pension funds and insurance companies) have grown tremendously in the past two decades (Blommestein, 1998). In addition, it is often argued that institutional investors play an important role in improving corporate governance (Del Guercio and Hawkins, 1999). In the following we try to assess to what extent institutional investors are already present in Central and Eastern Europe.

Table 12.6 Financial assets under institutional management (% of GDP)

	1993	1994	1995	1996	1997	1998	1999	2000	2001[a]
Czech Rep.	22.8%	17.3%	17.8%	21.4%	19.0%	16.8%	16.9%	15.4%	15.1%
Hungary	2.8%	3.9%	4.4%	6.1%	7.5%	8.9%	10.8%	12.7%	14.3%
Poland	0.6%	1.9%	1.5%	2.0%	2.6%	3.2%	4.6%	7.0%	9.6%
Germany	38.9%	41.3%	45.3%	50.6%	58.7%	66.1%	76.9%	79.8%	81.0%
Spain	29.3%	32.3%	33.4%	44.3%	56.0%	66.5%	67.7%	63.8%	61.9%
UK	163.0%	143.8%	164.0%	173.4%	195.5%	203.6%	227.7%	212.8%	190%
Austria	28.5%	30.4%	35.0%	40.3%	47.0%	54.6%	68.2%	72.5%	75.7%

Notes: [a] Data for 2001 are provisional. No data are available for the Slovak Republic.
Sources: IMF, OECD.

Table 12.6 shows the financial assets under institutional management, scaled by GDP. Among the CEE countries, assets under institutional management are the most significant in the Czech Republic with 15.1 per cent of GDP in 2001, but this ratio declined from a peak in 1993 (22.8%). One reason for this relatively large institutional involvement is the Czech voucher privatization scheme, which ultimately made the (mostly publicly owned) investment funds the new owners of the privatized companies. Institutional assets are slightly smaller in Hungary (14.3% of GDP) and in Poland (9.6%), but in both countries institutional ownership is steadily growing at high speed. For example, in Hungary the ratio almost doubled and in Poland even tripled between 1997 and 2001, following the pension reform.

Compared to major Western economies, institutional investment in CEE economies is still small. In Germany and the UK, institutional investors own financial assets worth 81.0 per cent and 190 per cent of GDP in 2001, respectively. Smaller European countries such as Austria or Spain have also experienced growing institutional investment over the past few years. Hence, it is reasonable to assume a similar development of institutional investment for the countries of Central and Eastern Europe. Factors driving this development are – compared to Western standards – a still young insurance sector, and in the cases of Hungary and Poland the reform of social security. In Hungary a pension reform introduced private pension funds in 1997 and in Poland in 1999. Recent statistics demonstrate that the Polish pension funds owned assets of over 2.6bn zloty (0.4% of GDP) in the year 2000, and the Hungarian pension funds about 13 per cent of GDP (National Bank of Poland; National Bank of Hungary).

An analysis of the composition of financial assets reveals that only a small fraction is invested in stocks. Among the CEE countries it is the largest for Poland (15%) and the Czech Republic (21%). The latter figure may be explained by the ownership-taking role of investment funds in the Czech privatization process. Institutional investors in Hungary appear to behave in a risk-averse manner, investing over three-quarters of financial assets in government bills or bonds, thereby financing the government deficit. Thus, Hungarian institutional investors play only an insignificant role in corporate finance. According to the National Bank of Hungary, in 2000 private and voluntary pension funds held the largest fraction of risky assets among institutional investors, with about 14 per cent in stocks. Compared to institutional investors in the UK, where 65 per cent are invested in stocks, institutional investment in the stock-market in CEE economies is small. But, as shown in Table 12.6, there is a clear trend towards a larger institutional engagement, particularly for those countries that implemented social securities reforms (see Zalewska in this volume).

The role of capital markets for corporate finance

In this section we try to evaluate to what extent firms from Central and Eastern Europe use capital markets for financing corporate investment. First we give an overview to the sources of corporate finance using information on bank credit as well as bond and share issues. The major advantage of this top-down approach is that it uses data aggregated at the country level and therefore covers *all domestic firms*. It also allows a comparison of the sources of finance between Eastern and Western European countries. In a second step, we make use of detailed firm-level data, and in a case-study framework we evaluate the sources of finance for *all non-financial corporations listed on the Warsaw Stock Exchange*, the largest CEE stockmarket.

Sources of finance

To obtain a comprehensive picture of the funding sources for corporate investment in the CEE economies, we collect information from a variety of data sources. The aim is to investigate to what extent investment in non-financial enterprises is funded by credit, bond issues and stock issues. We distinguish between three kinds of credit (credit by resident banks, credit by non-resident banks and inter-company loans), two kinds of bonds (domestic bonds and international bonds)[1] and share issues.[2] Credit by resident banks is defined as the change in the credit stock provided by the resident banking system to non-financial enterprises. Credit by non-resident banks is defined as the change in the loans taken abroad by 'other sectors', a sub-item of the countries' international liabilities.[3] Inter-company loans are loans of the parent company to a (non-financial) subsidiary. Complying to the methodology of the IMF, these loans are part of foreign direct investment (FDI). Funds from securitized debt can be originated from the issue of domestic bonds, which are mostly local-currency denominated, and from the issue of international bonds, which are mostly foreign-currency denominated. The Bank for International Settlements (BIS) provides information on the net issue value of both types of securities, separately for the corporate, financial and public sector. Since we are interested in the funding sources of the non-financial corporate sector, we

Table 12.7   Sources of funding (% of gross fixed capital formation), average for 1999–2000

	(1) *Credits from* *resident* *banks*	*(2)* *Credits from* *non-resident* *banks*	*(3)* *Intercompany* *loans*	*(4)* *Domestic* *debt* *securities*	*(5)* *International* *debt* *securities*	*(6)* *Sum of* *(1)–(5)*	*(7)* *IPO/* *SPO*
Czech Rep.	−2.6%	4.1%	4.4%	4.4%	n.a.	10.3%	1.1%
Hungary	18.6%	15.4%	5.6%	1.4%	0.9%	41.9%	7.6%
Poland	11.1%	6.7%	3.6%	0.0%	2.2%	23.6%	1.3%
Slovak Rep.	0.7%	−2.4%	3.0%	n.a.	2.6%	4.0%	0.0%
Germany	6.6%	1.8%	14.3%	2.3%	11.4%	36.4%	5.2%
Spain	44.6%	11.7%	2.6%	4.5%	10.3%	73.6%	67.8%
Portugal	36.7%	−0.9%	3.4%	2.6%	4.4%	46.2%	36.3%

Sources: Bank for International Settlements, national central banks, IMF.

focus on corporate sector debt securities. Finally, funds raised by share issues, both from initial and secondary public offerings, are reported by the International Federation of Stock Exchanges (FIBV). Table 12.7 reports the ratio of funds obtained from each of these sources to gross fixed capital formation, which is calculated as the average for the years 1999 and 2000 to smooth short-run fluctuations.

For the CEE economies, we find that the sum of capital raised by credits from resident and non-resident banks, inter-company loans as well as domestic and international debt securities varies greatly by country. It is the largest for Hungary with 41.9 per cent of gross fixed capital formation, the second largest for Poland with 23.6 per cent and much smaller for the Czech Republic (10.3%) and the Slovak Republic (4.0%). These results suggest that Hungarian non-financial firms fund a comparatively large fraction of corporate fixed investment by raising capital externally. In contrast, firms from former Czechoslovakia obviously have severe difficulties in raising funds externally and are likely to be constrained to using internally generated funds (for example retained earnings) for financing investment. The comparison with Germany, Spain and Portugal shows that Hungary has already reached a Western level of external funding.

Table 12.7 also provides evidence on the relative weight of each of the funding sources. For Hungary and Poland, credits by resident banks are the most important source of funding, credit by non-resident banks the second most important. In both countries, more than three-quarters of all external funds are raised in the form of bank credit. For Portugal, this dominance of funding by credit is similar, and to a lesser extent also for Spain. For the Czech Republic, financing by credit from domestic banks is even negative during the years 1999–2000. This signals severe credit constraints. High real interest rates – indicating the cost of capital – cannot be blamed for the lack of borrowing since real lending rates are only 100–150 basis points above the EU level

(Deutsche Bank Research, 2001). Rather, this shortfall appears to be a result of excessive lending in early years of transition, followed by a credit crunch and extreme risk aversion after the collapse of several financial institutions.

Czech firms are partially able to circumvent these credit constraints by accessing the market for debt securities. We find that Czech firms raise a larger amount of capital (relative to gross fixed capital formation) by issuing debt securities than firms from Hungary or Poland. This finding is consistent with the earlier result (p. 27) which shows that the Czech corporate bond market is the most developed among the CEE economies in terms of size and trading. Comparing the Czech bond market with Western markets, we find that only the Spanish market for corporate debt securities is similarly large. In contrast, firms from Germany and Spain are able to raise a much larger amount of capital by issuing international debt securities than firms from the CEE countries. One reason for this finding could be that for CEE firms the costs of issuing on foreign bond markets are too high compared to the domestic market (for example due to a larger risk premium or higher transaction costs); another reason could be that issuing in foreign currency is regarded as too risky due to increasing exchange rate volatility.

Additionally, the last column of Table 12.7 presents the amount of capital raised by newly or already listed companies via initial or secondary public offerings, again relative to gross fixed capital formation. We find that the largest amount of capital has been raised at the Budapest Stock Exchange, whereas raising funds via public stock offerings has been rather limited in the other three CEE countries. Note that extremely large amounts of capital are raised during 1999–2000 in Portugal and Spain. Partially this reflects a catch-up process for the respective stockmarkets. Taking Germany as the benchmark for the CEE countries, public stock issues do not contribute significantly to corporate finance in Poland, the Czech Republic and the Slovak Republic.

In sum, compared to Western countries only Hungarian firms finance a similarly large fraction of gross fixed capital formation externally (about 50%), that is without relying on internally generated funds such as retained earnings.[4] This fraction is much lower for Poland (25%), the Czech Republic (11%) and the Slovak Republic (4%). Whereas these ratios are only a very rough approximation for the sources of finance since they are based on highly aggregated data for each economy, the observed significant difference between these four CEE countries should be reliable. Among external funds, for Hungary and Poland the dominant sources of funding are domestic as well as foreign credits. In contrast, during the period 1999–2000 Czech and Slovak firms appear to have had major difficulties in financing investment by (particularly domestic) credit. Overall, usage of capital market funding is very limited: Financing by stock issues is the highest in Hungary (7.6% of gross fixed capital formation), and financing by domestic bond issues is the highest in the Czech Republic (4.4%).

Case study: sources of finance in Poland

To complement our top-down approach from the previous section, we now examine the sources of corporate finance in a bottom-up manner. Specifically, we examine all corporations listed at the Warsaw Stock Exchange over the period 1994–2000. The main reason for selecting Poland is that the Polish stockmarket is the largest and the best developed among the CEE markets. In addition, disclosure requirements are very strict, requiring firms to submit quarterly information to shareholders according to the International Accounting Standards (IAS). We investigate the financial statements for all non-financial corporations over the period 1994–2000 to obtain a detailed picture of the sources of finance available for investment.

Table 12.8 distinguishes between three sources of funding: internal funds (measured as net profit plus interest payments, taxes and depreciation), asset divestiture (measured as inflows from investment activity, especially from the sale of fixed and intangible assets and from the sale of marketable securities) and external funds (measured as inflows from financial activity, especially loans taken and issues of bonds and own shares). During the period 1998–2000, external funds play the dominant role among the three sources of gross finance. On average, for small and large firms more than 50 per cent of gross funds are external funds. Internal funding contributes much less to total funding, with on average 14.0 per cent for small firms and 24.7 per cent for large firms. Also not negligible are funds obtained from asset divestitures. A comparison with the period 1994–1997 shows that in this period internal funding constituted the main source of funding, with 57.0 per cent for small firms and 42.6 per cent for large firms. Hence, funding by internally generated

Table 12.8 Gross sources of funding of all Polish companies (non-financial) listed at the Warsaw Stock Exchange, 1994–2000

	1994–97		1998–2000	
	Small firms	*Large firms*	*Small firms*	*Large firms*
Internal funds	57.0%	42.6%	14.0%	24.7%
Asset divestiture	9.3%	17.5%	30.3%	24.3%
External funds	33.7%	39.9%	55.7%	51.1%
Total	100%	100%	100%	100%
Number of observations	380	382	344	345

Notes: All reported statistics are calculated at the mean. Gross sources of funding are measured as follows: internal funds (net profit + interest payments + taxes + depreciation), asset divestiture (inflows from investment activity, especially sale of fixed and intangible assets and sale of marketable securities) and external funds (inflows from financial activity, especially loans taken and issues of bonds and own shares). Statistics are calculated as the average for each of the four subsamples. Large/small firms are firms with total assets above/below the year-specific sample median.
Source: Notoria Serwis S.A.

funds declined sharply over the recent five years. In contrast, funding by asset divestitures became significantly more important. These findings are consistent with the notion that increasing product market competition eroded profit margins, thereby reducing the ability for internal funding. At the same time, Polish firms appear to have adapted their corporate structures by spinning off some assets or to have reduced free cash flow, as reflected in the increasing role of funds generated from asset sales. Overall, in recent years the largest volume of funds is, on average, not any longer generated internally but raised externally.

Table 12.9 investigates the inflows from financial activity more closely, essentially by splitting them into the contribution by loans taken, bonds and shares issued, and other sources. We find that the largest fraction of externally raised funds consists of new loans, with about 70 per cent during the years 1998–2000. The largest part of these loans is short-term (that is with maturity less than one year). Funding by bond issues is much smaller. This difference in the type of debt financing indicates that loans are still more popular and probably more easily accessible than bond issues. At the Warsaw Stock Exchange, only one corporate bond has been traded since April 2000, which suggests that Polish stock corporations are able to issue international bonds, which are not traded on the WSE. But clearly, the probability to make use of bond finance is positively related to firm size. Concerning the role of equity finance, share issues contribute to 18.4 per cent for small firms and 9.4 per cent for large firms. Hence, stock issues appear to be more relevant for smaller firms. This suggests that stock issues are used as a source of finance typically by smaller and probably younger firms, for example in the course of an initial public

Table 12.9   Composition of gross external funding of all Polish companies (non-financial) listed at the Warsaw Stock Exchange, 1994–2000

	1994–1997		1998–2000	
	Small firms	*Large firms*	*Small firms*	*Large firms*
Loans taken	56.3%	63.4%	69.8%	71.5%
thereof short-term	42.6%	45.0%	56.1%	54.7%
Bonds issued	3.2%	8.1%	5.0%	13.6%
thereof short-term	2.1%	5.9%	4.5%	10.7%
Shares issued	29.1%	22.1%	18.4%	9.4%
Other	11.4%	6.4%	6.7%	5.4%
Total	100%	100%	100%	100%
Number of observations	380	382	344	345

Notes: Composition of gross external funding is measured as follows: loans taken (long- and short-term loans taken), bonds issues (long- and short-term bonds issued), shares issued (inflows from issue of own shares). 'Short-term' means maturity is less than one year. Statistics are calculated as the mean for each of the four subsamples (median reported in parentheses). Large/small firms are firms with total assets above/below the year-specific sample median.
Source: based on Notoria Serwis S.A. data.

offering. Larger and probably older firms make less use of public stock offerings, although the fraction of 9.4 per cent is still significant.

A comparison with the respective figures for 1994–97 reveals that loan and bond financing has become more common, and equity financing less common. One reason for the decline in equity financing by stock issues is certainly the decline in going-public activity, which in turn reflects the slowdown in privatization activity. The increase in bond financing versus loan financing indicates that Polish stock corporations are not restricted to loan finance. On the contrary, the use of debt securities has increased by more than 50 per cent when comparing the fractions reported in Table 12.9 for the periods 1994–97 and 1998–2000.

Overall, this case study illustrates the funding sources for corporate investment using micro data for all non-financial corporations listed at the Warsaw Stock Exchange. We are able to confirm the dominance of loan finance, as documented earlier (p. 51). Hence, the dominance of loan funding appears to be similar for listed and non-listed Polish firms, but the results of this section indicate that internal funding plays a much smaller role for listed firms than for all other firms in the economy. Similarly, for listed firms we are not able to confirm that finance by the issue of debt or equity securities plays an almost insignificant role, as documented earlier (p. 51) for the entire Polish economy. For large listed firms, these two sources of funding contribute to about a quarter of all externally raised funds, which in turn make up for about 50 per cent of gross funding. Therefore, listed Polish corporations appear to differ substantially in terms of sources of finance from other Polish firms because the capital market plays an important role in their financing patterns. Nevertheless, loan finance is still the dominant source of funding also for listed firms. This stands in contrast to the situation of non-listed firms, which predominantly rely on internally generated funds.

Conclusion

The capital markets in Central and Eastern Europe are fast-growing emerging markets, although these markets still exhibit a relatively low market capitalization and turnover compared to Western European exchanges. The high speed of growth corresponds to strong economic growth in Central and Eastern Europe. Another important reason might be the membership in the European Union and expectations on a future EMU membership as well as an increasing integration into the world economy.

The best-developed stock exchanges are those of the Czech Republic, Hungary and Poland. Among these the Polish stock exchange clearly merits a top ranking. The Warsaw Stock Exchange has the highest capitalization, the largest official market segment which is particularly interesting for foreign and institutional investors, and a liquid index future on the blue-chip index WIG20 which allows investors to efficiently hedge stockmarket risk.

Regarding the sources of corporate finance, CEE firms finance the largest fraction of investment internally. Compared to Western countries, only Hungarian companies finance a similarly large fraction of gross fixed capital formation externally (about 50%), that is without relying on internally generated funds such as retained earnings. This fraction is much lower for Poland (25%), the Czech Republic (11%) and the Slovak Republic (4%). Closer analysis of the sources of external finance reveals that the largest part is obtained by taking new credits, and a much smaller part by issuing equity or debt securities. In Hungary and Poland, new credits significantly contribute to financing investment, while in the Czech Republic the issue of domestic debt securities is particularly relevant for corporate finance.

Overall, this dominance of credit finance is confirmed in a case study of all non-financial corporations listed at the Warsaw Stock Exchange. We find that in recent years Polish listed firms predominantly rely on credit finance. Compared to earlier years of transition, internal funding has declined significantly. Similarly, finance by equity issues has declined over the period 1994–2000 but still contributes strongly to corporate finance. This suggests that the Polish privatization scheme conducted by large-scale sales to strategic investors connected with a going public has benefited the Polish stockmarket, and the Polish stockmarket appears to be viable even in times of a slowdown in privatization activity. This finding contrasts with the evidence for the other CEE countries, which recently show a much larger decline in going-public activity than Poland.

Notes

1　*Domestic debt securities* are bonds issued by local issuers in local currency. *International debt securities* are (a) bonds issued by local residents in the domestic or international market, denominated in foreign currency, or (b) bonds issued by international issuers (corporates or other institutions such as the EBRD or the EIB) issuing in domestic markets, denominated in local or foreign currency. See Bank for International Settlements.
2　Below we also distinguish between capital raised through already listed firms (seasoned public offerings) and capital raised by newly listed firms (initial public offerings).
3　Using credits taken by 'other sectors' as proxy for borrowing by non-financial enterprises assumes that credits taken abroad by domestic households is negligible.
4　As a rough approximation, the fraction of internal finance can be calculated as 100% less the fraction observed for all external sources of finance including IPO/SPO.

13
A Comparative Study of Corporate Governance in the Czech Republic, Hungary and Poland

Robert W. McGee

Introduction: business environment indicators

The countries selected for this study – the Czech Republic, Hungary and Poland – have many things in common but they also have their differences. They are all located in Central Europe; they were all former Soviet satellite countries that had centrally planned economies but are now making the transition to some form of market economy; they all have large Catholic populations. But they have had different histories, there are some cultural differences and they speak different languages, which is a strong indicator of nationhood (Mises, 1944, 1957). The paths they have taken from central planning to a market economy have also been somewhat different, and they had different starting positions on that path (McGee, 1992). Table 13.1 compares some statistics for areas that touch on corporate governance and the business environment in which corporate managers must function.

Senior management in the Czech Republic, Hungary and Poland spends significantly less time dealing with the requirements of regulations (2.1%, 4.0% and 3.0% correspondingly) than management in the average country in the World Bank sample of 58 countries (6.7%), less than the average for the subsample of transition economies in Europe and Central Asia (4.5%), and much less than in Russia (6.3%). Comparison along other dimensions reported in Table 13.1 is also mostly favourable. In general, the economies of the Czech Republic, Hungary and Poland have a higher degree of economic freedom than most countries. That would have been unthinkable before 1989. This tentative conclusion is verified by the scores for the three countries given in the *Index of Economic Freedom*. Table 13.2 shows some relevant statistics for the three countries.

Presumably, there is a correlation between the degree of economic freedom a country has and the quality of corporate governance. Richer countries have a tendency to have more economic freedom, so it could be said that, as a general rule, richer countries and countries that have a high degree of economic freedom also have better corporate governance rules in place than do countries that are poor and lacking in economic freedom.

Table 13.1 Business environment: comparison of selected data (2005) for Czech Republic, Hungary, Poland and Russia

	Czech Republic	Hungary	Poland	Russian Federation	Average for transition economies in Europe & Central Asia
Senior management time spent dealing with requirements of regulations (%)	2.1	4.0	3.0	6.3	4.5
Consistency of officials' interpretations of regulations[a]	29.4	51.1	27.3	37.4	46.9
Unofficial payments for firms to get things done (% of sales)	0.4	0.5	0.4	1.0	0.8
Firms expected to give gifts in meetings with tax inspectors (%)	37.3	25.0	30.0	58.0	43.4
Value of gift expected to secure government contract (% of contract)	1.8	1.7	0.3	1.6	1.6
Internal finance for investment (%)	54.6	54.2	76.7	86.2	70.7
Bank finance for investment (%)	6.6	14.4	9.5	4.3	12.1
Informal finance for investment (%)	5.2	1.4	3.0	2.3	3.7
Supplier credit financing (%)	5.8	6.0	4.5	6.9	5.5
Collateral needed for a loan (% of loan)	123.2	164.5	151.5	147.0	153.7
Loans requiring collateral (%)	28.9	51.2	31.6	88.2	40.2
Sales reported by typical firm for tax purposes (%)	87.9	90.8	90.4	85.3	90.2
Delay in obtaining an electrical connection (days)	5.0	8.4	11.0	11.9	12.3
Electrical outages (days)	0.2	1.6	0.7	2.7	12.3
Value lost to electrical outages (% of sales)	1.6	1.4	1.6	2.0	3.0
Water supply failures (days)	0.1	0.2	0.1	1.3	4.4
Delay in obtaining a telephone connection (days)	4.3	8.3	12.7	16.5	13.8
Firms using the web to interact with clients/suppliers (%)	83.1	82.8	74.7	66.6	62.5
ISO certification ownership (%)	12.5	23.1	13.8	9.3	12.2
Spending on R&D (% of sales)	0.2	0.1	0.3	0.3	0.3
Firms offering formal training (%)	94.6	74.1	92.1	73.6	75.0
Permanent skilled workers receiving training (%)	52.6	27.3	35.4	18.6	24.6
Employment growth over the last 3 years (%)	20.9	6.6	6.7	30.8	19.2
Time spent in meetings with tax officials (days)	1.7	2.3	2.7	2.5	2.8

[a] Percentage of firms that agree with the statement 'In general, government officials' interpretations of regulations affecting my establishment are consistent and predictable.'
Source: Enterprise Surveys from World Bank & International Finance Corporation.

Table 13.2 Measurements of economic freedom: Czech Republic, Hungary and Poland

	Czech Republic	Hungary	Poland
Overall ranking for economic freedom (out of 161 countries)	21	40	41
Overall economic freedom score Categories: *free* (1–1.99), *mostly free* (2–2.99), *mostly unfree* (3–3.99), and *repressed* (4–5)	2.10	2.44	2.49
Score for banking and finance	1.0	2.0	2.0
Score for foreign investment	2.0	2.0	3.0

Note: (1 is best; 5 is worst).
Sources: Index of Economic Freedom 2006; Heritage Foundation.

Table 13.2 shows how the countries compare. Although all three countries are ranked more or less in the top quarter in terms of economic freedom world-wide, the Czech Republic is ranked much higher up the scale, in 21st place, compared to Hungary and Poland, which ranked 40th and 41st, respectively. All three countries fall into the *mostly free* category, although the Czech Republic, with an overall economic freedom score of 2.10, is closer to being a free economy than are Hungary and Poland.

There are some other interesting statistics in Table 13.1. The extent of unofficial payments required to get things done as a percentage of sales is about one-third of the average for the World Bank sample of transition and developing economies – 0.4 per cent for the Czech Republic and Poland and 0.5 per cent for Hungary, compared to 1.4 per cent on average.

The per cent of firms that are expected to give gifts to tax officials, however, is closer to the World Bank sample average – 37.3 per cent for the Czech Republic, 25.0 per cent for Hungary and 30.0 per cent for Poland, compared to a World Bank sample average of 33.8 per cent. Of the three countries in the present study, Hungary has the best score, although, with a percentage of 25.0 per cent, corporate management is still under pressure to engage in activities that are of questionable ethics, which tarnishes the quality of corporate governance.

In addition to the indicators discussed above, the European Bank for Reconstruction and Development issues annual reports on transition economies. Its 2005 Report (EBRD, 2005) reports progress for the Czech Republic, Hungary and Poland. The Czech Republic received upgrades for improvements in the areas of banking sector reform, and securities markets and non-bank financial institutions. Hungary earned upgrades for improvements in its governance, enterprise restructuring and maturing securities markets. Poland, which had not received any upgrades since 2001, received upgrades in 2005 for progress in the financial sector and for governance and enterprise restructuring.

Review of the literature on corporate governance practices in Central Europe

A number of general studies on corporate governance in transition economies have been made. An Institute of International Finance study (2002) provides a checklist for evaluating corporate governance practices in emerging markets for investors, governments and regulators. The Organization for Economic Cooperation and Development (OECD) published several major reports on the principles of corporate governance (1999d, 2004a). Various governments in transition economies have referred to these reports when constructing their own corporate governance rules. The OECD also published a report on corporate governance in South-East Europe (2003).

Oman, Fries and Buiter (2003) published an OECD Policy Brief that outlines the importance of corporate governance in transition economies. Oman and Blume (2005) discussed the challenges of corporate governance in developing economies. Ade-Ajayi (2004) discusses the difficulties that multinational corporations have with corporate governance issues when they do business in countries and regions where corporate governance standards are lacking. Gregory (2000) conducted a major study that made an international comparison of corporate governance guidelines and codes of best practices that focused on developing and emerging markets.

The World Bank's *Reports on the Observance of Standards and Codes* (ROSC) present detailed information following a template format, which makes it easier to compare specific corporate governance provisions between or among countries. Unfortunately, there are no ROSC reports for some transition economies, including two of the largest – Russia and Ukraine. However, ROSC reports do exist for the Czech Republic, Hungary and Poland. World Bank reports on corporate governance include: the Czech Republic (2002b), Hungary (2003) and Poland (2002c, 2005).

Scholars have made attempts to rate corporate governance. Strenger (2004) did so for Germany; Tsipouri and Xanthakis (2004) did so for Greece; and Sherman (2004) provides a general discussion on the issue. Bradley (2004) examined the link between corporate governance scoring and performance indicators.

A number of studies have been made of various aspects of corporate governance in one or more transition economies, including the three countries that are the subject of this chapter. Glaeser, Johnson and Shleifer (2001) compared the regulation of financial markets in the Czech Republic and Poland during the 1990s, and found that the Czech hands-off policy was associated with a moribund market whereas the Polish policy of strict enforcement of the securities laws was associated with a rapidly developing stockmarket.

Claessens, Djankov and Pohl (1996) showed that the massive Czech privatization programme was effective in improving firms' management. Their study of 706 firms found that large ownership by investment funds sponsored by banks and strategic investors played a significant role in improving corporate governance.

Blaszczyk, Hashi, Radygin and Woodward (2003) review the present state of knowledge on the interrelationship between emerging corporate governance mechanisms and ownership structure of privatised enterprises in post-communist countries. They examine corporate structure changes for companies in the Czech Republic, Poland and Slovenia. The latter theme is developed further in studies by Mickiewicz and by Andreff in this volume.

Roth and Kostova (2003) tested data from 1,723 firms in 22 transition economies in Central and Eastern Europe and the former Soviet Union using an institutional theory framework. Their study provides evidence that an enterprise's adoption of a new corporate governance framework will be helped or harmed by the institutional and cultural environment in which it operates.

Berglof and von Thadden (1999) argue that small investors are unlikely to play a significant role in most developing and transition economies and that they are more likely to come in as strategic investors or creditors. They propose a broader paradigm that includes other stakeholders to explain the problems these countries face.

Hashi (2003) identified the differences between corporate governance systems in various transition countries in order to highlight the progress made to date and the shortcomings of the existing framework. Issues examined included shareholder rights, equitable treatment of all shareholders, and disclosure, transparency and responsibilities of corporate boards.

The Budapest Stock Exchange issued a major report on corporate governance recommendations (2004) that focused on competencies of the board of directors and supervisory board, transparency and disclosure, shareholders' rights and treatment of shareholders and the role of stakeholders in corporate governance.

Dzierzanowski and Tamowicz (2002) drafted a corporate governance code that looked at various problems Poland has been having with protecting minority shareholder rights. Koladkiewicz (2001) discusses the process of building corporate governance systems in Poland. Dzierzanowski and Tamowicz (2004) looked at ownership and control of Polish companies and found that concentrated ownership structures result in major problems in the areas of minority shareholder rights and conflicts of interests among stakeholders. Kozarzewski (2003) analyses the legal framework of privatization and corporate governance in Poland and examines the post- privatization evolution of control structures in Polish privatized enterprises. He also shows the role of the regulatory framework in this process.

EBRD measures related to corporate governance

Table 13.3 shows the extent of progress of market reforms as measured by the EBRD in several key areas linked with corporate governance. The scale is from

Table 13.3   EBRD transition indicators related to corporate governance

	Private sector share of GDP %	Large-scale privatization	Small-scale privatization	Governance & enterprise restructuring	Banking reform & interest rate stabilization	Securities markets & non-bank financial institutions
Czech Republic	80	4	4+	3+	4	4−
Hungary	80	4	4+	4−	4	4
Poland	75	3+	4+	4−	4−	4−

Source: EBRD (2005).

1 to 4+, where 1 represents little or no change from a rigid centrally planned economy and 4+ represents the standards of a developed market economy.

As can be seen, substantial progress has been made. No score is below 3+ . In fact, 13 of the 15 scores are in the 4 range. The Czech Republic is somewhat lagging in the category of governance and enterprise restructuring, with a score of 3+ and Poland in the category of privatisation of large enterprises, which is consistent with data presented by Mickiewicz in this volume. None of the countries are quite at the level of a developed market economy, although a score of 4− in the governance and enterprise restructuring category is better than the score of 23 of the 27 countries listed in the EBRD study. Estonia and Slovakia are the only other countries that have a score of 4− and no country has a higher score. Thus, in comparative terms they are doing quite well in this category.

The Czech score for banking reform and interest rate liberalization was upgraded from 4− to 4 because of further financial deepening and significant growth in private sector credit. Its score for securities markets and non-bank financial institutions was upgraded from 3+ to 4− because of a substantial increase in liquidity and stockmarket capitalization associated with improvements in the regulatory regime.

The Hungarian score for governance and enterprise restructuring was upgraded because of the increased confidence resulting from becoming a member of the EU, which also helped investment and portfolio flows to increase. Its score for securities markets and non-bank financial institutions was upgraded from 4− to 4 because of the substantial increase in liquidity and stock market capitalization and the continued development of the insurance sector and tradable debt instruments.

Poland's score for governance and enterprise restructuring rose from 3+ to 4− due to the restructuring of its steel industry and its progress in reforming large state owned enterprises. Becoming an EU member also helped increase confidence in governance. Its score for banking reform and interest rate liberalization also increased from 3+ to 4−. The main reasons for the increase were growth in household lending, cumulative improvements in consumer protection and banking supervision, and progress in privatization.

The EBRD *Report* also looked at the extensiveness and effectiveness of corporate governance laws in transition economies, including the Czech Republic, Hungary and Poland. The *Report* measured extensiveness using the well-known OECD benchmarks and measured effectiveness using the EBRD's *Legal Indicator Survey*. The focus of the EBRD's 2005 *Report* is on the protection of minority shareholder rights in the context of related party transactions.

The EBRD *Report* ranked 27 transition countries into five categories based on the extent of their compliance with international corporate governance standards. The Czech Republic, Hungary and Poland all ranked relatively high. Here is the breakdown:

1 Very high compliance – None.
2 High compliance – Armenia, FYR Macedonia, Hungary, Kazakhstan, Latvia, Lithuania, Moldova, Poland and Russia.
3 Medium compliance – Albania, Bulgaria, Croatia, Czech Republic, Estonia, Kyrgyz Republic, Serbia and Montenegro, Slovak Republic, Slovenia and Uzbekistan.
4 Low compliance – Bosnia & Herzegovina, Georgia, Romania and Turkmenistan.
5 Very low compliance – Azerbaijan, Belarus, Tajikistan, Ukraine.

Although the Czech Republic did not rank quite as high as Hungary and Poland, it ranked higher than at least eight other countries. None of the transition countries made the top category, which could be expected, given the short time, in historical terms, since the collapse of central planning. It is also worth noting the relatively high position of Russia, in contrast to its lower scores in general business environment indicators discussed in the previous section (we will discuss Russian corporate governance in the next chapter).

The EBRD *Report* looked at a number of issues regarding the legal mechanisms available to minority shareholders seeking disclosure, and Table 13.4 summarizes some of the findings for the Czech Republic, Hungary and Poland.

If one were to assign a value of 1 for each *Yes* and 0 for each *No*, the scores for the three countries would be: 6 for the Czech Republic, 11 for Hungary, and 6 for Poland. Thus, it appears that Hungary protects minority shareholders better than the Czech Republic and Poland.

ROSC results

The rights of shareholders

The World Bank's *Reports on the Observance of Standards and Codes* (ROSC) project examined a number of aspects of corporate governance. Rights of shareholders is the first category to discuss.

Table 13.4   Legal mechanisms available to minority shareholders seeking disclosure

	Czech Republic	Hungary	Poland
Access to company books	No	Yes	No
Access to company's auditor	No	Yes	No
Independent auditor	No	Yes	No
Court-appointed independent audit	No	Yes	No
Extraordinary shareholders' meeting	Yes	Yes	Yes
Challenge to validity of a transaction	Yes	Yes	Yes
Derivative liability suit	Yes	Yes	Yes
Derivative liability suit against the parent company	No	No	No
Action against the parent company's subsidiary	No	Yes	No
National arbitration	Yes	Yes	Yes
International arbitration	Yes	Yes	Yes
Criminal prosecution	Yes	Yes	Yes

Source: EBRD (2005).

Czech Republic

Shareholders may transfer shares freely. They have access to court filings and other company documents, and companies are required to file unaudited quarterly financial statements. One possible problem area is the rule that allows companies to withhold damaging information.

Minority shareholders are protected from fundamental corporate changes such as bylaw changes, authorization of additional shares and extraordinary transactions such as the sale of the company. Bylaw changes and capital changes require a two-thirds vote of the shareholders attending the meeting. Shareholders have a pre-emptive right.

Shareholder meetings must be held at least once a year and there is a 30-day notice requirement. Although there are no restrictions on attending meetings or voting, shareholders have reported some difficulty gaining access to meeting and establishing their voting rights.

The takeover law requires the predator to notify the target, but the target may not adopt any measures to prevent shareholders from reviewing the offer and they may not do anything to frustrate the offer. Institutional investors are not very active in voting and they generally do not see any fiduciary duty to vote.

Hungary

There is an inconsistency between law and practice in updating the registry from KELER. (Organized as a private joint-stock company, KELER is the central background institution of the Hungarian capital market, which offers depository, settlement and clearing related functions.) Some voting is disallowed as a result. Some authority for capital increases can be delegated to the board.

There are some reports that companies set their meeting dates or locations so that they are difficult to attend.

Shareholders are required to disclose ownership interests exceeding 5 per cent. Companies disclose ownership in annual reports. There are strong takeover rules with squeeze-out provisions. Institutional investors tend to use exit over voice.

Poland

The system of ownership registration functions according to international standards. No problems were reported. Account holders are treated as the beneficial owners. Nominee owners are not recognized by law.

Listed shares must be freely transferable. Financial and non-financial information for public companies is freely available. Shareholders have the right to participate in general shareholder meetings. Public companies must have at least five board members. Shareholders are entitled to receive dividends, the amount of which is set at the annual general meeting.

Amending the articles requires the vote of a 75 per cent supermajority, as does the issuance of new shares. Shareholders must approve the management board's report and the financial statements. There is a pre-emptive right, which can be waived by an 80 per cent supermajority vote. There must be at least three weeks notice before the general meeting. If shareholders request it, they must be supplied with copies of board reports, financial statements and audit reports at least 15 days before the general shareholders' meeting.

Equitable treatment of shareholders

Equitable treatment of shareholders is another category of corporate governance the ROSC studies examine.

Czech Republic

Joint stock companies are permitted to issue only common and preferred shares. There is no requirement for the custodian to obtain the beneficial owner's permission before voting the shares. The report recommends laws or regulations to make sure that shareholder meetings are held at reasonably convenient locations. It also recommends allowing shareholders to vote by mail.

Self-dealing and insider trading are pervasive although they are illegal. Although the independent auditors are required to report such illegal activity, it is unclear what the penalties are for failure to do so. The supervisory board must approve the purchase or sale of assets if the market value exceeds one-third of the company's equity capital.

Hungary

Companies can employ voting caps. There are multiple voting rights, golden shares and veto shares, which complicate voting rights. There are strong definitions of insiders and inside information. There is limited disclosure of related party transactions under Hungarian accounting regulations. Perhaps the disclosure rules will improve now that Hungary is part of the EU, and must therefore adopt EU rules, including International Financial Reporting Standards (IFRS).

Poland

Although the securities law guarantees that all shareholders of the same class be treated equally, there are no sanctions in the law for violations of the act. Minority shareholders have several means of redressing grievances. Shareholders having more than 10 per cent of capital can demand a general meeting. Disgruntled shareholders can sue to overturn board decisions but there is a penalty of up to ten times legal fees for frivolous lawsuits.

There are laws against insider trading and insiders and their families must report sales of company stock within five days. Disclosure rules require issuers to disclose transactions over a certain amount.

The role of stakeholders in corporate governance

The ROSC studies also look at the role of stakeholders in corporate governance.

Czech Republic

Czech workers have rights similar to those in EU countries in the areas of equal opportunity, social security and health plans, labour law and working conditions. Workers may elect one-third of supervisory board members if they work for companies that have more than 50 employees.

Creditor rights have not been well respected in the past but measures have been taken to reduce this problem. The bankruptcy laws need to be reformed to provide alternatives to the liquidation of debtor assets. The judicial system needs to be reformed to protect creditor rights.

Although stock options are allowed and available, they are seldom used. Lack of liquidity makes them an unattractive method of rewarding employees.

Hungary

One-third of the supervisory board seats are reserved for employees. Employees can own shares and options.

Poland

Labour, environmental and bankruptcy laws protect stakeholders but they have limited direct involvement in the corporate governance process. Investors can own stock options, although options are rare. The EU directive on providing information about employees has not been implemented. There are some rules that protect whistleblowers.

Disclosure and transparency

Czech Republic

Czech disclosure requirements are similar to those of the EU's Fourth and Seventh Company Law Directives. Listed companies must file a report with the Securities Commission within four months of the end of their fiscal year. The report must provide a fair and true view of the company's financial situation. Listed companies must issue semi-annual audited statements, which is a more rigorous standard than what US listed companies must follow. Enforcement of financial disclosure regulation remains a problem. Czech companies have adopted IFRS, as have all other EU members. One issue that is unclear is how much in terms of resources should be devoted to developing national accounting standards, since the Czech Republic has moved to IFRS. Although Czech audit standards comply with International Standards on Auditing (ISA), application may not be consistent. Annual audits are required if any two of the following three conditions are met:

- net revenues are greater than $2.3 million in the current and prior year;
- aggregate capital is $1.1 million; and
- the average number of employees over the past two years exceeds 50.

Hungary

There are no disclosure requirements for material risk factors. Most companies use IFRS, according to the ROSC report. The EU has adopted IFRS as of 2005, which means that the use of IFRS will become more widespread. Most listed companies use one of the Big-4 accounting firms to conduct their audit. A review/oversight body was created in 2002.

Poland

Companies must issue annual, semi-annual and quarterly reports. The annual and semi-annual reports must be audited, and the annual report must be issued within six months after year-end. Reports must report significant successes and failures. Shareholder ownership information is publicly available and shareholders who own 5 per cent or more, either directly or indirectly, are listed in the annual and quarterly reports. Companies have been required to disclose board compensation in the aggregate since 2001 but only a few companies have actually done so. The securities commission will require the disclosure of individual compensation for reports filed starting in 2006.

Starting in 2005 all listed companies and banks must prepare their financial statements based on IFRS. Polish accounting standards can be used to prepare unconsolidated statements. One possible problem with this provision is that many Polish companies may not be prepared to make the transition to IFRS. Poland has adopted International Standards on Auditing (ISA) as of 2005.

Responsibilities of the board

Board responsibilities have come under increasing scrutiny by investors and regulators in recent years. There is pressure to make board members more responsible to the shareholders and other stakeholders and more independent.

Czech Republic

There must be at least three members on the supervisory board and employees can elect one-third of the supervisory board members if the company has more than 50 workers. The supervisory board is responsible for overall framework issues such as checking compliance with laws and regulations. It also is responsible for ensuring that the management board carries out corporate policies in the areas of strategy, risk management and corporate finance.

This two-tier board structure is consistent with that of Germany and other continental EU countries. Minority shareholders do not have much say over the appointment or removal of board members. Such decisions are generally made by the majority shareholders. Cumulative voting for directors is not permitted. The ROSC *Report* recommends removing the prohibition on cumulative voting, at least for directors who are not elected by the employees.

The management board is responsible for preparing the financial statements and sending them to shareholders at least 30 days before the general meeting. There have been cases where the information provided regarding risk factors and company objectives has been insufficient. Sometimes the management board does not have sufficient independence from management to perform its fiduciary duties properly. Having a nominating subcommittee is still the exception rather than the rule, although the larger companies are starting to form such committees.

Hungary

There is typically a two-tier board structure; although one-tier is optional, there are few supervisory boards in practice. A two-tier board means that the supervisory board is non-executive. The supervisory role is poorly defined. The fair treatment principle is often violated in practice. There are no barriers to preferential treatment. The board is required to comply with all legal requirements. Board and management nominations and remuneration are left to the general meeting, effectively to the management board. Liability for the nondisclosure of information is unclear.

Poland

Polish corporate boards are generally two-tiered, consisting of both management and supervisory boards. The supervisory board must have at least five members for public companies or three members for private companies. There is no minimum size requirement for the management board. The term for board members is five years and terms may be staggered.

Board members have a fiduciary duty to act in the best interests of the corporation, not necessarily the best interests of the shareholders. Although there is a principle of corporate governance requiring directors to treat all shareholders fairly, there is no legal provision making it compulsory.

The supervisory board is responsible for evaluating the management board's annual report. The supervisory board also has the responsibility of appointing or discharging members of the management board unless the articles state otherwise. Accounting and internal control functions are the responsibility of the management board.

Testing the difference in corporate governance practices

As already discussed, the World Bank's series on *Reports on the Observance of Standards and Codes* (ROSC) provides reports on a number of countries, including Poland (2002b, 2005), Hungary (2003) and the Czech Republic (2002c). They follow a template. Unfortunately, the templates for Poland, Hungary and the Czech Republic are not identical, making it impossible to do a perfect comparison. However, a good comparison can be made from the information given in their ROSC reports, and below is a summary of the information given in those reports. Table 13.5 combines the data for the three countries. The grids for the Czech Republic and Hungary are the same, which makes the comparison easy, but the Polish grid is different, and thus some minor adjustments have had to be made.

The next step is to determine which country has the best overall corporate governance system. That was done by assigning a point system to each category as follows: Observed = 5, Largely observed = 4, Partially observed = 3, Materially not observed = 2, Not observed = 1. Table 13.6 shows the number of points earned in each category as well as the overall score for each country.

The average scores for Hungary and Poland were both 3.7, compared to an average score of 3.0 for the Czech Republic, so it would appear that the corporate governance system in the Czech Republic is not as good as those for Hungary and Poland. But is it significantly worse?

A Wilcoxon test was conducted to determine whether the difference between the Czech and the Hungarian and Polish scores was significant. The Wilcoxon test is better than the Student t-test in this case because the Wilcoxon test is nonparametric and does not include the assumption that a normal distribution exists. According to the Wilcoxon test, the average scores for the Czech Republic and Hungary were significantly different ($p \leqslant 0.02365$). The averages for the Czech Republic and Poland were also significantly different ($p \leqslant 0.0173$) but the scores for Hungary and Poland ($p \leqslant 0.9524$) were not significantly different. Thus, we may conclude that the systems of corporate governance in Hungary and Poland are significantly better than the system in the Czech Republic. We can also conclude that the systems in Hungary and Poland are not significantly different.

However, we should point out some limitations. The Polish study was published in 2005, whereas the studies for the Czech Republic and Hungary were published in 2002 and 2003, respectively. It would have been better, for comparison purposes, if all three studies had been published in the same year, especially if corporate governance practices have been improving substantially from year to year. That way, any differences in scores would not be attributable to being at different points on the learning curve. However, we must go with the data we have, not the data we would like to have.

Table 13.5 Summary of findings, combined ROSC data (C = Czech Rep., H = Hungary, P = Poland)

	Observed	Largely observed	Partially observed	Materially not observed	Not observed
Ensuring the basis for an effective corporate governance framework					
Overall corporate governance framework	P				
Legal framework enforceable/transparent		P			
Clear division of regulatory responsibilities		P			
Regulatory authority, integrity, resources		P			
The rights of shareholders					
Basic shareholder rights	P	C	H		
Rights to participate in fundamental decisions	H	P	C		
Shareholders annual general meeting (AGM) rights		P	CH		
Disproportionate control disclosure		HP	C		
Control arrangements should be allowed to function	C	H	P		
Cost/benefit to voting				H	C
Exercise of ownership rights facilitated				P	
Shareholders allowed to consult each other					P
Equitable treatment of shareholders					
All shareholders should be treated equally		HP	C		
Prohibit insider trading	H	P		C	
Board/managers disclose interests			HP	C	
Role of stakeholders in corporate governance					
Stakeholder rights respected	P	H		C	
Redress for violation of rights	P	H	C		
Performance enhancement	P	H	C		
Access to information		CH			
Stakeholder disclosure		P			
'Whistleblower' protection				P	
Creditor rights law and enforcement			P		

Table 13.5   (*Continued*)

	Observed	Largely observed	Partially observed	Materially not observed	Not observed
Disclosure and transparency					
Disclosure standards		HP	C		
Standards of accounting and audit		P	H	C	
Annual independent audit		C	HP		
External auditors should be accountable			P		
Fair and timely dissemination	HP	C			
Research conflicts of interest			P		
Responsibilities of the board					
Acts with due diligence, care		P	CH		
Treat all shareholders fairly		H	CP		
Ensure compliance with law		H	C		
Apply high ethical standards			P		
The board should fulfill certain key functions			CP	H	
The board should be able to exercise objective judgment			CHP		
Access to information	HP	C			

Source: World Bank.

Table 13.6   Corporate governance system: computation of average scores

	Czech R.	Hungary	Poland
Observed (5 points)	5	20	35
Largely observed (4 points)	20	40	48
Partially observed (3 points)	36	21	30
Materially not observed (2 points)	8	4	4
Not observed (1 point)	1	0	1
Total points	70	85	118
Total observations	23	23	32
Average score	**3.0**	**3.7**	**3.7**

Fortunately, the World Bank also did a study of corporate governance in Poland in 2002, so it is possible to compare the 2002 and 2005 Polish studies to see how rapidly Poland has been going up the learning curve. Table 13.7 makes that comparison. However, this comparison is not perfect because the 2002 and 2005 studies used different classification systems for the various categories. The 2002 study used *Yes, No, Not Available* and *Incomplete* as categories, whereas the 2005 study used *Observed, Largely Observed, Partially Observed, Materially Not Observed* and *Not Observed* as categories. In order to make the two different classification systems compatible, Table 13.7 makes

Table 13.7 Comparison of Polish ROSC studies (P = 2005 study; D = 2002 study)

Principle	Observed	Largely observed	Partially observed	Materially not observed	Not observed
Ensuring the basis for an effective corporate governance framework					
Overall corporate governance framework	P				
Legal framework enforceable/transparent		P			
Clear division of regulatory responsibilities		P			
Regulatory authority, integrity,resources		P			
Ownership registration	D				
Share transfer	D				
Participation and voting at AGM	D				
Election of board	D				
Share in the profits	D				
The rights of shareholders					
Basic shareholder rights	P				
Rights to participate in fundamental decisions		P			
Amendments to the statutes	D				
Authorization of additional shares					D
Extraordinary transactions (resulting in the sale of the company)			D		
Shareholders annual general meeting (AGM) rights		P			
Sufficient and timely information about AGM	D				
Opportunity to ask questions and place items on the agenda	D				
Vote in person or in absentia			D		
Disproportionate control disclosure	D				
Control arrangements should be allowed to function			P		
Clearly articulated and disclosed rules and procedures,transparent prices and fair conditions					D
Cost/benefit to voting					D
Exercise of ownership rights facilitated				P	
Shareholders allowed to consult each other					P
Equitable treatment of shareholders					
All shareholders should be treated equally	D	P			
Same voting rights for shareholders within each class. Ability to obtain information about voting rights attached to all classes before share acquisition. Changes in voting rights subject to shareholder vote	D				
AGM processes and procedures allow for equitable treatment; avoidance of undue difficulties and expenses in relation to voting	D				

Table 13.7   (*Continued*)

Principle	Observed	Largely observed	Partially observed	Materially not observed	Not observed
Prohibit insider trading	D	P			
Board/managers disclose interests	D		P		
Role of stakeholders in corporate governance					
Stakeholder rights respected	P				
Redress for violation of rights	P				
Performance enhancement	P				
Access to information			D		
Stakeholder disclosure		P			
'Whistleblower' protection				P	
Creditor rights law and enforcement			P		
Disclosure and transparency					
Disclosure standards		P	D		
Standards of accounting and audit		P	D		
Annual independent audit			DP		
External auditors should be accountable			P		
Fair and timely dissemination	DP				
Research conflicts of interest			DP		
Financial and operating results	D				
Company objectives			D		
Major share ownership and voting rights	D				
Board members, key executives and their remuneration			D		
Material foreseeable risk factors					D
Governance structures and policies					D
Responsibilities of the board					
Acts with due diligence, care		P			
Treat all shareholders fairly			P		
Ensure compliance with law					
Apply high ethical standards			P		
The board should fulfill certain key functions			P		
The board should be able to exercise objective judgment			P		
Access to information	P				
Corporate strategy, risk policy,budgets, business plans, performance objectives, implementation and performance surveillance, major capital expenditures, acquisitions, divestitures			D		
Selection, monitoring, replacement of key management	D				

Sources: World Bank (2002c, 2005).

the *Yes* category equivalent to *Observed*, the *No* category equivalent to *Not Observed* and the *Incomplete* category equivalent to *Partially Observed*, with five, one or three points assigned, respectively. Data on the *Not Available* category was omitted.

Some of the items included in the two studies were also different. For example, the 2005 study had a subcategory titled *The right to participate in decisions on fundamental corporate changes*. The 2002 study did not have this category, *per se*, but did have three items listed within this category – (1) *Amendments to the statutes*, (2) *Authorization of additional shares*, and (3) *Extraordinary transactions*. It was possible to assign scores to each of these items but doing so makes the comparison less than totally homogeneous.

The average scores for the 2002 and 2005 studies were 3.8 and 3.7, respectively, which would seemingly indicate that the quality of corporate governance has been marginally declining with time. However, this conclusion must be heavily discounted, for several reasons. For one, the conversion of the 2002 template categories to correspond with the 2005 template categories is only an approximation. For example, the *Yes* category in the 2002 template was assigned a score of 5, when perhaps a score of 4 or 4.5 or 4.3 or 4.332 might have been equally appropriate. The *Incomplete* category was assigned a score of 3 when a score of 2.5 or 3.5 might have been more appropriate in certain cases. The Wilcoxon test showed no significant difference between the two average scores ($p \leqslant 0.3789$). Thus, we can conclude that corporate governance has not changed substantially in Poland between 2002 and 2005, which means the fact that the 2005 Polish data were being used to compare 2002 Czech data and 2003 Hungarian data does not weaken any conclusions that might be drawn.

Concluding comments on comparative corporate governance

Several conclusions can be drawn from this chapter. Corporate governance in Hungary and Poland is somewhat better than corporate governance in the Czech Republic. Corporate governance in Hungary and Poland is at about the same level in terms of quality.

Another conclusion that can be drawn is that all three countries are in need of improvement in some areas of corporate governance. In order to have excellent corporate governance systems they would need to have average scores of 5.0, or at least close to 5.0. The fact that their scores varied between 3.0 and 3.7 indicates the amount of improvement that is still required.

This study also points out which areas of corporate governance are strong and which are weak for each of the three countries and goes into a bit of explanation for why this is the case. It is difficult to pinpoint exactly why the Czech corporate governance system is weaker than those of Hungary and Poland. Many factors are undoubtedly at work. One factor to consider is the date of the World Bank studies. The Czech study was published in 2002, a year earlier than the Hungarian study and three years earlier than the Polish study. We demonstrated that the Polish 2002 and 2005 results are very similar, therefore the timing of the Polish study taken for comparison does not influence the results. On the other hand, if corporate governance practices were improving rapidly in the Czech Republic, the Czech scores could have been higher in 2003 or 2005. Thus, all we can conclude with confidence is that the Czech system of corporate governance in 2002 was significantly weaker than the corporate governance systems of Hungary in 2003 and Poland in 2005 (and 2002). If corporate governance practices do not change too rapidly, it would be fair to say that corporate governance practices in the Czech Republic are still weaker than those of Hungary and Poland.

It is likely that corporate governance practices in all three countries will continue to improve, perhaps markedly, in the next few years. One impetus for improvement is membership in the European Union. Pressure from EU bureaucrats will force changes in corporate structure and governance practices. The adoption and implementation of IFRS and International Auditing Standards will help improve corporate financial reporting practices. Assistance in the improvement process will also come from within, as top management seeks foreign investment. The Big-4 accounting firms, which audit most of the larger firms in these countries, will help enterprises in these countries climb the learning curve, thus facilitating the process of corporate governance reform and improvement.

It would not be too much of a stretch to predict that in a decade, if not less, the corporate governance practices of the Czech Republic, Hungary and Poland will be more or less on a par with practices in the older members of the EU, at least as far as the large companies are concerned.

14
Transparency and Disclosure in Russia

Robert W. McGee

Introduction

Corporate governance is a multi-faceted subject. It overlaps the disciplines of accounting, economics, finance, law, management, politics, sociology, history, cultural studies and even ethics and philosophy. Some aspects of marketing, public relations, journalism and corporate communications are also involved; especially in cases where a company has relatively good corporate governance, it wants to announce that fact to the international investment community. It is always easier to raise capital if a company is perceived as having a good system of corporate governance in place.

While all these disciplinary approaches remain valid, the typical assumptions made may not hold in the case of Russia. Samuel Huntington's book, *The Clash of Civilizations* (1998), which evolved from an earlier essay (1993), considers the Russian culture to be distinctly different from all other European or Asian cultures. When he divided the cultures of the world into seven or eight categories, he reserved one of those categories just for Russia. And while scholars have challenged parts of his thesis (Henderson, 2004; Imai, 2005; Novak, 2004; Seib, 2004/2005), no one has really challenged his assertion that Russia is a special case.

In particular, no one who is familiar with Russian culture would say that Russians like to disclose information, especially financial information. Even before communist times, there was a tendency to play financial matters close to the vest, so to speak. That being the case, one can imagine the hesitancy for post-communist, recently privatized Russian companies to disclose a plethora of financial information to the general public, which is what International Financial Reporting Standards (IFRS) and US GAAP (generally accepted accounting principles) require. But Russian companies that want to attract foreign investment, or even a loan from the local bank, need to disclose a certain amount of financial information. How do they measure up, compared to their competitors in the developed market economies? How do the quantity and quality of financial disclosure of Russian firms compare to that of the many other international firms they must compete with for capital?

Disclosure is a new concept for the Russians and it has taken them some time to learn how to deal with it. In the early days, shortly after Russian companies began to be privatized, they realized that they had to disclose financial information if they wanted to convince lenders or equity investors to give them the capital they needed. But the process was new for them, so in the early days they didn't get it quite right. They did not know what should be disclosed, so they sometimes disclosed information that was not of any interest to potential investors while failing to disclose important information. There was a tendency to report information they were familiar with rather than information that might be useful in rendering an investment decision (McGee and Preobragenskaya, 2005: 26).

That situation is changing however. The passage of time, moving up the learning curve through trial and error, plus advice from the large international accounting firms and various international organizations such as the World Bank, the International Monetary Fund, The United States Agency for International Development, TACIS and others have all helped the Russian companies increase both the quantity and quality of disclosure. But how far have they come? Have Russian company financial statements achieved parity with those of their competitors in the more developed market economies? *The Opacity Index*, which was a PricewaterhouseCoopers study (2001) of transparency in 35 countries, ranked Russia number 34, just ahead of China (Haigh, 2001). Kurtzman *et al.* (2004) expanded on that study by including 48 countries. Russia ranked 40.

One of the five components of the *Opacity Index* is accounting and governance practices. Table 14.1 shows Russia's score and relative rank in the accounting category for the 2004 survey.

Russia is tied for thirty-third place with several other countries. However, one may notice at the same time, that the score is now on a similar (or even higher) level than in several Central European countries, Poland in particular, and clearly higher than China.

How transparent are Russian financial reporting practices? This chapter attempts to partially answer that question. The financial statements of selected Russian companies are examined to determine whether the extent and timeliness of disclosure are comparable to that of companies in developed market economies. Luckily, the quality of Russian financial statements is getting better. An increasing number of Russian accountants are seeing the value of good reporting practices and are warming up to the idea of adopting and using IFRS (PricewaterhouseCoopers, 2004), although the implementation process has had some difficulties (McGee and Preobragenskaya, 2004; OECD, 2004b). Some Russian accountants (Schneidman, 2004) are even taking the position that it is immoral not to use IFRS because the Russian accounting standards are inefficient and misleading.

Table 14.1 Accounting and governance practices in selected countries

Rank	Country	Score
1	Finland	17
1	Belgium	17
1	Germany	17
4	USA	20
4	Canada	20
4	Chile	20
4	Israel	20
4	Thailand	20
9	Japan	22
9	Indonesia	22
11	Sweden	25
11	Switzerland	25
11	Ecuador	25
14	Colombia	29
15	Malaysia	30
15	Korea	30
15	Argentina	30
15	India	30
15	Venezuela	30
20	United Kingdom	33
20	Denmark	33
20	Hong Kong	33
20	Australia	33
20	Austria	33
20	South Africa	33
20	France	33
20	Mexico	33
20	Pakistan	33
20	Saudi Arabia	33
20	Philippines	33
31	Netherlands	38
31	Ireland	38
33	Taiwan	40
33	Brazil	40
33	Poland	40
33	**Russia**	**40**
33	Egypt	40
38	Czech Republic	44
38	Turkey	44
38	Lebanon	44
41	Singapore	50
41	Spain	50
41	Portugal	50
41	Hungary	50
41	Greece	50
46	China	56
47	Italy	63

Nigeria was not rated.

Source: Kurtzman *et al.* (2004).

Transparency is one of those terms that have many facets. It is used in different ways; it can refer to the openness of governmental functions; it can refer to a country's economy; or it can refer to various aspects of corporate governance and financial reporting. The OECD (1998) lists transparency as one element of good corporate governance. Kulzick (2004) and others (Blanchet, 2002; Prickett, 2002) view transparency from a user perspective. According to their view, transparency includes the following eight concepts: accuracy, consistency, appropriateness, completeness, clarity, timeliness, convenience, governance and enforcement.

This chapter focuses on just two aspects of transparency: completeness and timeliness.

Review of the literature

Financial transparency has its advantages. Ang and Brau (2002) examined 334 leveraged buyouts and found that the more transparent a firm was, the lower the costs of going public. Chiang (2005) found that analysts are able to make more accurate predictions when the firm has transparent financial statements. An OECD study (2002c) found that capital is more likely to flow to firms where transparency is high, corruption is low and the judicial system is efficient. Errunza and Losq (1985) found that companies in emerging market economies tend to report less information and take longer to report it than companies in more developed market economies.

A lack of transparency has its drawbacks. The lack of transparency and timeliness of financial reporting is cited as being one cause of the Asian financial crisis (Choi, 1998; Rahman, 1999; Ho and Wong, 2001).

Vishwanath and Kaufmann (2001) suggest that transparency may have its limits, especially in emerging economies because of inadequate enforcement. Before there can be adequate enforcement in the area of transparency, they argue that there must first be broader reforms in the public sector.

From reading the financial press and the comments by pundits one would assume that everyone champions more transparency and that more transparency is necessarily a good thing. However, not everyone favours more transparency and disclosure. In the case of segment reporting, for example, one argument against it is that it may provide information that is more useful to competitors than to shareholders. Disclosing such information may actually be against shareholder interests.

The type of investor also determines the desirability of the extent of transparency. Lenders may prefer less transparency, since it protects relatively weak firms, whereas equity investors would like more transparency. Perotti (2005) found that dominant creditors seek to decrease transparency below the level preferred by equity investors. However, Perotti and von Thadden (2003) argue that increased global trading and the entry into the market of transparent competitors may make it increasingly difficult for banks to keep firms opaque.

Transparency does not necessarily have to be imposed in a top-down fashion by government. The private sector can also put pressure on corporate management to have a transparent financial reporting system. Institutional investors are in a good position to do exactly that, since they have clout and can get the attention of top management. A study by Hebb (2006) found that pension funds can exert pressure on top management to more closely align their actions to the interests of shareholders by making the reporting system more transparent. Hebb concluded that transparency ensures that shareholder interests are the primary interests being served by the firm. When firms are opaque, decision-making distorts efficiency and secrecy is inefficient.

A study by Hunton, Libby and Mazza (2006) found that greater transparency in the reporting of comprehensive income reduces the probability that managers will engage in earnings management.

Ho and Wong (2001) conclude that having a top-down government imposed regulation approach to corporate financial disclosure would not be sufficient to solve the disclosure problem. They suggest that improving the quality of communication and the disclosure process by choosing more appropriate communication media, formulating a more proactive disclosure strategy, enhancing the relationship with investors and voluntarily reporting information desired by users would also be required.

Transparency is not free. It comes at a cost. The EU's decision to force the adoption of IFRS could cost non-EU companies up to $10 million in compliance costs if they want to list their shares in the EU. Thomas (2003) examined the cost-effectiveness of providing financial information in an attempt to determine ways to minimize the cost of providing useful information.

Berglof and Pajuste (2005) examined disclosure for 370 companies in Central and Eastern Europe and found widespread nondisclosure even of basic information, even where regulations required disclosure. They also found that the level of disclosure varies widely among firms and there is a country effect on what companies disclose. The legal framework in a country plays a large part in determining what is disclosed but disclosure did not correspond to a firm's financial performance. However, financial performance was strongly correlated to how easily information was available to the public. He also found that information is more available for larger companies, in firms where ownership was more concentrated, where leverage was lower and where the market-to-book ratio was higher. Bushman, Pietroski and Smith (2004) found that governance transparency is related to a country's legal system whereas financial transparency is primarily related to political economy.

Kang and Pang (2005) and others (Levine and Zervos, 1998; Rajan and Zingales, 1998; Salter, 1998) have found that the quality of disclosure and transparency tends to be higher for developed economies than for developing or transition economies and that quality improves as an economy develops. Lee (1987) contends that there is a direct correlation between the development of a country's stock market and the level of accounting disclosure.

Kim (2005) measured the transparency of Korean firms and found that firms are more transparent if they are members of chaebols. Firms with more assets tend to be more transparent than firms with fewer assets. In particular, the threshold level of assets where stricter financial reporting regulations start to kick in was associated with a shift towards greater transparency, which seems to indicate that stricter reporting requirements have some positive effect on the degree of transparency. Kim also found that the level of transparency differs across industries, with the telecommunications, finance and electronics industries being more transparent and the transportation, construction and paper industries being less transparent.

In APB Statement No. 4, the Accounting Principles Board (1970) in the USA listed timeliness as one of the qualitative objectives of financial reporting disclosure. APB Statement No. 4 was later superseded but the Financial Accounting Standards Board continued to recognize the importance of timeliness in its Concepts Statement No. 2 (1980). The US Securities and Exchange Commission also recognizes the importance of timeliness and requires that listed companies file their annual 10-K reports by a certain deadline.

The issue of timeliness has several facets. There is an inverse relationship between the quality of financial information and the timeliness with which it is reported (Kenley and Staubus, 1974). Accounting information becomes less relevant with the passage of time (Atiase, Bamber and Tse, 1989; Hendriksen and van Breeda, 1992; Lawrence and Glover, 1998).

There is some evidence to suggest that it takes more time to report bad news than good news (Bates, 1968; Beaver, 1968), both because companies hesitate to report bad news and because companies take more time to massage the numbers or resort to creative accounting techniques when they have to report bad news (Givoli and Palmon, 1982; Chai and Tung, 2002; Trueman, 1990). Stated differently, there seems to be a tendency to rush good news to press, such as better than expected earnings, and delay the reporting of bad news or less than expected earnings (Chambers and Penman, 1984; Kross and Schroeder, 1984). Dwyer and Wilson (1989) found this relationship to hold true for municipalities. Haw, Qi and Wu (2000) found it to be the case with Chinese companies. Leventis and Weetman (2004) found it to be the case for Greek firms.

However, Annaert, DeCeuster, Polfliet and Campenhout (2002) found that this was not the case for Belgian companies and Han and Wang (1998) found that this was not the case for petroleum refining companies, which delayed reporting extraordinarily high profits during the Gulf Crisis of the 1990s, perhaps because political repercussions outweighed what would otherwise have been a good market reaction. Rees and Giner (2001) found that companies in France, Germany and the UK tended to report bad news sooner than good news.

A study by Basu (1997) found that companies tend to report bad news quicker than good news, presumably because of conservatism. Gigler and Hemmer (2001) discuss this point in their study, which finds that firms with more conservative accounting systems are less likely to make timely voluntary disclosures than are firms with less conservative accounting systems.

Building upon the Basu study (1997), Pope and Walker (1997) found that there were cross-jurisdictional effects when extraordinary items were either included or excluded, using US and UK firms for comparison. Han and Wild (1997) examined the potential relationship between earnings timeliness and the share price reactions of competing firms. But Jindrichovska and Mcleay (2005) found that there was no evidence of conservatism in the Czech accounting system when it came to reporting bad news earlier than good news, presumably because the Czech tax system offers little incentive to do so. Ball, Kathari and Robin (2000) found that companies in jurisdictions that have a strong shareholder orientation tend to disclose earnings information sooner than companies in countries operating under a legal code system.

There is also a relationship between the speed with which financial results are announced and the effect the announcement has on stock prices. If information is released sooner, the effect on stock prices is more pronounced. The long the time lapse between year-end and the release of the financial information, the less effect there is on stock price, all other things being equal (Ball and Brown, 1968; Brown and Kennelly, 1972).

Some countries report financial results faster than other countries. DeCeuster and Trappers (1993) found that Belgian companies take longer to report their financial results than do Anglo-Saxon countries. Annaert, DeCeuster, Polfliet and Campenhout (2002) found this to be the case for interim information as well. Companies can report financial results faster on the internet and the information can be more widely disbursed but posting two-year-old annual reports does nothing to improve timeliness (Ashbaugh, Johnstone and Warfield, 1999).

Atiase, Bamber and Tse (1989) found that large companies report earnings faster than small companies and that the reporting of earnings results in a more significant market reaction for small firms than for large firms. In a study of Australian firms, Davies and Whittred (1980) found that small firms and large firms made significantly more timely reports than medium-size firms and that profitability was not a significant variable.

Whittred (1980) found that the release of financial information for Australian companies is delayed the first time an audit firm issues a qualified report and that the extent of the delay is longer in cases where the qualification is more serious. Keller (1986) replicated that study for US companies and found the same thing to be true. Whittred and Zimmer (1984) found that it took Australian firms in financial distress a significantly longer time to publish their financial information. A study of more than 5,000 annual reports of French companies found that it took longer to release audit reports where there had been a qualified opinion, and that the more serious the qualification, the greater the delay in releasing the report (Soltani, 2002).

Krishnan (2005) found that the audit firm's degree of expertise has an effect on the timeliness of the publication of bad earnings news. Audit firms that specialize in the industry in which the company operates are more timely in reporting bad financial news than are audit firms that have less industry expertise.

Disclosure

Financial disclosure consists of many elements. Issuing financial statements on a regular basis is only one aspect. But mere issuance is not enough. Statements must be issued in a timely manner and they must include information that is useful in arriving at investing and lending decisions. While more information is generally better than less information, mere quantity of information disclosed is not automatically transformed into quality.

Quantity is easier to measure than quality. Quantity is an objective number whereas quality is subjective. In the early days after Russian firms started to become privatized they were criticized for disclosing information that was not relevant to the investment and lending community. They have come a long way since those early days, although few would argue that the quality of financial reporting for the average Russian company is on a par with that of its Western and Japanese competitors.

For the purposes of this chapter we shall assume that the quality of the *best* Russian company financial statements is about equal to that of companies operating in the more developed market economies. That assertion is not too much of a stretch. The best Russian companies issue financial statements based on either International Financial Reporting Standards (IFRS) or US GAAP. Their financial statements are generally audited either by one of the Big-4 international accounting firms or by one of the second-tier international accounting firms. Thus, a certain level of quality must be present because international accounting firms would not allow their name to appear as auditor unless the financial statements met certain qualitative standards.

A survey of Russian company transparency was conducted by Standard and Poor's (Kochetygova *et al.*, 2005), to measure and rank transparency among Russia's 54 largest companies. Table 14.2 lists the companies' ranks and transparency scores.

As can be seen, some Russian companies have relatively high scores, while others do not. It is expected that overall scores will improve in future years because of the pressure being exerted on Russian companies in all industry sectors to improve their corporate governance practices and degree of transparency. This pressure is coming from the international investment community, the Russian government and internally, within the companies themselves. However, at present the high scores relate to a small number of top companies and drop off rather rapidly as soon as the sample size increases. Figure 14.1 illustrates how quickly the transparency scores decline.

For the purposes of our study, the *best* Russian companies are defined as the companies with the top ten scores in the Standard & Poor's study. If

Table 14.2   Transparency of Russia's largest companies, 2005

Rank	Company	Score	Rank	Company	Score
1	MTS	84	28	Baltika	50
2	Rostelecom	82	29	Kalina	49
3	Mechel	79	30	MGTS	48
4	Wimm-Bill-Dann Foods	77	31	Severstal	47
5	Golden Telecom	75	32	Tatneft	47
5	Vimpelcom	75	33	Kuzbassenergo	46
7	North-West Telecom	71	34	MMK	46
8	RosBusinessConsulting	69	35	Sberbank	45
9	Lukoil	68	36	Novatek	44
10	Southern Telecom	67	37	Pharmacy Chain 36,6	43
11	Volga Telecom	65	38	Yakutskenergo	43
12	Uralsvyazinform	64	39	KAMAZ	41
13	Centertelecom	63	40	GAZ	41
14	Sibirtelecom	63	41	Samaraenergo	39
15	Severstal Avto	60	42	AvtoVAZ	37
16	Gazprom	60	43	Lebedyanskiy	36
17	Power Machines	58	44	Krasnoyarskenergo	35
18	Norilsk Nickel	58	45	Surgutneftegaz	35
19	Mosenergo	58	46	Irkutskenergo	34
20	Sibneft	57	47	Sverdlovenergo	34
21	Dalsvyaz	55	48	YUKOS	33
22	Sistema	54	49	Irkut	30
23	TNK-BP	54	50	Bashkirenergo	27
24	OMZ	53	51	Bashneft	23
25	Lenenergo	52	52	Evrazholding	21
26	RAO UES	52	53	Pyaterochka	3
27	Aeroflot	51	54	Rambler Media	2
				Average score	**50**

transparency is defined as the extent of financial statement disclosure of relevant information, and if it is assumed that the big international accounting firms, the stock exchanges and the marketplace are forcing Russian firms to disclose the most relevant information, it then becomes a quantitative question. Are the best Russian companies disclosing as much relevant information as their non-Russian competitors?

Such a question is not impossible to answer, although there are some limitations. If it is assumed that companies report the most relevant information first, the second most relevant information second and the least relevant information last, or perhaps not at all, the quality of information being reported may be roughly measured by counting the number of pages of financial information that are reported in a company's annual report or similar document. A company that devotes 50 pages to the disclosure of such information is being more transparent than a company that devotes a mere 10 pages to such disclosure. However, total page count is a mere surrogate for quantity of disclosure. The

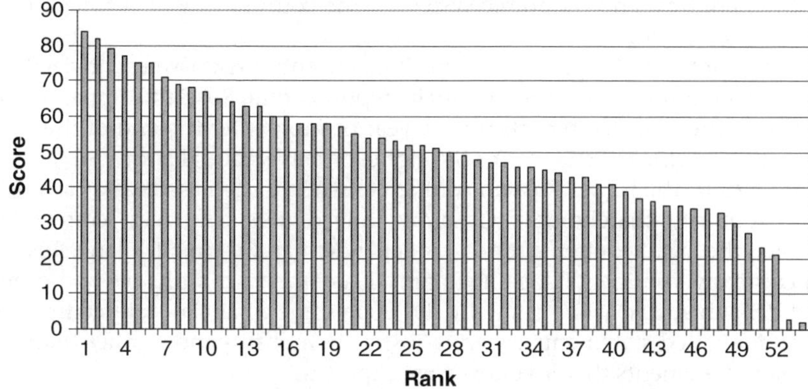

Figure 14.1   Transparency of Russian companies

size of the page, the size of the margins on the page and the size of the font also affect the amount of information that is disclosed on the page. These factors are all ignored for purposes of the present study and merely assumed to be equal between companies.

In order to determine the extent of financial disclosure, the most recent financial statements of the best Russian firms were examined and the number of pages devoted to the reporting of financial information in their annual reports or other relevant document were counted. The data that resulted from that count are presented below in Table 14.5.

Timeliness

Another measure of transparency and quality of financial reporting is timeliness. The lapse of time between a company's year-end and the date when financial information is released to the public is related to the quality of the information reported. Issuing excellent, accurate and comprehensive financial information two or three years after year-end is not as desirable as issuing less comprehensive and complete financial information a few months after year-end. Financial information becomes stale after a few months, and certainly after two or three years. The more stale it is, the less relevant it is to potential investors and creditors.

There are a number of reasons for the time lag between year-end and the issuance of the audit report and the publication of financial information. Ashton, Graul and Newton (1989) identified auditor size, industry classification, the presence or absence of extraordinary items and the sign of net income as some factors that influence timeliness. To that one might add the culture, political and economic system of the country in which the particular firm is located.

In the not too distant past, some Russian enterprises were criticized for waiting too long to issue their financial reports; some Russian companies did not issue their annual reports until a year or more after the end of the year, and in some cases Russian firms did not even have annual audits.

As of 2001, the largest Russian companies still hid their assets and cash flow from minority shareholders. Gazprom, one of Russia's largest companies, ignored the legal requirement of an independent audit. Lukoil, a large Russian oil company, routinely issued its financial statements months beyond promised deadlines, and when it finally did issue some financial statements, they were unaudited statements covering just a six-month period rather than the full-year statements that investors were expecting.

Measuring timeliness is relatively easy. The present study measures timeliness by computing the number of days that elapse between the company's year-end and the date of the auditor's report.

The study: Russian company financial data

The websites of the top-ten Russian companies were searched for financial information. Some websites posted information for more years than others, which accounts for the fact that the data listed below is more extensive for some companies than for others. In some cases, the consolidated financial statements were posted as separate documents and the annual reports were also posted. For companies that issued US GAAP financial statements the Securities and Exchange Commission reports were sometimes provided as well. Where the consolidated statements were published separately, those documents were used for purposes of this study.

A decision had to be made about how to treat the SEC reports. The main issue to decide was what information to include in the page count. On the one hand, it could be argued that every page of the SEC reports should be included because the SEC reports disclose financial information. But the more conservative approach would be to include only the pages containing the financial statements and their accompanying footnotes. Taking the conservative option would also increase the homogeneity of the comparison, since all companies issued financial statements and footnotes, but not all companies issued the information contained in the SEC reports.

It was not always possible to determine the name of the auditor because the name of the auditor is sometimes written in by hand at the bottom of the Auditor's Report and the version of the report that was posted to the company's website did not show that version of the report. In some cases, there were different auditors for the Russian financial statements (those prepared according to Russian Accounting Standards, whether published in Russian or English) and the IFRS or US GAAP financial statements. Where the auditor of the IFRS or US GAAP statements was known the name was listed. Otherwise, no auditor was listed.

MTS (Ranked #1)

Mobile Telesystems (MTS) posted its SEC Form 20-F for each year. The Form for 2004 was 502 pages, 60 pages of which consisted of financial statements and footnotes.

Rostelecom (Ranked #2)

Rostelecom is a telecommunications company. Its financial statements are based on IFRS with a US GAAP reconciliation. Its website included annual reports, IFRS statements and SEC reports going back to 1999 in some cases. The IFRS–US GAAP reconciliation for 2002–04 was as shown in Table 14.3. It is provided to show what such a reconciliation looks like and also to illustrate both the content and extent of the differences for a Russian company.

Mechel Steel Group (Ranked #3)

Although the Mechel Steel Group issued a 23-page annual report for 2004, it did not contain any financial information. It did post financial information on its website, but it was in html format, making it impossible to do a page count. It also posted an 11-page press release in the form of a pdf document on 27 June 2005 for the year 2004 that was based on US GAAP but also included some non-GAAP information. It did not post a full set of financials for years prior to 2004 other than the 2004 postings that had comparative data from 2003.

A 120-page audit opinion was issued 22 March 2005 by a Russian audit firm based on RAS. That audit opinion contained a large amount of financial

Table 14.3   Reconciliation of IFRS and US GAAP net income – Rostelecom (millions of rubles)

	2004	2003	2002
Net income under IFRS	4,298	398	739
US GAAP adjustments:			
Depreciation on reversed impairment charge	(889)	(800)	(602)
Unrealized gain on available for sale investments	(42)	(68)	(41)
Pension expense	–	(30)	(20)
Impact of difference in accounting for investments acquired for resale, net of minority interest	–	59	(59)
Impact of goodwill amortize, net of minority interest	135	92	35
Partial gain recognition	–	–	(3)
Reversal of impairment on investment in equity method	–	55	(55)
Deferred tax effects of US GAAP adjustments	177	123	140
Net income (loss) under US GAAP	3,679	(171)	134

data but it was not in a format that would be familiar to accountants who are familiar only with US GAAP. The website also posted a 407-page prospectus dated 29 October 2004. The basic financial statements were also posted separately but they were based on RAS rather than US GAAP or IFRS. However, all these postings made it difficult to find particular financial information because it was scattered around in different documents, some based on US GAAP and others based on RAS. No footnote disclosure could be found for 2004, although a great deal of information was posted on the website.

Wimm-Bill-Dann Foods (Ranked #4)

Wimm-Bill-Dan Foods issues financial statements using US GAAP. Although there were audit reports, the auditor's identity could not always be identified. Sometimes the financial statements were supplemented by a management discussion and analysis section. For 2002, for example, there were 59 pages of financial statements and footnotes and an additional 58 pages of management discussion and analysis. The website also included the corporate Code of Ethics and Corporate Governance Code.

Golden Telecom (Ranked #5)

Golden Telecom posted its SEC 10-K forms on its website. The 2004 Form was 177 pages in length; 43 pages consisted of financial statements and footnotes.

Vimpelcom (Ranked #5)

Vimpelcom is in the cellular telephone end of the telecommunications industry.

North-West Telecom (Ranked #7)

North-West Telecom posted its IFRS consolidated financial statements to its website. The auditor was not disclosed in some of its IFRS consolidated financial statements documents but the company also provided separate auditor opinion documents, which did include the name of the auditor. Annual reports were also included on its website.

Sometimes the auditor of the RAS statements was not the same as the auditor of the IFRS statements. For example, the 2002 RAS statements were audited by the firm of Nikolay V. Slavyaninov whereas the IFRS statements were audited by Ernst & Young.

The Annual Reports for North-West Telecom were also interesting. In 2002, and perhaps in other years, both the RAS and IFRS financial statements were published. The figures were significantly different. Table 14.4 shows selected financial statement data comparing the two sets of financial statements.

RosBusiness Consulting (Ranked #8)

RBC is a media and information technology company. The most recent annual report on its website was from 2003. The annual reports for 2001 and 2002

Table 14.4   Comparison of selected RAS and IFRS accounts – North-West Telecom, 2002 (000s rubles)

Account	Russian accounting standards	International financial reporting standards	Difference % IFRS – RAS IFRS
Revenue	10,091,841	10,790,609	6.5%
Net income	327,264	482,872	32.2%
Assets	14,938,041	19,661,170	24.0%

did not include financial information. KPMG was their auditor. The annual report for 2003 contained 28 pages of financial information. It took 141 days to publish the auditor's opinion.

Lukoil (Ranked #9)

Lukoil had both its annual reports and its US GAAP consolidated financial statements posted on its website. Its consolidated financial statements were used to determine page counts. Its auditor was KPMG for all reported years.

Southern Telecom (Ranked #10)

Southern Telecom retained Ernst & Young as its auditor for at least some years and issued financial statements based on IFRS for 2002–04 and US GAAP before that. Its financial statements went back to 1999. Although financial information was posted on its website, the information for some years was in the form of an Excel spreadsheet, which made it impossible to determine the number of pages. No information on the auditor or the date of the auditor's report was available for some years. The data for the Russian companies are given in Table 14.5

Summary results on timeliness and disclosure

It took Russian companies an average of 136.6 days after year-end to issue financial statements (actually, the date chosen was the date of the auditor's report). Assuming a 31 December year-end, the average Russian company released its financial results on 17 May. The top-10 companies listed in the 2006 Fortune 500 list took an average of 63.6 days to report, which means the average reporting date was 5 March, more than two months sooner than the average Russian company. Figure 14.2 shows the time lag between year-end and the date of the audit report for the 10 most transparent Russian companies.

   The next step was to count the number of pages of financial information issued by the top-ten Russian companies. It was thought that, since Russian culture is generally resistant to disclosure, and since Russian companies are not as familiar with financial disclosure as are non-Russian companies in

Table 14.5 Disclosure and timeliness data: top-10 Russian companies

Company	Year	Days	Pages	Auditor	Standards used
Golden Telecom (#5)	2004	70	43	Ernst & Young	US GAAP
	2003	70	31	Ernst & Young	US GAAP
	2002	65	49	Ernst & Young	US GAAP
Lukoil (#9)	2004	144	37	KPMG	US GAAP
	2003	173	46	KPMG	US GAAP
	2002	150	43	KPMG	US GAAP
	2001	176	38	KPMG	US GAAP
	2000	220	35	KPMG	US GAAP
	1999	81	28	KPMG	US GAAP
Mechel (#3)	2004	178	11	Unknown	US GAAP
MTS (#1)	2004	81	60	Deloitte & Touche	US GAAP
	2003	86	62	Deloitte & Touche	US GAAP
	2002	140	45	Deloitte & Touche	US GAAP
	2001	339	56	Deloitte & Touche	US GAAP
North-West Telecom (#7)	2004	166	54	Ernst & Young	IFRS
	2003	213	46	Ernst & Young	IFRS
	2002	212	43	Ernst & Young	IFRS
	2001	258	39	Unknown	US GAAP
RosBusiness (#8)	2003	141	28	KPMG	
	2002			No fin. Stmts.	
	2001			No fin. Stmts.	
Rostelecom (#2)	2004	174	60	Unknown	IFRS with US GAAP reconciliation
	2003	181	67	Ernst & Young	IFRS with US GAAP reconciliation
	2002	157	48	Ernst & Young	IFRS with US GAAP reconciliation
	2001	239	56	Ernst & Young	IFRS with US GAAP reconciliation
	2000	138	42	PWC	IFRS with US GAAP reconciliation
Southern Telecommunication (#10)	2004	177	46	Ernst & Young	IFRS
	2003			Unknown	IFRS
	2002	–	–	Unknown	IFRS
	2001	228	42	Unknown	US GAAP
	2000	110	25	Unknown	US GAAP
	1999	98	20	Unknown	US GAAP
Vimpelcom (#5)	2004	90	37	Ernst & Young	US GAAP
	2003	75	18	Ernst & Young	US GAAP
	2002	73	57	Ernst & Young	US GAAP
	2001	73	42	Ernst & Young	US GAAP
	2000	79	36	Ernst & Young	US GAAP
	1999	95	33	Ernst & Young	US GAAP
	1998	85	Unk.	Ernst & Young	US GAAP
Wimm-Bill-Dann Foods (#4)	2004	80	41	Unknown	US GAAP
	2003	60	44	Unknown	US GAAP
	2002	76	59	Ernst & Young	US GAAP
Average		136.6	42.4		

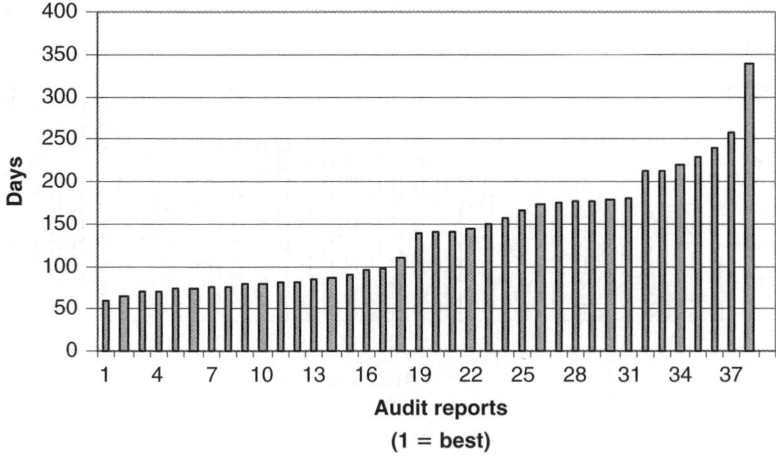

Figure 14.2   Days delay in issuing audit report

developed market economies, Russian companies would not disclose as much financial information as would non-Russian companies. The average Russian company published 42.4 pages of financial information, which is far less than many companies in developed market economies. Figure 14.3 shows the range of pages of financial disclosure.

The next test computed the number of days it took Russian companies to issue financial results if they used US GAAP and compared the results to Russian companies that used IFRS. It was thought that, since US GAAP has more rules and more complicated rules than IFRS, it would take Russian companies more time to issue their financial results if they used US GAAP. It took an average of 123.3 days for companies using US GAAP to release their financial results, compared to 184.1 days for companies using IFRS. This result was somewhat surprising, since it was expected that it would take longer to issue financial statements if they were based on a more complex and comprehensive set of accounting principles. It would be interesting to see whether this pattern is true for a larger sample of Russian firms. It would also be interesting to see whether this pattern is present for non-Russian firms.

The next test computed the number of pages of financial information Russian companies issued when using US GAAP and compared the results to those of Russian companies that used IFRS. It was thought that more pages of disclosure would be required when US GAAP was used, since US GAAP has more rules and more complicated rules than IFRS. It was found that Russian companies that used IFRS published significantly more pages of financial information than did companies that used US GAAP, which is just the opposite of the expected outcome. Table 14.6 summarizes the results.

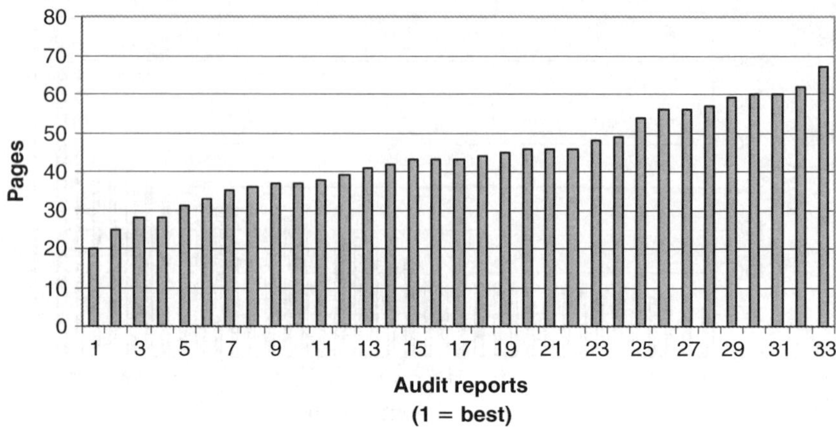

Figure 14.3 Number of pages of financial information

Table 14.6 Disclosure and timeliness: comparison between companies using US GAAP and IFRS

	Overall	US GAAP	IFRS
Days delay in reporting			
Average days after year-end before release of financial information	136.6	123.3	184.1
Day information released, assuming a December 31 year-end	17 May	4 May	1 July
Pages			
Average number of pages in financial statements	42.4	39.9	51.3

Concluding comments

The results of the present study show that even the best Russian companies take a long time to report financial results. The best Russian companies also do not disclose as much information as companies in mature market economies. These results were expected but this is the first study to confirm the expected result.

This study has some limitations. Only the ten best Russian companies were examined, as chosen based on a transparency index. A larger sample might have shown an even wider gap in comparison with their Western counterparts, but we have no quantitative measure of it.

There is room for further research on this topic. One methodology would be to choose Russian companies and non-Russian companies that are in the same industry. Some research has found that the timeliness of financial reporting is correlated with the industry in which the firm operates, so perhaps choosing samples from the same industry would produce interesting results.

Another methodology would be to compare Russian and non-Russian companies that are about the same size. There is some evidence to suggest that there is a correlation between firm size and the timeliness of financial reporting. It would be interesting to see if comparing Russian and non-Russian companies of similar size would produce the same result as other studies that have been conducted that compare firm size to the timeliness of financial reporting.

Another study could test the premise that Russian companies are reporting more information faster now than in the past. Such a study could be done by examining the page count of Russian financial statements for the current and prior years to see if the page count has increased substantially. Another test could be made by comparing the number of days it takes to release financial information for the most current year to past years.

The methodology used in the present study could also be used with data from other transition economies to see if the same pattern holds true. One might expect that the Russian case would be similar to the case in Ukraine and the other former Soviet republics, but this issue has not yet been examined, so it remains a mere assumption. It would also be interesting to do some comparative studies to see whether other countries, especially those in Central and Eastern Europe, are doing better in terms of the timeliness and extent of disclosure than Russia or some other former Soviet republic.

Bibliography

Abdel-Motaal, K. (2002) *Structural Change and Yield Curve Anomalies in the Mexican Local Market, Fixed-Income Research, Latin America* (New York: Morgan Stanley).

Accounting Principles Board (1970) *Basic Concepts and Accounting Principles Underlying Financial Statements of Business Enterprises – Statement No. 4* (New York: American Institute of Certified Public Accountants).

Adachi, Y. (2006) 'The ambiguous effects of Russian corporate governance abuses of the 1990s', *Post-Soviet Affairs*, 22(1): 65–89.

Ade-Ajayi, F. (2003) 'International corporate governance and the responsibility of the board', *Corporate Governance*, 12(2): 184–90.

Aghion, P. and Blanchard, O. (1998) 'On privatization methods in Eastern Europe and their implications', *Economics of Transition*, 6(1): 87–99.

Aghion, P. and Bolton, P. (1992) 'An incomplete contracts approach to financial contracting', *Review of Economic Studies*, 59: 473–94.

Aglietta, M. (1997) 'Le capitalisme au tournant du siècle', Preface to the new edition of *Régulation et crises du capitalisme* (Paris: Odile Jacob).

Aglietta, M. and Rebérioux, A. (2004) *Dérives du capitalisme financier* (Paris: Albin Michel).

Aguila, E. (2005) *Pension Reform and Savings*, University College London, mimeo.

Akerlof, G. and Romer, P. (1993) 'Looting: the economic underworld of bankruptcy for profit', *Brookings Papers on Economic Activity. Macroeconomics*, 2: 1–73.

Aldrich, H. (1979) *Organizations and Environments* (Englewood Cliffs, NJ: Prentice-Hall).

Allan, D. (2002) 'Banks and the loans-for-shares auctions', in D. Lane (ed.), *Russian Banking: Evolution, Problems and Prospects* (Cheltenham: Edward Elgar).

Allen, F. and Gale, D. (2000) 'Corporate governance and competition', in X. Vives (ed.), *Corporate Governance* (Cambridge: Cambridge University Press).

Almeida, H. and Wolfenzon, P. (2005) 'A Theory of pyramidal ownership and family business groups', *NBER Working Paper*, No. 11368, National Bureau of Economic Research.

Anderson, R., Mansi, S. and Reeb, D. (2003) 'Founding family ownership and the agency costs of debt', *Journal of Financial Economics*, 68: 263–85.

Andreff, W. (2005a) 'Post-soviet privatisation in the light of the coase theorem. Transaction costs and governance Costs', in A. Oleinik (ed.), *The Institutional Economics of Russia's Transformation* (Aldershot: Ashgate): 191–212.

Andreff, W. (2005b) 'Russian privatisation at bay: some unresolved transaction and governance costs issues in post-soviet economies', in A. Oleinik (ed.), *The Institutional Economics of Russia's Transformation* (Aldershot: Ashgate): 213–44.

Andreff, W. (1991) 'A francia privatizalas tanulsagai Kelet-Europa szamara' [The French privatisation experience and Eastern Europe] (Part 1), *Külgazdasag* (Budapest), Vol. xxxv, 1991/9: 53–66; Part 2, *Külgazdasag*, Vol. xxxv, 1991/10: 24–44.

Andreff, W. (1992) 'French privatization techniques and experience: A model for central-Eastern Europe?' in F. Targetti (ed.), *Privatization in Europe: West and East Experiences* (Dartmouth: Aldershot).

Andreff, W. (1993) *La crise des économies socialistes. La rupture d'un système* (Grenoble: Presses Universitaires de Grenoble).

Andreff, W. (1995) 'Les entreprises du secteur public: conditions du succès de la transition', in W. Andreff (ed.), *Le secteur public à l'Est. Restructuration industrielle et financière* (Paris: L'Harmattan).

Andreff, W. (1996) 'Corporate governance of privatized enterprises in transforming economies: A theoretical approach', *MOCT-MOST*, 6(2): 59–80.

Andreff, W. (1999a) 'Privatisation et gouvernement d'entreprise dans les économies en transition', *Economie Internationale*, 77: 97–129.

Andreff, W. (1999b) 'Nominal and real convergence – at what speed?' in J. van Brabant (ed.), *Remaking Europe: The European Union and the Transition Economies* (Lanham: Rowman & Littlefield).

Andreff, W. (2002) 'The new multinational corporations from transition countries', *Economic Systems*, 25(4): 371–9.

Andreff, W. (2003) 'Twenty lessons from the experience of privatisation in transition economies', in Y. Kalyuzhnova and W. Andreff, *op. cit.*

Andreff, W., Radygin, A. and Malginov, G. (1996) *The Typical Ownership of Russian Enterprises: Main Investors and Corporate Governance* Institute for the Economy in Transition, Moscow, mimeo.

Ang, J., Rebel, A., Cole, A. and Lin, J. (2000) 'Agency costs and ownership structure', *Journal of Finance*, 55(1): 81–106.

Ang, J. and Brau, J. (2002) 'Firm transparency and the costs of going public', *Journal of Financial Research*, 25(1): 1–17.

Annaert, J., DeCeuster, M., Polfliet, R. and Van Campenhout, G. (2002) 'To be or not be ... "too late": The case of the Belgian semi-annual earnings announcements', *Journal of Business Finance and Accounting*, 29(3/4): 477–95.

Aoki, M. (1995) 'Controlling insider control: Issues of corporate governance in transition economies', in M. Aoki and H.-K. Kim (eds), *Corporate Governance in Transitional Economies: Insider Control and the Role of Banks* (Washington, DC: The World Bank): 3–30.

Aoki, M. (2000) *Information, Corporate Governance, and Institutional Diversity* (Oxford: Oxford University Press).

Aoki, M. (2001) *Toward a Comparative Institutional Analysis* (Cambridge, MA: MIT Press).

Aoki, M. and Kim, H. (1995) *Corporate Governance in Transitional Economies: Insider Control and the Role of Banks* (Washington, DC: The World Bank).

Aron, L. (2003) 'The Yukos Affair', *Russian Outlook*, American Enterprise Institute for Public Policy Research, Fall.

Ashbaugh, H., Johnstone, K. and Warfield, T.D. (1999) 'Corporate reporting on the Internet', *Accounting Horizons*, 13(3): 241–57.

Ashton, R., Graul, P. and Newton, J. (1989) 'Audit delay and the timeliness of corporate reporting', *Contemporary Accounting Research*, 5(2): 657–73.

Atanasov, V. (2002) 'Valuation of large blocks of shares and the private benefits of control', *Tuck-JQFA Contemporary Corporate Governance Issues II Conference.*

Atiase, R., Bamber, L. and Tse, S. (1989) 'Timeliness of financial reporting, the firm size effect, and stock price reactions to annual earnings announcements', *Contemporary Accounting Research*, 5(2): 526–52.

Aukutsionek, S., Filatochev, I., Kapelyushnikov, R. and Zhukov, V. (1998) 'Dominant shareholders, restructuring and performance of privatised companies in Russia: an analysis and some policy implications', *Communist Economies and Economic Transformation*, 10(4): 495–517.

Bader, L. and Gold, J. (2003) 'Reinventing pension actuarial science', The Pension Forum, Society of Actuaries, January.

Balcerowicz, L. (1995) *Socialism, Capitalism, Transformation* (Budapest: Central European University Press).

Ball, R. and Brown, P. (1968) 'An empirical evaluation of accounting income numbers', *Journal of Accounting Research*, 6: 159–78.

Ball, R., Kothari, S. and Robin, A. (2000) 'The effect of international institutional factors on properties of accounting earnings', *Journal of Accounting and Economics*, 29(1): 1–51.

Bałtowski, M. and Mickiewicz, T. (2000) 'Privatisation in Poland: Ten years after', *Post-Communist Economies*, 12(4): 425–43.

Bałtowski, M. (1998) *Prywatyzacja przedsiebiorstw panstwowych. Przebieg i ocena* (Warsaw: PWN).

Bałtowski, M. (2003) *Przedsiebiorstwa sprywatyzowane w gospodarce polskiej* (Warszawa: PWN).

Balzer, H. (2003) 'Russia Opts for State Power over Free Markets or Why is Khodorkovskii in Jail?' Published. Available at www.gateway2russia.com/st/art_161898.php, 4 November.

Barnes, A. (2003) 'Russia's new business groups and state power', *Post-Soviet Affairs*, 19(2): 154–86.

Barney, J. and Hansen, M. (1994) 'Trustworthiness as a source of competitive advantage', *Strategic Management Journal*, 15(Special Issue): 175–90.

Basu, S. (1997) 'The conservatism principle and the asymmetric timeliness of earnings', *Journal of Accounting and Economics*, 24: 3–37.

Bates, R. (1968) 'Discussion of the information content of annual earnings announcements', *Journal of Accounting Research*, 6(Suppl.): 93–5.

Baums, T. (1993) 'Takeovers versus institutions in corporate governance in Germany', in P. Holland and D. Prentice (eds), *Contemporary Issues in Corporate Governance* (Oxford: Clarendon Press): 151–83.

Beaver, W. (1968) 'The information content of annual earnings announcements', *Journal of Accounting Research*, 6(Suppl.): 67–92.

Bebchuk, L. (1994) 'Efficient and inefficient sales of corporate control', *Quarterly Journal of Economics*, 109: 957–94.

Bebchuk, L. (1999) 'A rent-protection theory of corporate ownership and control', *NBER Working Paper*, No. 7203, National Bureau of Economic Research.

Becht, M. and Mayer, C. (2002) 'Corporate control in Europe', *Revue d'Economie Politique*, 112(4): 471–512.

Becker, F. (2000) 'Integrated portfolio strategies for dynamic organizations', *Facilities*, 18(10/11/12): 411–20.

Bednarova, E. (2001) La structure et les performances du système bancaire tchèque en transition, PhD dissertation, University Paris 1.

Bennedsen, M. and Wolfenzon, D. (2000) 'The balance of power in closely held corporations', *Journal of Financial Economics*, 58: 113–39.

Berglöf, E. (1990) 'Capital structure as a mechanism of control: a comparison of financial systems', in M. Aoki, B. Gustafsson and O. Williamson (eds), *The Firm as a Nexus of Treaties* (Cambridge, MA: MIT Press): 237–62.

Berglöf, E. and Pajuste, A. (2005) 'What do firms disclose and why? Enforcing corporate governance and transparency in Central and Eastern Europe', *Oxford Review of Economic Policy*, 21(2): 178–97.

Berglöf, E. and von Thadden, E. (1999) 'The changing corporate governance paradigm: implications for transition and developing countries', *Michigan Ross School of Business Working Papers*, No. 263.

Berglöf, E. and von Thadden, E. (2000) 'The changing corporate governance paradigm: implications for developing and transition economies', *Annual World Bank Conference on Development Economics 1999* (Washington, DC: World Bank).

Berglöf, E. and Perotti, E. (1994) 'The governance structure of Japanese keiretsu', *Journal of Financial Economics*, 35: 45–57.

Biloslavo, R. (2004) 'The systems thinking approach to development of the knowledge management framework', *International Journal of Learning and Intellectual Capital*, 1(2): 201–24.

Bishop, K., Filatotchev, I. and Mickiewicz, T. (2002) 'Endogenous ownership structure: factors affecting the post-privatisation equity in the largest Hungarian firms', *Acta Oeconomica*, 52: 443–71.

Black, B. (1998) 'Shareholder activism and corporate governance in the United States' in P. Newman (ed.), *The New Palgrave Dictionary of Economics and the Law*, Available at www.lawcolumbiaedu.

Black, B., Kraakman, R. and Tarassova, A. (2000) 'Russian privatisation and corporate governance: What went wrong?' *Stanford Law Review* 52(6): 1731–1808.

Blair, M. (1995) *Ownership and Control: Rethinking Corporate Governance for the Twenty-First Century* (Washington DC: Brookings).

Blanchard, O. and Aghion, P. (1996) 'On insider privatisation', *European Economic Review*, 40: 759–66.

Blanchet, J. (2002) 'Global standards offer opportunity', *Financial Executive* (March/April): 28–30.

Blanchflower, D., Oswald, A. and Stutzer, D. (2001) 'Latent entreprenership across nations', *European Economic Review*, 45: 680–91.

Blasi, J., Kroumova, M. and Kruse, D. (1997) *Kremlin Capitalism. Privatizing the Russian Economy* (Ithaca, NY: Cornell University Press).

Blaszczyk, B., Hashi, I., Radygin, A. and Woodward, R. (2003) *Corporate Governance and Ownership Structure in the Transition: The Current State of Knowledge and Where to Go from Here* (Warsaw: CASE, Center for Social and Economic Research).

Blies, P. (2000) *Corporate governance in deutsch-japanischen Vergleich Überwachungsmechanismen des Finanzsystems und interne Organüberwachung von Aktiengesellschaften* (Wiesbaden: Deutscher Universitäts-Verlag).

Blommestein, H. (1998) 'The new financial landscape and its impact on corporate governance', in M. Balling, E. Hennessy and R. O'Brien (eds), *Corporate Governance, Financial Markets and Global Convergence* (Kluwer Academic Publishers, Dordrecht): Chapter XVI.

Bodie, Z. (1995) 'On the risk of stocks in the long-run', *Financial Analysts Journal*, May/June: 18–22.

Bodie, Z. (2001) 'Financial engineering and social security reform' in J. Campbell and M. Feldstein (eds), *Risk Aspects of Investment-Based Social Security Reform* (Chicago, IL: University of Chicago Press).

Boehmer, E. (1998) 'Who controls Germany? An exploratory analysis', *Institut für Handels- und Wirtschaftsrecht Arbeitspapiere* (Universität Osnabrück).

Bonacich, P. (1972) 'Factoring and weighting approaches to status scores and clique identification', *Journal of Mathematical Sociology*, 2: 113–20.

Bonin, J. and Leven, B. (2000) 'Can banks promote enterprise restructuring? Evidence from a Polish bank's experience', *William Davidson Institute Working Paper*, No. 294, University of Michigan.

Boone, P. and Rodionov, D. (2001) 'Rent seeking in Russia and the CIS', Paper prepared for the *EBRD Tenth Anniversary Conference*, European Bank for Reconstruction and Development, London, December.

Boot, A. and Thakor, A. (1997a) 'Financial system architecture', *Review of Financial Studies*, 10: 693–733.

Boot, A. and Thakor, A. (1997b) 'Banking scope and financial innovation', *Review of Financial Studies*, 10: 1099–131.

Booth, J. and Deli, D. (1999) 'On executives of financial institutions as outside directors', *Journal of Corporate Finance*, 5: 227–50.

Bornstein, M. (2001) 'Post-privatization enterprise restructuring', *Post-Communist Economies*, 13(2): 189–203.

Boutillier, M., Labaye, A., Lagoutte, C., Lévy, N. and Oheix, V. (2002) 'Financement et gouvernement des entreprises: exceptions et convergences européennes', *Revue d'Economie Politique*, 112(4): 499–544.

Boycko, M., Shleifer, A. and Vishny, R. (1995) *Privatizing Russia* (Cambridge, MA: The MIT Press).

Bozec, R. and Breton, G. (2003) 'The impact of the corporatization process on the financial performance of Canadian state-owned enterprises', *The International Journal of Public Sector Management*, 16(1): 27–47.

Brada, J. and I. Singh, (1999) *Corporate Governance in Central Eastern Europe. Case Studies of Firms in Transition* (Armonk: M.E. Sharpe).

Bradley, N. (2004) 'Corporate governance scoring and the link between corporate governance and performance indicators: in search of the Holy Grail', *Corporate Governance* 12(1): 8–10.

Breach, A. (2005) 'Kremlin LBOs: The end of an era?', *Brunswick UBS Global Equity Research*, 1 September.

Brent, L. (2003) *The Rise and Fall of Financial–Industrial Groups: The Genesis of Russian Capitalism*, Unpublished PhD dissertation, University of Wisconsin-Madison.

Brickley, J., Lease, R. and Smith Jr, C. (1988) 'Ownership structure and voting on anti-takeover amendments', *Journal of Financial Economics*, 20: 267–91.

Brown, P. and Kennelly, J. (1972) 'The information content of quarterly earnings: an extension and some further evidence', *Journal of Business*, 45: 403–15.

Brunswick, U. (2000) 'Corporate governance analyzer', *Brunswick UBS Research*, May.

Budapest Stock Exchange (2004) *Corporate Governance Recommendations* (Budapest: Budapest Stock Exchange, with the co-operation of Ernst & Young Advisory Ltd. and Kapolyi Law Office).

Bureau of Economic Analysis (2001) *Problemy Sobstvennosti i Upravleniya v Protsessakh Restrukturizatsii Promyshlennykh Predpriyatij Rossii [Problems of Property and Management in the Process of Restructuring of Industrial Enterprises in Russia]*.

Burt, R. (1983) *Corporate Profits and Corporation* (New York: Academic).

Burt, R. (1992) *Structural Holes: The Social Structure of Competition* (Cambridge, MA: Harvard University Press).

Bushman, R., Pietroski, J. and Smith, A. (2004) 'What determines corporate transparency?', *Journal of Accounting Research*, 42(2): 207–52.

Campbell, J. and Viceira, L. (2002) *Strategic Asset Allocation: Portfolio Choice for Long-Term Investors* (Oxford: Oxford University Press).

Canner, N., Mankiw, N. and Weil, D. (1997) 'An asset allocation puzzle', *American Economic Review*, 87: 181–91.

Carlin, W. and Mayer, C. (2000) 'Finance, investment and growth', *Social Science Research Network Working Paper*.

Carroll, W. (1986) *Corporate Power and Canadian Capitalism* (Vancouver: University of British Columbia Press).

Chadam, J, (2002) 'Spółki żalezne w połskich grupach kapitałowych – wyniki badań', *Organizacja i Kierowanie*, 2.

Chadam, J. (2003a) 'Synergia w zarządzaniu organizacją holdingową', *Organizacja i Kierowanie*, 1.

Chadam, J. (2003b) 'Finansowe aspekty funkcjonowania mniejszych grup kapitalowych w Polsce', *Ekonomista*, 6: 876–90.

Chai, M. and Tung, S. (2002) 'The effect of earnings-announcement timing on earnings management', *Journal of Business Finance and Accounting*, 29(9/10): 1337–54.

Chambers, A. and Penman, S. (1984) 'Timeliness of reporting and the stock price reaction to earnings announcements', *Journal of Accounting Research*, 22(1): 21–47.

Chang, D. (1999) *Privately Owned Social Structures: Institutionalization – Network Contingencies in the Korean Chaebol*, Unpublished PhD dissertation, University of Chicago.

Chang, S. (2003) 'Ownership structure, expropriation, and performance of group-affiliated companies in Korea', *Academy of Management Journal*, 46: 238–54.

Chang, S. and Hong, J. (2000) 'Economic performance of group-affiliated companies in Korea: intragroup resource sharing and internal business transactions', *Academy of Management Journal*, 43: 429–48.

Charkham, J. (1994) *Keeping Good Company: A Study of Corporate Governance in Five Countries* (Oxford: Oxford University Press).

Chaston, I. and Mangels, T. (2000) 'Business networks: Assisting knowledge management and competence acquisition within UK manufacturing firms', *Journal of Small Business and Enterprise Development*, 7(2): 160–70.

Chen, H., Hexter, J. and Hu, M. (1993) 'Management ownership and corporate value', *Managerial and Decision Economics*, 14: 335–46.

Chew, D. (1997) (ed.), *Studies in International Corporate Finance and Governance Systems: A Comparison of the US Japan and Europe* (Oxford: Oxford University Press).

Chiang, H. (2005) 'Analyst's financial forecast accuracy and information transparency', *Journal of the American Academy of Business*, 7(2): 164–7.

Ching, C., Holsapple, C. and A. Whinston (1996) 'Towards IT support for coordination in network organizations', *Information Management*, 30(4): 179–99.

Choi, F. (1998) 'Financial reporting dimensions of Asia's financial crisis', *Proceedings of the Tenth Annual Conference of Accounting Academics* (Hong Kong: Hong Kong Society of Accountants), as cited by Ho and Wong (2001).

Chubais, A. and Vishnevskaya, M. (1993) 'Main issues of privatisation in Russia,' reprinted in A. Åslund (ed.), (1997) *Russia's Economic Transformation in the 1990s* (London and Washington: Pinter).

Chung, C. (2004) 'Institutional transition and cultural inheritance', *International Sociology*, 19(1): 25–50.

Chung, R., Firth, M. and Kim, J. (2002) 'Institutional monitoring and opportunistic earnings management', *Journal of Corporate Finance*, 8: 29–48.

Claessens, S., Djankov, S. and Pohl, G. (1996) 'Ownership and corporate governance: evidence form the Czech Republic', Presented at the *International Symposium on Capital Markets and Enterprise Reform*, Beijing, 8–9 November. Reprinted as *SSRN Working Paper*.

Claesens, S., Djankov, S. and Klingebiel, D. (2000) 'Stock markets in transition economies', *World Bank Financial Sector Discussion Paper*, 5.

Claessens, S., Djankov, S. and Lang, L. (2000) 'The separation of ownership and control in East Asian corporations', *Journal of Financial Economics*, 58: 81–112.

Clarke, D. (2003) 'Corporate governance in China: an overview', *China Economic Review*, 14(4): 494–507.

Coase, R. H. (1937) 'The nature of the firm', *Economica*, November, 386–405.

Coffee, J. (1991) 'Liquidity versus control: the institutional investor as corporate monitor', *Columbia Law Review*, 91: 1277–368.

Coffee, J. (1999) 'Privatisation and corporate governance: the lessons from securities market failure', *Working Paper*, No. 158, Columbia Law School, Center for Law and Economic Studies.

Commander, S., Dutz, M. and Stern, N. (1999) *Restructuring in Transition Economies: Ownership, Competition and Regulation* (Washington, DC: World Bank).

Conrad, J. (1999 [1911]) *Under Western Eyes* (London: Penguin Books).

Cornelius, P. and Kogut, B. (eds) (2004) *Corporate Governance and Capital Flows in a Global Economy* (Oxford: Oxford University Press).

Craswell, A., Taylor, S. and Saywell, R. (1997) 'Ownership structure and corporate performance: Australian evidence', *Pacific-Basin Finance Journal*, 5: 301–23.

Cull, R., Matesova, J. and Shirley, M. (2002) 'Ownership and the temptation to loot: evidence from privatised firms in the Czech Republic', *Journal of Comparative Economics*, 30: 1–24.

Dallago, B. and McIntyre, R. (eds) (2003) *Small and Medium Enterprises in Transition Economies* (Basingstoke: Palgrave Macmillan).

Davies, B. and Whittred, G. (1980) 'The association between selected corporate attributes and timeliness in corporate reporting: Further analysis', *Abacus*, 16(1): 48–60.

Davis, G. and Mizruchi, S. (1999) 'The money center cannot hold: commercial banks in the US system of corporate governance', *Administrative Science Quarterly*, 44: 215–39.

Dawson, I. (2000) 'Elektrim pulls of a surprise', *Euromoney*, January 2000, 70–74.

De Jong, H. (1997) 'The governance structure and performance of large european corporations,' *The Journal of Management and Governance*, 1(1): 5–27.

DeCeuster, M. and Trappers, D. (1993) 'Determinants of the Timeliness of Belgian Financial Statements', *Working Paper*, University of Antwerp, cited in Annaert *et al.* (2002).

Del Guercio, D. and Hawkins, J. (1999) 'The motivation and impact of pension fund activism', *Journal of Financial Economics*, 52, 293–340.

Demarzo, P. (1993) 'Majority voting and corporate control: the rule of the dominant shareholder', *Review of Economic Studies*, 60(3): 713–34.

Demsetz, H. and Lehn, K. (1985) 'The structure of corporate ownership: causes and consequences', *Journal of Political Economy*, 93: 1155–77.

Deutsche Bank Research (2001) 'EU enlargement monitor: central and eastern Europe', available at http://www.dbresearch.com.

Demsetz, H. and Villalonga, B. (2001) 'Ownership structure and corporate performance', *Journal of Corporate Finance*, 7: 209–33.

Dewatripont, M. and Tirole, J. (1994) 'A theory of debt and equity. Diversity of securities and management-shareholders congruence', *Quarterly Journal of Economics*, 109: 1027–54.

Dienes, L. (1996) 'Corporate Russia: privatisation and prospects in the oil and gas sector', *Donald W. Treadgold Paper No. 5*, Jackson School of International Studies, University of Washington.

Dienes, L. (2004) 'Observations on the problematic potential of Russian oil and the complexities of Siberia', *Eurasian Geography and Economics*, 45(5): 319–45.

Dittus, P. and Prowse, S. (1996) 'Corporate control in Central Europe and Russia: should banks own shares?' in R. Frydman, C. Gray and A. Rapaczynski (eds), *Corporate Governance in Central Europe and Russia* (Budapest: CEU Press), Vol. 1: 20–67.

Djankov S. and Murrell, P. (2002) 'Enterprise restructuring in transition: A quantitative survey', *Journal of Economic Literature*, 40: 739–92.

Doidge, C., Karolyi, A. and Stulz, R. (2004) *Why do Countries Matter so much for Corporate Governance?* University of Toronto, mimeo.

Dolgopiatova, T. (2001) 'Modeli korporativnogo kontroliya na rossiiskikh predpriyatiach', *Mir Rossii*, 10(3): (see www.socio.ru/wr/3-01/dolgop).)

Dolgopiatova, T. (2002) *Corporate Control in the Russian Companies: Models and Mechanisms.* Report, HSE.

Dolgopiatova, T. (2004) 'Corporate ownership and control in the Russian companies in the context of integration', *Russian Management Journal*, 2(2): 3–26.

Drygalski, J. 2002, 'W systemowym zawieszeniu. Klopoty z nadzorem panstwa', *Gazeta Wyborcza*, 1–2 June 2002.

Duchêne, G. and Rusin, P. (2003) 'New Private Sector and Growth. A Tale of Two Economies in Transition: Poland and Romania Compared', in Y. Kalyuzhnova and W. Andreff, *op. cit.*

Dudzinski A. and Szymkiewicz, K. (2003) *'Privatisation of Banks and Firms: the Polish Route'*, in W. Andreff and Y. Kalyuzhnova, *op. cit.*

Dunn, S. and Pressman, S. (2005) 'The economic contributions of John Kenneth Galbraith', *Review of Political Economy*, 17(2): 161–209.

Dwyer, P. and Wilson, E. (1989) 'An empirical investigation of factors affecting the time-liness of reporting by municipalities', *Journal of Accounting and Public Policy*, 8(1): 29–55.

Dynkin, A. and Sokolov, A. (2001) *Integrirovannyye biznes-gruppy – proryv k modernizatsii strany* (Moscow: Tsentr issledovaniy i statistiki nauki).

Dynkin, A. and Sokolov, A. (2002) 'Integrirovannie Biznes Gruppi v Rossijskoj Ekonomike [Integrated Business Groups in the Russian Economy]', *Voprosy Ekonomiki*, (4): 78–110.

Dzierzanowski, M. and Tamowicz, P. (2002) *The Corporate Governance Code for Polish Listed Companies* (Gdansk: The Gdansk Institute for Market Economics).

Dzierzanowski, M. and Tamowicz, P. (2004) 'Ownership and control of Polish corporations', *Corporate Ownership and Control*, 1(3): 20–30.

Earle, J., Frydman, R., Rapaczynski, A. and Turkewitz, J. (1994) *Small Privatisation* (Budapest: Central European University Press).

European Bank for Reconstruction and Development (1999a) *Law in Transition* (London: EBRD).

European Bank for Reconstruction and Development (1999b) *Transition Report 1999* (London: EBRD).

European Bank for Reconstruction and Development (2002) *Transition Report 2002* (London: EBRD).

European Bank for Reconstruction and Development (2004) *Transition Report 2004* (London: EBRD).

European Bank for Reconstruction and Development (2005) *Transition Report 2005* (London: EBRD).

Elektrim (2001) 'Stanowisko Elektrim SA w sprawie Umowy Inwestycyjnej z Vivendi', Press release, 25 February 2001.

Emerson, R.M. (1962) 'Power-dependence relations', *American Sociological Review*, 27(1): 31–40.

Encaoua, D. and Jacquemin, A. (1982) 'Organizational efficiency and monopoly power. The case of French industrial groups', *European Economic Review*, 19: 25–51.

Erickson, R. (2001) 'Is Russia in transition to a market economy?' in Archie Brown (ed.), *Contemporary Russian Politics* (Oxford: Oxford University Press).

Errunza, V. and Losq, E. (1985) 'The behaviour of stock prices on LDC markets', *Journal of Banking and Finance*, 9(4): 561–75.

Estrin, S. and Wright, M. (1999) 'Corporate governance in the former Soviet Union: An overview', *Journal of Comparative Economics*, 27: 398–421.

Estrin, S. (2002) 'Competition and corporate governance in transition countries', *Transition Newsletter*, May–June, The World Bank, Available at www.worldbankorg/transition-newsletter.

Exley, C., Mehta, S. and Smith, A. (1997) *The Financial Theory of Defined Benefit Pension Schemes*, Institute and Faculty of Actuaries, 28 April, mimeo.

Faccio, M. and Ameziane Lasfer, M. (2000) 'Do occupational pension funds monitors companies in which they hold large stakes?', *Journal of Corporate Finance*, 6: 71–110.

Faleye, O., Mehrotra, V. and Morck, R. (2005) 'When labor has a voice in corporate Governance', *NBER Working Paper*, No. 11254, National Bureau of Economic Research.

Fama, E. and Jensen, M. (1983a) 'Separation of ownership and control', *Journal of Law and Economics*, 26: 301–25.

Fama, E. and Jensen, M. (1983b) 'Agency problems and residual claims', *Journal of Law and Economics*, 26: 327–49

FCSM (Federal Commission for the Securities Market) (1999) *Regulatory Update*, October. Available at http://www.fcsm.ru/eregul/vol1/oct99.htm.

FCSM (Federal Commission for the Securities Market) (2002) *Corporate Governance Code* (Moscow: FCSM).

Fedorov, O. (2000) 'Three cases of abusive self-dealing', Paper presented at the *OECD 2nd Round Table on Corporate Governance in Russia*, Moscow, February 24–25.

Fenkner, J. (1999) 'How to steal an oil company', *Troika Dialog Market Weekly*, March 22–28.

Filatochev, I., Wright, M. and Bleaney, M. (1999) 'Privatization, insider control and managerial entrenchment in Russia', *Economics of Transition*, 7(2): 481–504.

Filatotchev, I., Piesse, J. and Lien, Y. (2005) 'Corporate governance and performance in publicly listed, family-controlled firms: evidence from Taiwan', *Asia-Pacific Journal of Management*, 22: 257–83.

Filatotchev, I., Hoskisson, R., Buck, T. and Wright, M. (1996) 'Corporate restructuring in Russian privatisations: implications for US investors', *California Management Review*, 38: 87–105.

Filatotchev, I., Kapelyushnikov, R., Dyomina, N. and Aukutsionek, S. (2001) 'The effects of ownership concentration on investment and performance in privatized firms in Russia', *Managerial and Decision Economics*, 22: 299–313.

Financial Accounting Standards Board (1980) *Statement of Financial Accounting Concepts No. 2, Qualitative Characteristics of Accounting Information* (Stamford, CT: Financial Accounting Standards Board).

Fitch, R. and Oppenheimer, M. (1970) 'Who rules the corporations?', *Socialist Revolution*, 1(4–6).

Fox, M. and Heller, M. (1999) 'Lessons from fiascos in Russian corporate governance', *William Davidson Institute Working Paper*, No. 282, University of Michigan.

Franks, J. and Mayer, C. (1997) 'Corporate ownership and control in the UK, Germany, and France', *Journal of Applied Corporate Finance*, 9: 30–45.

Frappaolo, C. (1998) 'Defining knowledge management: Four basic functions', *Computerworld*, 32(8): 44–60.

Fraser, D. and Zardkoohi, A. (1996) 'Ownership structure, deregulation and risk in the savings and loan industry', *Journal of Business Research*, 37: 63–9.

Freeland, C. (2000) *Sale of the Century: the Inside Story of the Second Russian Revolution* (London: Little, Brown & Co.).

Freeland, C. (2003) 'A Falling Tsar', *Financial Times*, November 1.

Frenkel, M. and Menkhoff, L. (2004) 'Are foreign institutional investors good for emerging Markets?', *The World Economy*, 27(8): 1275–93.

Frydman, R., Rapaczynski, A. and Earle, J. (1993) *The Privatisation Process in Central Europe* (Budapest: Central European University Press).

Frydman, R., Pistor, K. and Rapaczynski, A. (1996) 'Exit and voice after mass privatisation: the case of Russia', *European Economic Review*, 40: 581–8.

Frydman, R., Gray, C., Hessel, M. and Rapaczynski, A. (1999) 'When does privatization work? The impact of private ownership on corporate performance in the transition economies', *Quarterly Journal of Economics*, 114(4): 1153–91.

Frydman, R., Hessel, M. and Rapaczynski, A. (2000) 'Why ownership matters? Entrepreneurship and the restructuring of enterprises in Central Europe', *Economic Research Reports*, CV, Starr Center for Applied Economics, New York.

Frye, T. (2002) 'Capture or Exchange? Business lobbying in Russia', *Europe–Asia Studies*, 54(7): 1017–36.

Frye, T. and Shleifer, A. (1997) 'The Invisible hand and the grabbing hand', *American Economic Review*, 87(2): 354–8.

Gadomski, W. (2002) '4 zycia kota, czyli fascynująca historia wzlotu i upadku Elektrim' *Gazeta Wyborcza*, 27 February..

Garibaldi, P., Mora, N., Sahay, R. and Zettelmeyer, J. (2001) 'What moves capital to transition countries?' *IMF Staff Papers*, 48(Special Issue): 109–45.

Geoffron, P. (1999) 'Quelles limites à la convergence des modèles de corporate governance?' *Revue d'Economie Industrielle*, 90: 77–89.

Gerlach, M. (1992) 'The Japanese corporate network: a blockmodel analysis', *Administrative Science Quarterly*, 37: 105–39.

Gerschenkron, A. (1962) *Economic Backwardness in Historical Perspective* (Cambridge, MA: Harvard University Press).

Ghemawat, P. and Khanna, T. (1998) 'The nature of diversified business groups: a research design and two case studies', *The Journal of Industrial Economics*, 46(1): 35–61.

Gibbs, P. (1993) 'Determinants of corporate restructuring: the relative importance of corporate governance, takeover threat, and free cash flow', *Strategic Management Journal*, 14: 51–68.

Gigler, F. and Hemmer, T. (2001) 'Conservatism, optimal disclosure policy, and the timeliness of financial reports', *The Accounting Review*, 76(4): 471–93.

Gillian, S. and Starks, L. (2000) 'Corporate governance proposals and shareholder activism: the role of institutional investors', *Journal of Financial Economics*, 57: 275–305.

Gilson, R. and Roe, M. (1993) 'Understanding the Japanese Keiretsu: overlaps between corporate governance and industrial organization', *Yale Law Journal*, 102: 871–906.

Gilson, S. (1990) 'Bankruptcy, boards, banks and blockholders', *Journal of Financial Economics*, 27: 355–87.

Givoli, D. and Palmon, D. (1982) 'Timeliness of annual earnings announcements: some empirical evidence', *The Accounting Review*, 57(3): 486–508.

Glaeser, E., Johnson, S. and Shleifer, A. (2001) 'Coase versus coasians', *The Quaterly Journal of Economics*, 116(3): 853–99.

Gnezditskaia, A. (2003) 'Russian banks' profit strategies: the evidence from various types of banks', *Communist and Post-Communist Studies*, 36: 163–91.

Gokhberg, L. (1999) *Russia: A Science and Technology Profile* (London: British Council).

Gold, J. (2001) 'Accounting/actuarial bias enables equity investment by defined benefit pension plans', *Discussion* Paper, 2001–5, Pension Research Council.

Golubkov, D. (1999) *Osobennosti korporativnogo upravleniia v Rossii* (Moscow: Alpina).

Goriaev, A. and Sonin, K. (2005) 'Is Political Risk Company-Specific? The Market Side of the Yukos Affair', *CEPR (Centre for Economic and Policy Research) Discussion Paper*, No. 5076, London.

Goskomstat (2003) *Sotsial'no-economicheskoe polozhenie Rossii: Yanvar'- Iyul' 2003 goda* (Moscow: Goskomstat).

Grabher, G. and Stark, D. (1997) *Restructuring Networks in Post-Socialism: Legacies, Linkages, and Localities* (New York: Oxford University Press).

Gregory, H. (2000) *International Comparison of Corporate Governance Guidelines and Best Practice: Developing and Emerging Markets* (New York: Weil, Gotshal & Manges).

Grosfeld, I. and Tressel, T. (2001) 'Competition and corporate governance: Substitutes or Complements? Evidence from the Warsaw Stock Exchange', *Social Science Research Network Working Paper*.

Grossman, S. and Hart, O. (1986) 'The costs and benefits of ownership: a theory of vertical and lateral integration', *Journal of Political Economy*, 94(4): 691–719.

Grossman, S. and Hart, O. (1988) 'One share-one vote and the market for corporate control', *Journal of Financial Economics*, 20: 175–202.

Grzeszak, A. (1999) 'Polowanie na dinozaury', *Polityka*, 02/2175.

Gupta, B., Iyer, L. and Aronson, J. (2000) 'Knowledge management: practices and challenges', *Industrial Management and Data Systems*, 100(1/2): 17–21.

Guriev, S. and Rachinsky, A. (2005) 'The role of oligarchs in Russian capitalism', *Journal of Economic Perspectives*, 19(1): 131–50.

Guriev, S., Lazareva, O., Rachisnky, A. and Tsukhlo, S. (2003) 'Corporate governance in Russian industry'. *CEFIR Working Paper*, Moscow.

Guseva, A. (2004). *Russian Insurance Market in the Transitional Period*. Paper presented at the *American Sociological Association Meeting*, San Francisco.

Gustafson, T. (1999) *Capitalism Russian-Style* (Cambridge: Cambridge University Press).

Haigh, A. (2001) 'We view Russia's future with optimism', *Kommersant-Daily*, 26 January. Available at www.pwcglobal.ru/.

Halpern, P. (2000) 'Systemic perspectives on corporate governance', in S. Cohen and G. Boyd (eds), *Corporate Governance and Globalization. Long Range Planning Issues* (Northampton, MA: Edward Elgar).

Hamilton, G. (1996) *Asian Business Networks* (Berlin, New York: Walter de Gruyter).

Han, J. and Wild, J. (1997) 'Timeliness of reporting and earnings information transfers', *Journal of Business Finance and Accounting*, 24(3/4): 527–40.

Han, J. and Wang, S. (1998) 'Political costs and earnings management of oil companies during the 1990 Persian Gulf crises', *The Accounting Review*, 73: 103–17.

Hanousek, J. and Kočenda, E. (2003) 'The impact of Czech mass privatisation on corporate governance', *Journal of Economic* Studies, 30(3/4): 278–93.

Hanson, P. (2004) 'Putin and Russia's economic transformation', *Eurasian Geography and Economics*, 45(6): 421–8.

Hanson, P. (2005) 'Observations on the costs of the Yukos affair to Russia', *Eurasian Geography and Economics*, 46(7): 481–94.

Hanson, P. and Teague, E. (2005) 'Big business and the state in Russia', *Europe–Asia Studies*, 57(5): 657–80.

Hargadon, A. and Sutton, R. (2000) 'Building innovation factory', *Harvard Business Review*, 78(3): 157–66.

Harris, M. and Raviv, A. (1988) 'Corporate governance voting rights and majority rights', *Journal of Financial Economics*, 20: 203–35.

Harris, M. and Raviv, A. (1990) 'Capital structure and the information role of debt', *Journal of Finance*, 45: 321–50.

Hart, O. (1995a) 'Corporate governance: Some theory and implications', *The Economic Journal*, 105(430): 678–89.

Hart, O. (1995b) *Firms, Contracts and Financial Structure* (Oxford: Oxford University Press).

Hart, O. (2001) 'Financial contracting', *Journal of Economic Literature*, 39: 1079–100.

Hashi, I. (2003) *The Legal Framework for Effective Corporate Governance: Comparative Analysis of Provisions in Selected Transition Economies* (Warsaw: CASE, Center for Social and Economic Research).

Haw, I., Qi, D. and Wu, W. (2000) 'Timeliness of annual report releases and market reaction to earnings announcements in an emerging capital market: the case of China', *Journal of International Financial Management and Accounting*, 11(2): 108–31.

Hay, J., Shleifer, A. and Vishny, R. (1996) 'Toward a theory of legal reform', *European Economic Review*, 40: 559–67.

Hebb, T. (2006) 'The economic inefficiency of secrecy: pension fund investors' corporate transparency concerns', *Journal of Business Ethics*, 63(4): 385–405.

Heck, U. and Rogger, A. (2004) 'Knowledge management for E-service-delivery – a conceptual approach within E-government', in *Knowledge Management in Electronic*

Government: Proceedings of 5th International Working Conference, KMGov 2004, Krems, Austria, 17–19 May, 1–8.

Hellman, J., Jones, G. and Kaufmann, D. (2000) 'Seize the state, seize the day: state capture, corruption and influence in transition', *World Bank Policy Research Working Paper*, No. 2444, World Bank.

Hellman, J. (1993) *Breaking the Bank: The Political Economy of Banking Reform in the Soviet Union*, Unpublished PhD dissertation, Columbia University.

Henderson, E. (2004) 'Mistaken identity: testing the clash of civilizations thesis in light of democratic peace claims', *British Journal of Political Science*, 34(3): 539–63.

Henderson, J. and Radosevic, S. (2004) 'Restructuring and growth of post-socialist enterprises through alliances: LUKoil and Yukos', in S. Radosevic and Bert M. Sadowski (eds), *International Industrial Networks and Industrial Restructuring in Central and Eastern Europe* (Dordrecht: Kluwer).

Hendriksen, E. and van Breda, M. (1992) *Accounting Theory*, 5th edn (Burr Ridge, IL: Irwin).

Heritage Foundation (2005) Index of Economic Freedom 2005, *The Wall Street Journal*, January 12, 2005. Available at http://www.heritage.org/research/features/index/countries.cfm?sortby=country.

Heritage Foundation (2006) Index of Economic Freedom (Washington, DC & New York: Heritage Foundation and *The Wall Street Journal*). Available at www.heritage.org.

Hilferding, R. (1981) *Finance Capital* (Boston: Routledge & Kegan Paul).

Himmelberg, C., Hubbard, R. and Palia, D. (1999) 'Understanding the determinants of managerial ownership and the link between ownership and performance', *Journal of Financial Economics*, 53: 353–84.

Ho, S. and Wong, K. (2001) 'A study of corporate disclosure practice and effectiveness in Hong Kong', *Journal of International Financial Management and Accounting*, 12(1): 75–102.

Hodges, R., Wright, M. and Keasey, K. (1996) 'Corporate governance in the public sector', *Public Money and Management*, 16(2): 7–13.

Hoffman, D. (2002) *The Oligarchs, Wealth and Power in the New Russia* (Oxford: Public Affairs).

Holderness, C. and Sheehan, D. (1988) 'The role of majority shareholders in publicly held corporations', *Journal of Financial Economics*, 20: 317–46.

Holland, J. (1994) 'Bank lending relationships and the complex nature of bank-corporate relations', *Journal of Business Finance and Accounting*, 21: 367–93.

Holmstrom, B. (1979) 'Moral hazard and observability', *Bell Journal of Economics*, 10: 74–91.

Holtzmann, R. (1999) 'The World Bank approach to pension reform', *Social Protection Discussion Paper Series*, 9807, World Bank.

Holtzmann, R. (2000) 'Can investments in emerging markets help to solve the aging problem?' *Social Protection Discussion Paper Series*, 0010, World Bank.

Hoskisson, R., Cannella, A., Tihanyi, L. and Faraci, R. (2004) 'Asset restructuring and business group affiliation in French civil law countries', *Strategic Management Journal*, 25: 525–39.

Hoskisson, R., Johnson, R. and Moesel, D. (1994) 'Corporate divestiture intensity in restructuring firms: Effects of governance, strategy, and performance', *Academy of Management Journal*, 37: 1207–51.

Humphreys, P., Shiu, W. and Chan, F. (2001) 'Collaborative buyer-supplier relationships in Hong Kong manufacturing firms', *Supply Chain Management: An International Journal*, 6(4): 152–62.

Huntington, S. (1993) 'The clash of civilizations?' *Foreign Affairs*, 72(3): 22–49.

Huntington, S. (1998) *The Clash of Civilizations and the Remaking of World Order* (New York: Simon & Schuster).

Hunton, J., Libby, R. and Mazza, C. (2006) 'Financial reporting transparency and earnings management', *The Accounting Review*, 81(1): 135–57.

Hussain, F., Lucas, C. and Asif, A. (2004) 'Managing knowledge effectively', *Journal of Knowledge Management Practice*, 5, May. Available at http://www.tlainc.com/articl66.htm.

IFAC (2000) *Corporate Governance in the Public Sector: A Governing Body Perspective*, IFAC (The International Federation of Accountants). Available at http://www.ifac.org.

Iglesias, A. (2002) Limites de Inversion para los Fondos de Pensiones en America.

Ikonnikov, A. (2001) 'The long road towards good corporate governance practices', in Marat Terterov (ed.), *Doing Business with Russia*, 2nd edn (London: Kogan Page).

Imai, K. (2005) 'Economic globalization and state control in different cultures; testing the *Clash of Civilizations* Thesis', Midwestern Political Science Association Annual Meeting, Chicago, Conference Paper.

International Monetary Fund (2004) *Global Financial Stability Report* (Washington, DC: IMF).

Impravido, G., Musalem, A. and Vittas, D. (2003) 'Promoting pension funds in countries with small financial systems', *World Bank Policy Research Working Paper*.

Indermit, G., Packard, T. and Yermo, J. (2005) *Keeping the Promise of Social Security in Latin America* (Palo Alto: Stanford University Press).

Institute of International Finance (2002) *Policies for Corporate Governance and Transparency in Emerging Markets* (Washington, DC: Institute of International Finance).

Jackson, J., Klich, J. and Poznanska, K. (2005) *The Political Economy of Poland's Transition: New Firms and Reform Governments* (Cambridge: Cambridge University Press).

James, E. (1996) 'Protecting the old and promoting growth', *Policy Research Working Paper*, No. 1570, World Bank.

Jeffers, E. and Plihon, D. (2001) 'Investisseurs institutionnels et gouvernance des entreprises', *Revue d'Economie Financière*, 63: 137–52.

Jensen, M. (1986) 'Agency costs of free cash flow, corporate finance, and takeovers', *American Economic Review*, 76: 323–29.

Jensen, M. and Meckling, W. (1976) 'Theory of the firm: managerial behavior, agency costs, and ownership structure', *Journal of Financial Economics*, 3: 305–60.

Jensen, M. and Warner, J. (1988) 'The distribution of power among corporate managers, shareholders, and directors', *Journal of Financial Economics*, 20: 3–24.

Jindrichovska, I. and Mcleay, S. (2005) 'Accounting for good news and accounting for bad news: some empirical evidence from the Czech Republic', *European Accounting Review*, 14(3): 635–55.

Johnson, J. (2000) *A Fistful of Rubles: The Rise and Fall of the Russian Banking System* (Ithaca and London: Cornell University Press).

Johnson, R. and Greening, D. (1999) 'The effects of corporate governance and institutional ownership on corporate social performance', *Academy of Management Journal*, 42(5): 564–76.

Johnson, S., Kaufmann, D. and Shleifer, A. (1997) 'Politics and entrepreneurship in transition economies', *William Davidson Institute Working Paper*, No. 57, University of Michigan.

Kang, T. and Pang, Y. (2005) 'Economic development and the value-relevance of accounting information – a disclosure transparency perspective', *Review of Accounting and Finance*, 4(1): 5–31.

Kapelyushnikov, R. (2001) 'The largest and dominant shareholders in the Russian industry: evidence of the Russian economic barometer monitoring', *Journal of East–West Business*, 6(4): 63–88.

Kapelyushnikov, R. (2002) 'Sobstvennost' i kontrol' v rossiiskoi promyshlennosti,' *Voprosy ekonomiki*, 12: 103–24.

Keller, S. (1986) 'Reporting timeliness in the presence of subject to audit qualifications', *Journal of Business Finance and Accounting*, 13(1): 117–24.

Kenley, W. and Staubus, G. (1974) 'Objectives and concepts of financial statements', *Accounting Review*, 49(4): 888–9.

Kester, C. (1992) 'Industrial groups as systems of contractual governance' *Oxford Review of Economic Policy*, 8: 24–43.

Khanna, T. and Palepu, K. (1997) 'Why focused strategies may be wrong for emerging markets', *Harvard Business Review*, 75(4): 41–51.

Khanna, T. and Palepu, K. (1999) 'The right way to restructure conglomerates in emerging markets', *Harvard Business Review*, 77(4): 125–34.

Khanna, T. and Palepu, K. (2000) 'The future of business groups in emerging markets: long-run evidence from Chile', *Academy of Management Journal*, 34: 268–85.

Kim, J. (2005) 'Accounting transparency of Korean firms: measurement and determinant analysis', *Journal of American Academy of Business*, 6(2): 222–9.

Kirchmaier, T. and Grant, J. (2005) 'Corporate ownership structure and performance in Europe', *European Management Review*, 2: 231–45.

Klein, B., Crawford, R. and Alchian, A. (1978) 'Vertical integration, appropriable rents and the competitive contracting process', *Journal of Law and Economics*, 21: 297–326.

Klipper, M. (1998) 'The governance of privatized firms: Authority, responsibility and disclosure', *Economics of Transition*, 6(1): 101–11.

Kochetygova, J., Popivshchy, N., Shvyrkov, O., Kazakov, D., Kuzmina, O. and Rozanova, A. (2005) *Russian Transparency and Disclosure Survey 2005: Continuing Progress in Transparency, but Mainly among Weaker Disclosers*', 21 September.

Kogut, B. and Spicer, A. (2002) 'Capital market development and mass privatization are logical contradictions: lessons from Russia and the Czech Republic', *Industrial and Corporate Change*, 11(1): 1–37.

Koładkiewicz, I. (2001) 'Building of a corporate governance system in Poland: initial experiences', *Corporate Governance*, 9(3): 228–37.

Koładkiewicz, I. (2002) *Nadzór korporacyjny w Narodowych Funduszach Inwestycyjnych* (Warszawa: Wydawnictwo WSPiZ).

Könden, J. (1994) 'Duties of banks in voting their clients' stock', in T. Baums, R. Bauxbaum and K. Hopt (eds), *Institutional Investors and Corporate Governance* (Berlin and New York: Walter de Gruyter).

Konings, J. (2001) 'The effects of foreign direct investment on domestic firms', *Economics of Transition*, 9(3): 619–33.

Konstantinov, G., Lipsits, I. and Filonovich, S. (2002) 'Kak vybrat'sia iz lovushki molodosti,' *Ekspert*, 5. Available at http://www.expert.ru/rus_business/2002/02/08ex-lipsic/.

Kornaï, J. (1990) *The Road to a Free Economy. Shifting from a Socialist System. The Example of Hungary* (New York: W.W. Norton).

Kotz, D. (1978) *Bank Control of Large Corporations in the United States* (Berkeley, CA: University of California Press).

Kozarzewski, P. (2002) 'Changes in corporate governance structures in Polish privatised companies', *Working Paper*, No. 8, Centre for the Study of Economic and Social Change in Europe, School of Slavonic and East European Studies.

Kozarzewski, P. (2003) *Corporate Governance and Secondary Privatisation in Poland: Legal Framework and Changes in Ownership Structure* (Warsaw: CASE, Center for Social and Economic Research).

Krasnitskaya, E. (2000) 'Corporate governance in Russia: still clowning around?' *Troika Dialog Research*, November.

Kraus, E. (2003) 'Truth and beauty ... (and Russian Finance): Yukos follies', *Sovlink Desknote*, 7 July.

Krishnan, G. (2005) 'The association between big 6 auditor industry expertise and the asymmetric timeliness of earnings', *Journal of Accounting, Auditing and Finance*, 20(3): 209–28.

Kross, W. and Schroeder, D. (1984) 'An empirical investigation of the effect of quarterly earnings announcement timing on stock returns', *Journal of Accounting Research*, 22(1): 153–76.

Kryshtanovskaya, O. (1996) 'The financial oligarchy in Russia', *Izvestiia*, 10 January, p. 5, in *CDPSP*, XL VIII, 4 February.

Kryshtanovskaya, O. and White, S. (1996) 'From Soviet Nomenklatura to Russian Elite', *Europe–Asia Studies*, 48(5): 711–33.

Kryukov, V. and Moe, A. (1998) *The Changing Role of Banks in the Russian Oil Sector* (London: Royal Institute of International Affairs).

Kulzick, R. (2004) 'Sarbanes-Oxley: Effects on financial transparency. S.A.M.', *Advanced Management Journal*, 69(1): 43–9.

Kurtzman, J., Yago, G. and Phumiwasana, T. (2004) 'The Opacity Index 2004: the global costs of opacity: measuring business and investment risk worldwide', *MIT Sloan Management Review*, 46(1): 38–44.

Kuznetsov, A. and Kuznetsova, O. (2003) 'Corporate governance: Does the concept work in transition countries?' *Journal for East European Management Studies*, 8(3): 244–62.

Kuznetsova, O. and Kuznetsov, A. (1999) 'The state as a shareholder: responsibilities and objectives,' *Europe–Asia Studies*, 51(3): 433–45.

Kuznetsova, O. and Kuznetsov, A. (2001) 'The virtues and weaknesses of insider shareholding,' *Journal of East–West Business*, 6(4): 89–106.

La Porta, R., Lopez-de-Silanes, F., Shleifer, A. and Vishny, R. (1997) 'Legal determinants of external finance', *Journal of Finance*, 52: 1131–150.

La Porta, R., Lopez-de-Silanes, F., Shleifer, A. and Vishny, R. (1998) 'Law and finance', *Journal of Political Economy*, 106: 1113–55.

La Porta, R., Lopez-de-Silanes, F. and Shleifer, A. (1999a) 'Corporate ownership around the world', *Journal of Finance*, 54: 471–517.

La Porta, R., Lopez-de-Silanes, F., Shleifer, A. and Vishny, R. (1999b) 'Investor protection and corporate valuation', *NBER Working Paper*, No. 7403, National Bureau of Economic Research.

La Porta, R., Lopez-de-Silanes, F., Shleifer, A. and Vishny, R. (2000) 'Investor protection and corporate governance', *Journal of Financial Economics*, 58: 3–27.

Labaronne, D. (1998) 'Les lenteurs de la privatisation en Europe de l'Est: une conséquence de la stratégie d'enracinement des managers', *Revue d'Economie Politique*, 108(5): 672–89.

Lane, D. (2003) 'The evolution of post-communist banking', in D. Lane (ed.), *Russian Banking: Evolution, Problems and Prospects* (Cheltenham, UK: Edward Elgar): 9–35.

Lane, D. and Seifulmulukov, I. (1999) 'Structure and Ownership', in D. Lane (ed.), *The Political Economy of Russian Oil* (Lanham, MD: Rowman & Littlefield).

Latynina, I. (1999) 'Mikhail Khodorkovskii: Khimiia i Zhizn', *Sovershenno Sekretno*, August 8.

Lawrence, J. and Glover, H. (1998) 'The effect of audit firm mergers on audit delay', *Journal of Managerial Issues*, 10(2): 151–64.

Ledeneva, A. (1998) *Russia's Economy of Favours: Blat, Networking and Informal Exchange* (Cambridge: Cambridge University Press).

Ledeneva, A. (2001) *Unwritten Rules: How Russia Really Works* (London: Centre for European Reform).

Lee, C. (1987) 'Accounting infrastructure and economic development', *Journal of Accounting and Public Policy*, 6(2): 75–85.

Leitch, J. and Rosen, P. (2001) 'Knowledge management, CKO, and CKM: the keys to competitive advantage', *The Manchester Review*, 6(2/3): 9–13.

Lelyveld, M. (2003) 'Russia: Moscow hails oil merger but pursues probe', *RFE/RL, News and Analysis*, April 24. Available at www.rferl.org/features/2003/04/24042003182018.asp

Leuz, C. and Oberholzer-Gee, F. (2003) 'Political relationships, global financing and corporate transparency', *Working Paper*, No. 03–16, Wharton Financial Institutions Center, The Wharton School, University of Pennsylvania.

Leventis, S. and Weetman, P. (2004) 'Timeliness of financial reporting: Applicability of disclosure theories in an emerging capital market', *Accounting and Business Research*, 34(1): 43–56.

Levine, R. and Zervos, S. (1998) 'Stock markets, banks, and growth', *American Economic Review*, 88(3): 537–58.

Lin, C. (2001) 'Corporatisation and corporate governance in China's economic', 2001, *Transition Economics of Planning*, 34(1/2): 5–35.

Lorsch, J. and MacIver, E. (1989) *Pawns and Potentates: The Reality of America's Corporate Boards* (Boston, MA: Harvard Business School Press).

Loughran, T. and Ritter, J. (1995) 'The new issues puzzle', *Journal of Finance*, 50(1): 23–51.

Loughran, T. and Ritter, J. (2000) 'Uniformly least powerful test of market efficiency', *Journal of Financial Economics*, 55(3): 361–89.

Loughran, T. and Ritter, J. (2002) 'Why don't issuers get upset about leaving money on the table in IPO's?' *The Review of Financial Studies*, 15(2): 413–43.

Lucas, R. (1988) 'On the mechanics of economic development', *Journal of Monetary Economics*, 22: 3–42.

Macey, J. and Miller, G. (1997) 'Universal banks are not the answer to America's corporate governance "problem": a look at Germany, Japan and the US', *Journal of Applied Corporate Finance*, 9: 57–73.

MaCurdy, T. and Shoven, J. (2001) 'Asset allocation and risk allocation: Can social security improve its future solvency problem by investing in private securities?' in J. Campbell and M. Feldstein (eds), *Risk Aspects of Investment-Based Social Security Reform* (Chicago: University of Chicago Press).

Makarenko, B., Urnov, M. and Shevtsova, L. (2003) 'My ne sdaem imena v arendu', *Moskovskie novosti*, no. 30. Available at www.mn.ru/issue.php?2003-30-18

Mambula, C. and Sawyer, F. (2004) 'Acts of enterpreneurial creativity for business growth and survival in a constrained economy. Case study of a small manufacturing firm (SMF)', *International Journal of Social Economics*, 31(1/2): 30–55.

Marangos, J. (2005) 'Alternative paths to the transition process', *International Journal of Social Economics*, 32(4): 307–24.

Mariolis, P. (1975) 'Interlocking directorates and control of corporations: the theory of bank control', *Social Science Quarterly*, 56: 425–39.

Mathieson, D., Roldos, J., Ramaswamy, R. and Ilyina, A. (2004) *Emerging Local Securities and Derivatives Markets: Developments and Policy Issues* (Washington, DC: World Economic and Financial Surveys, International Monetary Fund).

Maug, E. (1997) 'Boards of directors and capital structure: alternative forms of corporate restructuring', *Journal of Corporate Finance*, 3: 113–39.

Maug, E. (1998) 'Large shareholders as monitors: Is there a trade-off between liquidity and control?' *Journal of Finance*, 53: 65–92.

Mcalister, D., Ferrell, O. and Ferrell, L. (2003) *Business and society: a strategic approach to corporate citizenship* (Boston, MA: Houghton Mifflin).

McCarthy, D. and Puffer, S. (2003) 'Corporate governance in Russia: a framework for analysis', *Journal of World Business*, 38: 397–415.

McConnell, J. and Servaes, H. (1990) 'Additional evidence on equity ownership and corporate value', *Journal of Financial Economics*, 27: 595–612.

Mc-Dermott, G. (2000) 'Network restructuring and firm creation in Eat-Central Europe: a public-private venture', *William Davidson Working Paper*, No. 361, University of Michigan.

McDermott, G. (2002) *Embedded Politics: Industrial Networks and Institutional Change in Postcommunism* (Ann Arbor: The University of Michigan Press).

McFaul, M. (1997) 'When Capitalism and Democracy Collide in Transition: Russia's "Weak" State as an Impediment to Democratic Consolidation', *Working Paper*, No. 1, Program in New Approaches to Russian Security, Harvard Russian Center.

McGee, R. (1992) (ed.), *The Market Solution to Economic Development in Eastern Europe* (Lewiston, NY: The Edwin Mellen Press).

McGee, R. and Preobragenskaya, G. (2004) 'Problems of implementing international accounting standards in a transition economy: a case study of Russia', *Presented at the Eighth International Conference on Global Business and Economic Development*, Guadalajara, Mexico, 7–10 January. Available at www.ssrn.com.

McGee, R. and Preobragenskaya, G. (2005) *Accounting and Financial System Reform in a Transition Economy: A Case Study of Russia* (New York: Springer).

Megginson, W. and Netter, J. (2001) 'From state to market: a survey of empirical studies on privatization', *Journal of Economic Literature*, 39: 321–89.

Megginson, W., Nash, R. and Van Randenborgh, M. (1994) 'The financial and operating performance of newly privatized firms: an international empirical analysis', *The Journal of Finance*, 49(2): 403–52.

Menshikov, S. (1969) *Millionaires and Managers* (Moscow: Progress Publishers).

Mertlik, P. (1996) 'Czech privatization: from public ownership to public ownership in five years?', in B. Blaszczyk and R. Woodward (eds), *Privatization in Post-Communist Countries* (Warsaw: CASE).

Mesnard, M. (1999) 'Emergence des groupes et *corporate governance* en Russie', *Economie Internationale*, 77: 131–60.

Mickiewicz, T. (1996) 'The state sector during economic transformation: Employment, wages and investment', *Communist Economies and Economic Transformation*, 8(3): 393–410.

Mickiewicz, T. (2005) *Economic Transition in Central Europe and the Commonwealth of Independent States* (Houndmills: Palgrave Macmillan)

Mickiewicz, T. and Bałtowski, M. (2003) All roads lead to outside ownership: Polish piecemeal privatisation, in D. Parker and D. Saal (eds), *International Handbook on Privatisation* (Cheltenham: Edward Elgar): 402–26.

Mickiewicz, T., Gerry, C. and Bishop, K. (2005) 'Privatisation, corporate control and employment growth: evidence from a panel of large Polish firms, 1996–2002', *Economic Systems*, 29: 98–119.

Mikkelson, W. and Partch, M. (1989) 'Managers' voting rights and corporate control', *Journal of Financial Economics*, 25: 263–90.

Mileusnic, N. (1996) 'The great boardroom revolution', *Moscow Times*, 16 July.

Milgrom, P. and Roberts, J. (1992) *Economics, Organisation and Management* (Englewood Cliffs, NJ: Prentice Hall).

Millstein, I., Albert, M., Cadbury, A., Denham, R., Feddersen, D. and Tateishi, N. (1998) *Corporate Governance: Improving Competitiveness and Access to Capital in Global Markets, A Report to the OECD by the Business Sector Advisory Group on Corporate Governance* (Paris: OECD).

Mintz, B. and Schwartz, M. (1985) *The Power Structure of American Business* (Chicago, IL: University of Chicago Press).

Mintzberg, H. (1983) *Power In and Around Organizations* (Englewood Cliffs, NJ: Prentice Hall).

Mises, L. (1944) *Omnipotent Government: The Rise of the Total State and Total War* (New Haven: Yale University Press).

Mises, L. (1957) *Theory and History: An Interpretation of Social and Economic Evolution* (New Haven and London: Yale University Press).

Mizerski, S. (2005) 'Człowiek dobry na wszystko', *Polityka*, 10/2494.

Mizobata, S. (2003) 'Bank Sector Restructuring', in D. Lane (ed.), *Russian Banking: Evolution, Problems and Prospects* (Cheltenham, UK: Edward Elgar): 36–55.

Mizruchi, M. (1982) *The American Corporate Network, 1904–1974* (Beverly Hills, CA: Sage).

Mizruchi, M. (1996) 'What do interlocks do? An analysis, critique, and assessment of research on interlocking directorates', *Annual Review of Sociology*, 22: 271–98.

Mizruchi, M. and Stearns, L. (1994) 'A longitudinal study of borrowing by large American corporations', *Administrative Science Quarterly*, 39: 118–40.

Mizruchi, M. and Bunting, D. (1981) 'Influence in corporate networks: an examination of four measures', *Administrative Science Quarterly*, 26: 475–89.

Mizruchi, M. and Stearns, L. (1988) 'A longitudinal study of the formation of interlocking directorates', *Administrative Science Quarterly*, 33: 194–210.

Mobius, M. and Filatov, R. (2001) 'Corporate governance in Russia: the battle for share-holders' rights', in Peter Westin (ed.), *The Wild East: Negotiating the Russian Financial Frontier* (London: Pearson).

Modigliani, F. and Perotti, E. (1997) 'Protection of minority interest and the development of security markets', *Managerial and Decision Economics*, 18: 519–28.

Moe, A. and Kryukov, V. (1994) 'Observations on the reorganization of the Russian oil industry', *Post-Soviet Geography*, 35(2): 89–101.

Moerland, P. (1995) 'Alternative disciplinary mechanisms in different corporate systems,' *Journal of Economic Behavior and Organization*, 26(1): 17–34.

Monks, R. and Miw, N. (1994) *Watching the Watchers* (Oxford: Blackwell Business).

Moors, K. (1999) 'Landmark shareholder battle heats up at Yukos oil holding', *Russia/Central Europe Executive Guide*, 30 June. Available at http://www.wtexec.com/ew063099.html.

Morck, R. and Steier, L. (2005) 'The Global History of Corporate Governance: An Introduction', *Working Paper No. 11062*, National Bureau of Economic Research.

Morck, R., Shleifer, A. and Vishny, R. (1988) 'Management ownership and market valuation: an empirical analysis', *Journal of Financial Economics*, 20: 293–316.

Morck, R., Nakamura, M. and Shivdasani, A. (2000) 'Banks, ownership structure and firm value in Japan', *Journal of Business*, 73(4): 539–67.

Moser, N. (1996) 'The privatization of the Russian oil industry 1992–1995 – Façade or Reality?' MPhil dissertation, Oxford University.

Moser, N. and Oppenheimer, P. (2001) 'The oil industry: structural transformation and corporate governance', in B. Granville and P. Oppenheimer (eds), *Russia's Post-Communist Economy* (Oxford: Oxford University Press).

Myers, S. and Majluf, N. (1984) 'Corporate financing and investment decisions when firms have information that investors do not have', *Journal of Financial Economics*, 20: 187–221.

Nash, R. (2001) 'Corporate consolidation: Russia's latest lurch towards capitalism', in P. Westin (ed.), *The Wild East: Negotiating the Russian Financial Frontier* (London: Pearson).

Nechaev, T. (1999) 'Korporativnye voiny: nepokorennaia vertikal', *Nefte-Gazovaia Vertikal*, 4. Available at http://www.oil-equip.ru/ngv/4-99/war/war.html

Negodonov, S (2001) 'Fenomen Iukosa. Byvshii izgoi neftianogo sektora vykhodit v lidery otrasli', *RusEnergy*, 27–28 June.

Nellis, J. (1999) 'Time to rethink privatization in transition economies?' *Transition*, 10(1): 4–6.

Nellis, J. (2002a) 'The World Bank, privatization, and enterprise reform in transition economies. A retrospective analysis', *Transition Newsletter*, 13(1): 17–21.

Nellis, J. (2002b) *The World Bank, Privatization and Enterprise Reform in Transition Economies: A Retrospective Analysis* Center for Global Development, Washington DC, mimeo.

Nelson, E. and Tylor, J. (1995) 'New ventures and enterpreneurship in an Eastern European context: a training and development programme for managers in state-owned firms', *Journal of European Industrial Training*, 19(9): 12–22.

Nestor, S. (2002) 'Corporate reform in Russia and the Former Soviet Union: The first ten years', in G. Tumpel-Gugerell, L. Wolfe and P. Mooslechner (eds), *Completing Transition: The Main Challenges* (Heidelberg: Springer).

Nestor, S. and Jesover, F. (2000) 'OECD Principles of Corporate Governance on Shareholder Rights and Equitable Treatment: Their Relevance to the Russian Federation', Paper presented at the *2nd Meeting of the Corporate Governance Round Table on Shareholder Rights and Equitable Treatment*, 24–25 February.

Neun, S. and Santerre, R. (1986) 'Dominant stockownership and profitability', *Managerial and Decision Economics*, 7: 207–10.

NIK (2003) *Report on Findings of Inspection at Business Entities Described in the Government's Opening Report of 7th May, 2002* (Warsaw: NIK [Supreme Audit Commission]).

Nonaka, I. (1994) 'A dynamic theory of organizational knowledge creation', *Organizational Science*, 5(1): 14–37.

Nonaka, I. and Takeuchi, H. (1995) *The Knowledge-Creating Company* (Oxford: Oxford University Press).

Novak, M. (2004) *Universal Hunger for Liberty: Why the Clash of Civilizations is Not Inevitable* (Washington, DC: AEI Press).

Nunnenkampf, P. (1996) 'The German model of corporate governance, basic features, critical issues and applicability to transition economies', *Working Paper*, No. 713, Kiel Institute of World Economics.

Nwankwo, S. (1996) 'Public-to-private organizational transition. A reconceptualization of conventional paradigms', *International Journal of Social Economics*, 23(7): 25–38.

O'Sullivan, S., Kushnir, P. and Danilenko, O. (2003) 'Yukos: leading the pack', *United Financial Group-Russia: Oil & Gas*, 20 February.

Organisation for Economic Co-operation and Development (1998) Global Corporate Governance Principles (Paris: OECD).

Organisation for Economic Co-operation and Development (1999a) *OECD Principles of Corporate Governance* (Paris: OECD).

Organisation for Economic Co-operation and Development (1999b) 'Corporate Governance: Getting it right in Russia', *OECD Observer*, 1 August.

Organisation for Economic Co-operation and Development (1999c) 'Synthesis Note from 1st Russian Corporate Governance Roundtable', 31 May–2 June.

Organisation for Economic Co-operation and Development (1999d) *OECD Principles of Corporate Governance* (Paris: OECD).

Organisation for Economic Co-operation and Development (2002a) *White paper on corporate governance in Russia* (Paris: OECD).

Organisation for Economic Co-operation and Development (2002b) *Country Report Poland* (Paris: OECD).

Organisation for Economic Co-operation and Development (2002c) 'Transparency for FDI', *OECD Observer*, 25–26 October.

Organisation for Economic Co-operation and Development (2003) *White Paper on Corporate Governance in South East Europe* (Paris: OECD).

Organisation for Economic Co-operation and Development (2004a) *OECD Principles of Corporate Governance* (Paris: OECD).

Organisation for Economic Co-operation and Development (2004b) 'Implementing International Financial Reporting Standards (IFRS) in Russia: 25 Recommendations to Facilitate the Transition to IFRS' (Paris: OECD).

Okhmatovskiy, I. (2003) *Records of interviews with executives and board members of Russian banks*, Moscow, mimeo.

Olcott, M. (2004) 'Vladimir Putin and The Geopolitics of Oil', *The Baker Institute Energy Forum Paper Series*, The James A. Baker III Institute for Public Policy, Rice University, October.

Olsson, M. and Alasheyeva, J. (2000) 'Market transparency, ownership concentration and harmonisation of law in some East European accession countries', *Conference Economic Aspects of European Integration: The Swedish Research Frontier*, Mölle, 15–18 May.

Oman, C. and Blume, D. (2005) 'Corporate Governance: A Development Challenge', OECD Development Centre, Policy Insights, 3.

Oman, C., Fries, S. and Buiter, W. (2003) 'Corporate Governance in Developing, Transition and Emerging-Market Economies', OECD Development Centre, Policy Brief, 23.

Pahor, M., Prasnikar, J. and Ferligoj, A. (2004) *'Building a corporate network in a transition economy: The case of Slovenia'*, *Post-Communist Economies*, 16(3): 307–31.

Pajuste, A. (2002) 'Corporate governance and stock market performance in Central and Eastern Europe', *Social Science Research Network Working Paper*.

Pappe, I. (2000) *Oligarkhy: Ekonomicheskaia Khronika 1992–2000 [The Oligarches: Economic Chronicle 1992–2000]* (Moscow: GU-VSE).

Parthiban, D., Kochhar, R. and Levitas, E. (1998) 'The effect of institutional investors on the level and mix of CEO compensation', *Academy of Management Journal*, 41(2): 200–8.

Patrick, H. (2000) 'Corporate governance and the Indonesian financial system: a comparative perspective', *Discussion Paper Series*, 16, University of Columbia.

Peek, J. and Rosengren, E. (2005) 'Unnatural selection: Perverse incentives and the misallocation of credit in Japan', *American Economic Review*, 95: 1144–66.

Peng, M. (2004) 'Outside Directors and firm performance during institutional transitions', *Strategic Management Journal*, 25: 453–71.

Peng, M. and Heath, P. (1996) 'The growth of firms in planned economies in transition: institutions, organisations, and strategic choice', *Academy of Management Review*, 21: 492–528.

Peng, M., Au, K. and Wang, D. (2001) 'Interlocking directorates as corporate governance in third world multinations: theory and evidence from Thailand', *Asia Pacific Journal of Management*, 18: 161–81.

Pennings, J. (1980) *Interlocking Directorates* (San Francisco: Jossey-Bass).

Perotti, E. (2005) 'Dominant investors and strategic transparency' *Journal of Law, Economics and Organization*, 21(1): 76–102.

Perotti, E. and Gelfer, S. (1999) 'Red barons or robber barons? Governance and financing in Russian FIG', *CEPR Discussion Paper Series*, 2204.

Perotti, E. and Gelfer, S. (2001) 'Red barons or robber barons? Governance and investment in Russian financial – industrial groups', *European Economic Review*, 45: 1601–17.

Perotti, E. and von Thadden, E. (2000) 'Outside finance, dominant investors and strategic transparency', *Tinbergen Institute Discussion Paper*, TI 2001-019/2.

Perotti, E. and von Thadden, E. (2003) 'Strategic transparency and informed trading: Will capital market integration force convergence of corporate governance?' *Journal of Financial and Quantitative Analysis*, 38(1): 61–85.

Perotti, E.C. and von Thadden, E. (2005) 'Dominant invertors and strategic transparency', *The Journal of Law, Economics, and Organization*, 21(1): 76–102.

Petkoski, D. (1997) *Financial Industrial Groups in Russia: Key Drivers Behind their Formation'* Economic Development Institute, World Bank, mimeo.

Pfeffer, J. (1972) 'Size and Composition of Corporate Boards of Directors', *Administrative Science Quarterly*, 17: 218–28.

Pfeffer, J., and Salancik, G. (1978) *The External Control of Organizations: A Resource Dependence Perspective* (New York: Harper & Row).

Pinto, B. and van Wijnbergen, S. (1995) 'Ownership and Corporate Control in Poland: Why State Firms Defied the Odds', *CEPR Discussion Paper Series*, 1273.

Pissarides, F. (1999) 'Is the lack of funds the main obstacle to growth? EBRD's experience with small- and medium-sized businesses in Eastern and Central Europe', *Journal of Business Venturing*, 14: 519–39.

Pistor, K. (2003) 'Enhancing corporate governance in the new member states: Does EU Law Help?' *Conference 'Law and Governance in the Enlarged Europe'*, Columbia University, 4–5 May.

Pistor, K., Raiser, M. and Gelfer, S. (2000) 'Law and finance in transition economies', *Center for International Development at Harvard University, CID Working Papers*, No. 49.

Plihon, D., Ponssard, J. and Zarlowski, P. (2001) 'Quel scénario pour le gouvernement d'entreprise? Une hypothèse de double convergence', *Revue d'Economie Financière*, 63: 35–51.

Pohl, G. and Claessens, S. (1994) 'Banks, capital markets, and corporate governance. Lessons from Russia for Eastern Europe', *Policy Research Working Paper*, No. 1326, World Bank.

Pollin, J. (2003) 'Quel système de gouvernement d'entreprise pour l'Europe?' in Le Cercle des Economistes, *L'Europe et la gouvernance mondiale* (Paris: Descartes & Cie).

Pope, P. and Walker, M. (1999) 'International differences in the timeliness, conservatism, and classification of earnings', *Journal of Accounting Research*, 37(Suppl.): 53–87.

Porter, M. (1985) *Competitive Advantage* (New York: Free Press).

Porter, M. (1990) *The Competitive Advantage of Nations* (New York: Free Press).

Potthof, E. (1996) 'Board-system versus duales system der unternehmungsverwaltung,' *Betriebswirtschfliche Forschung und Praxis*, 3: 253–68.

Pound, J. (1988) 'Proxy contests and the efficiency of shareholder oversight', *Journal of Financial Economics*, 20: 237–65.

Presidential decree 1403, 17 November 1992, '*Ob osobennostiakh privatizatsii i preobrazovaniia v aktsionernyie obschestva gosudarsvennykh predpriiatii, proizvodstvennykh i nauchno-proizvodstvennykh ob'edinenii neftianoi, neftepererabatyvaiushchei promyshlennosti i nefteproduktoobespechenii'*.

Prevezer, M. and Ricketts, M. (1994) 'Corporate governance: the UK compared with Germany and Japan', in N. Dismsdale and M. Prevezer (eds), *Capital Markets and Corporate Governance* (Oxford: Clarendon Press).

Pricewaterhouse Coopers (2001) *The Opacity Index*, January.

Pricewaterhouse Coopers (2004) *Accounting Reform II: Complex Survey Results*, May 20, prepared by Romir Monitoring.

Prickett, R. (2002) 'Sweet Clarity', *Financial Management*, September, 18–20.

Pye, R. (2000) 'The evolution of insurance sector in Central and Eastern Europe and the former Soviet Union', *William Davidson Institute Working Paper*, No. 336, University of Michigan.

Queisser, M., and Vittas, D. (2000) *The Swiss Multi-Pillar Pension System: Triumph of common sense?* Mimeo, Development Research Group, Washington DC, World Bank.

Radaev, V. (1998) *Formirovanie novykh rossiiskikh rynkov: transaktsionnyje izderzhki, formy kontrolia i delovaia etika* (Moscow: CIPE/Tsentr politicheskikh tekhnologiy).

Radaev, V. (2002) 'Rossijskij biznes: na puti k legalizatsii?' *Voprosy ekonomiki*, 1: 68–87.

Radosevic, S. (2004) 'The dynamics of international industrial networks in central Europe', in Radosevic S. and B. Sadowski (eds), *International Industrial Networks and Industrial Restructuring in Central and Eastern Europe* (Dordrecht: Kluwer): 41–58.

Radosevic, S., Yoruk, D. and Dornisch, D. (2001) 'The issues of enterprise growth in transition and post-transition period: the case of Polish "Elektrim"', *Centre for the Study of Social and Economic Change in Europe Working Paper*, No.1. Available at http://www.ssees.ac.uk/economic.htm

Radygin, A. (1999) Ownership and control in the Russian industry, Paper presented at the *OECD Conference on Corporate Governance*, Moscow, 31 May–2 June.

Radygin, A. (2000) 'Ownership and control of the Russian industry', OECD Roundtable on Corporate Governance. Available at www.oecd.org/daf/corporate-affairs

Radygin, A. (2003) 'Delo Iukos: popytka interpretatsii', *Ekonomiko-politicheskaia situatsiia v Rossii*, Institute of Economic Transition, July: 36–8.

Radygin, A. and Sidorov, I. (2000) 'Rossiiskaia korporativnaia ekonomika: sto let odinochestva?' *Voprosy ekonomiki*, 5: 45–61.

Radygin, A., Entov, R., Gontmakher, A. and Turuntseva, M. (2004) *Ekonomiko-Pravovye Faktory i Ogranicheniya v Stanovlenii Modelej Korporativnogo Upravleniya [Economic and Legal Factors and Limitations in the Development of the Corporate Governance Models]* (Moscow: Institute of Transitional Economy).

Radyign, A. (2004) 'Rossiia v 2000–2004 godakh: na puti k gosudarsvennomu kapitalizmu?' *Voprosy ekonomiki*, 4: 42–65.

Rahman, M. (1999) 'The role of accounting disclosure in the East Asian financial crisis: lessons learned?' A paper prepared for the United Nations Conference on Trade and Development (March), cited by Ho and Wong (2001).

Rajan, R. and Zingales, L. (1995) 'What do we know about capital structure? Some evidence from international data', *Journal of Finance*, 50: 1421–60.

Rajan, R. and Zingales, L. (1998) 'Financial dependence and growth', *American Economic Review*, 88: 559–86.

Rees, W. and Giner, B. (2001) 'On the asymmetric recognition of good and bad news in France, Germany and the UK', *Journal of Business Finance and Accounting*, 28(9/10): 1285–332.

Rice, J.A. (1995) *Mathematical Statistics and Data Analysis* (Belmont, California: Duxbury Press).

Ritter, J. and Welch, I. (2002) 'A review of IPO activity, pricing, and allocations', *Journal of Finance*, 57(4): 1795–828.

Roe, M. (1990) 'Political and legal restraints on ownership and control of public companies', *Journal of Financial Economics*, 27: 7–42.

Roe, M. (1997) 'The political roots of American corporate finance', *Journal of Applied Corporate Finance*, 9: 8–22.

Roemer, P. (1989) 'Capital accumulation and the theory of long-run growth', in R. Barro (ed.), *Modern Business Cycle Theory* (Cambridge, MA: Harvard University Press).

Roldos, J. (2004) 'Pension reform, investment restrictions and capital market', *IMF Policy Discussion Paper*, No. 04/4.

Rona-Tas, A. (1998) *Persistence of Networks in the Post-Communist Transformation in Eastern Europe*. Research Report, University of California, San Diego.

Rosefielde, S. (2005) 'An abnormal country', *The European Journal of Comparative Economics*, 2(1): 3–16.

Roth, K. and Kostova, T. (2003) 'Organizational coping with institutional upheaval in transition economies', *Journal of World Business*, 38(4): 314–30.

Rozman, R. (2000) 'The organizational function of governance,' *Management*, 5(2): 99–115.

Rusin, P. (2002) La privatisation de l'économie par création d'entreprises: Une nouvelle approche de la transition. Le cas de la Pologne, PhD dissertation, University Paris 1.

Russian Institute of Directors (2004) *Praktika Korporativnogo Upravleniya v Rossijskikh Aktsionernykh Obshchestvakh [Corporate Governance Practices in Russian Corporations]* (Moscow: Russian Institute of Directors).

Rutland, P. (2001) 'Introduction: business and the state in Russia', in P. Rutland (ed.), *Business and the State in Contemporary Russia* (Boulder, CO: Westview Press).

Rutland, P. (2005) 'Putin's economic record', in S. White, Z. Gitelman and R. Sakwa (eds), *Developments in Russian Politics 6* (Badingstoke: Palgrave).

Rzeczpospolita (2002) 'Zakręćic się na karuzeli stanowisk', *Rzeczpospolita*, 30th September.

Sachs, J. (1991) 'Accelerating privatization in Eastern Europe', *World Bank Conference on Development Economics*, Washington, DC, 25–26 April.

Salter, M. (2002) 'OAO Yukos Oil Company', Case study report, Harvard Business School, 29 January.

Salter, S. (1998) 'Corporate financial disclosure in emerging markets: Does economic development matter?' *The International Journal of Accounting*, 33(2): 211–34.

Saunders, A. and Sommariva, A. (1993) 'Banking sector and restructuring in Eastern Europe', *Journal of Banking and Finance*, 17: 931–58.

Schneidman, L. (2004) 'Corporate reporting and morality', *Vedomosti*, 13 April. Available at www.pwc.com.mu/ru/eng/ins-sol/issues/04-04-13_ls_ve.html.

Scott, J. (1985) 'Theoretical Framework and Research Design', in F.N. Stockman, R. Ziegler and J. Scott (eds), *Networks of Corporate Power* (Cambridge, England: Polity): 1–19.

Scott, J. (1997) *Corporate Business and Capitalist Classes* (New York: Oxford University Press).

Seib, P. (2004/2005) 'The News Media and the "Clash of Civilizations"', *Parameters* (U.S. Army War College) 34(4): 71–85.

Selznick, P. (1949) *TVA and the Grass Roots* (New York: Harper & Row).

Shelley, L. (1997) 'The price tag of Russia's organized crime,' *Transition: The Newsletter About Reforming Economies*, February, World Bank.

Sherman, H. (2004) 'Corporate Governance ratings', *Corporate Governance* 12(1): 5–7.

Shipley, D., Hooley, G., Beracs, J., Fonfara, K. and Kolos, K. (1995) 'Marketing organizations in Hungarian and Polish firm: part 1', *Journal of Marketing Practice: Applied Marketing Science*, 1(2): 39–54.

Shleifer, A. and Vishny, R. (1997) 'A survey of corporate governance', *Journal of Finance*, 52 June, 737–83.

Shleifer, A. and Treisman, D. (2000) *Without a Map: Political Tactics and Economic Reform in Russia* (Cambridge, MA: MIT Press).

Shleifer, A. and Tresman, D. (2004) 'A Normal Country', *Foreign Affairs*, 84(2): 20–38.

Shleifer, A. and Wolfenzon, D. (2002) 'Investor protection and equity markets', *Journal of Financial Economics*, 66: 3–27.

Shleifer, A. and Vishny, R. (1986) 'Large shareholders and corporate control', *Journal of Political Economy*, 94: 461–88.

Shleifer, A. and Vishny, R. (1994) 'Politicians and firms', *Quarterly Journal of Economics*, 109, 995–1025.

Short, H. (1994) 'Ownership, control, financial structure and the performance of firms', *Journal of Economic Surveys*, 8: 203–49.

Simatupang, T., Wright, A. and Sridharan, R. (2002) 'The knowledge of coordination for supply chain integration', *Business Process Management Journal*, 8(3): 289–308.

Singh, A. (1996) 'Pension reform, the stock market, capital formation and economic growth: a critical commentary on the World Bank's proposals', *CEPA Working Paper*, No. 2.

Singh, M. and Davidson III, W. (2003) 'Agency costs, ownership structure and corporate governance mechanisms', *Journal of Banking and Finance*, 27: 793–816.

Sizov, Y. (2004) 'Novyi vitok korporativnykh konfliktov,' *Aktsionernoe obshestvo: voprosy korporativnogo upravleniia*, November. Available at http://www.sovetnik.orc.ru/texts/sizov.htm

Slater, S. and Narver, J. (1995) 'Market orientation and the learning organization', *Journal of Marketing*, 59: 63–74.

Smith, A. (1990) 'Corporate ownership structure and performance', *Journal of Financial Economics*, 27: 143–64.

Smith, A. (2000) *The Return to Europe. The Reintegration of Eastern Europe into the European Economy* (London: Palgrave Macmillan).

Soltani, B. (2002) 'Timeliness of corporate and Audit Reports: some empirical evidence in the French context', *The International Journal of Accounting*, 37: 215–46.

Spicer, A. and Pyle, W. (2002) 'Institutions and the vicious circle of distrust in the Russian household deposit market: 1992–1999', *Advances in Strategic Management*, 19: 373–98.

Sprenger, C. (2000) 'Corporate governance in Russia', *Russian Economic Trends*, No. 2, 6–20.

Srinivas, P., Whitehouse, E. and Yermo, J. (2000) *Regulating Private Pension Fund's Structure, Performance, and Investments: Cross-Country Evidence*, World Bank Pension Primer (Washington, DC: World Bank).

Standard & Poor's (2002) 'S&P Corporate Governance Scores – Criteria, Methodology and Definitions'. Available at http://www2.standardandpoors.com/servlet/Satellite?pagename=sp/sp_article/ArticleTemplate&c=sp_article&cid=1021558139012&s=&ig=&b=2&dct=24

Stanton, W., Etzel, M. and Walker, B. (1994) *Fundamentals of Marketing* (New York: McGraw-Hill).

Stark, D. (1996) 'Recombinant property in East European capitalism', *American Journal of Sociology*, 101(4): 993–1027.

State Treasury (2002) *Opening Report – Information on the Situation in Selected State Treasury Companies and State-Owned Enterprises* (Warsaw: Ministry of the State Treasury).

Steele, M. (2005) 'Time for investors to come in from the cold', *Financial Times*, 19 May.

Stephen, F. and Backhaus, J. (2003) 'Corporate governance and mass privatisation. A theoretical investigation of transformations in legal and economic relationships', *Journal of Economic Studies*, 30(3/4): 389–468.

Stiglitz, J.E. (2002) *Globalization and Its Discontents* (New York: W.W. Norton).

Stiglitz, J. (1985) 'Credit markets and the control of capital', *Journal of Money, Credit and Banking*, 17: 133–152.

Stiglitz, J. (2000) '*Quis custodiet ipsos custodes*? Les défaillances du gouvernement d'entreprise dans la transition', *Revue d'Economie du Développement*, 1–2 June, 33–70.

Stockman, F., Ziegler, R. and Scott, J. (1985) *Networks of Corporate Power* (Cambridge, UK: Polity Press).

Strenger, C. (2004) 'The corporate governance scorecard: A tool for the implementation of corporate governance', *Corporate Governance*, 12(1): 11–15.

Stultz, R. (2005) 'The limits of financial globalization', *Journal of Finance*, 60(4): 1595–1638.

Stulz, R. (1988) 'Managerial control of voting rights financing polices and the market for corporate control', *Journal of Financial Economics*, 20: 25–54.

Sullivan, J.D. (2002) 'Democracy, governance and the market', Center for International Private Enterprise. Available at http://www.cipe.org/publications/fs/articles/article3162.htm

Szczurek, M. (2000) 'Investing II pillar pension fund – Polish experience', ING Bank.

Taniura, T. (1993) 'The lucky Goldstar group in the Republic of Korea', *Developing Economies*, 31: 465–84.

Teramishi, J. (1995) 'Saving mobilization and investment financing during Japan's post-war economic recovery', in M. Aoki and H. Kim (eds), *Corporate Governance in Transitional Economies: Insider Control and the Role of Banks* (Washington, DC: The World Bank): 405–34.

Thomas, A. (2003) 'Assessing the benefits of corporate transparency', *International Journal of Business Performance Management*, 5(2/3): 174–87.

Thomas, L. and Waring, G. (1999) 'Competing capitalisms: capital investments in American, German and Japanese firms', *Strategic Management Journal*, 20: 729–48.

Thompson, J. and McEwen, W. (1958) 'Organizational goals and environment: Goal-setting as an interaction process', *American Sociological Review*, 23: 23–31.

Thomsen, S. and Pedersen, T. (2000) 'Ownership structure and economic performance in the largest European companies', *Strategic Management Journal*, 21(6): 639–705.

Tian, L. (2005), *Bank Lending, Corporate Governance and Government Ownership in China*, Institute of Finance and Accounting, London Business School, mimeo.

Tiwana, A., (2001) *The Essential Guide to Knowledge Management. E-business and CRM Applications* (Prentice Hall: Pearson Education).

Tobin, J. (1958) 'Liquidity preference as behavior towards risk', *Review of Economic Studies*, 25: 68–85.

Tompson, W. (2002) 'Putin's challenge', *Europe–Asia Studies*, 54(6): 933–57.

Tompson, W. (2003) 'Putin's Success', *The World Today Essay*, 8 June. Available at http://observer.guardian.co.uk/worldtoday/story/0,11726,972697,00.html

Tompson, W. (2003) 'The Present and Future of Banking Reform', in D. Lane (ed.), *Russian Banking: Evolution, Problems and Prospects* (Cheltenham, UK: Edward Elgar), 56–78.

Tompson, W. (2005a) 'Putting Yukos in perspective', *Post-Soviet Affairs*, 21(2): 159–81.

Tompson, W. (2005b) 'Putin and the "Oligarchs": a two-sided commitment problem', in Alex Pravda (ed.), *Leading Russia: Putin in Perspective: Essays in Honour of Archie Brown* (Oxford: Oxford University Press).

Troika Dialog (2001) 'Russian corporate governance', *Troika Dialog Research*, May.

Trueman, B. (1990) 'Theories of earnings-announcement timing', *Journal of Accounting and Economics*, 13: 285–301.

Tsipouri, L. and Xanthakis, M. (2004) 'Can corporate governance be rated? Ideas based on the Greek experience', *Corporate Governance*, 12(1): 16–28.

Tsygankov, A. (2005) 'Vladimir Putin's visions of Russia as a normal great power', *Post-Soviet Affairs*, 21(2): 132–58.

United Nations Conference on Trade and Development (UNCTAD) (1999) *World Investment Report 1999. Foreign Direct Investment and the Challenge of Development* (New York and Geneva: UN).

United Nations Conference on Trade and Development (UNCTAD) (2002) *World Investment Report. Transnational Corporations and Export Competitiveness* (New York and Geneva: UNCTAD).

Useem, M. (1996) 'Shareholders as strategic assets', *California Management Review*, 39(1): 8–27.

Vagliasindi, M. and Vagliasindi, P. (2003) 'Privatisation Methods and Enterprise Governance in Transition Economies', in Y. Kalyuzhnova and W. Andreff (2003).

Vasiliev, D. (2001) 'Korporativnoe upravlenie v Rossii: Est' li shans dlia uluchshenii?' in E. Iasin (ed.), *Investitsionny klimat i perspektivy ekonomicheskogo rosta v Rossii* (Moscow: HSE).

Vedres, B. (2000) 'The Constellations of economic power: the position of political actors, banks and large corporations in the Networks of Directorate interlocks in Hungary, 1997', *Connections*, 23(1): 44–9.

Vincensini, C. (2003) Les trajectoires nationales de propriété en Pologne, Hongrie et République tchèque. Une analyse comparative du changement institutionnel post-socialiste, PhD dissertation, Universitssy Paris 1.

Vishwanath, T. and Kaufmann, D. (2001) 'Toward transparency: new approaches and their application to financial markets', *The World Bank Research Observer*, 16(1): 41–57.

Vittas, D. (2000) 'Pension reform and capital market development: "Feasibility" and "impact" preconditions', *World Bank Policy Research Working Paper*, No. 2414.

Volkov, V. (2003) 'The Yukos affair: terminating the implicit contract', *PONARS Policy Memo* No. 307, Center for Strategic and International Studies, Washington, DC.

Walendziak, W. and Bałtowski, M. 'Państwo rządne i efektywne', *Rzeczpospolita*, 7–8 June.

Walter, I. (2000) 'Capital markets and control of enterprises in the global economy', in S. Cohen and G. Boyd (eds), *Corporate Governance and Globalization. Long Range Planning Issues* (Northamptom, MA: Edward Elgar).

Wasserman, S. and Faust, K. (1994) *Social Network Analysis: Methods and Applications* (Cambridge: Cambridge University Press).

Wawrzyniak, B. (2003) *Zarządzanie wiedzą w przedsiębiorstwie* (Warszawa: Wyższa Szkola Przedsiębiorczzosci i Zarządzania im. Leona Koźmińskiego).

Weafer, C. (2005) 'State Control Over Lock, Stock and Barrel', *Moscow Times*, 14 February. Available at www.themoscowtimes.com/stories/2005/02/14/006.html

Weston, F., Slu, J. and Johnson, B. (2001) *Takeovers, Restructuring and Corporate Governance* (Saddle River, NJ: Prentice Hall).

Whittred, G. (1980) 'Audit Qualification and the Timeliness of Corporate Annual Reports', *The Accounting Review*, 55(4): 563–77.

Whittred, G. and Zimmer, I. (1984) 'Timeliness of financial reporting and financial distress' *The Accounting Review* 59(2): 287–95.

Wielinga, B., Sandberg, J. and Schreiber, G. (1997) 'Methods and techniques for knowledge management: What has knowledge engineering to offer?' *Expert Systems With Applications*, 13(1): 73–84.

Wiig, K. (1995) *Knowledge Management. The Central Management Focus for Intelligent-Acting Organizations* (Arlington, TX: Schema Press).

Williamson, O. (2002) 'The theory of the firm as governance structure: from choice to contract', *Journal of Economic Perspectives*, 16(3): 171–95.

Windolf, P. (2002) *Corporate Networks in Europe and the United States* (Oxford: Oxford University Press).

Winiecki, J. (2002) 'The Polish generic private sector in transition: developments and characteristics', *Europe–Asia Studies*, 54: 5–29.

Woidtke, T. (2002) 'Agents watching agents? Evidence from pension fund ownership and firm value', *Journal of Financial Economics*, 63: 99–131.

Woodruff, D. (2003) 'Khodorkovsky's Gamble: From Business to Politics in the YUKOS Conflict', *PONARS Policy Memo No. 308*, Center for Strategic and International Studies, Washington, DC.

World Bank (1995) *Bureaucrats in Business. The Economics and Politics of Government Ownership* (New York: Oxford University Press).

World Bank (2000) *Corporate Governance: A Framework for Implementation* (Washington, DC: World Bank).

World Bank (2001) *World Development Report* (Washington, DC: World Bank).

World Bank (2002a) *Transition – The First Ten Years: Analysis and Lessons for Eastern Europe and the Former Soviet Union* (Washington, DC: World Bank).

World Bank (2002b) *Corporate Governance Country Assessment. Czech Republic* (Washington, DC: The World Bank).

World Bank (2002c) *Poland. Corporate Governance Assessment and ROSC Module* (Washington, DC: The World Bank).

World Bank (2003) *Corporate Governance Country Assessment. Hungary* (Washington, DC: The World Bank).

World Bank (2004) *From Transition to Development: A Country Economic Memorandum for the Russian Federation* (Moscow: World Bank, April).

World Bank (2005) *Corporate Governance Country Assessment. Poland* (Washington, DC: The World Bank).

Wright, M., Buck, T. and Filatotchev, I. (2003) Is stakeholder corporate governance appropriate in Russia?' *Journal of Management and Governance*, 7: 263–90.

Wruck, K. (1989) 'Equity ownership concentration and firm value. Evidence from private equity financing', *Journal of Financial Economics*, 23: 3–28.

Yakovlev, A. (2003) 'Interaction of interest groups and their impact on economic reform in contemporary Russia', *Working Paper, No. 51*, The Research Centre for Eastern European Studies, Bremen.

Yakovlev, A. (2004) 'Evolution of corporate governance in Russia: government policy vs real incentives of economic agents', *Post-Communist Economies*, 16(4): 387–403.

Yim, N., Kim, S., Kim, H. and Kwahk, K. (2004) 'Knowledge based decision making on higher level strategic concerns: system dynamics approach', *Expert Systems with Applications*, 27: 143–58.

Yoshimori, M. (1995) 'Whose company is it? The concept of the corporation in Japan and the West,' *Long Range Planning*, 286(4): 33–44.

Yousef-Martinek, D., Minder, R. and Rahim, R. (2003) 'Yukos oil: a corporate governance success story?' *Chazen Web Journal of International Business*, Columbia Business School, Fall.

Yuganskneftegaz (1994) 'Memorandum ob AO Yuganskneftegaz', April.

Yukos (2002) *Yukos Annual Report 2001*.

Yukos (2003) *Yukos Annual Report 2002*.

Zajac, E. (1988) 'Interlocking directorates as an interorganizational strategy: a test of critical assumptions', *Academy of Management Journal*, 31: 428–38.

Zalewska, A. (2005) 'Is locking domestic funds into the local market beneficial? Evidence from the Polish pension reforms', *LIFE Working Paper*, 05-004.

Zang, X. (2000) 'Intercorporate ties in Singapore', *International Sociology*, 15(1): 87–105.

Zeckhauser, R., and Pound, J. (1990) 'Are large shareholders effective monitors? An investigation of share ownership and corporate governance', in R. Hubbard (ed.), *Asymmetric Information, Corporate Finance and Investment* (Chicago: University of Chicago Press): 149–80.